GENERAL VINOY.

RÉPUBLIQUE FRANÇAISE

FÉLIX DOUAY.

MARECHAL MAC-MAHON.

GENERAL LADMIRAULT.

DÉLIVRANCE DE PARIS MAI 1871

GENERAL DE CISSEY.

Mrs. Geo. W. Carpenter
Paris Nov. 1871

THE RISE AND FALL

OF

THE PARIS COMMUNE

IN 1871;

WITH A FULL ACCOUNT OF

THE BOMBARDMENT, CAPTURE, AND BURNING OF THE CITY.

By W. PEMBROKE FETRIDGE,

EDITOR OF "HARPER'S GUIDE-BOOK TO EUROPE AND THE EAST," "HARPER'S PHRASE-BOOK," &c.

ILLUSTRATED WITH A MAP OF PARIS AND PORTRAITS FROM ORIGINAL PHOTOGRAPHS.

NEW YORK:
HARPER & BROTHERS, PUBLISHERS,
FRANKLIN SQUARE.
1871.

PREFACE.

AS accuracy is the principal merit in a work of this description, the author, who remained in Paris from March 6th until after the capture of the city by the Government troops, which was completed May 29th, 1871, has diligently examined and carefully sifted all reports published by the different writers in the Paris journals, as well as those of foreign correspondents, with whom he was brought in hourly contact. Naturally, there was much discrepancy in the various accounts given, as the scene of action covered so large a space of territory. Each succeeding day corrections were made in the original reports, of which readers in the United States could never be thoroughly informed through the newspapers. Three days in succession three different first-class Paris journals gave the last dying words of General Dombrowski, one of the chiefs of the insurrection, all entirely different. So it was in every instance connected with the arrest or execution of the different members of the Commune, the storming of the different barricades, and the multitude of heroic and daring actions performed throughout the city. These accounts have been corrected by facts since brought to light; and this material, with what the author personally saw, is now brought before the public. The record is probably the saddest which has ever appeared on the page of history.

PARIS, *August, 1871.*

CONTENTS.

CHAPTER I.

CHAPTER II.

CHAPTER III.

CHAPTER IV.

CHAPTER V.

CHAPTER VI.

CHAPTER VII.

CHAPTER VIII.

CHAPTER IX.

CHAPTER X.

CHAPTER XI.

CHAPTER XII.

CHAPTER XIII.

CHAPTER XIV.

CHAPTER I.

Causes of the insurrection—War with Prussia—Fall of the Empire—Clause in the Treaty of Brussels, leaving the National Guard in arms—Letter of Prince Napoleon to Jules Favre—Mistake made by Jules Favre in signing the treaty—Fears entertained regarding the return of the soldiers—Weakness shown by the Government—Council of Ministers held at Versailles—Meeting of National Guards at Montmartre—Election of members for the Central Committee—A Prefect of Police appointed by the Government—Protest of the National Guards—They insist upon their right to elect municipal officers—They protest against the introduction of regular troops into the city—Organization of the National Guard—Necessity for its dissolution—Refusal of the Guards to deliver up their guns—The Government proposes to stop their pay—Prussian sentry killed by a National Guard—Arrest of the latter—Arrest of two Germans by the malcontents—Their trial and condemnation by the Central Committee—Their release—Conditions of their release unfulfilled by the Prussians—Proclamation of M. Thiers—Proclamation to the National Guards—Determination of the Government to subdue the insurrection—Attempt made to secure the guns in the Place des Vosges—They are removed to Belleville—Erection of barricades—Occupation of Montmartre by the troops—Mismanagement shown—Hostile attitude assumed by the National Guard—They oppose the removal of the guns—Refusal of the soldiers to advance—The 88th regiment of the line fraternizes with the insurgents—Withdrawal of the troops who remain faithful—They are fired upon by the insurgents.

THE unfortunate war which France declared against Germany in the month of July 1870, was indirectly the cause of the late insurrection, the most formidable and criminal the world has ever seen. The head that had so long controlled the ruthless desperadoes of Paris, most of whom have by this time expiated their fearful crimes, was in exile—the defeat of Sedan had set them at liberty.

Although the insurgents had always been strictly opposed to the Empire, they were the first and loudest in their shouts of "*On to Berlin*" when marching through the boulevards, although the last to try and get there; and happy were they at the defeat of the brave and gallant army, overmatched by numbers and military organization.

After the overthrow of the Imperial dynasty, September 4th, 1870, by a greater *coup d'état* than that practiced by the Emperor, the chiefs of that movement, many of whom were leaders in the late insurrection, proclaimed to the world that Napoleon III was the prime mover in the declaration of war. Most people, residents of France, knew to the contrary; the English Government knew to the contrary when Lord Lyons' dispatches were read in the House of Commons, declaring that the French people had taken the reins out of the Emperor's hands. The armies of the Empire were defeated, the Republic was proclaimed, its armies defeated, its military and political leaders overpowered by the surrender of Paris and the treaty of Brussels—then was committed the crowning error of leaving armed a National Guard, a large portion of which was the refuse of France, and the scum of different European countries, who, getting the upper hand of the more respectable portion of the Republicans in the city, loosened the *bagne* of some thirty thousand of its frequenters, and, led by instigators of murder and rebellion —assassins like Eudes and Mégy—released from prison by the Committee of National Defence, in which they had been confined under the Empire, committed, under the name, and for the purpose of protecting the Republic, every species of crime and blasphemy.

Prince Napoleon, cousin of the Emperor, and who, in the event of the death of the Prince Imperial, would be the next heir to the Imperial crown, addressed the following letter to Jules Favre, in which he accused that statesman with all the misery lately brought upon France. Its publication will throw considerable light on the origin of events proposed to be illustrated:

PRINCE NAPOLEON'S LETTER.

"LONDON, May, 1871.

"Peace is signed with the conqueror. Paris, the great capital, burns—its finest edifices, which have existed for centuries, are reduced to ashes—blood flows in torrents—your work is complete.

"The affliction which oppresses every French mind ought not to obscure one's reason, which has the right to demand from you an account of the disasters which you have accumulated.

"The 4th September—the armistice discussed at Ferrières—the defence of Paris—the preliminaries of Versailles—the 18th March—the peace of Frankfort—the burning of the metropolis;—such are your ill-omened dates. History will call you *l'homme fatal,* and will find in you only one motive—hate for the name of Napoleon.

"The disastrous war commenced the 19th July, 1870, by the Empire, terminated on the 10th of May by the government without name, to which you belong. What is that régime? Is it the national defence? No;—for you only capitulated. Is it a national restoration? No; for disorganization and anarchy have seized on France. Is it a Monarchy? No. Is it a Republic? Still less. Is it liberty? Certainly not. Look at the elections oppressed by decrees of ostracism, withdrawn at the last hour, after having perverted the choice of the citizens.

"All those are the evils accumulated on one another by the absence of order, security, liberty, and strength.

"Let us go over the steps by which you conducted us to the bottom of the abyss.

"On the 4th September you proposed the deposition of the Emperor. The insurrection, led on by you, drove away your colleagues; you violated your oath, and you usurped power at the Hôtel de Ville against universal suffrage.

"The Empire had committed faults, our defeats were great, but our disasters date from you—to each, his share. Doubtless the error was most unfortunate to count too much on the forces of France, and to commit in 1870 the mistake made by Prussia in 1806; to think too much of the victories of the great Republic and the first Empire; to forget too much the powerful enemy we had to combat; to contemplate the Crimea of 1854 and the Italy of 1859, instead of looking firmly at the strength of Germany in 1870, and the remarkable men whom she had at her head.

"I do not wish to deny, nor can I, those faults which the Napoleons pay still more dearly for by their heart-felt grief than by their exile; but the Emperor did not seek to cling to the throne by a peace which might save his power in imposing heavy sacrifices on France.

"At all events, we have one consolation, that of having fallen with the country, whereas your elevation dates from her misfortunes.

"Better than any one, you know the conditions which Napoleon III could have obtained from Prussia at Sedan; certainly they were hard, but incomparably less so than those accepted by you. Our sacrifices were not to be compared to those which you signed, without reckoning that we should have avoided the months of disorder entailed by the government of the non-defence of Paris, and by the dictatorship of those of your colleagues who emigrated in balloons to pillage and oppress our provinces. Down to the fall of the Empire, we had suffered great misfortunes, but capable of being repaired, as may be found in the history of many great nations. Since the 4th September, on the contrary, those which have occurred can no longer be so termed—they are disasters unexampled in history.

"To the Empire falls the responsibility of faults, to you that of positive disasters; and I ask, if, amongst the former, the greatest is not to have tolerated your criminal attempts in the interior.

"The inevitable consequence of your usurpation was

the revolution of the 18th March, which you now accuse, and the burning of Paris, for which you are responsible.

To defend Paris, you confined yourself to proclaiming fictitious successes. You did not utilize those terrible but vigorous elements which you have unchained, and which lately held the soldiers of France in check during two months; and, however they were the same men, misled since by democratic folly, amongst whom you could have excited the patriotic passion, they were the same national guards, cannons, muskets, forts, ramparts, barricades, all those forces which remained paralyzed in your weak hands, and which might have been sublime against the foreigner.

"Know this fact, that the Napoleons would have been patriotic enough to have blessed your triumph and their fall, if you had freed France, but history will say that having promised to save the country, you destroyed it.

"In the interval, you went to Ferrières to shed tears! and I really pity you. You pronounced there the dangerous words which are not those of a statesman: 'Not a stone of our fortresses, nor an inch of our territory.' Your conscience ought to feel oppressed by them. For the honor of a French Minister, you should have had the modesty to place some other name than your own at the foot of the act recording the grievous sacrifices rendered indispensable by often-repeated faults.

"At Versailles the conqueror proposed the disarming of the National Guard or of the army, and you chose that of the soldiers, because you feared Bonapartist tendencies among the troops; at the same time that you never paid the slightest attention to the elements of disorder in an irritated crowd, dissatisfied with itself, badly led, humiliated, and unfortunate, all of which causes were destined to lead to that terrible explosion of the Commune.

"You sold France to the representative of the enemy,

in exchange for your personal Republic. Why did you give way? I will tell you—because the Foreign Minister hinted at the possibility of assembling the former Legislative Body. Then you signed everything.

"To continue. Your incapacity led to the triumph of the Commune in Paris, and to daily increasing demands on the part of the Germans. The negotiations languished at Brussels, and nothing was accomplished. You went to Frankfort, but what was done there? You signed an aggravation of the preliminaries of peace, first, by shortening the time for the payment of the indemnity; secondly, by prolonging until December, 1871, the occupation of the northern forts, which were to have been evacuated after the payment of the first 500 millions; and, thirdly, by not making Prussia take to her charge so much of the former national debt of France as belonged to the departments ceded, in proportion to the territory and the number of the inhabitants, which is a principle of public law, and which was admitted on the cession of Lombardy, Savoy, Nice, and Venetia.

"Did not Prussia in 1866 accept the liabilities of Hanover, Electoral Hesse, and the Grand-Duchy of Nassau? The Prussian negotiators, even in their victorious ascendency, could not openly refuse you that point. You bowed your head because you feared an appeal to the French nation. You then conceded everything; and again at Frankfort, as at Versailles, you sacrificed France to your inveterate hatred. The mode of proceeding never varied to obtain everything from your government; all that was required was to show you the possibility of the triumph of the national will.

"I do not condemn those who, in a terrible conjuncture, accepted the preliminaries, perhaps inevitable, of Versailles, and still less the Assembly which ratified them; I do not consider I have the right to do so. But you are inexcusable for having brought about the 4th September, badly defending Paris, engaging the country by empty phrases, maintaining an excited population in arms, which were useless against the foreign enemy, and a danger to itself; for having aggravated the preliminaries by the treaty of peace; and, lastly, for having ended by the destruction of Paris.

"You have filled up the measure. France is indignant, and posterity will judge you. In the darkness in which the country is now plunged; in presence of those maniacs who, in their fury, burn our public buildings, throw down the column, and break up that glorious bronze, the fragments of which inflict a wound on the heart of each of our soldiers, some issue of safety must be found. It is not in the intrigues of pretenders, but in the will of the country; apart from that, there can be only conflict and confusion.

"The wished-for haven is not to be found in a principle which is the negation of modern society; in the white flag which France knows no longer, nor in a denial of universal suffrage; in a white terror succeeding the red; in the fusion of the contending claimants, and the return of the French Stuarts. No;—to a new society a fresh symbol is necessary. What is required, and modern right demands it, is the abdication of all before the will of the people, freely and directly expressed. Once more I say, apart from that, there is only chaos.

"Monarchical faith cannot be decreed. The only basis on which a government in France can establish its principle, and the only source from which it can derive force and legality, is an appeal to the people, which we demand, and which France ought to exact.

"NAPOLEON (JEROME.)"

Many who are not the political opponents of Jules Favre blame him much for his course of action while he remained in power; it would certainly have been in better taste, had he permitted some other Frenchman to sign his name to a treaty of peace which gave away many inches of territory and numerous stones of fortresses; but he was fond of power and wished to retain it—so fond of it, that at his request, the Germans permitted the National Guards to retain their arms, most of whom were the same men who attempted to overthrow the government during the funeral of Victor Noir, and who were ignominiously defeated in their attempt to establish a commune during the siege; but these men were Favre's electors and the electors of Gambetta and Rochefort, and they must be armed, as the soldiers of the empire would soon be back from Germany, and they must be prepared to meet them. It is to be hoped that the result of the late struggle will prove to the advocates of socialistic and communist ideas that the good sense of the people of France will never permit a repetition of the past lamentable events; and should an attempt again be made, the recollection of the destruction of property and loss of life, of the blasphemy and horror, will cause every citizen with a social position to maintain and a dollar to lose, to rise and crush the monster in its infancy. Had this been done by the government of M. Thiers, how different would have been the result; but M. Thiers was old and tender-hearted, and Favre had too much consideration for his friends; and as late as March 16, two days before the outbreak, a council of ministers was held at Versailles, when it was determined, "seeing the state of affairs at Montmartre, to let matters take their natural course and not interfere," and the *Constitutionnel*, a leading Paris journal, in alluding to this resolution, observed: "The majority of the Paris population will applaud this resolution, and the provinces also, when better informed as to the scope of manifestations which have caused too much alarm, will shortly admit that temporization was, after all, the best course to adopt.

On the same day a meeting was held, in the open air, by the National Guards at Montmartre. The principal business was the election of members of the Central Committee; Garibaldi was unanimously elected general-in-chief of the National Guard; Flourens also was elected to an important office; and all present pledged themselves to obey in future no orders but those of the Committee. Generals Paladine and Vinoy were declared to be dismissed from their functions, and these were generals commanding the French army then stationed in Paris; and still M. Thiers, the veteran statesman, the head of the French executive, who had shown such temper, promptitude and adroitness in all his transactions, who had steered the country through its recent crisis, did not have the courage to grapple with the rising difficulty.

The executive government now determined to appoint a Prefect of Police, and their choice fell upon General Valentin, a former colonel of gendarmerie, a man of fine abilities, who had distinguished himself during the siege. The National Guard, encamped at Montmartre, protested against this appointment—they wished not only to exercise military but political rights, and insisted in electing their own municipal officers. They also protested against the introduction of regular troops into the city—rights which neither the city of New York nor London possess—and aspired to revive the days of the Revolutionary Commune. Their organization represented the various districts and wards of the city, and was originally intended to assist in defending the capital against the Prussians. Upon the ratification of peace by the National Assembly and the withdrawal of the enemy, this organization should have been dissolved; but the chiefs, having the power in their own hands, felt the regular government was not sufficiently strong to enforce their surrender, consequently refused to break up, and held their own on the heights of Montmartre and in the quarters of Belleville and Vilette, the first at the north, the other two quarters at the east of the city, the residence of the lowest classes of Paris and the hot-bed of insurrections; and the red flag, the symbol of the Commune, remained hoisted on the column of July in Place Bastille. The authorities tried to coax them to deliver up those cannon of which they had over four hundred pieces, with an endless stock of ammunition; but they would not be coaxed—they maintained that they were Paris, and that Paris was France, and that an ultra-social republic was the only government possible in the country.

The mutineers had thus organized a Republic within a Republic, setting the authority of the National Government at defiance. It was argued by many of the advisors of the government that by withholding the pay of thirty sous (thirty cents), on which the National Guard had been supported from the beginning of the siege, a bloodless victory might be obtained, as they were still receiving this pay from the government against which they were almost in open rebellion. Had this been stopped, many thought that the workman would be obliged to return to his ordinary avocations, from which the government allowance had weaned him, or be starved into submission; but the pay was not stopped, and 40,000 men, well armed and well fortified, remained at the call of a few reckless and desperate individuals, with 100,000 more ready to join them on their first success against the established authorities. The latter had not long to wait.

During the first few days of the armistice, a National Guard passed the French lines, and fired a revolver at a Prussian sentinel, who was mortally wounded. The National Guard, who was an officer, was immediately arrested, and conveyed to the fort of Aubervilliers. Some time after, two Germans were arrested in Paris by the malcontent National Guards, and taken to the Central Committee, by which they were tried, and sentenced to death the following morning. The Prussian military authorities, on learning this fact, demanded the immediate restoration of the condemned men. General Paladines sent a captain of the staff of the National Guard to claim the prisoners; but the application was refused, the envoy was dismissed, the chiefs declaring that they refused to recognize the authority of the General. A Commissary of Police was then deputed to continue the negotiation, and finally the committee offered to give up the Germans on condition that the National Guard above mentioned, who was an officer in the 147th battalion, should be set at liberty. The offer was accepted by the French authorities, and the prisoners were handed over to them. The officer was still retained by the Prussians; and the commander of the fort declared that he should be tried by a court-martial, and, if found guilty, shot; whereas the National Guards declared they only gave up their two prisoners on condition that their officer should be set at liberty, and were loud in the denunciations of the Government. Whereupon M. Thiers, chief of the Executive Power, issued, March 17th, the following proclamation:

"INHABITANTS OF PARIS,—We address ourselves to you, to your reason, to your patriotism, and we hope to be heard. Your great city, which can only live by order, is being deeply disquieted in some districts. This state of things, without spreading to other districts, is, however, sufficient to prevent the resumption of labor and comfort. For some time past some ill-intentioned persons have, under the pretense of resisting the Prussians, who are no longer before your walls, constituted themselves masters of a part of the city, have constructed fortifications on which they keep guard, and on which they force you to mount guard with them by order of an unknown committee. They pretend alone to command a part of the National Guard, and do not recognize the authority of General d'Aurelle des Paladines, who so nobly deserves to be at your head. Their wish is to institute a government in opposition to the legal government instituted by universal suffrage. Those persons who have already done you so much harm—those persons who on the 15th of December last you yourselves scattered, after they had pretended that it was their intention to defend you against the Prussians who did but appear inside your walls, and whose final departure is only delayed by these disorders—those persons have turned their guns so that, if they fired, they would reduce your homes to ruins, kill your children and yourselves. Finally, they have compromised the Republic instead of defending it, because if it once becomes the opinion of France that the Republic is necessarily accompanied by disorders, the Republic is lost. Do not believe them. Hear the truth which we tell you in all sincerity. The government, established by the entire nation, could have retaken the cannon robbed from the state, and which actually threaten you. It could have removed these ridiculous intrenchments which stop your commerce, and have placed in the hands of justice the criminals who do not fear to make civil war succeed foreign war; but it has wished to give to the deceived time to separate from those who deceive them. Still, time is granted to the good men to separate from the bad, and you are entreated by your love of peace, by your own well-being, by the well-being of all France, not to prolong indefinitely the duration of this state of things. Commerce is stopped; the shops are deserted; large orders, which would arrive from all parts, are suspended; your arms are

A. THIERS

Chef du Pouvoir Exécutif

de la République Française.

paralyzed; credit will not revive in capitals, the government of which, while the territory of the country needs to be delivered from the presence of an enemy, hesitates to come forward.

"In your interest, and in that of the city, and in that of France, the Government has resolved to act. The criminals, who affect to institute a government, must be delivered to regular justice, and the cannon taken away must be restored to the arsenals. To carry out this act of justice and reason, the Government counts upon your assistance, and that the good citizens will separate from the bad, that they will support instead of resist public opinion, that they will thus hasten to restore peace in the city, and render a service to the Republic which, in the opinion of France, must be ruined by disorder. Parisians! we speak to you thus, because we esteem your good sense, wisdom and patriotism, but having given you this warning, we shall proceed to have recourse to force, because there must be peace at all hazards without a day's delay, so that order, the condition of well-being, may return—order, complete, immediate, and unalterable."

The following proclamation, signed by all the members of the National Government, was posted during the day on the walls of Paris:

"National Guards of Paris,—An absurd report is being circulated that the Government is making preparation for a *coup d'état*. The Government of the Republic neither has nor can have any other object than the safety of the Republic. The measures it has taken were indispensable for the maintenance of order; it intended and still intends thoroughly to put down the Insurrectionary Committee, whose members are almost all unknown to the inhabitants of Paris; they represent nothing but

Communist doctrines, and would hand over Paris to pillage and send France to her grave, if the National Guard and the army did not rise to defend with one common accord their country and the Republic."

The government now feeling with justice that they could no longer countenance the presence in Paris of a party which openly defied them and held the city in terrorism, resolved on the morning of the 18th of March to take possession of the cannon planted on Montmartre, and reduce to obedience the National Guard who presumed to dictate to the authorities. An attempt had been made the evening before to obtain possession of fifty-six guns in the Place des Vosges by a number of artillery-drivers with horses, protected by a detachment of the Republican Guard, but the National Guard refused to open the gates leading to the square, and the regular troops, not wishing to assume the responsibility of shedding blood, withdrew. These cannon were removed in the night to Belleville and the Buttes Chaumont—an elevated portion of the city, in the vicinity of Père la Chaise, and in possession of the National Guards—and the Committee of Direction at Montmartre were advised of the attempt; so when the troops appeared, the sentinels on guard over the artillery, were fully prepared to meet them.

It became absolutely necessary after this failure, and in view of the meeting of the National Assembly to be held on Monday, to adopt at once a more vigorous course. It was accordingly decided, at a meeting of general officers, to bring into requisition the whole military force of the government, and put an end at once to the existing state of affairs.

At 4 o'clock A.M. the *rappel* was heard in all the streets, a sound indicative of barricades and murder. An attack was to be simultaneously made, on Montmartre by

General Susbielle, of the 2d army corps; another by General Faron, on Belleville; a third by General Wolff, of the 1st army corps, on the Place de la Bastille; and a fourth, under General Hanrion, of the same corps, on the cité. At 4 o'clock the Buttes of Montmartre were completely surrounded by the 88th, 137th and 122d regiments of the line, a battalion of the 17th *chasseurs à pied*, and a few guardians of the peace. Mitrailleuses were in battery in Rue Houdon, Rue Durantin, Rue des Martyrs, and Rue Virginie, seven-pounder guns were planted in all streets leading up to Montmartre, and soldiers of the line were posted in the streets as sentinels to prevent pedestrians from going towards the Buttes. The windows were crowded with spectators, and groups of women and children were formed in the streets discussing, some with frightened and others with angry looks, the events which were transpiring.

A regiment of the army of Faidherbe, the 88th of the line (since disbanded for fraternizing with the insurgents, and never more to exist in the French army), which had only arrived the day before in Paris, made its appearance at the base of Montmartre, and separating into different columns, arrived by the Rue Lepic, Chaussée Clignancourt, and Boulevard Ornano, forming their junction at the Tour of Solferino, the culminating point of the Buttes, which was occupied by some fifty National Guards, who were disarmed before they had time to give the understood signal.

This signal consisted in three discharges of cannon, fired in quick succession. From this moment the heights were occupied in a military point of view.

The women of the neighborhood were loud in their denunciations against the National Guards who had surrendered, declaring, if they had been left in charge, the *canaille* of Versailles would have met with some resistance. One immense virago was gesticulating in a most fearful manner, calling the regular officers of the line scoundrels, assassins, and dogs.

There seems to have been some mismanagement in the organization of the plan of attack, as it is evident that many of the cannon seized at Montmartre as early as 5 o'clock A.M. were still guarded by the troops at 8 A.M.; no horses, or not sufficient in number, had arrived to remove them all. At this hour the National Guards began to show themselves, one at a time, crawling out of all sorts of places, to mix with a crowd of other guards and soldiers of the line coming up the hill with their muskets *la crosse en l'air* (reversed), shouting "*Vive la Ligne,*" and "*Vive la Garde Nationale,*" while others, who had captured a lieutenant-colonel of the line, were shouting "*à mort! à mort!*" and not a soldier came to succor him. Seeing matters were assuming a serious aspect, the regulars in charge of the cannon commenced harnessing the horses to the gun-carriages, and some twelve pieces began moving down toward the city by the Rue Lepic, but at the corner of the Rue des Abbesses another crowd opposed the passage of the guns. Men, women and children caught hold of the bridles of the horses, and the artillerymen, not wishing to run over them, desisted in their attempt to make a passage. A moment after, a company of sixty infantry arrived to protect the artillerymen and force a passage. They had hardly commenced to move when a heavy column of the National Guards of Belleville arrived to help their friends of Montmartre. At the same moment General Susbielle, appearing with an escort of *gendarmerie* and *Chasseurs d'Afrique,* gave them an order to form in sections and occupy Place Pigalle. The National Guards commenced now to arrive in great numbers, fraternizing with troops of the line who had either reversed their muskets or abandoned them altogether.

The General gave the order to the troops of the line to advance and open a passage for the guns; the soldiers refused to move, shouting "*Vive la Garde Nationale!*" The *Chasseurs d'Afrique* received the order to "draw sabres," but the line refused to open for them, and several shots were fired from the body of insurgents, when the captain gave the order "*En avant!*" and all the swords issued from their scabbards. "*Vive la République!*" cried the crowd, "*La Ligne et la Garde Nationale!*" The chasseurs hesitated, as before them were many men of the regular army, and in the end they sheathed their swords. "*En avant!*" repeated the captain, when several balls whistled past his head. Five or six men only followed him, but they were received with blows from the soldiers' muskets; one of the insurgents seized the reins of the captain's horse, but he fell, his head cleft in two; another grasped the reins on the other side, and in an instant the arm was severed from the body, and for a moment still hung quivering to the reins; two others shared the fate of the first, when the rider and horse both fell pierced by a shot at the same time, the insurgents discharging their pieces in the midst of the chasseurs and gendarmes, killing and wounding great numbers. The attack of the regular troops on the crowd was repulsed, the fraternizing soldiers firing on the former without hesitation, the crowd shouting "*Vive la République!*"

The excitement of the masses was now extreme. The 152d battalion of the National Guards arrived, having forced a post of the line and captured a mitrailleuse. Two other posts in that vicinity were also forced, and the crowd received the insurgents with "*Vive la République!*" The 88th regiment of the line, which was stationed at the corner of Boulevard Ornano and Rochechouart, withdrew their bayonets from their muskets, shouting "*Vive la Garde Nationale!*" The officers endeavored to resist, but were made prisoners and carried off. The soldiers then fraternized with the new comers, and seizing two mitrailleuses, were joined by a portion of the 87th of the line, to whom the pieces had been confided. The officers then, in consequence of the wavering of the troops who had up to this time remained faithful, or in consequence of the menacing appearance of a large and compact body of insurgents from Belleville, issued the order to retire, and thus permitted the new comers to occupy the place without firing another shot. At the same time the artillerymen at the corner of the streets removed their pieces rapidly towards the Place de Clichy. This retrograde movement began between eight and nine o'clock; and the calm and sensible citizens of this quarter had commenced to congratulate themselves that the horrors of the morning had subsided, when from the Place Pigalle a mitrailleuse was heard belching out wounds and death. Belleville representatives were firing on troops of the line who refused to fraternize. A panic now seized the crowd, and the masses fled in every direction.

CHAPTER II.

Elation of the National Guards—Erection of new barricades—Battery surrendered by its escort to the insurgents—Arrest of Generals Lecomte and Thomas—Their assassination—Brave attitude of the murdered officers—Two aides-de-camp of General Lecomte narrowly escape the same fate—The Central Committee assume the direction of affairs—Excitement at Montrouge—Barricades erected in the Faubourg Saint-Antoine—Gendarmes dismounted and disarmed—Proclamation of the Government—Events at the Hotel de Ville—All access to the Buttes Chaumont forbidden by the National Guards—Two regiments of the line surrounded and disarmed—The insurgents take possession of the Place Vendome—Evacuation of the 11th Arrondissement—Meeting of Paris Deputies, Mayors and Adjoints—Concessions proposed to the Government and accepted, but withdrawn after news received of the murder of Generals Lecomte and Thomas—The Central Committee take possession of the Hotel de Ville—Arrest of General Chanzy—Official journal seized by the insurgents—Proclamation of the Central Committee—City entirely abandoned by the troops—Public buildings occupied by the insurrection—Decree for the elections—Communication cut off with the provinces—The Government officials summoned to Versailles—The Prussians return to St. Denis—Their despatch to M. Jules Favre—His reply—Great military preparations—Sitting of the Assembly—The department of the Seine declared in a state of siege—Children of General Lecomte adopted by the country — Prussian communication to the Central Committee — Reply of Paschal Grousset.

PLACE PIGALLE, the centre of the Montmartre insurrection, had now commenced to assume its ordinary movement. The corpse of the brave but unfortunate officer of chasseurs had been deposited in one of the wooden huts constructed for the lodgement of soldiers, and a crowd of idlers passed in to see the victim. Some women cried "*Vive la ligne!*" to soldiers of the 88th who had fired on the staff and the chasseurs, to which one of them responded that he would sooner shoot himself than shoot his countrymen; and what cowards and *canaille* his officers were.

What a change since the morning. The streets so deserted, except an occasional red-trousered soldier of the line, were now swarming with National Guards flushed with victory, swaggering round superintending the construction of barricades, erecting batteries in which to place the captured cannon. Instead of the government blocking up every street, and placing a cordon of soldiers around Montmartre, with cannon pointing up, the insurgents were blockading them now with barricades and batteries, in which were guns pointing *down!* Drums were beating, trumpets braying, with every indication of very serious work.

Several pieces of the artillery of General Susbielle were lost while the cannon were being removed from the Buttes. Some boys had cut the traces, unseen by the drivers, and a number of National Guards suddenly fell on the guns and carried them off.

By two o'clock the troops had all been withdrawn from the vicinity of Montmartre. Several cannon which the artillerymen had retaken were abandoned by them near the Mairie, where the women and children precipitated themselves on the pieces to preserve them.

At this moment the Butte Montmartre and the artillery in the intrenched camp were completely in the power of the insurgents, who continued the erection of barricades in view of a renewed attack. The horse of the captain of chasseurs was cut up by the soldiers of the line who had mutinied, and sold on the Place, the proceeds of which they used for the purchase of liquor to cement their criminal union with the insurgents, who assured them the committee had plenty of money, or would soon have; and that the continuance of their pay, or better, was a certainty, with less to do and better food. The 100th and 181st battalion of the National Guard now arrived by the *Rue des Martyrs,* to take possession of the Heights of Montmartre. They were received with the loudest applause.

Captain Douradon, of the artillery, had been sent the previous night with a battery to the Boulevard Rochechouart. General Lecomte sent to him in the morning for two pieces to place them nearer to the Butte. The guns were escorted by a company of the line to support them. When the insurgents appeared, these soldiers raised the butts of their muskets in the air, and the cannons were taken by the rioters. The General, who occupied the Tour of Solferino, was arrested by some National Guards, and conducted to the Chateau Rouge, his only crime being that he refused to cry "*Vive la Republique!*" on compulsion. A short time after General Clement Thomas, lately commander-in-chief of the National Guards of Paris, was also made prisoner. He was passing in an inoffensive manner through the Rue Marie-Antoinette, when one of the insurgents having recognized him by his large white beard, went straight to him, saying,

"You are General Clement Thomas? I don't think I can be mistaken. That beard of yours betrays you."

"Well, supposing I am General Thomas. Have I not always done my duty?"

"You are a traitor and a *miserable!*" said the insurgent, grasping the old man by the collar. He was immediately assisted by others, who helped to drag the General in the direction of Rue des Rosiers, in No. 6 of which street the Republican Central Committee of Montmartre was holding its sittings. After the parody of a trial, he and General Lecomte were both hauled along the garden, and being tied together, were placed against the wall to be shot. An officer of the Garibaldian Legion implored to have the execution suspended, but his entreaties were drowned in shouts of "*A mort!*" "*A mort!*" In this supreme and horrible hour General Thomas exhibited proofs of heroic bravery. He stood facing his murderers, holding his hat in his hand. Instead of firing in a body, according to military usage, they fired one after the other. Each ball that struck him, some in the arms, others in the legs, caused a convulsive tremor of the body. The only words he uttered were "*Lâches! lâches!*" ("Cowards! cowards!"—a word of much stronger significance in the French than in the English language). At the end of the *fourteenth shot* he was still standing erect—still holding his hat in his hand, regarding his executioners with a look of horror. The fifteenth shot struck him under the right eye, when he fell to the ground.

General Lecomte was very pale. He stood erect—his arms crossed over his breast. He uttered a few words of expostulation, but fell almost instantly, pierced by a bullet behind the ear. It is said that both their corpses were then mutilated with bayonet thrusts.

There is a question whether General Lecomte had even a mock trial. Some say yes—others, no; but the fact that a lieutenant of the 269th battalion, who was present at these massacres, cried out, "To be shot without being heard! 'tis too horrible!" makes one incline to the latter report.

The two aides-de-camp of General Lecomte were about to undergo the same fate as their General, when they were saved by the intervention of a young man of seventeen, who cried out that what was taking place was horrible, and that no one knew the men who were ordering them to be put to death. He succeeded in saving the lives of the two young officers.

Towards four o'clock, the National Guards of Montmartre, who had collected since the forenoon, commenced a descent on Paris. About three battalions took the Rue des Martyrs, where the groups cried out, without much enthusiasm, "*Vive Garibaldi!*" "*Vive la Republique!*" The first body of these men marched very well, the second worse, and the third carried their weapons with a carelessness and indifference which had nothing terrifying, except to those in the rear.

At two o'clock the Central Committee of Montmartre had assumed the entire direction of affairs—had appointed committees of defence and of barricades—many of which were erected there and in other parts of Paris. A body of men, protected by a line of National Guards, raised a barricade at the end of the Rue des Martyrs, at the junction of that street with the Boulevards Rochechouart and Clichy. Behind it was placed a cannon on its carriage. Other barricades were erected on Rue Germain-Pilon, as also on all the different strategic points in that quarter of Paris.

The quarter Montrouge was also up and stirring; and though it had surrendered its cannon to the authorities a few days before, at two o'clock P. M. the Barrière-d'Enfer was in the hands of its battalions; the women and children were all in the streets; the walls were covered with proclamations from a committee stating that the National Guards were the protectors of the Republic; and that their officers ought to be appointed by them, and them alone. The streets were crowded with the insurgents coming and going to the headquarters of their commander-in-chief, which were situated in a shop in Rue Rochefoucault; and their appearance was anything but encouraging to the friends of law and order. They all carried chassepots, but that was the only thing in which they were all alike. They mostly wore slouched hats, with long hair. Your true insurgent favors that style; and in the absence of cartridge-pouches, stuffed that needful article in their pockets. Many wore high boots, with a brace of pistols stuck in their belts; and a line soldier who had become demoralized was a small deity among them. The beer and wine shops were all doing a thriving business, but their customers did not have the appearance of men bent on sustaining the proper authorities.

In the Faubourg St. Antoine numerous barricades were raised. One of the largest was in the Rue de Charonne, near the fountain; it was defended by several cannon from La Roquette, and was manned by National Guards. All circulation was prevented, and well-dressed people were obliged to shoulder a musket or be sent to work on some barricade; mounted gendarmes were obliged to surrender their horses and sabres. Barricades were erected on Rue Piat with one piece of cannon, on Rue Delamarre, Rue Godfrey, Rue de la Roquette, Rue de Flandres, Rue Vincent de Paul, Faubourg du Temple, Faubourg Saint Martin, Place de la Barrière Blanche, and several other points of importance.

In the course of the afternoon the following proclamation, addressed to the National Guards of the Seine, was posted up in Paris:

PARIS, 18th March 1871.

"The Government calls on you to defend your city, your homes, your property, and your families. Some misguided men, placing themselves above the law and obeying only a secret authority, are pointing against Paris the guns which have been saved from the Prussians. They are resisting by force the National Guard and the army. Will you permit such an act? Will you in sight of the foreigners, ready to take advantage of our disorders, abandon Paris to sedition? If you do not stifle it in the bud, the Republic will be lost, and perhaps France also! You have your future in your hands. The Government has allowed you to retain your arms. Take them up resolutely to re-establish the regime of the law, and to save the Republic from anarchy, which would be its ruin. Rally round your chiefs, for it is the only means of escaping ruin and the domination of the foreigner.

"ERNEST PICARD,
"Minister of the Interior.

"D'AURELLE,
General Commanding-in-Chief of the National Guards of the Seine."

Events of great importance were occurring in other parts of the city, away from the principal scene of disturbance. As early as nine o'clock A. M., groups were formed in the square before the Hotel de Ville, discussing the events of the morning. The words "treason" and "coup d'etat" being frequently heard. At about half past eleven a battalion of the line and one of the National Guard, headed by their drums and carrying their muskets upside down, arrived to protest against the attack at Montmartre. Cries of "*Vive la ligne!*" "*Vive la Republique!*" were heard on all sides, when suddenly a shot was fired by an individual in plain clothes. The mob rushed on the aggressor, who was at once seized; some persons were for throwing him into the river, but moderate counsels prevailed and he was removed in custody. Another well-dressed person, about sixty, took advantage of a moment of silence to raise the cry of "*Vive l'Empereur!*" "*A bas la Republique!*" In an instant he was knocked down and maltreated by the mob, his clothes being torn to shreds. The Office of Public Assistance and the Octroi were occupied by regiments of the line, whilst artillery and cavalry were massed in the Place of the Hotel de Ville. But when calm became re-established General Vinoy ordered them to be sent to other points. Later in the afternoon another deputation, of about 200 officers of the National Guard, line, and franc-tireurs, and accompanying several individuals, wounded in the Rue Legendre, came to protest against the "surprise" and "treason" of Montmartre.

At the junction of the Boulevards Voltaire (formerly Prince Eugene) and Richard Lenoir, women and children were at work constructing a barricade. All circulation was stopped, and about one hundred soldiers who were stationed here withdrew to the Bataclan café-concert. The entire district comprised between the Faubourg St. Martin, Rue Lafayette, the outer boulevards and Rues de Flandres, d'Allemagne and de Puebla, was entirely closed by double barricades, constructed of omnibuses and artillery-wagons filled with paving-stones. All access to the Buttes Chaumont was forbidden by the National Guards, to whom the protection of the guns there was confided.

The regiments of the line, among others the 35th, which had occupied the outer boulevards in the morning, were surrounded and confined between the barricades until they had given up their arms, when they were set at liberty. On the other hand, bodies of well-affected National Guards held various posts of importance. At 5 o'clock the 6th battalion guarded the Rue Drouot; the 10th and 227th the Place de la Bourse; the 149th the Mairie of the Bank Quarter; the 1st and 5th the Place Vendome; the 13th on the Rue de la Paix, on the side of the Rue Rivoli; the 12th the Rue de Marengo. Toward six o'clock a considerable affluence was to be seen on the Place de la Concorde; several battalions arrived there in succession, and among them the 81st, 82d, 131st, 156th, 165th and 178th; the reason for their presence was not clearly explained, and most of the men were themselves ignorant of what they were about to do.

During the whole day the gates of the Louvre, those of the Pavilion de Rohan looking on the Palais Royal as well as those of the Tuileries, were completely closed. The 89th of the line guarded the Place du Carrousel and the Tuileries. During the evening, among the groups formed at different points, the principal topic of conversation was the abominable act perpetrated in the afternoon at Montmartre, and of which Generals Lecomte and Clement-Thomas were the victims.

Early in the evening a body of some three thousand National Guards, composed of the 64th and 172d battalions, belonging to the Montmartre quarter, approached the Place Vendome without having encountered the slightest resistance in the way. Arriving at the Rue de la Paix, they found themselves confronted by the 1st battalion, Commandant Barré, who ordered the Montmartre men to halt; but as they manifested the intention of continuing their march, the 1st were ordered to load. This show of firmness brought the others to a stand-still, and they raised the butts of their muskets in the air, asking the 1st to do the same. The latter, however, remained resolute and awaited the orders of their chief. After having argued for some time and taken the instructions of the superior officers of the staff, the commandant of the 1st gave his men orders to retire, and the Place Vendome was abandoned to the others, who shortly after occupied the Etat-Major and the headquarters of the first military division.

The eleventh arrondissement, which is populated by most advanced republicans, who were positive that a *coup d'etat* was intended, seeing the streets occupied by cavalry, infantry and artillery, was spared a scene of bloody strife by the action of M. Mottu, Mayor of the arrondissement. He immediately waited on Ernest Picard who assured him of his republican sentiments, "Then do not defy the people. Why and against whom this display of force? I answer for the maintenance of order and peace in my arrondissement, if you do not yourselves offer provocations to disorder and civil war." "The general command," was the reply, "is in the hands of General Vinoy." M. Mottu went to the General and represented to him in warm language the grave responsibility he was incurring. Already, no doubt, the first account of the dispositions of the troops had reached the General, as, after a little hesitation, he decided on signing an order for the evacuation of the arrondissement, which was immediately executed.

Later in the day a meeting of Paris Deputies, Mayors and Adjoints was convened at the Mairie of the Second Arrondissement. The gravity of events gave to this assembly an unusual importance. After discussion, a deputation was sent to M. Picard to come to an understanding with him on the modifications to be introduced into the government system. Several proposals were made, but without any result; as the Minister of the Interior could not come to any decision without the assent of his colleagues. The deputation next waited on General De Paladines, who declared that he could not apply any remedy to the situation, which, besides, was not of his creating. The General declared that the fate of France was in the hands of the municipalities, and that he abandoned all initiative. Jules Favre afterward received the deputation, who proposed the following as the bases of the concessions claimed—1. The nomination of M. Langlois as the commander-in-chief of the National Guards; 2. M. Edmond Adam as Prefect of Police; 3. M. Dorian, Mayor of Paris; 4. M. Billot, member of the National Assembly, commander of the army of Paris. M. Jules Favre replied that he would submit those propositions to the government. On that declaration the delegates returned to the Mairie of the Second Arrondissement, where they found a letter from Jules Ferry, declaring to the mayors of Paris, that he abandoned the Hotel de Ville and delivered up his powers into the hands of those elected. He accordingly withdrew during the night to Versailles. The acceptance of these conditions were sent in the evening to the official journal of the government, but on hearing of the murder of the two generals, it was withdrawn.

The Hotel de Ville was taken possession of about 4 o'clock, the Mayor of the 24th Arrondissement, wearing his scarf, presented himself at the building and demanded admission, which was refused; a crowd collected and cheered him, and at last the doors were opened and he entered. The people then went to the Napoleon barrack and cheered the soldiers of the 109th regiment who were at the windows. The latter replied with cries of "*Vive la Republique!*" The commanding officer ordered the windows to be closed, and the troops disappeared. The mob then tried to break open the gates, and seizing a sentry-box, used it as a battering-ram. At this moment a door of the Hotel de Ville opened, and a company of gendarmes fell upon the crowd with the butt-ends of their muskets. An indescribable scene of tumult occurred. Women, children, and National Guards fled in every direction amidst screams and cries. The gendarmes afterward entered the building, and at a later hour, on the resignation of Jules Ferry becoming known, the doors were opened and the Central Committee took possession.

General Chanzy, Commander of the Army of the Loire, returning from Tours in the afternoon, was totally in the dark as to the events that had taken place during the day. The insurgents, evidently forewarned of his arrival, took possession of the Orleans station, and when the train stopped, a number of individuals, armed with revolvers, presented themselves at the door of the compartment in which the General was seated in full uniform, and ordered him to alight; resistance was useless, and he was carried off to the Chateau-Rouge and there confined, a prisoner in the hands of the Central Committee.

The evening of this eventful day was perfectly calm, although the crowds were great on the streets and boulevards, every one in search of news. The omnibuses had ceased to run, fearing they would be requisitioned for barricades; but in the centre of the city circulation was nowhere impeded.

In the morning of the 19th March the following proclamation was posted on the walls of Paris, addressed to the National Guards of the city, signed by all the members of the government present:

March 19, 1871.

"A body, assuming the name of Central Committee, after having seized on a certain number of cannon, has covered Paris with barricades, and has taken possession, during the night, of the Ministry of Justice. It has fired on the defenders of order; it has made prisoners and has murdered in cold blood Generals Clement-Thomas and Lecomte. Who are the members of that committee? No one in Paris knows them; their names are new to every one. No one can even say to what party they belong. Are they Communists, Bonapartists, or Prussians? Are they the agents of a triple coalition? Whoever they may be, they are the enemies of Paris, for they are giving it up to pillage; of France, for they are handing her over to the Prussians; and of the Republic, for they are abandoning it to despotism. The abominable crimes they have committed deprive of all excuse those who would dare to follow them or to submit to them. Will you accept the responsibility of their murders, and of the ruin they are bringing on the country? If so, remain at home. But if you have any regard for your most sacred interests, rally around the Government of the Republic and the National Assembly."

During the night the office of the *Journal Officiel* had been seized by the insurgents, and that paper appeared in the morning as the exclusive organ of the Central Committee, holding its sittings at the Hotel de Ville, with the following heading:

"*Republican Federation of the National Guard.*
Organ of the Central Committee."

HOTEL DE VILLE, March 19.

"CITIZENS:—You had charged us with organizing the defence of Paris and of its rights, and we are convinced that we have fulfilled this mission. Aided by your generous courage and your admirable *sang-froid*, we have expelled the government which was betraying us.

"At this moment our mandate has expired, and we again deliver it up to you, inasmuch as we do not pretend to take the place of those whom the popular breath has just overthrown. Prepare yourselves, and immediately make your communal elections, and give us for recompense the only one we ever hoped for—the true Republic. In the meantime we retain, in the name of the people, the Hotel de Ville.

"*Assi, Bilhoray, Ferrat, Babick, Edouard, Moreau, C. Dupont, Varlin, Boursier, Martier, Gushier, Lavalette, Fr. Jourde, Rousseau, Ch. Lullier, Blanchet, J. Grollard, Barroud, H. Geresme, Fabre, Pougerot.*"

The following proclamation was also posted on the walls of the city, addressed to the people, and signed by the same names as above:

"CITIZENS:—The people of Paris have shaken off the yoke sought to be imposed upon it. Calm, impassible in its strength, it awaited without fear as without provocation the shameless madmen who would destroy the Republic.

"This time our brothers of the army were unwilling to lay a hand on the sacred ark of our liberties. Thanks be to all, and let Paris and France together establish the basis of a Republic, acclaimed with all its consequences the only government that will forever close the era of invasions and civil wars.

"The state of siege is raised. The population of the capital is convoked in its sections for its communal elections. The safety of the citizen is assured by the assistance of the National Guard."

At 10 o'clock in the morning the last of the regular soldiers had quitted the capital, and were on the way to Versailles. The Ministry of Finance had been abandoned in the morning by the soldiers who there kept guard, and was occupied about noon by the National Guard. The specie on hand, which amounted to two and a half millions of francs, had been removed in the night to Versailles.

About the same hour the Ministry of the Interior, Ministry of Marine and Prefecture of Police were all occupied by the insurgents, and the entire public service was in the power of the Central Committee, who drew up the following explanation which was posted on the walls and appeared in the official journal:

"If the Central Committee of the National Guard were a government, it might, out of respect for the dignity of its electors, disdain to justify itself; but as it does 'not pretend to take the place of those whom the popular breath has overthrown,' but, in its simple honesty, desires to remain exactly within the express limits of its powers, it remains a compound of individualities which have the right to defend themselves.

"A child of the Republic, whose motto is the great word 'Fraternity,' it pardons its detractors; but it wishes to convince honest men who have accepted the calumny through ignorance, it has not acted in secret, for the names of its members were on all its proclamations. If the individuals were obscure, they did not shun the responsibility, which was great. It was not unknown, for it was the free expression of the suffrages of 215 battalions of the National Guard. It has not provoked disorders; for the National Guards, which have done it the honor to accept its direction, have committed neither excesses nor reprisals, and have owed their strength to the wisdom and moderation of their conduct.

"And yet provocations have not been wanting; the Government has not ceased, by the most shameful means, to attempt the most horrible of crimes—civil war; it has calumniated Paris, and has excited the provinces against the capital; it has drawn up against us our brothers of the army, and has left them to perish with cold in the streets while their homes were waiting them; it has attempted to impose on you a General-in-Chief; it has, by nocturnal attacks, tried to disarm us of our cannons, after having been prevented by us from delivering them up to the Prussians; in fine, with the aid of its affrighted accomplices of Bordeaux, it has said to Paris: 'Thou hast just been heroic; therefore we are afraid of thee, and tear from thy brow thy crown of capital.'

"What has the Central Committee done to reply to those attacks? It has founded the Federation; it has preached moderation and generosity. At the moment when the armed attack commenced it said to all: 'Refrain from aggression, and defend yourself only at the last extremity.' It summoned to its aid all men of intellect and capacity; it invited the co-operation of the corps of officers; it opened its door to whoever knocked in the name of the Republic. On which side, then, was right and justice, and on which deception?

"One of the greatest causes of anger against us was the obscurity of our names. Alas! how many were known—too well known, and that notoriety has often been fatal to us. One of the last means they employed against us was to refuse bread to the troops who preferred to allow themselves to be disarmed rather than fire upon the people; and they who punish by hunger the refusal to murder, call us assassins! In the first place—we say it with indignation—the sanguinary filth with which they attempt to sully our honor is an ignoble infamy. No order of execution was ever signed by us; the National Guard never took part in the execution of the crime. What interest would it or ourselves have had in doing so? The charge is as absurd as it is base.

"We are indeed almost ashamed to defend ourselves. Our conduct shows what we are. Have we ever sought after emoluments or honors? If we are unknown, although we have obtained the confidence of 215 battalions, it is because we have disdained to make any propaganda. A few hollow phrases or a little cowardice is sufficient, as is shown by recent events.

"We who were charged with a task which imposed on us a terrible responsibility have accomplished it without hesitation and without fear; and now that we have arrived at the goal, we say to the people who have esteemed us sufficiently to listen to our counsels: 'Here is the authority which thou hast confided to us; where our personal interest commences our duty ends; do this well; Master, thou hast recovered thy liberty. Obscure a few days back, we are about to return obscure to thy ranks, and show to those who govern that we can descend proudly the steps of the Hôtel de Ville, with the certainty of finding at the bottom the grasp of the loyal and robust hand.'

"*Ant. Arnaud, Assi, Billioray, Ferrat, Babick, Ed. Moreau, C. Dupont, Varlin, Boursier, Mortier, Gouhier, Lavalette, Fr. Jourde, Rousseau, Ch. Lullier, Henri Fortune, G. Arnold, Viard, Blanchet, J. Grollard, Barroud, H. Géresme, Fabre, Pougeret, Bouit—Les membres du Comité central.*"

The following decree was also issued:

"The Central Committee of the National Guard, seeing there is urgent necessity for immediately constituting the communal administration of the city of Paris, decrees—

"1. The elections of the Communal Council shall take place Wednesday, March 22.

"2. The vote shall be taken by ballot and by arrondissement, a councillor being named for twenty thousand inhabitants, or fraction in excess of ten thousand.

"3d. The voting shall take place from eight in the morning to six in the evening, the examination being made immediately after.

"4th. The municipalities of the twenty arrondissements are charged as concerns each with the execution of the present decree. An ulterior notice will indicate the number of councillors to be elected."

Signed as before.

Several other important decrees were published on the same day, abolishing military tribunals in the army, granting full amnesty for all political crimes and offences. Nearly all crimes were construed to be political ones, and directors of prisons were instructed to set at liberty all persons detained on political grounds.

The members of the Central Committee met on Monday morning, March 20th; the tricolor flag had been hauled down, and the red hoisted in its place. The Place de la Mairie de Paris was filled with National Guards, who discussed the state of affairs in front of their piled arms. All the shops were shut at that part of the Rue Rivoli. Barricades were raised with paving stones in the Avenue Victoria, Rue de Rivoli, on the quay, Place Lobau, and all the environs. After the National Guard had taken possession of the Prefecture of Police, they established pickets on the Place Dauphine, and numerous detachments were posted on the Quais des Lunettes and De l'Horloge, the Rue Sainte Chapelle, the Boulevard Sevastopol, and the Rue de Jerusalem. In the interior, sentinels were placed at every door, and in all directions National Guards were to be seen armed, many with two muskets.

The Etat-Major and Ministry of Justice in Place Vendome were occupied by the 91st battalion from Montmartre and the 174th from Belleville. The sentinels were doubled, and a duplicate supply of cartridges distributed to the men.

All the members of the government had left on Sunday, the 20th, for Versailles. M. Thiers left about noon. One of the first acts of the government installed at Versailles was to interrupt, by cutting the telegraph wires, all communication between Paris and the departments. The prefects in the provinces were also informed that any one of them who should publish the acts emanating from the Central Committee would be immediately arrested. The Ministers met in council under the presidency of M. Thiers, at the Hotel of the Prefecture, and decided that Paris must be left to itself until further orders, and that the government would remain on the defensive until the well-disposed National Guards made an energetic manifestation against the new power installed by the revolt at the Hotel de Ville and the Ministries.

M. Thiers telegraphed to all the different staffs at the Ministries to go and resume their posts at Versailles.

The Prussians, on hearing of the revolt in Paris, advanced nearer to the capital, and re-occupied St. Denis, which they had evacuated. They also telegraphed Jules Favre from Rouen the following despatch:

"ROUEN, March 21, 1871.

"I have the honor to inform your Excellency that, in in presence of the events which have just taken place in

Paris, and which appear no longer to ensure the execution of the conventions as regards the future, the commander-in-chief of the army before Paris interdicts all approach to our lines in front of the forts occupied by us, demands the re-establishment, within twenty four hours, of the telegraphs destroyed at Pantin, and declares that he will treat the city of Paris as an enemy if it shall still adopt any measures in contradiction to the negotiations engaged, and the preliminaries of peace, which circumstance would lead to an opening of the fire from the forts in question.

"FABRICE."

To which Jules Favre, Minister of Foreign Affairs, returned the following answer:

"VERSAILLES, March 21.

"I received only very late this evening the telegram which your Excellency does me the honor to address to me this day at 12 h. 20 m. The insurrectional movement triumphant in Paris has been only a surprise, before which the Government has momentarily retired to avoid a civil war. It is the work of a handful of factious men disavowed by the great majority of the population, and energetically combated by the mayors, who resist with courage. The departments are unanimous in condemning the movement and in promising their support to the Assembly. The government will make itself master of the situation; and if it does not do so to-morrow, the reason is that it desires to spare the effusion of blood. Your Excellency can therefore be assured that our engagements shall be kept, and you will doubtless be unwilling, in presence of these facts and of our formal declaration, to inflict on the city of Paris, protected by the preliminaries of peace, the calamity of a military execution. To do this would be to make the dying expiate the crime of a few perverse enemies of their country. As to the damage done to the telegraph at Pantin, the government, unfortunately, has not at present the means of repairing it. Notice has been sent to the mayors, who perhaps will be able to do what is demanded. But I have the honor to repeat to your Excellency, that, owing to the good sense of the great majority of the Paris population, to the firmness of the Assembly, and the support given by the departments, the cause of right will prevail, and that in a few days I shall have the power of giving entire satisfaction to your Excellency in respect to the claims justified by our engagements.

"JULES FAVRE."

The streets of Versailles soon became filled with soldiers from Paris, and no great alarm was manifested by the population at what was transpiring in that ill-fated city. Great military preparations, however, were being made, and arms and artillery were demanded from the departments.

The provinces were firmly determined to resist what was taking place in the capital, and to support their deputies. The Mobiles of the departments, stimulated by their representatives, commenced arriving by all the lines of railway.

A stormy debate took place at the sitting of the National Assembly on the 20th, on a motion brought up for the purpose of putting the department of the Seine and Oise in a state of siege. Louis Blanc violently opposed the measure, which he stated to be one of most aggressive character. He thought a policy of conciliation should be adopted with respect to Paris, the situation of which was extremely grave.

General Trochu declared the bill was not one of aggression but protection, and said that he was astonished, with respect to the measure, that no one had spoken of the murder of Generals Lecomte and Thomas. The executioners of these two brave men had repeatedly endeavored, during the siege, to get the Prussians into Paris, and it was that step which they were now again endeavoring to compass. He added further that General Lecomte, who has left six children, died a victim to duty, and the other officer had devoted his whole life to the Republic in the most courageous and generous manner; that the Assembly should, by a solemn vote, declare the country adopted the family of the first, and that the murder of the second was a cause of public mourning, in which all France took part! His expressions were received with the most enthusiastic applause by the entire Assembly, and the state of siege was declared almost unanimously. The Assembly declared it would make itself respected, and would succeed in founding the Republic which was now compromised by nefarious insurgents.

In the meantime the Central Committee received the following communication from the Prussian headquarters at Compiègne:

"COMPIEGNE, 21st March.

"The undersigned, commanding-in-chief, takes the liberty to inform you that the German troops which occupy the forts to the north and east of Paris, as well as the environs of the right bank of the Seine, have received orders to maintain an amicable and passive attitude so long as the events of which the interior of the city is the theatre shall not assume—with regard to the German armies—a hostile character, and of a nature to place them in danger; should such be the case, they will observe the terms determined by the preliminaries of peace.

"But, in the case these events should have a character of hostility, the city of Paris will be treated as an enemy.

"For the Commander-in-Chief of the 3d corps of the Imperial armies.

"VON SCHLOTHEIM,
Major-General."

To which Pasqual Grousset, Delegate for Foreign Relations, returned the following answer:

"PARIS, 22d March.

"The undersigned, delegated by the Central Committee to the department of Foreign Affairs, in answer to your despatch, informs you that the revolution accomplished here having a character essentially municipal, is not in any way aggressive against the German armies.

"Furthermore, we have no authority to discuss the preliminaries of peace voted by the Assembly at Bordeaux."

CHAPTER III.

Admiral Saisset appointed Commander-in-Chief of the National Guards—The Law and Order Party endeavor to overcome the insurrection—Concessions obtained by Admiral Saisset from the National Assembly—His proclamation —The insurrectionists still unsatisfied—The elections postponed by decree until March 26th—Declaration of the press—It calls forth a threat from the Central Committee—Procession of the Order Party—Passage through the Place Vendome—Citizen Tony-Mollin appointed Mayor of the 6th Arrondissement—M. Leroy takes possession of the Mairie—Is ejected by citizen Lullier —Warehouses broken into by the mob—Chassepots sold for ten francs—Deputation sent to Valerien—Second procession of the Order Party—Endeavor made to disperse the crowd—Shots fired—Frightful massacre—Ambulances collect the dead—Differences of opinion with regard to which party fired the first shot—Account given by the official journal—General Bergeret's view of the question—Requisitions—Executions at Montmartre—Deputation of Mayors to the Assembly demanding a compromise concerning the day of the elections—Hostile attitude of the Assembly—Address of M. Arnaud—Tribune assigned to the Mayors—Their entrance—Their observations resented by the Right—Violent agitation—The meeting dissolved—Evening sitting—Resolutions presented by the Mayors for approval—Several Mayors on their return to Paris make an arrangement with the Central Committee—The citizens exhorted to vote—Discrepancy in the statement of the Mayors and that of the Central Committee—The resolutions of the Mayors rejected in the Assembly by a large majority—Decrees in the official journal—Insurrectional movement in Lyons—In Marseilles—Toulouse—St. Etienne—Fusion of the Mayors and Central Committee—Version of the Committee—That of the Mayors—Proclamation of the Deputies of Paris—Resignation of Admiral Saisset—Proclamation of the Central Committee.

THERE were now published daily two official journals, one emanating from the Hotel de Ville in Paris, the other published in Versailles by order of the National Assembly. The last-named, after publishing an announcement that Admiral Saisset had been named Commander-in-Chief of the National Guards of the Seine, a leader who, the government thought, would rally the men of order, published the following declaration:

"The Government wished to avoid bloodshed, even when provoked to it by the unexpected resistance of the Central Committee of the National Guard. That opposition, skilfully organized, and directed by conspirators as audacious as they were treacherous, was carried into effect by the invasion of a mass of National Guards without arms, and of the population, rushing on the soldiers, breaking their ranks and depriving them of their arms. Led away by those guilty manœuvres, many of the men forgot their duty. The National Guard which had been convoked, also held back, and during the whole day only came out in insignificant numbers. In that serious conjuncture the Government, not wishing to engage in a sanguinary encounter in the streets of Paris, and considering that it was not strongly enough supported by the National Guard, decided on withdrawing to Versailles, near the National Assembly, the only legal representation of the country. On leaving Paris, the Minister of the Interior, at the request of the Mayors, delegated to a commission to be appointed by them the power of provisionally administering the affairs of the city, but the authorities met several times without arriving at any understanding. While those events were going on, the insurrectionary committee installed itself at the Hotel de Ville, and published two proclamations—one, to announce its assumption of the chief authority; and the other, to convoke the electors of Paris to appoint a Communal Assembly.

"This shameful state of anarchy is, however, beginning to move the good citizens, who are perceiving too late the fault they have committed in not immediately giving their material aid to the Government appointed by the Assembly. Who can, in fact, without a shudder, accept the consequences of that deplorable sedition, descending on a city like a sudden tempest, irresistible and inexplicable? The Prussians are at our gates, and we have treated with them. But if the Government which signed the preliminaries of peace, is overthrown, the convention is broken. The state of war recommences, and Paris is fatally condemned to an occupation. Thus the long and painful efforts by which the Government succeeded in avoiding that irreparable misfortune will be rendered fruitless; but that is not all—with this lamentable disorder credit is destroyed and labor suspended. France not being able to meet her engagements will be abandoned to the enemy, who will reduce her to a cruel state of servitude. Such are the bitter fruits of the criminal folly of some, and of the deplorable supineness of others. The time has come to return to reason and to take courage. The Government and the Assembly do not despair. They appeal to the country and lean on it, decided as they are on following it resolutely, and on striving boldly against sedition."

The law and order men of the National Guards, with several of the leading citizens of Paris, encouraged by the government, made for a few days a spasmodic exertion to overthrow the insurrection, and bring back affairs to their old state. Admiral Saisset was popular, a true republican and a patriotic man, his only son had been killed during the late siege, and it was thought that he stood well with all the different elements of the National Guard; he had obtained, in conjunction with the Mayors and Deputies of Paris, very important concessions from the National Assembly, concessions which ought to have satisfied any true republican, concessions that were all which the Central Committee at one time wanted—the recognition of its municipal franchise and the election of the officers of the National Guard. Much importance was therefore attached to the following proclamation, which was thought would serve as a base for a compromise:

"PARIS, March 23, 1871.

"DEAR FELLOW-CITIZENS:—I hasten to inform you that, in accord with the Deputies of the Seine and the Mayors of Paris, we have obtained from the Government of the National Assembly:

"1. The complete recognition of your municipal franchise;

"2. The election of all the officers of the National Guard, including the Commander-in-Chief.

"3. Certain modifications of the measure in commercial bills;

"4. A law of rents favorable to tenants paying any sum as far as and including 1,200 francs.

"Until you have confirmed my nomination or shall have replaced me, I remain at my post of honor to watch over the execution of the conciliatory measures which we have obtained, and thus contribute to the consolidation of the Republic.

SAISSET,

Vice-Admiral, Prov. Commander-in-Chief of the National Guard of the Seine.

What more could the chiefs of the revolt have demanded. If they had been sincere, as they declared themselves to be, they were bound to adhere to these dispositions which would have given satisfaction at once to the interests of law and order—but they were not sincere, neither did General McMahon, nor the other military leaders, believe them; but M. Thiers was willing to go to any length to prevent the effusion of more blood.

The Central Committee sitting at the Hotel de Ville issued the following proclamation relating to their forthcoming election:

"HOTEL DE VILLE, 22d March, 1871.

"CITIZENS:—Your legitimate anger placed us on the 18th of March at the post which we will only occupy until the necessary arrangements can be made for the forthcoming communal elections.

"Your mayors and your deputies, repudiating the engagements they had just made as candidates, have tried to fetter the elections, which we wish to hold in the briefest possible time.

"The reaction raised by them declares war against us.

"We will accept the struggle, and will crush all resistance, that you may proceed to the vote in the serenity of your will and your power.

"In consequence, the elections are postponed until Sunday next, March 26th.

"Up to that time the most energetic measures will be taken to cause to be respected the rights you have assumed.

"*Avoine fils, Ant. Arnaud, G. Arnold, Assi, Andignoux, Bouit, J. Bergeret, Babick, Boursier, Baron, Billioray, Blanchet, Castioni, Chouteau, C. Dupont, Ferrat, Henri Fortuné, Fabre, Fleury, Pougeret, C. Gaudier, Gouhier, Guiral, Géresme, Grollard, Josselin, F. Jourde, Maxime Lisbonne, Lavalette, Ch. Lullier, Maljournal, Moreau, Mortier, Prudhomme, Rousseau, Ranvier, Varlin, Viard—Le Comité Central de la Garde Nationale.*

In the meantime, the principal Paris journals entered into a combination to resist the holding of the elections by the insurgents, and issued the following

"DECLARATION OF THE PRESS.

"To the Paris Electors:—Seeing that the convocation of electors is an act of national sovereignty;

"That the exercise of this sovereignty appertains to the powers emanating from universal suffrage;

"That, in consequence, the committee which is installed at the Hotel de Ville has neither the right nor the quality to make this convocation.

"The representatives of the undersigned journals consider the convocation announced for the 22d of March as null and void, and request the electors to regard it in that light.

(Signed)

"*Journal des Débats, Constitutionnel, Electeur Libre, Petite Presse, Vérité, Figaro, Gaulois, Paris Journal, Petit National, Rappel, Presse, France, Liberté, Pays, National, Univers, Cloche, Patrie, Français, Bien Public, Union, Opinion Nationale, Journal des Villes et Campagnes, Journal de Paris, Moniteur Universel, France Nouvelle, Gazette de France, Messager de Paris, Soir.*"

This collective declaration of the Paris journals does them great honor, as they embody every shade of politics. The committee, however, threatened with severe repression any resistance to its authority, and announced that the reactionary journals had recourse to falsehood and calumny to cast a slur on the patriots who had ensured the triumph of the people's rights. "We cannot attack the liberty of the press," it said; "only, the Government of Versailles having suspended the ordinary course of the tribunals, we warn all badly-intentioned writers to whom would be applicable in other times the common law on slander and insult, that they will be immediately tried by the Central Committee of the National Guard."

Assi, one of the chiefs of the insurrection, a leading member of the International Society, the instigator and promoter of nearly all the "strikes" that have occurred throughout Europe, made his appearance in the streets in one of the late Emperor's carriages; it had passed, inside the year, through the hands of Napoleon III., Gambetta, Glais-Bizoin, Rochefort, Etienne Arago, Jules Ferry, and Assi. Nearly all the other carriages had been sent to Versailles for the use of the government.

Soon after a numerous column of peaceable citizens, which increased at each instant, composed of National Guards without arms, artisans, tradesmen and soldiers, traversed the boulevards and descended the Rue Vivienne as far as the Place de la Bourse. They carried a tricolored flag, with an inscription "*Union of the Men of Order,*" "*Vive la République!*" On their arrival at the Place, the battalion on guard there had an instant's hesitation, but on hearing shouts in favor of order and the National Assembly, they turned out and presented arms. The manifestation, which became more important every instant, then resumed its march, and passing by the Rue Montmartre and the boulevard of that name, came to the Rue Drouot. At the Mairie, in that street, the guard, which was composed of the 117th battalion (one of the insurgent battalions) attempted to prevent the procession from passing; but its members held firm, and insisted on pursuing their way to the Rue Lafayette. In the end the malcontents gave way, and the others went on with the same cry of "*Vive l'Ordre!*" They afterward traversed another part of the boulevard and went down the Rue de la Paix. On arriving at the entrance of Place Vendome, they found all passage barred, but they went in resolutely and passed unmolested through the guard. A man who strove to speak from the balcony of the Etat-Major in the name of the insurgents, was hooted down with cries of "*A bas le Comité!*" The guardians of the place put themselves in position near their guns, and a panic took place among the crowd. Fortunately the procession took a prudent course and proceeded on its route, avoiding the horrible massacre which took place at the same point on the following day.

At 5 o'clock, when the cortège descended the Boulevard St. Michel and passed before the Palais de Justice, the numbers exceeded five thousand, and the people who thronged the steps manifested open sympathy, particularly at each cry of "*Vive l'Assemblée Nationale!*"

After the passage of the friends of order, the battalions in charge of the Etat-Major in the Place Vendome took formidable precautions. Two pieces of cannon threatened the Rue de la Paix, and two more the Rue Castiglione; the circulation was also stopped, and piquets were placed at the corners of the streets leading to those localities.

The Central Committee now commenced to make many arbitrary arrests and requisitions, among the latter one million francs from the Bank of France; also to occupy the different posts by National Guards, strangers in the districts; in consequence of which the men of order belonging to the Guards, held public meetings in the various arrondissements, and decided upon energetic measures for the protection of their respective quarters.

The Central Committee had delegated the citizen Tony-Mollin as Mayor of the 6th Arrondissement, in place of M. Hérisson. A short time after M. Herbert Leroy, one of the Adjoints of the Mairie, accompanied by a numerous crowd, arrived and took possession of his municipal cabinet, Tony-Mollin being at that moment absent. But this success was of short duration; for shortly after, Citizen Lullier, one of the chiefs of the insurgents, presented himself with three battalions of the National Guard and reinstated M. Tony-Mollin.

A large storehouse of arms, belonging to the Government, in the Rue St. Dominique, and another on the Boulevard de Latour-Maubourg, was broken into by a mob in sympathy with the insurgents, and completely plundered of all their contents. Several officers of the National Guard attempted to introduce some order in the appropriation of the objects belonging to the state; but each individual took the article he pleased, and carried it off to sell or give away, and then returned to the depot to make a fresh selection. Boys of thirteen or fourteen were seen marching off with pistols, revolvers or muskets. On the Avenue de Latour-Maubourg, in the building of the Invalides, which lately served as the arsenal for the Garde Mobiles, the chassepots left by a regiment of the Line were taken, and might be purchased in the evening for from one to ten francs each. The stock of arms was soon exhausted, and the late-comers had to content themselves with belts, cartridge-boxes, and other articles of equipment. A serious danger of explosion existed for a long time, as many of the people who had made the irruption did not take the precaution of putting out their pipes or cigars, while open cases of cartridges were lying about in all directions. The rush was so great that one National Guard had his leg broken, and several were almost squeezed to death.

The forts on the south of Paris being all in the possession of the National Guards, they sent a deputation of three thousand men to demand the delivery of Mount Valerien, the greatest stronghold in the vicinity of Paris, situated at the west, and dominating nearly the whole city. The regular troops in the fort were much irritated at the demand. The colonel in command having consented to parley with three of the National Guard, declined their advances, ushered them through the gates, and the 3000 men returned to the city. Had the insurgents gained possession of Valerien, the situation of Paris would have been much more grave.

On the following day, March 22d, a large mass of people belonging to the party of "Order," many of whom were probably the same persons who had paraded the streets on the previous day, assembled on the Place de l'Opera about one o'clock. They were without arms, and most respectable in appearance—few blouses, if any, were to be seen. Their intention was the same as the day before, viz., to promenade the boulevards in crying "*Vive la République!*" "*Vive l'Ordre!*" "*Vive l'Assemblée Nationale!*" Between one and two o'clock a picket of insurrectionary National Guards advanced by the Rue de de la Paix, with an order to disperse this peaceable multitude. At sight of the menacing attitude of these armed men, the crowd commenced to shout: "*Vive l'Ordre!*" "*Vive l'Assemblée Nationale!*" and succeeded by their words in causing the National Guards to retire towards Place Vendome. When it was seen that these guards thus gave way before words of conciliation, the crowd entered in a body, with the object of passing through the Place. Among the multitude no other cry was heard but "*Vive l'Ordre!*" "*Vive la République!*" "*Vive l'Assemblée Nationale!*" It thus proceeded to the entrance of Place Vendome, a distance of about three hundred yards, when it was opposed by the National Guards, who stood at "charge bayonets," drums beating "to arms;" but the noise was drowned in the continued cries of "*Vive l'Ordre!*" "*Vive l'Assemblée Nationale!*" A group of citizens, who had arrived by the way of Rue Neuve des Capucines, carrying a tricolored flag, advanced to the front, where the Guards barred the passage. As they advanced, the cries of "*Vive l'Ordre!*" were redoubled, and a general waving of handkerchiefs and hats, hoisted on the end of sticks, took place—and every one looked forward to a happy *denoûment* of the affair. Vanquished by this pacific and patriotic manifestation, some of the guards raised the butt-end of their muskets, others peaceably crossed their bayonets; and it was seen and felt that in a few more minutes the insurrection would melt away before the right and legality of conciliation; but, alas! at the corner of Place Vendome a shot was fired. The crowd remained impassible. This first shot was immediately followed by five others, which caused the multitude to retreat; but on the exhortation of several men of decision and courage, it again advanced, holding firm its original position, when a fearful discharge of musketry took place, causing a general flight of the masses. In the twinkling of an eye Rue de la Paix was covered with the bodies of the wounded, dead, and those overthrown in the panic. The flight of the crowd did not arrest the fire of the National Guards, who continued to shoot on every side of the street, in many instances killing their own men. One splendid looking fellow, dressed in the costume of the French navy, bravely stood his ground, holding the tricolor in his left hand, and striking his breast with his right, crying "*Vive la Republique!*" "*Tirez donc, tas d'assassins.*" A rush was then made by the National Guard, who arrested all who had not run away, and conveyed them inside the Place Vendome. In an instant the greatest alarm prevailed everywhere in the neighborhood, and all the shops were at once closed. Groups collected, and the words "Assassins!" "Brigands!" were heard on every side. The men of the Place Vendome then cleared the Rue Castiglione, and posted sentinels at the end towards the Rue Rivoli, to prevent any one from passing. Half-an-hour afterwards a strong body escorted the persons made prisoners to the end of the street, and then set them at liberty. The excitement was everywhere intense, and fear was entertained of further bloodshed before the morning.

The ambulances soon began collecting the bodies which were lying in the Rue de la Paix and in the adjoining streets. They were mostly carried inside the Place Vendome, and ranged in a row upon a long table in the building of the Credit Mobilier; others, that were at once recognized, were carried off on brancards in different directions. Two workmen in blouses carried off one poor fellow who was screaming in the most horrible manner, the blood having completely saturated his clothes and the mattress upon which he was lying; he was dead before they had arrived at his home, which was in the immediate vicinity. On their return for more wounded, as they passed in front of the American Club on the Place de l'Opera, they met a body of the National Guards coming from Place Vendome; the brave fellows set down the brancard in such a position that the Guards were obliged to make a detour in order to pass, and turning over the mattress they pointed to the gory bed of the murdered man, and shouting "Look there! murderers and assassins! Look at the blood of Place Vendome!" the soldiers seemed sobered and scared at the terrible tragedy their folly had brought about; but two or three loaded their chassepots, pointing them at the men, when the officer in command stepped in front, and, waiving his sword, ordered his men to advance.

There has been considerable debate and altercation as to which party fired the first shot, the Men of Order or the National Guards. The defenders of the National Guards (when they have defenders) say that the Order party, under pretence of a friendly unarmed remonstrance, attempted to force the ranks of the National Guards and get possession of their rifles, some of which had actually been thus carried away, and that one or two of their men had been shot before they fired a gun. Lieutenant-General Sheridan, who was stopping at the time in the Westminster Hotel, situated in Rue de la Paix, and who saw the whole affair, says the crowd fired first on the National Guard; but another American gentleman, who was standing on his balcony in the same hotel, thinks the National Guard fired first on the crowd. The official journal of the Committee published an account of the unhappy affair after an inquiry into the matter, the translation of which is the following:

"The Central Committee at once ordered an inquiry into the events which occurred on the Place Vendome on the 22d. It was unwilling to publish an immediate recital, which might have been accused of being influenced by foregone conclusions. The following are the facts as they result from the evidence taken on the investigation:

"At half-past one the manifestation, which had been collecting since noon on the Place du Nouvel Opera, descended the Rue de la Paix. In the first ranks an excited group, amongst whom the National Guards assert that they recognized MM. de Heeckeren, De Cœtlegon, and H. de Pène, former supporters of the Empire, was violently agitating a flag, bearing no inscription. On arriving at the Rue Neuve-Saint-Augustin, the demonstrators surrounded, disarmed, and maltreated two men detached as advanced sentinels. Those citizens only owed their safety to retreat to the Place Vendome, and without their muskets, their clothes torn. Immediately the National Guards seized their arms and advanced as far as the Rue Neuve-des-Petits-Champs.

"The first rank had received orders to raise the butt-ends of their muskets in the air if it was broken, and to fall back behind the third; the same for the second; whilst the last of all was to cross bayonets, but expressly recommended not to fire.

"The foremost amongst the crowd, which amounted to about 800 or 1,000 persons, were soon face to face with the defenders. The character of the demonstration was then clearly defined. Cries were raised of '*A bas les Assassins! A bas le Comité!*' and the nationals were grossly insulted. They were called 'Murderers!' 'Cowards!' 'Brigands!' Some furious individuals seized their muskets, and an officer's sword was wrenched from him. The shouts were redoubled, and the affair became, instead of a manifestation, a veritable riot. In fact, a revolver shot wounded in the thigh Citizen Maljournal, Staff-Lieutenant of the Place, member of the Central Committee. General Bergeret, commander of the forces, hastened at the commencement to the front rank and summoned the rioters to withdraw. During nearly five minutes the roll of the drum was to be heard. Ten times the order was repeated, and was replied to by cries and abuse. Two National Guards fell seriously wounded; but, however, their comrades hesitated, and fired in the air. The agitators strove to break the lines and disarm the National Guard. Some shots were heard, and the crowd suddenly dispersed. General Bergeret instantly ordered the firing to cease, and his officers aided his efforts. However, other detonations were heard in the interior of the Place, and the fact is only too true that the National Guards were fired upon from the houses. Two of them were killed: the citizens Wahlin and François, belonging to the 7th and 215th battalions; eight were wounded: namely, Maljournal, Cochet, Miche, Ancelot, Legat, Reyer, Train, and Laborde.

"The first of the dead taken to the ambulance of the Crédit Mobilier was Viscount de Molinet, struck at the back of the head, in the front rank of the crowd. He fell at the corner of the Rues de la Paix and Neuve-des-Petits-Champs, on the Place Vendome side, with his face to the ground. The fact is clear that he was struck by his companions, for had he fallen in flying the body would have lain in the direction of the New Opera. On the corpse was found a poignard attached to the waist-belt by a chain.

"A large number of revolvers and sword-sticks were picked up in the Rue de la Paix and taken to the Etat-Major.

"Doctor Rambow, formerly surgeon at the camp of Toulouse, living 32 Rue de la Victoire, and a number of other medical men, hastened to attend the wounded and sign the official reports.

The valuables found on the rioters were placed in sealed packets and deposited at the Etat-Major.

"Owing to the coolness and firmness of General Bergeret, who was able to restrain the just indignation of the National Guards, more serious accidents were avoided."

Most of the men killed and wounded, judging from their appearance, were men of respectability, and not likely to take part in an ordinary street row. Nearly all had been struck in the upper parts of the body, about the heart or head, and in the back, as if they were turning to escape. A great deal of the firing had evidently been aimed at the windows, as many of the panes of glass in the Rue de la Paix and Place Vendome had been shivered by bullets.

General Bergeret, who figured later as a conspicuous member of the Commune, gave the following account of the affair:

"For some days we were endeavoring to overthrow the illegal government of Paris, and establish one founded on universal suffrage. This effected, the elections will approve everything we have done. We intend to ratify the peace made with the Prussians, and heal the wounds of France. The mad population are ready to take advantage of the situation to rob and murder. On Tuesday a large crowd approached the Place Vendome, shouting and hissing the government of the Central Committee, and showed a disposition to drive the National Guards from their position.

"I wished to parley with them, but they refused, with characteristic monarchical intolerance, and hissed and shouted. They retired, threatening to return the following day. On Wednesday they again prepared a demonstration, and some were armed. I placed men in the Rue de la Paix to keep back the mob, if any attempted to invade the Place Vendome, with orders not to fire. At one o'clock a large crowd of ten thousand advanced and overpowered the first line, wrenched the rifles from the troops, beat and maltreated them. I ordered the second line to retire slowly on Place Vendome, and to keep back the crowd, without violence. The guns were taken from more soldiers, upon which I ordered the line to take up a position across the road in sufficient numbers to resist the crowd by force; but I told them to throw up their rifles, so as to show the people that we wished to avoid an effusion of blood. They remained face to face some minutes. The crowd tried to break the cordon; and, yelling against the Government and the National Guard, at last they commenced using their revolvers, so that four of our men fell. One died immediately, shot through the brain, and the others are very seriously wounded. The National Guard, finding that the mob meant bloodshed, fired first in the air. Some, enraged at seeing their comrades fall, fired at the crowd, and killed five and wounded fifteen or twenty. The mob then dispersed in great confusion, and I hope will attempt nothing of the kind in future. We do not want war, nor do we want to kill each other; for our enemies are scarcely out of the city. What can we do? The Government attempted to take our cannon, and to prepare for a monarchy. The Assembly has a fixed determination to force a king upon us. We will avoid further bloodshed."

The situation in Paris remained for several days about the same. The supporters of the law had taken up arms, and were occupying the principal quarters of the capital. All parts of France were rallying round the National Assembly and the Government. A proposition had been passed in the Chamber that the National Guards of France should be summoned to assist in the defence of the representatives of the country. The army at Versailles was hourly being reinforced, and the head of the Executive Power was accused of lack of energy in not at once attacking the insurgents; but he, or the generals in command, knew their duties better. It would have been sheer madness to make an attack on 100,000 men fighting in forts, defended by ramparts, or behind barricades, even if the 25,000 National Guards who remained loyal could have opened the gates. The army did not yet muster over 50,000 men, many of whom had probably not yet been cured of their fraternizing propensities.

In the meantime the requisitions of the Committee kept increasing. The insurgents had used up one million three hundred thousand francs, which were on deposit at the Comptes d'Escomptes to the credit of the International Society, in addition to the loose change they had found lying at the different public offices. Many of the shopkeepers were hesitating about laying in further supplies, and all of them manifested the intention of defending their property. The following is a specimen of one of the orders issued by the Committee of the Hotel de Ville:

"LIBERTY, EQUALITY, FRATERNITY.
"IN THE NAME OF THE REPUBLIC.
"REQUISITIONS.
"MONEY—PROVISIONS.

"In case of refusal, Citizen Albert, charged with the commission, may get himself assisted by the National Guards of the quarter. (Signed) "LULLIEN,
"Member of the Federation."

There were two stamps on this paper—one with the words "*République Française*," and the other "*Federation Républicaine*." Thus had a revolution of blood and violence fully commenced. The insurgents were now the declared enemies of peaceful Paris, and must succeed, in order not to be called to account for the blood shed and robberies committed. They now held Paris in their grasp, utterly despising the National Assembly and its power.

The following is a copy of a report made by the General in command (formerly a dealer in old iron), at Montmartre.

"Report from 20th to 21st. Nothing new. I have received communications from the chief of ports. At five minutes past ten, two sergeants-de-ville, disguised as simple citizens, were brought up by some franc-tireurs, and immediately shot. At twenty minutes past twelve, a gardien-de-la-paix, accused of firing off a revolver, was also shot. At seven in the evening a gendarme, brought in by some Guards of the 28th battalion, was similarly put to death."

Seeing the danger of allowing matters to proceed in the above manner, the principal mayors of Paris, in conjunction with the deputies of the city, most of whom were advanced Republicans, desired to make a compromise with the Committee, and hold the elections at once; but the Government of Versailles refused to sanction this compromise, and issued a decree to hold the elections on the 3d of April, the day on which they were to be held throughout France. The Committee insisted they should be held in Paris on the 26th of March; consequently, a deputation, consisting of fourteen of the mayors of Paris, visited Versailles, to represent to the Assembly the advantages of compromising with the insurgents; but their arrival was ill-timed—the Assembly was in no mood for compromising with rebels. M. Sarget, a member of the Chamber, had just finished a speech, in which he said that "General Trochu lately proposed to the Assembly to declare General Clement-Thomas' death a cause of public mourning, and to adopt the family of General Lecomte. Yesterday an infinitely more tragical event took place near the Place Vendome, where a number of inoffensive citizens, without arms, and crying '*Vive la France!*' '*Vive l'Assemblée Nationale!*' were fired at by pretended National Guards, and mercilessly slaughtered" (great agitation). "I propose that France should adopt the families of the unfortunate victims who thus lost their lives when protesting in favor of order" (renewed approbation). A voice replied "that the whole budget would not suffice at the rate the insurgents were going on."

M. Arnaud, who, in addition to being a mayor of Paris, was also deputy, rose and said that, "in common with his colleagues, mayors in Paris (Paris is divided into twenty arrondissements, each having its mayor appointed by the government), he had, in consequence of the gravity of existing circumstances, come to Versailles to place himself in communication with the Assembly. He was quite sure that none but members had a right to take a seat there, but he thought his duty required him to ask that an exception should be made in favor of the municipal functionaries. (Protests on the Right.) The fact would be sufficient that one of them, who was a Deputy, should make the communication, so as to prevent any idea of disorder. The Assembly would decide as it thought proper. He had been charged with a commission, which he had fulfilled conscientiously. He wished to observe, as they had all come together, and been jointly delegated—

On the Right.—"By whom?" (Great noise.)

4

Several Voices.—"Was it by the existing executive?"

M. Flouquet.—"You desire, then, the continuation of the civil war?" (Renewed disturbance.)

M. Arnaud believed he had no occasion to give any explanations, as, in speaking of delegation, he recognized no other power than that issuing from universal suffrage. He was anxious to state that he and his friends had come to state the results of their common efforts, and that they hoped to triumph; but they were anxious to be strengthened by the sentiment and assistance of the Assembly. He left the matter in the hands of the President, and asked at least that a tribune should be assigned to the various representatives of the municipal bodies of Paris.

The President.—Nothing could be more simple than to reconcile the rights, prerogatives, and interests of the Assembly, which must never be sacrificed, with the deference due to the mayors of Paris. M. Arnaud had said that they had a communication to make. Amongst them were several members of the Chamber; let one of them read the document. As to the respect due to the municipal functionaries, that would receive full satisfaction. A tribune should be placed at their disposal, and he believed that the questers had already taken the necessary measures.

M. Baze, a member, said he would give the mayors the most distinguished places in the house.

At that moment fourteen members of the municipality of Paris entered, each wearing the tricolored scarf, which forms the insignia of their office. The whole Assembly at once rose and welcomed them with loud applause, the Left with cries of "*Vive la France!*" and "*Vive la République!*" and the Right with the former alone. The mayors responded with some exclamations for France and the Republic, when fifty or sixty members of the Right, pointing to them, called out: "Order! order! They do not respect the Assembly! Have the hall evacuated! They have no right to speak! they are only admitted as spectators!" The members of the Left protested in favor of the mayors, and for a time the tumult was so great that the words used in the altercation going on between the two sides of the Chamber could not be heard. About thirty deputies put on their hats, although the President was still sitting. The Left cried out, "Hats off! Respect your President!"

M. Floquet, to the Right.—"You are insulting Paris!"

A Voice.—"And you are insulting France!"

The agitation, instead of calming down, continued to increase, and the President, despairing of being able to restore order, declared the sitting to be at an end, but that the members would again meet in the evening.

The Deputies met again at ten o'clock in the evening—the mayors were not present, having returned to Paris.

M. Arnaud presented a series of resolutions agreed upon by the mayors of Paris, who were convinced that the re-establishment of order required the following measures:

1. That the Assembly should place itself in more frequent and closer communication with the municipalities of Paris.

2. That it should authorize the mayors to adopt such measures as circumstances might require.

3. That the elections of officers in the National Guard should take place before the 28th inst.

4. That the municipal councils should be chosen before the 3d of April, if possible, and the qualifications for being elected should consist merely in six months' residence.

A number of the mayors, immediately after their return to Paris, without waiting for any action to be taken on the above propositions, entered into an arrangement with the Central Committee that the election should take place on the 26th.

The walls of Paris were covered with placards exhorting all citizens to go and vote at the municipal elections. At the first glance it would appear that all parties were unanimous in giving this advice. The Central Committee stated that the mayors and deputies had rallied to it. On the other hand, these last, in a rival notice entitled, "The only authentic text of the Convention," whilst endeavoring to show it was not they who had gone over to the Committee, but the latter to them, also came to the conclusion that all ought to take part in the ballot. But in looking a little more closely, it was seen that this unanimity was much less perfect than at first appeared.

Louis Blanc made it known to the Assembly that it had been decided to hold the elections on Sunday, March 26th, notwithstanding that body had as yet taken no action in the matter; but he had thought there was danger in postponing that proceeding, and in consequence asked, in the name of the Deputies of the capital, the Assembly to declare that the mayors and adjoints, in consenting to that course, acted like good citizens. The Chamber rejected the proposal by a large majority.

The official organ of the Central Committee continued to publish daily decrees of more or less importance. Following the announcement of the municipal elections on the 26th, there was one encouraging the National Guard to persist firmly in their service, although they were opposed by several battalions of that body and a portion of the press, which stigmatized the movement of the Committee as the act of communists, pillagers, and insurgents; another implored the citizens of Paris to repair in crowds to the voting places; another appointing commanders of their forces, which said: "Considering that the situation exacts rapid measures; that on all sides the superior commanders, continuing the routine of the past, have by their inaction produced the present state of affairs; that the monarchical reaction has hitherto prevented, by riot and falsehood, the elections which would have constituted the sole legal power in Paris; the Committee decrees that the military powers of the capital are placed in the hands of the Delegates Brunel, Eudes, and Duval. They have the title of General, and will act in concert while waiting the arrival of General Garibaldi, acclaimed as General-in-Chief. Courage now and always, and the traitors will be foiled. '*Vive la République!*' The Committee learns that some men wearing the uniform of the National Guards, and who have been recognized as former gendarmes or sergeants-de-ville, have fired on the Prussian lines. Should a similar circumstance again occur, the Committee will itself take the necessary measures for seizing on the culprits, and having them shot immediately. The security of the whole city demands vigorous measures.

"The fugitive government at Versailles has sought to create a void around you, and the provinces are entirely deprived of all news from Paris. But that attempt has not succeeded in preventing a revolutionary sentiment from forcing a passage through all those precautions. The Central Committee has received delegations from the cities of Lyons, Bordeaux, Marseilles, Rouen, &c., which came to know what was the nature of our movement, and which have left in haste to give the signal for an analogous one, already prepared everywhere. '*Vive la France!*' '*Vive la République!*'"

The Central Committee was perfectly correct in its proclamation that many other cities of France had been prepared, and were acting in concert with Paris. An insurrectionary movement now commenced in Lyons, which has always been the hot-bed of riots and revolutions. A number of delegates from different political groups proceeded to the Hotel de Ville on the afternoon of the 22d of March, and demanded that the Prefect should recognize as the legal government the Central Committee installed in Paris. That injunction not being obeyed, the malcontents left, declaring that they could, if necessary, carry their point by force. Crowds having begun to assemble on the Place des Terreux, the authorities ordered the National Guard to be called out. During the evening cries of "*Vive la Commune!*" and "*Vive le Comité de Paris!*" were raised in the streets, and the *Marseillaise* was sung. One or two companies of a battalion from La Guillotière also went over to the rioters. About midnight a delegate of the Committee was introduced into the Hotel de Ville, then occupied by three battalions, and proclaimed from the balcony the insurrectionary government of Paris. Many of the National Guards protested, but abstained from offering any opposition to the movement, in order to avoid a collision. One shot was fired, but apparently by accident, and no person is known to have been wounded. Great incertitude existed in the minds of the population, and the insurgents took advantage of the hesitation to impose their own will. The red flag was hoisted the following morning on the Hotel de Ville. The Prefect was made prisoner, and the Municipal Council dissolved and replaced by a Provisionary Committee. This Committee, after pronouncing numerous decrees and several capital condemnations (which fortunately were never executed), finding themselves gradually abandoned by the very National Guards who had at first supported them, decided to retire, which they did after drawing up a paper declaring that, being no longer supported by the National Guards, they considered themselves as released from all engagements with their constituents, and threw up all their powers. The next morning a battalion devoted to the cause of order came to take possession of the municipal edifice, and re-establish the tri-colored flag, in the midst of cries, a thousand times repeated, of *"Vive la République!" "Vive l'Assemblée Nationale!"*

At Marseilles the same attempt was made with rather more serious results. The insurgents took possession of the Prefecture, hoisted the red flag, and for some time controlled the destinies of the city; but they were finally put down by the regular forces.

Toulouse and St. Etienne also followed the lead of Paris, both declaring the Commune, but both were convinced of the error of their ways by more or less loss of life.

At St. Etienne the Prefect of the Loire was most basely murdered in the night, at a moment when all was supposed to be over. The murderer, however, was immediately executed.

The fusion between the Central Committee and some of the Mayors and Deputies of Paris in regard to holding the elections, took place on Saturday night, March 26th, the day before the elections were to take place. This fusion, however, was by no means unanimous. Out of the twenty Mayors of Paris there were only seven who adhered to the manifesto, and out of sixty adjoints only thirty-one. Some of them were absent and could not be called upon to take any decision. Others had protested publicly against this convocation of electors, in which they persisted in seeing a serious encroachment on the rights of the National Assembly, and consequently on the sovereignty of the people. Out of forty-three deputies nominated in Paris on February 8th, there were only ten, or less than a fourth, who consented to unite with M. Assi, his comrades, and a portion of the elected municipalities.

A proclamation was prepared in common between the

fusionists. The committee, however, in publishing their version, modified and changed the wording, without giving any notice to the mayors, making it read:

"The Central Committee of the National Guard *to which the deputies, mayors, and adjoints of Paris have rallied*, being convinced that the only way to avoid civil war, and also strengthen the Republic," etc.; whereas the proper wording and the one agreed to, read: "The deputies of Paris, the mayors, and the elected adjoints, reinstalled in the mairies of their arrondissements, and the members of the Central Federal Committee of the National Guard, convinced that in order to prevent civil war and the effusion of blood, as well as to strengthen the Republic, it is necessary to proceed immediately to the elections, convoke the electors for Sunday in their respective colleges.

"Signed by the representatives of the Seine present in Paris—

"*E. Lockroy, Ch. Floquet, G. Clémenceau, Tolain, and Greppo—also by some of the mayors and adjoints.*"

A deputation was sent to inform the Government of this resolution, and a notice was forwarded to the National Printing Office, and posted up in the evening.

M. Tiraud, mayor of the second arrondissement, also issued from Versailles an address, in which he announced that being convinced of the imminent necessity for the measure, he had just signed, with several deputies for Paris, a demand presented by M. Louis Blanc to obtain from the Assembly a declaration to justify the course adopted by the mayors and adjoints. We have seen in what manner this demand was rejected by the Assembly.

Six deputies of the Assembly, nominated from Paris, published the following proclamation to the electors on the eve of the election:

"PARIS, March 25th, 1871.

"CITIZENS:—The question of the moment in Paris, where the legislative power has refused to sit, and from which the executive is absent, is whether the conflict which has arisen between citizens equally devoted to the Republic should be decided by material or moral force. We have the consciousness of having done all that we could for the ordinary law to be applied in the exceptional crisis through which we are passing. We have proposed to the National Assembly all the measures of conciliation of a nature to appease the public mind, and avoid civil war. Your elected mayors have gone to Versailles to convey the legitimate complaints of those who wish that Paris should not be at the same time deprived of its situation as capital and of its municipal rights, which belong to all the towns and communes of the Republic. Neither your elected mayors nor your representatives in the Assembly have succeeded in obtaining a reconciliation. To-day, placed between civil war for our fellow-citizens and a serious responsibility for ourselves, decided on anything rather than permit the shedding of one drop of that Parisian blood which you lately offered for the defence and honor of France, we say to you, Let us terminate the conflict by a vote, and not by arms. We shall thus be investing with the municipal authority honest and energetic Republicans, who, by preserving order, will spare France the terrible danger of an offensive return of the Prussians, and the rash attempts of dynastic pretensions. We said yesterday in the National Assembly that we would take on ourselves the responsibility of all measures that could prevent an effusion of blood. We have done our duty in opening to you our minds. *Vive la France! Vive la République!*

"*Schœlcher, Floquet, Lockroy, Clemenceau, Tolain, Greppo—the Representatives of the Seine present in Paris.*"

Admiral Saisset, in whom so much hope was centered, resigned his commission as Commander-in-Chief of the National Guards of Paris. He had seen the immense organization of the insurgents, and the lukewarmness with which the National Guard rallied round his standard. The mayors also, who were specially lukewarm on the question of law and order, thought it better that he should resign, before doing which he issued the following order:

"I have the honor to inform the chiefs of corps, officers, and National Guards of the Seine, that I authorize them to return to their homes, from Saturday the 25th, at seven in the evening.

"SAISSET,
"Vice-Admiral, Commander-in-Chief."

All the inhabitants of Place Vendome were obliged to leave their apartments in the charge of domestics. The National Guards or insurgents of the Place turned out these latter at two hours' notice on the 25th March, and took up their quarters in the houses, at the same time issuing a notice that, guided by a desire for conciliation, and happy in bringing about a union, the incessant object of all their efforts, they frankly offered a fraternal hand to all who were opposed to them; but that the continuance of certain manœuvres, and especially the removal by night of mitrailleuses to the mairie of the first arrondissement, obliged them to maintain their first resolution. The elections will positively take place to-morrow, 26th March. If they have mistaken the intention of their adversaries, they invited them to prove their error, and to join them in the general vote to-morrow.

On Sunday morning the voting places were opened at eight o'clock, but at that hour scarcely any one attended. At the same time the following proclamation from the

Central Committee attracted crowds of readers in the streets:

"PARIS, 26th March.

"At the moment we write the Central Committee will have *de jure*, if not *de facto*, ceded its place to the Commune. Having fulfilled the mission imposed upon it by necessity, it will reduce itself to the special functions for which it was called into existence; and which, violently disputed by the Executive, obliged it to struggle to conquer or to die with the city, whose armed representative it was.

"Expression of the municipal liberty legitimately, judicially, insurgent against governmental arbitrariness, the Committee had no other task than to prevent, at any price, that Paris should be deprived of the primordial right it had triumphantly conquered. The day after the vote it may be said to have done its duty.

"As to the elected Commune, its part will be very different, and perhaps its means also. Before everything it will have to define its mandate and determine its attributes. That constituent power which is accorded so wide, so indefinite, so confused to a French National Assembly, it will have to exercise for itself, that is to say, for the city of which it is the representative.

"Therefore, its first work will be the discussion and preparation of a Charter, of that act which our ancestors of the Middle Ages called their commune. That accomplished, it will have to consider the means of making recognized and guaranteed by the central power, whatever that may be, this statute of municipal autonomy. This portion of its task will be none the less arduous if the movement, localized in Paris and one or two large cities, permits the present National Assembly to prolong a mission which good sense and the force of things limited to the conclusion of peace, and which has already been some time accomplished.

"To a usurpation of power the new body will not have to respond by a similar step. Federated with the communes of France already freed, it will have in its own name, and those of Lyons, Marseilles, and perhaps soon of ten large towns, to study the clauses of the contract which will unite them to the nation and to draw up the ultimatum of the treaty they intend to sign.

"What will the terms of it be? First of all the fact is clear that it will have to contain the guarantee of the autonomy and sovereignty reconquered by the municipality. In the second place, it will have to assure the free play of the relations between the Commune and the representatives of the national unity.

"Finally, it will have to impose on the Assembly, if it consents to negotiate, the promulgation of an electoral law such that the representation of the towns shall not in future be absorbed, and as it were drowned in that of the country districts. So long as a measure conceived in that spirit shall not have been applied, the broken national unity, the destroyed social equilibrium, cannot be re-established.

"On those conditions, and those only, the insurgent city will again become the capital. Its spirit, circulating more freely throughout France, will soon become that of the nation itself, the sentiment of order, progress, justice, that is to say, of revolution.

"*Avoine Fils, Ant. Arnaud, G. Arnold, Assi, Andignoux, Bouit, J. Bergeret, Babick, Barou, Billioray, Blanchet, Castioni, Chouteau, C. Dupont, Ferrat, Fabre, Fleury, Fougeret, C. Gaudier, Gouhier, Guiral, Géresme, Grolard, Josselin, F. Jourde, Lavalette, Maljournal, Ed. Moreau, Prudhomme, Rousseau, Ranvier, Varlin, Viard—Le Comité de la Garde Nationale.*"

CHAPTER IV.

Successful results obtained by the Committee on the elections—Small number of voters—List of the Commune—Delescluze resigns his seat in the Assembly and becomes member of the Commune—Ceremony at the Hotel de Ville—Commissioners appointed by the Commune—Proclamations—Decrees—The red flag floats from the Tuileries—Absolute Power of the Commune—Sub-Committee of eleven members—Garibaldi—Opinions of the Communist Journals—Post-office Director appointed by the Commune—Imprisonment of Sullier—Situation of Paris—Preparations of the insurgents—Concentration of their troops—Plan of attack—Engagement at Meudon—Chatillon—Sortie by the Port Maillot—The insurgents met by the Versailles troops—Bearer of a flag of truce shot by the insurgents—Their precipitate retreat—Charge of the gendarmes—False bulletins of the Commune—Arrival of the insurgents, commanded by Flourens, at Reuil—Barricades erected in the streets—Arrival of the gendarmes and capture of the barricades—Utter rout of the Federals—Search for Flourens—He is discovered and killed—His aide-de-camp taken prisoner.

THE elections passed off quietly throughout the city, except in one or two quarters where the controversy between the adherents of the Commune, or insurgents, and the Order party was exceedingly bitter, and even blows were resorted to—a very unusual thing in Paris or among the French people. The Committee candidates were returned by large majorities. The Conservative or Order party were only successful in the 1st, 2d, and 16th arrondissements. These represent the quarters of the Louvre, the Bourse, and Passy. Two arrondissements elected candidates representing the fusion between the Committee and the Advanced Republicans; the other fifteen returned Committee candidates. The number of votes cast was comparatively small—180,000 only voting. At the elections on the 12th of February, 620,000 electors were inscribed. Out of the 180,000 votes the Commune received 120,000, or less than one-fifth of the whole number of votes. Thus the party of Order having refused to vote, or fled their posts, the authority of the city was left in the hands of an insurrectionary minority, who, taking advantage of this parody of an election, sought not only to control the destinies of Paris, but the rest of France.

The triumph of the Committee was most decisive in Vilette, Montmartre, Belleville, and Montrouge, where the voting was unanimous.

With the exception of Felix Pyat, Delescluze, Blanqui, Flourens, and Gambon, the successful candidates were mostly unknown to fame, but known to be men belonging to different international societies, or societies of "Trades-Union." As all these societies in Europe are political, the ambition of their chiefs is the primary object; the benefit of the workingman (if he ever receives any benefit from his connection with such a society), the secondary. The leading members of the Commune, or International, wished to introduce into society what is called "Socialism," supposed to be founded in a love of liberty, equality, and respect for human life. This Socialism is a misnomer, which the actions of its adherents has always proven; it is an empty sound full of wickedness and deceit, and may be summed up in this axiom: "The right of those who have not, to take from those who have." What the Commune or Committee wanted was to keep the power in their own hands. Their disinterestedness was as pure as their love of liberty, which consisted in arresting citizens on the slightest provocation.

Out of thirty-seven members of the Central Committee twenty were elected as members of the Commune. The Committee were *supposed* to withdraw and leave the Hotel de Ville to the newly constituted authorities. Such, however, was not, it would seem, their intention, as everything remained on Monday morning guarded as before.

MIOT
Commune of Paris.
1871

The day after the Commune was elected it composed one hundred and six members. At the end there were but fifty. One by one they had retired, some from disgust, others from horror, the greater part from prudence. Many gave their *démission* at once, and are noted in the following list as *démissionnaires:*

Adam, démissionnaire; Amouroux; Arnauld (Antoine); Arnould (Arthur); Alix, à Mazas; Andrieux; Arnold; Assi; Avrial.

Babick; Barré, démissionnaire; Brelay, démissionnaire; Blanchet, à Mazas; Beslay, démissionnaire; Brunel; Billioray; Bouteiller (de), démissionnaire; Blanqui, détenu; Briosne, a refusé; Bergeret.

Chéron, démissionnaire; Clémence; Champy; Chardon; Clément (J. B.); Chalain; Clément (Victor); Cluseret, à Mazas; Courbet; Clément (Emile); Cournet.

Demay; Dupont; Desmaret, démissionnaire; Duval, mort; Decamp; Dereure; Durand; Delescluze; Dupont (Clovis).

Eudes.

Ferry, démissionnaire; Fortuné (Henry); Fruneau, démissionnaire; Frankel (Léo); Ferré; Flourens, mort.

Gérardin; Goupil, démissionnaire; Gambon; Géresme; Gérardin (Charles), en fuite avec Rossel; Grousset (Paschal); Garibaldi (M.), a refusé.

Jourde; Johannard.

Loiseau, démissionnaire; Lefrançais; Ledroit; Leroy, démissionnaire; Lefévre, démissionnaire; Langevin; Lonclas; Longuet.

Méline, démissionnaire; Murat, démissionnaire; Mortier; Meillet (Léo); Martelet; Marmottan, démissionnaire; Malon; Miot (Jules).

Nast, démissionnaire.

Ostyn; Oudet.

Protot; Puget; Pillot; Pyat (Felix); Philippe; Parent (Ulysse), démissionnaire; Parisot; Pottier; Pindy.

Ranc, démissionnaire; Ranvier; Rogeard, a refusé; Rochard, démissionnaire; Régère; Robinet, démissionnaire; Rossel, en fuite; Rigault (Raoul); Rastoul.

Serrailler; Sicard.

Tirard, démissionnaire; Tridon; Theisz; Trinquet.

Urbin.

Vaillant; Verdure; Varlin; Vallès (Jules); Vermorel; Vésinier; Viard.

These individuals formed the Commune, which was only a new name for the Central Committee, whose members, instead of retiring into private life, as was inferred from their official announcement the day before the election, evidently intended to stay where they were. On the Place Vendome the precautions taken were considerably more minute and searching than previously, and an immense barricade was erected at the southern end, furnished with pieces of cannon pointed against the Rue Castiglione, and the Rue St. Honore, both to the east and west.

Delescluze, one of those few who formed part of a sort of secret committee for the Central Committee, was elected in several arrondissements. He wrote to the President of the National Assembly resigning his seat in that body, where he declared he had only remained to impeach the dictators of the 4th of September. He added that being unwilling to associate himself with the insanities and passions of the Chamber, and having been returned by several arrondissements of Paris to the Commune, he had decided upon giving the preference to the latter delegation.

The announcement of the vote for the Commune was made at the Hotel de Ville on the 28th with considerable ceremony. The gate below the clock-tower was hung with red, blue, and green drapery, whilst the statue of Henry IV above was concealed with a crimson curtain. A platform ornamented with a bust of a female figure representing the Republic, had been erected in front of the building, and on it were placed arm-chairs for the accommodation of the Committee. Cannon were drawn up on the square, which was also occupied by about 20,000 National Guards in close ranks. Other battalions waited in the adjacent streets and on the quay. At four o'clock Citizen Assi rose and announced that the power of the Central Committee had transpired and was now transferred to the Commune. He then read aloud the names of the Councillors elected. Cries of "*Vive la République!*" were raised, the trumpets sounded, drums beat, and caps were waved in the air. About four o'clock salvos were fired from the Hotel de Ville, and answered by the guns at Montmartre. This cannonade created considerable alarm among the inhabitants, who imagined that the troops of Versailles had arrived at Paris, or that the Prussians had returned to restore order. All the National Guards present, to the number of 60,000, then marched past the dais on which the Committee was seated. In the evening the Arc de Triomphe, barracks, and principal public buildings were illuminated.

It will be remembered that the Committee had solemnly promised to retire on the new election; that it had represented such precipitate resignation as one of its highest titles to glory. However, after reading the official organ of the insurgents, one was led to believe that the occupants of the Hotel de Ville had already reconsidered their determination. In fact that body, after having declared that it ceded its place to the Commune, added: "Having fulfilled the extraordinary mission imposed upon it by necessity, it will reduce itself to the special functions for which it was called into existence." Thus admitting that it had at the same time an *extraordinary* mission and a *special function.* It abdicated the first, but retained the *second.* What did that mean, and in what consisted that attribution which escaped the Commune? The sequel will illustrate.

The Communists were divided into the following committees, the record of which is taken from the first number of the official Journal of the Commune, published the 30th of March, 1871.

COMMISSION EXÉCUTIVE.

Les citoyens: Eudes, Tridon, Vaillant, Lefrançais, Duval, Felix Pyat, Bergeret.

COMMISSION DES FINANCES.

Les citoyens: Victor Clément, Varlin, Jourde, Beslay, Régère.

COMMISSION MILITAIRE.

Les citoyens: Pindy, Eudes, Bergeret, Duval, Chardon, Flourens, Ranvier.

COMMISSION DE LA JUSTICE.

Les citoyens: Ranc, Protot, Léo Meillet, Vermorel, Ledroit, Babick.

COMMISSION DE SÛRETÉ GÉNÉRALE.

Les citoyens: Raoul Rigault, Ferré, Assi, Cournet, Oudet, Chalain, Gérardin.

COMMISSION DES SUBSISTANCES.

Les citoyens: Dereure, Champy, Ostyn, Clément, Parizel, Emile Clément, Henry Fortuné.

COMMISSION DU TRAVAIL.—INDUSTRIE ET ÉCHANGE.

Les citoyens: Malon, Frankel, Theisz, Dupont, Avrial, Loiseau-Pinson, Eug. Gérardin, Puget.

MÉGY
Commune of Paris
1871

COMMISSION DES RELATIONS EXTÉRIEURES.

Les citoyens: Delescluze, Ranc, Paschal Grousset, Ulysse Parent, Arthur Arnould, Ant. Arnauld, Ch. Girardin.

COMMISSION DES SERVICES PUBLICS.

Les citoyens: Ostyn, Billoray, J. B. Clément, Mardelet, Mortier, Rastoul.

COMMISSION DE L'ENSEIGNEMENT.

Les citoyens: Jules Vallès, Docteur Goupil, Lefèvre, Urbain, Albert Leroy, Verdure, Demay, Docteur Robinet.

Also the following proclamations:

"The Central Committee has remitted its powers to the Commune.

"COMMUNE OF PARIS.

HOTEL DE VILLE, 29th Mar., 1871.

"CITOYENS:—Your Commune is constituted.

"The vote of the 26th of March has sanctioned the victorious revolution.

"A cowardly aggressive power had taken you by the throat. You have in your legitimate defence repulsed from your walls this Government which wished to dishonor you by imposing upon you a king.

"To-day these criminals, whom you have no desire to pursue, abuse your magnanimity in organizing, even at the gates of your city, a monarchical conspiracy. They invoke civil war; they set at work every corruption; they accept all accomplices; they have dared even to ask aid from the foreigner. We cite these execrable underhand plotters to judgment before France and before the world."

"CITOYENS:—We are about to confer on you institutions that will defy all attacks.

"You are masters of your destinies. Strong in your

support, the representatives whom you have just elected are about to repair the disasters caused by the forfeited Government. Compromised industry, suspended labor, paralyzed commercial transactions, will all receive a vigorous impulse.

"To-day the awaited decision on rents—to-morrow, that of payment of bills due.

"All public service re-established and simplified.

"The National Guard reorganized without delay, will remain the only armed force of the city.

"These will be our first acts.

"The elected of the people only wish the confidence of their electors to assure the triumph of the Republic. They will be sure to do their duty.

"LA COMMUNE DE PARIS."

"HOTEL DE VILLE, 29th Mar., 1871.

"THE COMMUNE OF PARIS DECREES—

"1st. The Conscription is abolished.

"2d. No military force other than the National Guard can be created, or can enter the city.

"All valid citizens will form a part of the National Guard.

"LA COMMUNE DE PARIS."

"HOTEL DE VILLE, 29th Mar., 1871.

"THE COMMUNE OF PARIS—

"Considering that labor, industry and commerce have supported all the changes of the war—that it is only just that property should make some sacrifice to the country,

"DECREES—

"Art. 1st. A general remission is made to the tenant of the three-quarters rent due October 1870, January 1871, and April 1871.

"Art. 2. Any sum paid by the tenant during these nine months will be deducted from future payments.

"Art. 3. Equally are remitted any sums due for furnished apartments.

"Art. 4. All leases are renewable only at the pleasure of the tenant (they could be renewed only on his terms, whether unexpired or not), which may be done any time during six months from date of present decree.

"Art. 5. All notices to quit may be prorogued for three months, at the pleasure of the tenant.

"LA COMMUNE DE PARIS."

There were several other decrees issued the first day of more or less importance: one prohibiting government officials from receiving orders from the Versailles government; another prohibiting any proclamation emanating from Versailles being posted on the walls; another appointing General Bergeret Commandant la Place de Paris, *Etat-Major* at Place Vendome, whence all military orders, watch-words, etc., must emanate.

One of the first acts of the Commune was to display the red flag from the Palace of the Tuileries. Hearing also that the Duke d'Aumâle was in France, the official journal, speaking on the subject, said: "Society has only one duty towards princes—death! It is only bound to observe one formality—the proof of identity. The Orleans are in France; the Bonapartes desire to return; *let all good citizens be warned and act!!!*"

In reading the official organ of the Commune, one cannot be mistaken as to the scope of the movement of which Paris had taken the initiative. The business of the newly elected members was to discuss and draw up, like Frenchmen in the middle ages, their charter and constitution, and to devise means for getting them recognized and guaranteed by the central power. Thus France, without suspecting the fact, and without the movement having been prepared or indicated by any book, journal, speaker, meeting, club, or tendency, just on the morrow of a war of invasion which ravaged her territory,—France was invited to pass from unity, the work of so many ages, to the federation of mediæval times! Strange indeed are the surprises in the lives of nations, and above all, in the movements of great cities!

The working engineer Assi, one of the chiefs of this great revolt—a man without instruction or judgment, but of an energetic character, has avowed that he never read but one book—the "*Revolutions of Italy*," a work by Edgar Quinet, which he was incapable of understanding by reason of his inadequate information, but by which his imagination was much affected. Italy, which in three hundred years up to the time of Charles V, presents the spectacle of seven thousand revolutions, must most assuredly have offered to Citizen Assi the complete model of an entire system. The elected Commune had to draw up its charter. The watchmaker Tirard, the dyer Loiseau-Pinson, sat side by side as members of the Central Committee, and disposed of Paris, the capital of a great nation, as Congress would have disposed of a nuisance in the District of Columbia.

In a word, the new Commune was constituent, and acknowledged no other authority than its own—a spectacle unique in the world. Neither in the United States nor Switzerland, where communal liberties are so great, has anything of the kind ever existed. Such was the situation—a return to the middle ages—a retrogression of eight centuries—federation substituted for unity—universal suffrage become a dead letter—the Prussian invasion considered as one of those accidents from which Paris had to disengage its responsibility, as the Assembly at Versailles only existed on condition of being an annex to the Commune.

It has been well said of the newly elected Commune

what Emile de Girardin said in 1848 to the orators of the Socialist School and to Louis Blanc: "You are agitators, but will never be reformers."

A Central Sub-Committee was formed at the Hotel de Ville, on the proposal of Assi, and was composed of himself and eleven other members, viz., Cluseret, Bergeret, Henry, Gasnier, Babick, Avoine, Jr., Avrial, Maljournal, Duval, Géresme, and General Garibaldi as honorary president. That body took the direction of the National Guard, the elections of which it prepared, and was charged with the protection of the Municipal Council, the maintenance of order in the city, and the payment of the civic force. All accusations of treason against the Republic were also referred to it.

As the Central Committee had, and the Commune was making, considerable capital by invariably associating the name of Garibaldi with the insurgent National Guards, M. Jules de Précy, editor of the *Liberté*, published the following, for which and other articles in opposition to the Commune that journal was suppressed:

"The journal official of the Commune has confided the military powers to three delegates, '*in awaiting the arrival of General Garibaldi, proclaimed General-in-Chief.*' Now, men of the Committee, we say to you, *Never—Never!* Do you hear? Garibaldi will never associate himself with this civil war, of which you are the authors.

"We, who know him—we, who have on so many occasions admired his resignation, his patriotism, his abnegation, his tolerance—we proclaim it before the world that he execrates as much as we your bloody dictatorship. The great citizen, whom you trumpet in all your faubourgs, marching on Rome, found himself at Aspromonte, in the midst of inaccessible mountains, surrounded by 10,000 volunteers ready to the last man to die for their beloved

General; he could with a gesture, with a single word, have stirred up to rebellion Sicily, Naples, and Central Italy; all this he could have done, but he scorned the action; he surrendered himself and his voluuteers after having received, without returning it, the fire of the royal troops.

"One month later, Garibaldi, wounded, lay upon his bed in the prison of Fort Varignano. We ran to shake him by the hand; he gave us a lengthy account of this unfortunate epoch, and, with sparkling eye and beating heart, he terminated his narrative with these words: 'I have yielded; civil war....never! never!' Garibaldi will never come; your works to him are horrible.

"Not only will he never come, but we defy you to draw from him a single line—a single word—which will not be a disavowal of your acts, a reprobation of your indulgences."

The different Communist journals which were started in Paris for the support of the insurrection, demanded the immediate dissolution of the National Assembly. The *Vengeur*, on the ground that it was incomplete, in consequence of the resignation of the deputies of Paris—that it no longer represented the country, and, therefore, its pretensions to enact laws and govern France was usurpation and high treason. The *Cri du Peuple* recommended the "*rurals*" of Versailles to go and die in their cow-houses. The *Nouvelle République* considered that the accession of the Commune would revive confidence; and expressed the opinion that a "timid capital" would reappear if the "*rurals*" of the Assembly would permit it; but as they were not disposed to do so, these "fugitives must be run to earth" in the indispensable interest of labor and commerce. The *Mont-Aventin*, in its turn, urged the Chamber to "depart," under penalty of being "thrown out of the window;" however, it consented to allow the "peasants of Versailles" a week to pack up their trunks. The *Père Duchene* advised the Commune to dissolve the Assembly, which, "after having subscribed to the shame of France, was conspiring for the destruction of the Republic."

The Commune, wishing to take possession of the Post-office, sent word to the director that, considering the disorder that prevailed in the postal service, it was necessary to make a change in the administration, and that Citizen Theisz was charged with the direction.

The postal service was the best managed in France, but the director was obliged to give place to the insurrection. The director, chief clerk, and all the heads of offices, left the next day for Versailles.

Internal dissension had already commenced among the members of the Commune; and M. Lullier was sent to the Conciergerie, whence he wrote a long protest to the journals, complaining of the treatment he had met with from the Central Committee. According to his account, the entire defence of Paris was organized and successfully carried out by him; but that when his colleagues had no further need of him, and he had recommended them to exercise moderation in their conduct, they had thrown him into prison, where he still remained.

It would be necessary to go back some fifteen centuries to find in the celebrated city of Syracuse a case parallel to that of Paris on the first day of April, 1871. The Prussians held the northern and eastern forts, the insurgents were masters of the southern forts, the city, and its walls; and the regular Government was reduced to the possession of Mont Valérien, situated at the west, but the most powerful of all the forts.

The insurgents, emboldened by their success, commenced to make most important preparations, with a view of attacking the Assembly at Versailles. They disarmed all the National Guards suspected of any attachment to the cause of order. They reorganized the franc-tireurs, created twenty war battalions, twenty batteries of cannon, and fifteen of mitrailleuses. They requisitioned horses, pillaged the arsenals, gave orders for immense supplies of powder, petroleum, gun-cotton, and nitro-glycerine; and on the 30th of March the preparations were completed, and active operations commenced. They had 70,000 National Guards in marching order, furnished with rations for eight days, and excited to the highest possible pitch of enthusiasm.

On the 31st their plans were developed, and on the 1st of April they had concentrated their troops to the south and northwest of Paris. On the morning of the 3d the whole army of the insurgents set out for Versailles by three different routes—one column by the St. Germain road, a second by that of Sèvres and a third, commanded by Duval, by that of Chevreuse. Three simultaneous attacks appear to have been contemplated in the plan devised by the Commune. The first commenced toward Sèvres, early in the morning; and the musketry fire was so sharp that as the Versailles train arrived the passengers were obliged to put up the cushions against the windows to protect themselves from the shower of balls. The train from Paris was obliged to put back.

Numerous battalions of National Guards issued from the forts of Issy and Vanves, but on that side the engagement was one principally of artillery. The insurgents, in advancing on Meudon were fired on by the cannon of the regulars, and much damaged. The first moment of surprise being passed, the battalions formed themselves in line of battle along the road; but the palace battery on the heights of Meudon raked the valley, and obliged them to fall back on the reinforcements arriving by the gates on the south of Paris. An attempt was then made to open fire with the pieces of cannon brought with them, but the shot was found to be not of the right calibre, so that the guns were useless. Fort Issy replied with considerable vigor, and in a short time a fire of musketry became general from Meudon to Chatillon, where a second column attempted to gain Versailles by the road through Clamart and Velizy.

The first battalions, engaged towards Meudon, had, however, started too early and in too small numbers, and were in a very short time completely disorganized. At 8 o'clock reinforcements arrived and raised the number of the insurgents to 20,000 men, with thirty-six guns. They re-formed ranks by degrees, and again assumed the offensive. Scattered bands concealed in the woods, in gardens, behind walls, and in the old Prussian trenches, kept up a desultory fire on the regular troops, who continued to increase in numbers as they advanced, and eventually became masters of the ground. But towards four o'clock new reinforcements having been sent to the insurgents, who had fallen back on the village of Issy, the latter resumed the offensive, and advanced in their turn to scale the heights of Meudon. In this attack they gave proof of the greatest amount of courage and personal daring; but the Versailles troops were in admirable order and admirably commanded, and numbers were compelled to give way before discipline. For the second time they were driven back behind the fortress of Issy, exasperated beyond all bounds at their defeat, putting to death wounded men whom they found on the field of battle. Meudon and Issy kept up an artillery duel more or less violent until seven o'clock. The ambulance service had not been prepared, and the wounded were not all brought in until late in the night. Until four in the afternoon the gates were closed to all who wished to enter, but after that hour the different battalions and fugitives entered the city pell-mell.

The column commanded by *General* Eudes (a liberated

murderer in the service of the Commune), numbering some 35,000 men, passed by Fontenay-au-Roses and Plessis-Piquet, and entered the road from Sceaux to Versailles. They arrived without difficulty at Le Petit Bicêtre, where the road is joined by that of Choisy-le-Roi. Here they were met by some other battalions coming from La Croix de Berney. They were about to proceed, as they thought, in an uninterrupted manner to Versailles, when they were suddenly attacked by the regular troops from the woods of Verrières on the left, and Meudon on the right. The road was well guarded, and it was impossible to proceed further. They immediately began a precipitate retreat, and at four o'clock had arrived at the plateau of Chatillon in a complete state of disorder. During the whole of that evening and night a stream of tired, dusty and desperate men passed the different draw-bridges, many without arms and with torn clothes, and all demoralized, declaring that they had been betrayed—that their leaders were cowards or traitors, and ought to be shot.

Early on Tuesday morning the whole plateau of Chatillon was evacuated by the insurgents, and later in the day occupied by the regular troops without a blow being struck; and on that prominent position the batteries were planted which, with the help of Meudon, eventually silenced the forts of Vanves and Issy.

The column commanded by General Bergeret, a master mason, with Gustave Flourens, a hot-brained traitor, originator and stirrer-up of revolutions, second in command, left Porte Maillot on the night of the 2d of April, intending to pass through Neuilly, Nanterre and Rueil, and attack Versailles in the rear. It was thought by some that it intended to take Mont Valérien on its route, the men having been informed that the commandant of that fort was more anxious to deliver it up to the insurgents than they were to take it. This column had made itself most talked about. It was not the one, however, on which the most reliance was placed. If it were successful, it was to push its advantage—if not, to return in good order.

The column started headed by Bergeret in a victoria drawn by two horses. He was surrounded by his staff, dressed up in the most gorgeous and theatrical costumes, their belts filled with immense revolvers, and brandishing large sabres, shouting "*à Versailles!*" "*à Versailles!*"

The Government of Versailles, which had been informed on the previous day that the insurgents were having large bodies of men concentrated at Puteaux and Surennes preparatory to marching on Versailles, decided to send a division of men to meet the battalions from Paris and summon them to lay down their arms. In consequence, some troops, under the order of Captain Bruat of the Navy, and composed of two regiments of the line, some sailors, mounted gendarmes, chasseurs d'Afrique, and two mitrailleuses, were sent in the middle of the night to Mont Valérien.

About six in the morning some shots were exchanged between the outposts. At seven, General Vinoy arrived at the fort and gave his orders. Soon after Dr. Pasquier, of the mounted gendarmes, preceded by a trumpeter and accompanied by two men, presented himself with a flag of truce at the bridge of Courbevoie. Two of the insurgents met him, and after a few words had passed, one of the latter drew a revolver and shot Dr. Pasquier dead on the spot. Fire was immediately opened on all sides, and the news that the bearer of a flag of truce had been killed caused extreme indignation.

The gendarmes, especially, swore to avenge their doctor, whom they adored, and when the order was given to charge they did so with the greatest fury. At first the combat was one of skirmishes. The sailors and the regular troops formed one long line of constant fire, which closed in continually and directed its aim on the head of the columns of the Commune, which were effecting a movement toward Courbevoie. At the same time Mont Valerien sent at them a few shell and *boite-ă-mitraille* (grape-shot). About nine o'clock the action became general along the line of the insurgents, when the mitrailleuses were brought forward, and a few well-directed discharges threw confusion into their ranks. Their retreat commenced in the greatest disorder, soon becoming a total route. The mounted gendarmes charged in pursuit, engulfing one portion of the insurgents in the ravines of Malmaison, and driving the other toward the city in the wildest confusion. After entering the city the fugitives described the battle as a great success, and the official organ of the Commune, in its issue of the 4th April, says: "*Generals Bergeret and Flourens have effected their junction. They are marching on Versailles. Success is certain.*" And again at 2 P. M. the following official announcement was issued:

"Towards four this morning the columns of General Duval and Colonel Flourens made their junction at the rond-point of Courbevoie. Just as they had arrived they sustained a heavy fire from Mont Valérien. The troops sheltered themselves behind walls and houses. Thus protected, the commanders were able to organize a movement which completely succeeded, and the two columns passed the lines and resumed their march on Versailles. General Bergeret, who led them on with shouts of '*Vive la République!*' had two horses killed under him. The fire of the Versailles army has not caused us any appreciable loss."

Notwithstanding these official reports, there was an air about the *conquerors* who had returned that did not savor strongly of victory.

At 3 o'clock a courier passed by the Arc de Triomphe

on his way to the Hotel de Ville, announcing to the crowd that Flourens had entered Versailles at the head of 40,000 men—that they had captured one hundred deputies, and M. Thiers was a prisoner!

Some one suggested that "there were not over 20,000 men who went out this way."

"Where did he get the men?"

"Oh, he has them!" and "General Bergeret fought like a tiger. He had two horses killed under him."

"*Before* him you mean," shouted one of the crowd; "as he went out in a victoria."

That portion of the advancing column of insurgents which had passed Valerien under the command of Flourens amounted to 5,000 men. Accelerated considerably in their motions by the retreat of the larger portion of their troops, they arrived at Rueil, which was guarded by only a small post of cavalry, which at once fell back in the direction of Versailles. The National Guards spread through the town, some occupying the barracks, others entering the wine-shops and private houses; the bread and provision shops were requisitioned, the dealers receiving tickets of the Commune in payment for their wares. Barricades were constructed in the streets and across the wide avenue in the direction of St. Germain; scouts were thrown out along the Seine, and Flourens took up his headquarters near the railway station. They were, however, suddenly attacked by some detachments of mounted gendarmes and regiments of the line, and defeated on every side. The barricade in the direction of St. Germain, which was armed with two pieces of cannon and strongly defended, was captured by the gendarmes sword in hand. They took 200 prisoners; among them there were several soldiers—deserters—who were at once shot, and the National Guards were conducted to Versailles as prisoners.

At 4 o'clock P. M. of this eventful day, as the mounted

gendarmes were searching the village of Châtou for run-away or secreted insurgents, the celebrated Flourens was tracked to his hiding-place by some soldiers. On entering the room where he had taken refuge, the first gendarme received a bullet in the shoulder, fired from a revolver by Flourens. Before he could draw again, an officer of gendarmes, Captain Desmerest, ran forward and cut the insurgent leader through the skull with a single stroke from his sabre. His aide-de-camp Cypriani, a young Garibaldian, also received a sword-cut on the thigh, and was made prisoner. He was in plain clothes, but wore the képi of a chef-de-bataillon. Flourens was still in military dress, but had with him a leather bag containing private clothes for the purpose of disguising himself.

Thus while the Commune at Paris were posting an account of the success of this leader, his body was being taken to Versailles, where it was deposited in the hospital —a melancholy example of *universal republicism, cosmopolitan revolutions, and misdirected intellect.*

CHAPTER V.

Proclamation of the Marquis de Gallifet—Threat of the Communists—Imprisonment of Assi—Grade of General abolished—Dombrowski appointed Commandant of Paris—Attack on Chatillon—Death of General Duval—Decree rendering military service obligatory for all men between the ages of nineteen and forty—Pretexts adopted for escape from the city—Rochefort instigates the demolition of M. Thiers' house—Letter of Garibaldi—Decree relative to prisoners—Cluseret's report—Note of Paschal Grousset to the Foreign Representatives—Bergeret's Letter—Capture of Courbevoie by the Versailles troops—The bridge of Neuilly taken—Shells fall at the Arc de Triomphe—Persecution of the Clergy—Imprisonment of the Archbishop of Paris—Conflict of the Commune and Central Committee—Bergeret incarcerated—Despatch of Dombrowski—The fight at Courbevoie—Attack on the insurgent outposts at Issy—Account given by General Cluseret—The Committee of Conciliation.

THE shooting of Dr. Pasquier and some soldiers who fell into the hands of the insurgents caused the Marquis de Gallifet to issue the following proclamation in the village of Châtou:

"War has been declared by the bands of Paris. Yesterday, the day before, and to-day, they have assassinated my soldiers.

"It is a war without truce or pity that I declare against these murderers. I have had to make an example this morning; may it be a salutary one! I do not desire to be again reduced to such an extremity.

"Do not forget that the country, the law, and right are at Versailles and in the Assembly, and not with the grotesque body at Paris which calls itself the Commune.

"GALLIFET,

"General of Brigade."

This proclamation was made known to the inhabitants of Châtou by the public crier, who, after each beat of the drum, added:

"The President of the Municipal Committee of Châtou warns the inhabitants in the interest of their own safety, that those who offer an asylum to the enemies of the Republic will render themselves subject to the laws of war.

"LAUBEUF,
"President."

None of the three columns had been successful. The sortie *en masse* had failed; a few thousand insurgents had reached Versailles, but in a character totally different from that in which they had hoped to arrive. Compared with the number of troops engaged, the losses in killed and wounded were small; but it was the commencement of a furious strife, and one of the most inauspicious and saddest days in the history of France—the beginning of fearful civil war, brother literally fighting against brother; and well might the poor old lady of Neuilly say, "Thank God my poor boy was killed by the Prussians; *this* would have been too dreadful." Still the Commune, instead of stopping this bloodshed at the beginning, stimulated its adherents by reports of success or of deeds of murder and retaliation supposed to have been committed by the Versaillists.

The official journal of the Commune, published the 7th of April, contains the following:

"CITIZENS:—The *Journal Officiel* of Versailles contains the following: 'Some men recognized as belonging to the army and seized with arms in their hands, have been shot, in accordance with the rigor of military law which condemns to death all soldiers fighting against their flag.'

"That horrible avowal requires no commentary, and

each word of it cries loudly for justice and vengeance, which will not be delayed. The violence of our enemies proves their weakness. They murder whilst the Republicans combat. The Republic must conquer!"

"The people of Versailles murder the Republican prisoners and mutilate the corpses in a horrible manner, eye for eye, and tooth for tooth. The gates of Paris are closed, and no one can leave. We have hostages in our hands. Let the Commune issue a decree, and let its men act. For every head of a patriot which falls under the hands of the Versailles authorities, let that of a Bonapartist, Orleanist, or Legitimist of Paris roll in the dust as a reply. Well! So be it. The Assembly wills it. A reign of terror!"

In the mean time Citizen Assi, the late President of the Central Committee, had been committed to prison for having made a speech at one of the sittings of the Commune, in which he declared that that body was going beyond its legal powers, and that it had no right to march on Versailles; that they should not give way too much to the ignorant masses, and that the better class of men were becoming alienated, instead of converted by their decrees. For this intemperate speech he was quietly placed in prison, where he remained several days before it was known outside the Commune. General Cluseret's star was now in the ascendant, and, as delegate of war, he covered the walls of Paris with decrees emanating from the War Department. He issued an address to the National Guards, in which he blamed the increasing use of gold bands, stripes, etc., on their uniform; pointed out to them, that as working men, who have accomplished a great revolution, they should not blush for their origin; the movement had been made in the name of virtue against vice, of duty against abuse, of honesty against corruption, and had triumphed for that very reason, and concluded by announcing that any officer who added embellishments to the regulation dress, should be sent before a council of discipline. He also issued the following decree:

"Considering that the grade of General is incompatible with the democratic organization of the National Guard, and can only be temporary, the members of the Commune decree as follows:

"Art. 1. The rank of General is suppressed.

"Art. 2. Citizen Ladislas Dombrowski, commandant of the 12th legion, is appointed commander of the garrison of Paris, in the place of Citizen Bergeret, summoned to other functions."

On the 4th of April, the day following the combined movement for the capture of Versailles, numerous fresh battalions were sent out to reinforce those which had been dispersed by the panic, and the struggle recommenced, but without being more fortunate. Notwithstanding an obstinate resistance, the insurgents were obliged to give way in every direction.

Fourteen pieces of cannon placed in battery at Issy, and protected by earthworks thrown up during the night, opened fire upon the heights of Chatillon, and were answered by a strong battery on the terrace of Meudon. At four in the afternoon considerable reinforcements having arrived from Belleville, a strong attack was made on Chatillon, but unsuccessfully. The fort of Vanves kept up a vigorous fire during the rest of the day. Towards night the insurgents brought in a mitrailleuse, which they had captured, but left 250 men in the hands of the Versailles troops, in addition to the commandants of the 127th and 104th battalions. Their loss in killed was about one hundred.

No other military operations took place with the exception of those on the side of Clamart and Meudon.

The Versailles troops confined themselves to a defensive attitude, having had no intention at this time to march on Paris. They were satisfied at stopping the offensive movement of the battalions of the Commune, which had attempted in every direction to force a passage to Versailles.

The fire on Chatillon having produced but little effect, the Communist generals adopted another plan, namely, to turn the position by Clamart and Bagneux, instead of attacking in front; but this movement also failed, as at night the regular troops still held the strong positions of Chatillon and Meudon, which kept up during the day a continuous artillery fire on the forts of Vanves and Issy. Thus the march on Versailles proved a complete failure, as, after three days' fighting, the troops of the insurgents were thrown back on Paris, and the regular army held the three positions which commanded the road to Versailles, viz., Mont Valérien, the Château of Meudon, and the plateau of Chatillon. Of the three columns of attack, the first directed on Rueil by Mont Valérien, was dispersed on the first day; the other two, sent by Chatillon and Sevre, were effectually checked on the two following days.

General Duval was killed the first day at Chatillon, and his colleague, General Henry, captured and sent to Versailles. The Versailles journals spoke very highly of the heroic manner of the former's death.

About this time the great desire in life among the better class of young and middle-aged men was to get out of the city, produced by the following proclamation of General Cluseret:

"Considering the patriotic reclamations of a large number of National Guards who are anxious, although married, to share in the honor of defending their municipal independence, even at the price of their life, the decree of the 5th instant is modified thus:

"From the age of seventeen to nineteen service in the war companies will be voluntary; and from nineteen to forty obligatory for the National Guards, married or not.

"I urge all good patriots to themselves perform the police of their quarters, and to force the disobedient to serve.

G. CLUSERET,
"Delegate to the War Office."

This continual menace of an armed requisition was to all men of a certain age a veritable punishment. The Octroi gates and railway stations were held by the insurgents, and every sort of ruse was invented to escape this danger or vexation—the most common one, until discovered, was that of hiring a fiacre with an old driver, changing clothes and putting the coachman inside, then changing back when outside the walls. Another—still more ridiculous—was that of buying a *return* ticket at the station. The stupid blockheads sometimes at the door thought one would never buy a return ticket unless he intended coming back!

The poet Bergerat passed through the gate in a charcoal cask.

The Belgium and Swiss legations were invaded by young men with all their papers in order, showing they were citizens of those countries. As for our own legation, it was next to an impossibility to catch a glimpse of Mr. Washburne. His doors were always surrounded by a crowd of from five hundred to a thousand Alsatians or Lorrainians. The German authorities having claimed these provinces, the officer in command of the Prussian forces at St. Denis had notified the Commune that these citizens must be exempt from all military service; and it was truly surprising what a number of young men spoke

French with an accent peculiar to the borders of the Rhine.

The insurgents now commenced making requisitions upon different schools and theological institutions. Among others, they entered the establishment of the Jesuits in the Rue Lhomond, and placed all the fathers under arrest. They then searched the house from top to bottom, breaking the furniture and sacking the cupboards; and finally descended to the cellars, where they gorged themselves with wine destined for the use of the establishment. They then carried off the Superior and seven others to the Prefecture of Police in an omnibus requisitioned for the purpose. Similar outrages were also committed amongst the fathers of the Saint-Esprit and the Dominicans, who were also taken to prison.

These and similar acts of plunder were the result of Rochefort's articles in the *Mot d'Ordre,* which, abandoning the comparative moderation which it had lately observed, now stimulated to pillage in every number which it issued, at one time saying:

"M. Thiers possesses in the Place St. George a marvelous hotel, full of works of art of all sorts. M. Picard possesses in the streets of Paris, which he has deserted, three houses, which bring him in a large income; and M. Jules Favre occupies in the Rue d'Amsterdam a sumptuous habitation, belonging to him. What would these statesmen proprietors say if, to their destruction outside, the people were to respond by the blows of a pickaxe; and if each time a house at Courbevoie was touched by a shell a wall was to be knocked down of the palace in the Place St. George, or the hotel in the Rue d'Amsterdam?"

It was only necessary in moments like those, to indicate certain proceedings to an excitable people, to produce the most deplorable consequences.

The Central Committee received a letter from Garibaldi thanking the members for the honor done him in offering him the command of the army of Paris, but declining the proffered post. In his letter he pointed out that a Commander of the National Guard, a General-in-Chief of the forces, and a Directing Committee, as they existed, were incompatible with the present situation of France; the advantage possessed by despotism was the concentration of power; and in a crisis like the existing one, a similar centralization should be opposed to the enemies of the Republic. He recommended them to choose a citizen such as Victor Hugo, Louis Blanc, Felix Pyat, Edgar Quinet, or some other of the democratic leaders—or even Generals Cremer or Billot, who appear to possess the confidence of the people; and to place the supreme power in a single hand. He added, that if France had the good fortune to find a Washington, she would speedily rise greater than ever.

The official organ of the insurgents published the following proclamation:

"Whereas the Government of Versailles is openly trampling under foot the rights of humanity and the laws of war, and has been guilty of atrocities such as have not even been perpetrated by the foreign invader, the Commune decrees as follows:

"Art. 1. All persons charged with complicity with the Government of Versailles shall be incarcerated.

"Art. 2. They shall be deferred within twenty-four hours to a jury of accusation.

"Art. 3. The jury shall give its judgment within twenty-four hours.

"Art. 4. All accused retained in custody by the verdict of the jury will be made the hostages of the people of Paris.

"Art. 5. The execution of a prisoner of war or of a partisan of the regular Government of the Commune shall be followed by that of a triple number of the hostages.

"Art. 6. Every prisoner of war shall be sent before a jury of accusation, which shall decide whether he is to be set at liberty or kept as a hostage."

The Delegate of War also published the following report, addressed to the members of the Executive Commission:

"CITIZENS: Since my entrance into the Department of War, I have sought to render an exact account of the military situation, the cause of the aggression, which nothing can justify, and its results.

"The motive seems to be, in the first place, to frighten the population; in the second, to cause us needlessly to waste our ammunition, and to mask a movement on the right for the purpose of occupying the forts on that side of the river.

"Up to this day, the culpable hopes of the enemy have been frustrated, and his attempts repulsed.

"The population has remained calm and dignified, and if our munitions have been wasted by some of our youngest soldiers, they acquire each day, in the practice of firing, the coolness and steadiness indispensable in war.

"As to the third it will depend more upon the Prussians than upon us; however we shall be on our guard.

"The active point of view may be summed up as follows: Excellent soldiers, with officers—some very good, others very bad. Much dash, but little firmness. When the war companies are formed, and separated from the sedentary element, we shall have a select body of troops of more than 100,000 men. I cannot too much recommend the National Guards to direct all their attention to the choice of their chiefs. At present, the respective positions of the two armies may be thus described: The Prussians of Versailles occupy the positions of their congeners from beyond the Rhine. We hold the trenches, Molineaux, and the Clamart railway station. In fine, our position is that of men who, strong in their rights, await patiently for the attack, contented with defending themselves. In concluding, Citizens, I believe that if our troops preserve their coolness and husband their ammunition, the enemy will be tired out before we are. There will then only remain, of this mad and criminal attempt, the widows and the orphans, the recollection of an atrocious action, with the contempt which it involves.

GENERAL E. CLUSERET,
"The Delegate of War."

The following note was addressed to the representatives of the foreign powers then in Paris by the Citizen Paschal Grousset, member of the Commune and Delegate of Exterior Relations:

"PARIS, April 5, 1871.

"The undersigned Member of the Commune of Paris and Delegate for Foreign Relations, has the honor to notify you officially of the constitution of the Communal Government of Paris. He begs you to inform your Government of it, and takes this opportunity of expressing the desire of the Commune to draw closer the ties of fraternity which unite the people of Paris to the ——— nation.

"Accept, &c., &c.,
"PASCHAL GROUSSET."

It has been thoroughly demonstrated that the illusions fostered by the portion of the Paris population which supported the Commune were vain. That body could do nothing against Versailles. Such was the truth. Nevertheless, the struggle still continued, and the army of Versailles, remaining on the defensive, Paris, as every one knew, could only subsist materially by commerce and manufactures. The city not producing any objects of

PASCHAL GROUSSET
Commune of Paris
1871

consumption was obliged to draw them from without, and to furnish in exchange the produce of its own handicraft. But Paris could neither work nor barter; so that commerce and industry were both at a stand-still.

Paris, already more than half exhausted by five months of blockade, subsisted only by expending the relics of its savings. Every day that passed constituted a dead loss for the city, and involved the destruction of a capital which was not replaced. The most sanguine of the partisans of the Commune could not contradict it when it was affirmed, that the prolongation of the situation discarded absolutely all hope of a resumption of labor. Total ruin and famine was therefore at the end. Against this fatal consummation it was useless to contend. If Paris was not subjected to the material blockade of the siege, the reason was, that the Government of Versailles did not choose to have recourse to that extremity. An order would have sufficed to stop the arrival of all provisions. The military impotence of the Commune reduced Paris to subsisting only at the good pleasure of Versailles.

Early on the morning of the 7th of April, Mont Valérien awoke the inhabitants of Paris with its thunder, and crowds rushed towards the Arc de Triomphe, from which spot the fort was visible. The National Guards who had supported the Commune had been continually worsted by the regular troops. The latter had gradually advanced, and had, during the last twenty-four hours, gained some decided advantages, particularly at Courbevoie and Neuilly, both in a direct line with the Champs Elysées, and both distinctly visible from the Arc de Triomphe. It was evident that no defeat was anticipated by the Commune in that quarter, as, on the preceeding day, the General commanding the troops in Paris addressed the following letter to the Executive Committee:

"Dear Citizens:—The fears of certain persons are exaggerated. I am aware that our brave National Guard requires a new organization; but the situation of our beloved Paris is excellent; our forts are provided with ammunition, and valiantly resist the insensate and criminal attacks of the men I am ashamed to call the French of Versailles. As for Neuilly, the great aim of our adversaries, I have fortified it formidably, and I defy any army to take it. I have placed there a firm and intelligent man, Citizen Bourgoin; he maintains there with a firm hand the flag of the Commune, and no one will come and tear it from him. Therefore, dear citizens, let us organize our battalions in the calm and vigilant security of our strength, and leave to time—a few days only—thè task of showing to our enemies their weakness and our force.

"Jules Bergeret."

It will be seen, however, that Bergeret was laboring under a most erroneous idea of the strength of the position.

The village of Courbevoie had been confided to four battalions, numbering about 2,500 men, whilst two others occupied the houses in the Avenue of Neuilly. The National Guards were stationed on the *demi-lune*, at the head of the avenue, with their arms piled, when suddenly a detachment of regular troops appeared, and Valérien commenced to throw grape-shot into the place, which was precipitately evacuated by the insurgents.

The holders of the village were without cannon, and had no serious defensive works, and, as usual, at the moment of combat, were without orders and without a chief. The companies soon rallied in the adjoining avenue and fell back slowly, sheltering themselves as well as they could behind the trees, and firing on the Versailles forces as the latter arrived on the plateau. When these last had taken up their position, Mont Valérien ceased firing, but the cannon and mitrailleuse supplied its place.

The insurgents then tried to protect themselves behind the barricade at the end of the bridge, but ineffectually, as that construction, badly put together, and made up of timber and paving-stones, could not resist cannon-balls, and was speedily demolished. At that moment the men of the Commune experienced their severest losses, the mitrailleuses making fearful havoc in their ranks, and a moment of indescribable confusion ensued. Several pieces of cannon had stood for a long time behind the bridge, but could not be used, as the road was encumbered with fugitives. At last some artillery-men arrived to remove the pieces, but a shell dropping in their midst, killing and wounding large numbers, they were compelled to drag their guns into the side-streets.

The insurgents being obliged to abandon the bridge, took refuge in the houses, and continued to fire on the soldiers who had adopted a similar measure on the other side of the river. Eight pieces on the ramparts around the Porte Maillot (the gate of the barricade connecting the Avenue de la Grande Armée with the Avenue Neuilly) then commenced to shell the Avenue Neuilly, and for a long time prevented the troops from reconstructing the barricade. Gradually the insurgents abandoned the combat, and some companies re-entered Paris. At five o'clock the fusillade recommenced, the soldiers issuing in force from the houses, and, covered by the fire from the *demi-lune*, restored the barricade, and established themselves behind it, though not without considerable loss.

At the close of the day, Neuilly was completely abandoned by the National Guards. Colonel Bourgoin, who was intrusted with the defence of the barricade by Bergeret, died bravely fighting behind it. This officer was formerly an aide-de-camp to Flourens, when he was fighting the Turks in the Cretean insurrection.

During the afternoon, while the combat was taking place at the bridge of Neuilly, all the space between the Arc de Triomphe to within a short distance of the Maillot gate was filled with a crowd of men, women, and children, probably ten thousand people, all looking at the fight with the greatest anxiety. Telescopes, field-glasses, tables, chairs, and benches, were for hire, as for fireworks, or at public fêtes. The gratification of this feeling of curiosity was not, however, accomplished without some risk. During the afternoon a shell burst in the Avenue de la Grande Armée, which caused a considerable scattering of the crowd, but they all returned. Another burst within three hundred yards of the Arc de Triomphe, and prudent persons were thinking it advisable to leave, when suddenly an immense *obus* came screeching through the air, and passing five feet above the heads of the immense mass, exploded with a fearful noise on the Arc de Triomphe. Five feet lower, and there would have been five hundred victims. One-half of the crowd fell on their faces, another portion fell long after the explosion, when all danger was over, and the remainder made a rush for the side-streets. Men on horseback, cabs, and carts, public and private conveyances, every thing that was left standing, started over the fallen masses, and in an instant sabots, canes, umbrellas, and cloaks were the only things visible on the avenue. The Prussian bombardment had taught the Parisians that the danger from shells is lessened three-quarters by falling on the face as a shell arrives; but many forget until all danger is over, and then it appears most ridiculous to see them drop. The experience is one of which it is to be hoped few readers will ever be compelled to avail themselves. A battery placed at two and a half miles distant, as was Valérien from the Arc de Triomphe, may be seen to fire some twenty seconds before the sound arrives, and there is an interim of four or five seconds between the sound and the arrival of the shell, giving one plenty of time to dodge; but it is necessary that both eyes and ears be kept wide open.

The shells fell for some time in quick succession in the vicinity of the Arc de Triomphe, Avenue de l'Impératrice, and Champs Elysées, killing and wounding great numbers.

A belt of insurgents was stationed midway up the Champs Elysées to prevent the people from advancing, and it was necessary to make a long detour to arrive at the Arc de Triomphe. Numerous battalions of insurgents were encamped on the Champs Elysées.

During the following day the regular troops continued to strengthen their positions outside the fortifications on the west of the city. On the southwest the forts of Vanves and Issy continued to send shells on the plateau of Chatillon, which did not reply. The insurgents, thinking they had dismounted the guns of the regular troops, were on the point of making an attack, when a sharp fusillade was heard in the direction of the viaduct; in an instant after the Versailles outposts had passed Le Val and dislodged the insurgents from the slope nearest Issy.

A veritable persecution had now commenced against the churches and clergy of Paris by order of the Commune. Monseigneur Darboy, the Archbishop of Paris; M. Deguerry, curé of the Madeleine, the curé of Notre-Dame-des-Victoires, the curé of Saint Séverin, the curé of Saint Eustache, and a number of other respectable ecclesiastics in Paris, were all arrested, the object being to hold them as hostages. The Archbishop's sister was also arrested, and the following notice stuck up in many of the churches: "*Boutique á loué*"—"This shop to let." Not only was the wealth of the different churches declared the property of the Commune, but also the private property of the clergy was confiscated, and no ecclesiastic could consider himself safe from the unjustifiable violence of the Commune. It was rumored that one million francs were demanded as ransom from the Archbishop.

A serious conflict had arisen between the Central Committee and the Commune, in consequence of the attempt of the former to seize the Hotel de Ville, also on account of conflicting authority in the War Department. On the night of the 7th of April several orders of General Cluseret's (Delegate of War) had not been executed by the staff; and General Bergeret, substituting his authority for that of his colleague, had sent to the battalions orders so different from those which he had received, that there was much confusion in the military operations. In the morning Bergeret was replaced by General Dombrowski, a Polish citizen formerly an officer in the Russian service, and the ex-commander was sent for by General Cluseret, who addressed to him such violent reproaches that the interview soon degenerated into a sharp dispute. Citizen Bergeret then raising his voice, told General Cluseret that he (the speaker), a Frenchman and a patriot, could not consent to obey a man who had fought in America for the cause of slavery against liberty, and who had repudiated his quality of Frenchman to become a citizen of another country.—Bergeret was in error as to the side on which Cluseret fought during the American civil war, the error at that time being very prevalent in Paris. He fought on the Northern side, and was for some time attached to the staff of General Fremont. Bergeret was immediately arrested and thrown into prison, and the Polish exile or convict was appointed to his place. It was said that the new commander, Dombrowski, was much feared by the Russian authorities. He had been transported to Siberia and escaped, after having traversed all Russia at the peril of his life, arriving in France in 1865.

A despatch from the new commandant, Dombrowski,

was received on the morning of the 10th of April, announcing that his men had occupied Asnières and that the enemy was in flight, adding that his own loss was small, the enemy's great. This was followed by the following announcement:

"April 10.

"The troops have definitely installed themselves in their positions at Asnières. Iron-plated wagons are commencing their operations, and by their movement on the lines of Versailles and Saint-Germain, cover that between Colombes, Garennes, and Courbevoie.

"Our posts at Villiers and Levallois have advanced, and we are in possession of the whole of the northeast part of Neuilly. I have executed with my whole staff a reconnaissance by Levallois, Villiers, and Neuilly, as far as the Rond-point of the Boulevard du Roule, returning by the gate of the Ternes. The situation at the Porte-Maillot is much improved, in consequence of the diminution of the bombardment during the night.

"We have been able to repair the damage caused by the enemy's fire, and we have begun the construction of fresh batteries in front of the gate in question.

"Perfect order prevailed during the night at all the posts; and the rumors about the abandonment of the different positions are only inventions of the reaction, devised for the purpose of demoralizing the population.

"DOMBROWSKI."

According to the *Mot d'Ordre*, Rochefort's paper, the losses of insurgents at Neuilly bridge amounted to 225 killed and 435 wounded, although officially the insurgents announce only a few wounded, and instead of a defeat a very decided victory. It was easy to be seen from many points in the vicinity of the Arc de Triomphe that the

Communists had met with a decided defeat, and the following correspondence from the Versailles army verifies the view as seen from Paris:

"At none of the encounters between the Prussians and the French around Paris did I see more severe fighting than on Friday evening at the Courbevoie end of the bridge of Neuilly. There was one barricade there and another on the middle of the bridge; it had been resolved to carry those barricades on Friday, with the view of opening a way to Paris by the Avenue de Neuilly. The division of General Montaudon was marched to Courbevoie for the purpose, and that General directed the movements. Generals Pechot and Besson were also on the ground. I saw the action from the glacis of Valérien. At 3 o'clock the enemy opened fire, Valérien throwing 14 and 28 pound shells from 7 and 14 pound guns against Porte Maillot and the insurgents' batteries on the ramparts close to that gate. At the same moment the fire of eight 7-pounders and of four 12-pounders was directed on the *tête de pont* at the right bank of the river from the Courbevoie road and open space to the left, and the cannon and mitrailleuses of Montaudon's division enfiladed the avenue leading down to the *enceinte*.

"The insurgents vigorously replied with heavy guns from Porte Maillot and the ramparts, and with a mitrailleuse battery on the banks of the river close to the island. The troops possessed themselves of the houses at the angles of Puteaux and Courbevoie, and from these, at half-past three, commenced a chassepot fire on the insurgents. Dreadful was the thunder of artillery, the running scream of mitrailleuses, and the shrill whizzing of chassepots for a quárter of an hour; the whole of the region of Courbevoie and Neuilly was enveloped in a smoke so thick that one could see the fire blaze from the cannon's mouth and from exploding shells as if it had been night. Insurgents were seen collecting in the Bois de Boulogne. Valérien shelled them, but they got under cover.

"Troops entered the wood and gave them chase; they ran across towards the Porte Maillot. The National Guards there fired, and so stopped the pursuit, but the shots from the fort brought down friends and foes alike. When the terrific din had somewhat abated, and the smoke partially cleared away, I saw a body of troops, each furnished with a sand-bag, approach the barricade at the end of the bridge. The insurgents had retreated to the second barricade. Putting the sand-bags on the top of the barricade, the infantry crouched behind it and fired volley after volley along the bridge, while Valérien and all the military batteries kept sweeping the avenue. In half an hour the troops were on the bridge. A column of them was marched over it, and proceeded to occupy the houses at St. James on the right and at Neuilly on the left. A caisson left by the insurgents on the bridge exploded and killed General Besson on the spot. The firing of artillery was still very hot; but at four o'clock the fusillade had ceased near the bridge.

"General Pechot was found to be badly wounded. He died in the Press Ambulance a short time after he was carried in there. It was nearly six o'clock when the artillery fire slackened, and the struggle came to a conclusion for the day. Just then two rifled 24-pounders arrived at Valérien, and were at once placed in position.

"During the fight no fewer than twenty-one officers were killed or wounded on the Government side. The bridge and the entrance of the Avenue were strewn with dead and wounded insurgents. At eleven at night the division of General Grenier was marched out from Versailles to supply the place of the division of General

Montaudon, who had been wounded. By some bad management, the insurgents were allowed to regain possession of a barricade on the Neuilly side, but they were driven from it again yesterday morning. It was reported that Porte Maillot was to be taken. I was near the ground from morning till night, but no attempt at storming the insurgent position was made. The artillery combat was renewed early and continued till dark, and the troops succeeded in occupying the houses in the Avenue de Neuilly as far as the church; but the infantry operations were confined to firing from windows and from behind walls. The batteries at Porte Maillot and close to the ramparts on the right of the gate shelled Courbevoie and the other positions of the troops. Valérien, with 48-pound shells, kept up a constant fire on Porte Maillot and its redoubts, and the field batteries of the Grenier Division swept the Avenue up to the Arc de Triomphe. One shell struck the Arc itself. On both sides hundreds of spectators were out to witness the performance. I saw a large body of National Guards prepare to march down from the Arc de Triomphe at about four o'clock. They were arrested by the shelling of the troops."

The following morning a warm fusillade took place in the Bois de Boulogne, and soon extended along the river to Clichy and Asnières. Mont Valérien continued to throw shells from time to time into the wood, and in the direction of the Bois de Colombes and Gennevilliers. The guns on the rampart kept up a continual fire on Courbevoie and the bridge at Neuilly. The insurgents were busily occupied in fortifying Asnières, which place seemed likely to become the base of future operations. The gate of the fortifications in that direction was open, and vehicles laden with ammunition and stores were passing out. The villages of Levallois and Champerret were strongly occupied by National Guards. To the south of Paris the Versailles troops had opened a murderous fire from the plateau of Chatillon, which had remained entirely silent for two days. They had profited by the leisure allowed them by the forts of Vanves and Issy to place naval guns in the works established by the Prussians. The first battery unmasked was on the right of the Moulin, and fired on what remained of the barracks of Vanves. The insurgents were obliged to retire to the casemates. Later in the day the fusillade commenced from the advanced posts, and the mitrailleuses were heard resounding in the woods of Clamart. The action extended to Montrouge and Bagneux and the left, whence the insurgents were seen retreating. They soon halted, however, Cluseret having sent large reinforcements to their aid. There seemed to be a mutual lull on both sides, but soon after dark there suddenly broke out a furious discharge of musketry, cannon, and mitrailleuses, such as had not been heard even during the siege by the Prussians. For nearly two hours the peals succeeded each other at intervals of only a few seconds; and as the clouds were dark and low, the sky was lit up each moment with flashes of light like summer lightning. A serious attack had been made by the Versailles troops on the insurgent outposts before Issy. Some battalions were surprised, and were obliged to retreat precipitately behind the forts. In the meantime a severe contest ensued between the outposts of both parties. After a desperate struggle in the village of Issy, all the approaches to which were barricaded or pierced for musketry, the insurgents fell back under cover of the forts, which kept up a strong fire to protect their retreat. The mitrailleuses, with which the barricades were armed, also opened fire on two strong columns of troops which were marching on Issy.

A despatch from the Commander Dombrowski, received

during the action, stated that the situation presented no gravity; that Paris could preserve its confidence; that the attack of the Versailles forces, which had been expected for two days, would not succeed.

A despatch from the commander of Fort Issy, dated one o'clock, April 13th, states that the Versailles troops made three successive attacks, but were repulsed with heavy loss. The plateau of Chatillon, he wrote, was covered with dead which the enemy could not remove. A similar report was also sent from Fort Vanves. There the troops appear to have attacked the insurgents in the trenches. General Cluseret, Delegate of War, issued the following official report of the engagement on the evening of the 11th:

"The enemy, profiting by the obscurity of the night, unmasked all his batteries, and attempted a violent attack on the gates of the southwest, but was repulsed with disgrace. Our losses are *two* wounded and *one* killed (there were seldom more than that number killed in any action, according to the Commune) as far as is known at present. In this nocturnal assault—an operation always difficult to be repelled by very young troops—there was not a moment of hesitation, and the *Enfants de Paris* behaved most bravely. I mention in the order of the day the 208th and 179th battalions on account of their ardor."

The official Journal of the Commune, commenting on the attack, says:

"The cannonade of Monday evening against the forts of the south was as useless as it was furious. The attack was vigorously repulsed, and the fire of the enemy soon ceased. Much noise and little work; but certainly no small loss for the assailants. The Ministry of War is of opinion that this grand demonstration is meant to cover a surprise towards the Porte Maillot and Neuilly, which will not have any better success. We are ready here as elsewhere. Versailles is void of troops. The whole royal army is said to be under the walls of Paris, which expects them with the calmness and confidence of right and force."

The same organ adds:

"The attack of Tuesday evening took place between the forts of Issy and Vanves. The Versailles troops advanced to within a hundred yards of the trench, but they were vigorously repulsed, and in their flight sustained considerable loss."

The Commune having accused the Government of Versailles of introducing agents into the National Guards for the purpose of propagating disorder, published a decree instituting a Council of War in each legion, to be composed of seven members—a president, two officers, two sub-officers, and as many privates. A Council of Discipline was also formed in each battalion, composed of as many members as there were companies, nominated by election, and revocable on the proposition of the Delegate of War. The Council of War could pronounce all penalties *en usage*, subject to the ratification of a Court of Revision.

The Chambers of Commerce of Paris, representing nearly eight thousand merchants, manufacturers and traders, appointed a delegation to proceed to Versailles and endeavor to bring about some amicable settlement of the conflict now dividing the insurgents of Paris and the legal Government. The bases on which the envoys were to endeavor to bring about a reconciliation were these:

"The maintainance and affirmation of the Republic.

The possession by the city of Paris of the most extended municipal liberties, distinct from all action or interference from the central power." These delegates state that they arrived at Versailles, and placed themselves in communication with a committee of seven members of the Left, in conjunction with whom they drew up the following outline of the compromise:

"The formation of a Committee of Conciliation, the functions of which would be to place in communication the members of the Government and of the Commune of Paris, each preserving entire freedom of action, and to seek in that exchange of ideas the means of a pacific solution. The course by which that result is to be arrived at appears to consist principally in these dispositions: 'The acceptance by the city of Paris of the Municipal Bill which is about to be voted by the Assembly; elections in Paris in conformity with that law, that is to say, in a few days, under the direction of the Committee of Conciliation; recognition of the right of the Municipal Council thus chosen to submit to the Assembly certain propositions relative to the particular conditions of the city of Paris, the necessity of which the bill already admits in certain respects; and consequently, in order to facilitate the negotiations, the suspension of military operations immediately after the acceptance of those preliminaries at Paris, without prejudice for the present to the question of the arming or organization of the National Guard, which subject shall be reserved for the subsequent examination of the Municipal Council, and for the decision of the National Assembly, when the latter body shall have under consideration the reconstitution of the armed force in France. A general political amnesty!" The report of the delegates then goes on to say: "We waited on M. Barthélemy Saint-Hilaire, who manifested the greatest sympathy with the object of our mission, and procured for us an interview with M. Thiers. The Chief of the Executive Power, to whom the terms of the powers we had received from the Syndical Chambers had been communicated, replied very categorically to the two points mentioned above. With respect to the maintenance of the Republic, he affirmed to us, 'on his honor,' in the clearest and most positive language, that never, he living and in power, the Republic in France should fall! He reminded us that he had already said the same in the Chamber, and authorized us to repeat it, in his name, to the persons who had sent us and to the public. He added that, notwithstanding the personal tendencies of certain individuals or groups in the Chamber, 500 deputies at least would support him in that order of ideas; and that, in fine, the Republic, if it had reason to mistrust the excesses of factions, had nothing to fear from the disposition of the Chamber. These assurances, which we received with joy, were besides on every point in conformity with the confidence testified on the previous evening by the deputies of the Left. On the second point, that of the municipal liberties of Paris, the Chief of the Executive Power declared to us that the city could not expect anything more from the Government than the application of the common law, as established by the municipal bill which the Chamber was about to vote. On that subject we avoided entering on a discussion which could not lead to any result, for we did not hope to convert to municipalist or federalist ideas the well-known centralism of M. Thiers. We, however, thought right to communicate to him the note drawn up with the deputies of the Left. M. Thiers listened attentively to the reading of the paper; he neither ratified explicitly any of its dispositions, nor formally contested any of them; and the explanations exchanged on various paragraphs, especially on that relative to the armistice, left us under this impression—that the terms of the note in question might, so far as the executive power was concerned, serve as the basis for the ulterior discussion of an arrangement." The delegation not possessing any authority to treat further, thought fit to return to Paris and report progress.

CHAPTER VI.

M. Jules Favre at Prussian headquarters—Letter of Paschal Grousset to the Prussian Commander—Proclamation posted at St. Denis—Sacrilege of the Communists—Religious services discontinued—Decree ordering the destruction of the Column Vendome—Article in the *Mot d' Ordre*—Shells fall far into Paris—Report of General Cluseret—Battery at Trocadero—Marshal de McMahon appointed Commander-in-Chief of the army of Versailles—Formation of that army—The army of reserve—Fighting on the 15th—Elections of the 16th—Fighting at Asnières—The Chateau de Bécon carried by the troops—The Government accused of procrastination—Deputations to Versailles—Address of the Republican League—Programme of the Commune—Severe firing on the 19th—Losses of the insurgents—Attack of the insurgents on the bridge at Neuilly—Their defeat—Letter from the Archbishop to M. Thiers—Damage caused in Paris by shells—Engagement at the bridge of Clichy—Explosion of a powder magazine—Convents and nunneries invaded—Atheism of the Communists—The Executive Committee—Suppression of journals—Insurgent batteries at Lavallois and Clichy—Attack on the Park of Neuilly—Proclamation announcing an armistice at Neuilly—Expectation of a grand attack—Attack on Levallois by the troops—Repulsed by Dombrowski.

M. JULES FAVRE, Minister of Foreign Affairs, passed the entire day of the 9th of April with General Fabrice in the German headquarters at Rouen. The object of his journey was to ascertain for the Government of Versailles the nature of the communications recently made by the Commune of Paris to the German military authorities at St. Denis, and he at once obtained all the information he required. It appeared that on the 4th of April, Paschal Grousset, acting for the Commune as Delegate of Foreign Affairs, sent to the German headquarters at St. Denis a note in these words:

"The Commune wishes to know at what point have arrived the negotiations between Germany and the Government of Versailles for the execution of the preliminaries of peace, and in case the latter should have effected the payment of a sum of 500 millions of francs, the Communal delegate demands the evacuation by the Prussians of the forts on the north side, which are dependencies of the territory of Paris."

This document is a specimen of the stupid arrogance of some of the members of the Commune. They did not recognize the Versailles Government, but if that Government had paid any portion of the war debt, they wished to take advantage of it.

M. Jules Favre, in communicating to the National Assembly the result of his mission, added that the German authorities sent no reply; and the Minister then, referring to the attitude of Prussia relating to the events then going on in Paris, declared that the Cabinet at Berlin had repeatedly offered its service to the Government of Versailles for the re-establishment of order in the French capital, but that those overtures had been declined.

The commander-in-chief of the 3d army corps had the following proclamation posted at St. Denis:

"Compiegne, April 6, 1871.

"Art. 1. The state of siege is declared in those parts of the departments of the Seine, Seine-et-Oise, Seine-et-Marne, and Oise, occupied by the troops of the 3d army.

"Art. 2. The powers with which the civil authority was invested for the maintenance of order and police, are consequently transferred entirely to German military commanders. The civil authority will, nevertheless, continue to exercise those functions of which it has not been deprived by the military governors.

"Art. 3. The German military tribunals are competent to try crimes and offences against the safety of the German troops, or against public order, whatever may be the position of the principal accused or their accomplices.

"Art. 4. The German military authority has the right—1. To make perquisitions by day or by night in the dwellings of the inhabitants; 2. To remove released convicts and individuals not having a residence in the localities subject to a state of siege; 3. To order the delivery of arms and ammunition, and to search for and remove them; and 4. To prohibit such publications and meetings as may seem to it of a nature to produce or protract disorder.

"ALBERT,
"Prince Royal of Saxony."

The disgraceful and sacrilegious conduct of the Commune became more and more disgusting to that respectable portion of the citizens who were compelled to remain in Paris. A number of its soldiers went on the morning of the 9th of April to the church of Notre-Dame-de-Lorette, and, after blocking up the approaches, proceeded to make requisitions under the pretext of seeking for mitrailleuses. They also arrested one of the priests, and seized on the papers of the curé. The search lasted several hours, during which time some of the party were playing cards in the vestry, others proceeded to dress up the figure of the Virgin Mary as a vivandière, while that of Jesus was clothed in the uniform of a Versailles soldier, a pipe stuck in his mouth, and then shot at by the insurgents present.

All the clergy of Montmartre, including M. Protot, the venerable curé of St. Pierre, were also arrested. The motives may be seen from the following curious placard, posted on the closed doors of the church:

"APRIL 10, 1871.

"Whereas priests are thieves, and churches are haunts where the masses have been morally assassinated in dragging France under the heels of the scoundrels Bonaparte,

Favre, and Trochu, the delegate of Les Carrières at the ex-Prefecture of Police orders the church of St. Pierre to be closed, and decrees the arrest of the ecclesiastics and ignorantins.—Le Moussu."

Two Commune seals were affixed to the paper.

One of the venerable fathers was conducted to the ex-Prefecture of Police and brought before the citizen delegate, the notorious atheist, Raoul Rigault, who demanded his name.

"My children," replied the venerable man, whose hair was whitened with the frost of eighty winters.

"Citizen," interrupted the delegate Rigault, who was not quite thirty years old, "you are not before children, but in presence of a magistrate." "What is your profession?"

"I am a servant of God."

"Where does he live?" interrogated Rigault.

"Everywhere," responded the pious old priest, noted for his deeds of charity for over half a century.

"Send this man to the Conciérgerie, and issue a warrant for the arrest of his Master, one called God, who has no permanent residence, and is consequently, contrary to law, living in a perpetual state of vagabondage," replied the infamous blasphemer.

The following day the Commune ordered the religious service to be discontinued in all the prisons. It also ordered the destruction of the Column Vendôme. This decree was probably the most remarkable, as well as the most dastardly, of all the proclamations of these vandals:

"PARIS, April 12, 1871.

"THE COMMUNE OF PARIS—Considering that the imperial column in the Place Vendôme is a monument of barbarism, a symbol of brute force and false glory, an affirmation of militarism, a negation of international law, a permanent insult cast by the victors on the vanquished, a perpetual attack on one of the great principles of the French Republic Fraternity, decrees the column of the Place Vendôme shall be demolished.

This beautiful column took its name from the hotel of Duke Vendôme, the illegitimate son of Henry IV., which formerly stood here. The form of the Place is a perfect octagon, 420 by 450 feet. The buildings bordering on the Place are very beautiful, and of Corinthian architecture. In the centre formerly stood an equestrian statue of Louis XIV; this was demolished by the people during the first revolution, the base only being saved. In 1806, the Emperor Napoleon I. gave orders for the erection of a triumphal monument in honor of the successes of the French armies. The column was of the Tuscan order, and copied after Trajan's Pillar at Rome. Its height was 135 feet; in circumference at the base, 35 feet; the base was 21 feet high and 20 square. The summit was reached by a winding staircase of 176 steps. The column was covered with bas-reliefs in bronze, composed of 276 plates, made out of 1200 pieces of cannon taken from the Russians and Austrians, representing the victories of the French armies in the German campaign of 1805. There were over 2,000 figures of three feet high, and the metal used weighed 1,800,000 pounds. The column was surmounted by a colossal bronze statue of Napoleon I, 11 feet high, in a Roman toga; this was erected by Napoleon III, in 1863, replacing the old familiar statue with the cocked hat and military surtout. The Emperor's statue was hurled to the ground during the revolution of 1814, but France was not satisfied until a finer one was placed upon the summit. The whole cost was about $300,000.

The Commune did not decide the destruction of the national monument without some opposition. A small minority argued that it was not the moment to waste time on such trifling questions. The reasons which preceded the text of the decree were also the subject of a long discussion. Although monuments commemorative of victories are of a nature to perpetuate insatiable animosities between nations, if they are to disappear, the national representation of the whole of France ought to order their suppression, the whole of France having contributed to their erection.

Paschal Grousset, in his paper, the Vengeur, says:

"At last that Column Vendôme is to be removed—a ridiculous and monstrous trophy, erected at the command of a blind despot, to perpetuate the remembrance of his insensate conquests and his culpable glory—a monument, moreover, destitute of all artistic value—a cantata in bronze, a daub in metal instead of on canvas—in short, a wretched imitation of Trajan's column. Art will lose nothing by its destruction; good sense and patriotism will gain. For the fact is injudicious to leave under the eyes of the ignorant and the simple the stupid glorification of a cursed past. That Column of Vendome . . I have never been able to look at it without my heart bounding with indignation and disgust. In the time of the Empire there was always to be seen hanging on the railings and rotting in the rain, innumerable wreaths of a flaunting yellow or a dirty white: Souvenir, Regrets, Gloire, Victoire. Without the sentinel who watched over this rubbish with jealous care, one might have taken the place for the traditional shop always to be found next door to the marble-mason's at the gates of the cemeteries."

The seizure of the public treasures of the Paris churches created an intense excitement, and most of the respectable journals which still remained unsuppressed were loud in their complaints against Rochefort, a supporter of the

Commune and editor of the *Mot d'Ordre,* for having denounced the treasures, and indicating where different sacred vessels were hid away for safety. In his turn he replied that, not only was it proper to make the seizures, but he gloried in having been the means of assuring that result. His reasoning was characteristic of the men with whom he associated at the time—men whose blasphemous words and atheistical opinions were far in advance of the revolutionists of 1789, and of such a character as to make all true Frenchmen weep for their country. His article on the subject ran thus:

"Not only does the *Mot d'Ordre* refuse to disavow the co-operation which it gave for the seizure in question, but it declares that if it knew of any other treasure belonging to the clergy elsewhere, it would again hasten to inform the Commune. Our eternal creed will be, that as Jesus Christ was born in a stable, the only treasure that Notre-Dame ought to possess is a truss of straw. As to the sacred vases studded with emeralds, or the emeralds enriched with finely-chased vessels, we do not hesitate to declare them national property, from the simple reason that they are derived from the generosity of those to whom the Church promised Paradise; and that an assurance of imaginary blessings, given to extort money or articles of value, is designated in all codes as swindling. Why is a physician interdicted from inheriting from his patient? Because the supposition is that he may have been able, by the dread of death, to turn the brain of the sick man and induce him to put the doctor's name in his will in exchange for the preservation of his life. The priests, and the church which enrolls them, are just in the same case. We cannot say how the first Christians understood religion, which has been since so strangely revised, corrected, and augmented; but at this hour, and for many centuries past, it has become the pretext for all sorts of extortions and intimidations. For that reason we infinitely prefer seeing the Commune make requisitions on the churches rather than on merchants and manufacturers."

The *Moniteur*, of Versailles, made the following comment on the above article:

"Where did M. Rochefort learn that the crucifixes carved by Bouchardon, and the sacred vessels chased by the most celebrated artists, were swindled, as he elegantly puts it, out of the dying, by working on their fears? When Philippe-le-Bel, after his victory of Mons-en-Puelle, Louis XIII, after the glorious combats of Pont-de-Suse, Condé, Turenne, and Luxemburg, whom the Parisians proudly named the Decorator of Notre-Dame, enriched our temples with their voluntary offerings, or with standards taken from the enemy, was their conduct caused by terror or cheating? And if those recollections do not touch M. Rochefort, let him at least respect in those works of art, so admirably executed, the glory of the artists. The handicraftsman has also his glory, often more durable than that of conquerors, pretended legislators, and self-called politicians; he transmits it to posterity in the masterpieces which, if a painter, he has fixed on canvas; if a sculptor, he has created from the shapeless block of marble; or, if a goldsmith, he has hammered or chiselled out with delight. In the name of industry and its glorious inheritance, respect at least those so-called treasures of the churches, which are, in reality, only magnificent works of art, and which, at least, unlike those carefully preserved in the cabinets of celebrated collectors, are open to all. Democrats, respect democratic art, which, perhaps, the Christian religion alone has placed at the service of the poor as well as of the rich."

The advantage round the walls of Paris, for one or two days, was not decidedly with the Versailles troops. Nearly all their attacks on the southern forts of Issy, Vanves and Montrouge had been repulsed. On the morning of the 13th, the engagement became general along the west side of Paris. The object of the regular troops was to release, by a flank movement, a detachment which had been driven on the Grande Latte, an island in the Seine, between the bridges of Asnières and Neuilly. This was a body of men who had recently arrived at Versailles from Breton. At the same time a severe encounter of infantry was going on in the streets of Neuilly and Levallois; the National Guards were obliged to give way, and General Dombrowski was under the necessity of sending for reinforcements. The Avenue de la Grande Armée, and the neighborhood of the Arc de Triomphe, continued to receive its share of projectiles from Mont Valérien and from the bridge at Neuilly. One shell fell as far down the Champs Elysées as the corner of the Rue de Morny, smashing a lamp-post and the butt and truck of a water-carrier. It fortunately did not burst; and a group of spectators, who were standing near, escaped unhurt. Another shell fell in the midst of a battalion of insurgents in Place de l'Etoile. The soldiers were on their way to Port Maillot, beating drums and waving several new flags. Seven men were killed and twenty wounded with the single shell. From that moment spectators were not allowed to go nearer the firing than the Rond-Point on the Champs Elysées. The fusillade continued during the afternoon, but it was difficult, from the ramparts, to form any idea of the result of the fighting near the barricade of the Pont de Neuilly. Later in the day the engagement extended to the left side of the Avenue de Neuilly, which district was still occupied by the Versailles troops.

M. Rossel, chief of the insurgent staff, published the following military report:

"April 13th.

"The fighting has continued all day at Neuilly. The troops of the Commune have preserved an offensive attitude, and the town is attacked and defended foot by foot. At Asnières the struggle is less obstinate.

"On the side of the southern forts, the day has passed without any remarkable incident. General Eudes is making active dispositions for the night, as the movements of the enemy seem to presage an attack. Reinforcements have been sent to the points already assailed. The morale of the troops is excellent.

"The progress of organization admits of a gradual diminution of the excessive fatigue imposed on the troops."

General Cluseret's report, the same day, addressed to the Commune, says:

"I return from an inspection of the southern forts, and of the general line of defence from Montrouge to La Muette, and my impression is most favorable.

"The attacks of Tuesday and Wednesday, made with a great number of men on the enemy's side, were repulsed with so much ease and so little loss that they ought to inspire an entire confidence in the future.

"The battery of 24, on the Trocadéro, has sent balls into the barracks of Mont Valérien. That range was all we wished to obtain for the moment.

"I invite the attention of the Commune to the manly aspect of the troops, and the exceptional order prevailing at the Point du Jour. Both men and materials are in good order, and denote energy, activity, and competence on the part of the commander. Vanves and Montrouge are in good condition. On the side of the enemy there is the same disposition of artillery as in the time of the

Prussians. As to their infantry, it is not numerous, and without much consistence. When the critical moment arrives, I have every reason to believe that the resistance of the Versaillaise will not be found superior to our efforts."

General Cluseret in his reports did not deem it necessary to be controlled in any measure by the *facts* in question. A proposition had been made in the Commune to abolish the French Grammar, leaving to citizens the privilege of spelling as they pleased; also expunging from the dictionary such words as king, duke, sir, servant, equipage, conscription, etc.; it would have been as well to have included truth, veracity, etc.

The large guns in position on the Trocadero (the heights above Passy at the extreme west of the city), and pointed at Mont Valérien, commenced firing during the afternoon of the 13th. The fort replied feebly; and, not being able to discover the exact position of this new battery, which was concealed behind the wall of the Passy Cemetery, threw a few shells on the neighboring houses. A crowd of idlers, who had collected in the rear of this battery, immediately dispersed. About half-past four the guns there ceased firing, probably because none of the shot had reached high enough up the mountain to touch the fort at the top. Of the eighteen shells, the flight of which was observed, some fell in the Bois de Boulogne, one at Suresnes, some in the vineyards at the foot of Valérien, and four were not followed by any explosion, and probably dropped into the river. The fort, being at a higher elevation, had the neighborhood of the Trocadéro within range, and its projectiles damaged houses in the Rues Scheffer, Pétrarque, and Vineuse.

The military operations being about to assume a new and more important phase, to assure their success, M. Thiers, by an official decree, appointed Marshal de

McMahon commander-in-chief of the army of Versailles, an appointment that gave the greatest amount of satisfaction to all lovers of law and order in France. The illustrious Duke of Magenta, ever since the fatal day of Froeschwiller, was the most popular man in France, and the prestige of his name was immense. He had not yet thoroughly recovered from the wound received at the battle of Sedan when he was called to this new command.

The composition of the army of Versailles, placed under the command of Marshal de McMahon, was as follows: The active army consisted of three corps—two of infantry and one of cavalry—commanded respectively by Generals Ladmirault, De Cissey, and Du Barail. General Borel was chief of staff; General Princeteau, commandant of artillery; and General Brettevillois, commandant of engineers.

The 1st corps was formed of three divisions, commanded by Generals Grenier, Laveaucoupet, and Montaudon. Its chief of staff was General Saget; General Laffaille, commandant of artillery; and General Dubost, commandant of engineers.

The second corps, as the first, numbered three divisions, commanded by Generals Lavasson-Sorval, Susbielle, and Lacretelle. Its chief of staff was General de Place; General de Berckheim, commandant of artillery; and General Séré de Rivière, commandant of engineers.

The third corps was composed of three divisions of cavalry, commanded by Generals Halna du Fretay, De Preuil and Ressayre. Its chief of staff was Colonel Balland. It had also a battery of artillery attached to each division.

The Army of Reserve was under the immediate direction of General Vinoy. It was formed of three divisions, under the command of Generals Faron, Bruat, and Vergé. Its chief of staff was General de Valdan; General Réné commandant of artillery; General Dupouët, commandant of engineers. To which force was added, towards the end of April, two other corps, viz., those of Generals Douay and Clinchant.

It was thus, with six army corps, that Marshal de McMahon commenced active operations for the suppression of the insurrection of Paris.

The morning of the 15th commenced with a sharp cannonade, which lasted about four hours. The Versailles batteries then ceased firing, but for a considerable time the insurgent guns continued to batter the defences at Neuilly and Courbevoie. In the meantime rapid musketry firing was kept up in the Bois de Boulogne and and Levallois, where the combatants, posted at the windows and concealed in the streets and gardens, kept up a constant fusillade. In the afternoon the batteries of Mont Valérien and Courbevoie recommenced their fire.

The guns of Trocadéro were tried during the morning, not on the fortress, as before, but on Longchamps, where reserved troops were encamped. From the Trocadéro to Mont Valérien the distance is a little over three miles and a quarter, which was quite within reach of long range guns. Shells had already fallen at Chaillot which is in the rear of Trocadéro. Passy also commenced to suffer from the fire in this new direction, as the projectiles intended for the battery on the Trocadéro frequently fell there. The fighting was very obstinate during the afternoon at Levallois, a part of which village was occupied by the troops and part by the insurgents. At four o'clock two iron-clad locomotive batteries left the Batignolle's station in the direction of Levallois, and shortly after the noise of the mitrailleuses, with which they were armed, could be heard. Two heavy ship guns placed on the bastion at the Porte St. Ouen also took part in the combat, which terminated by the insurgents falling back behind their barricades.

On the morning of the 16th the cannonade recommenced at four, and continued without intermission until eight in the evening. The firing was chiefly from the insurgent batteries. An incident occurred during the morning at the station of Colombes beyond the Seine. The insurgents had advanced up the line to see whether it was cut, in order to manœuvre the iron-clad railway batteries. A body of Versailles cavalry made a dash to cut off the retreat of the National Guards, but the locomotive which was waiting toward Asnières came to the rescue, and, sending a volley from a mitrailleuse among the mounted troops, drove them back. The insurgents then retreated under cover of the engine, but without ascertaining how far beyond the station the line was open.

The elections held on the 16th, for the purpose of filling up the vacancies in the Commune caused by resignations, was a strong rebuke to those who had usurped the power of the capital. The partisans of the Commune had announced that the ballot on the 16th would be a striking triumph for them, that all Paris would rush to the urns in crowds, and nominate by acclamation the Communal candidates. They found themselves in front of a pitiable result. In most of the arrondissements the persons who had come forward had not received one-eighth of the number of voters on the electoral lists. This government had been at work nearly a month, and the people had been able to judge of its merits. General Cluseret, who gave orders to 150,000 men, had difficulty in obtaining 1,968 votes; General Dombrowski, in spite of the aid of the biographies in the official organ of the Hotel de Ville, presents himself escorted by 65; M. Courbet, the patriotic promoter of the demolition of the Vendôme Column, recruited as many as 2,418 supporters; and Colonel Razona is obliged to avow that with his 972 he had fewer electors than soldiers.

RAZOUA
Commune of Paris
1871.

The comments of various journals on these elections, produced the following decree from the Commune:

> The Commune, which cannot possibly tolerate in besieged Paris journals which openly preach up civil war, give military information to the enemy, and propagate calumny against the defenders of the Republic, has decided that the *Soir*, the *Cloche*, the *Opinion Nationale*, and the *Bien Public* are hereby suppressed."

One of the most important engagements of the siege took place on the 17th between the regulars and the advanced posts at Asnières. During the morning the troops from Versailles attacked the federal outposts on the railway, guarded by the 77th battalion, which at once retreated, abandoning the barricades and trenches. Four other battalions on the farther bank of the Seine, seeing their comrades fall back, and being attacked by mitrailleuses, fled to the bridge of boats; a detachment of cavalry made a dash, cutting off a large number and making them prisoners. The insurgents then endeavored to bring their locomotive batteries into action, but a shot from a battery established at the Château de Bécon seriously damaged one of those engines, and drove it off the rails; the line in consequence became blocked, and the other locomotives had to return to Paris. The insurgents on the right bank, fearing that the troops might cross the pontoon bridge, severed it in the middle; but at that moment many insurgents still remained on the opposite side. Some of these men threw themselves into the river to endeavor to cross the gap in the chain of boats by swimming; others tried to climb up the slope of the railway bridge, on which they were exposed to the fire of the troops; whilst many were carried away by the stream and drowned.

By noon the whole of Asnières had been evacuated by the insurgents, leaving 150 killed and 50 prisoners in the hands of the regular troops, who contented themselves with strengthening their positions in the vicinity of Gennevilliers. The insurgents stopped in their retreat before arriving at the ramparts, and the officers reformed their companies as well as they could. During the afternoon they advanced again to the river, and a fire was kept up between them and the troops until evening. During the day the Chateau of Bécon, a most important position, was carried by the young Colonel Davoust, at the head of the 36th regiment. This officer is a grandson of the celebrated Marshal of the first Napoleon of the same name. M. Thiers made the action the subject of the following despatch to the Sub-Prefects:

"April 17th, 7.20 P.M.

"Our troops to day executed a brilliant feat of arms in the direction of Courbevoie. The division of General Montaudon captured the Chateau of Bécon after a sharp cannonade. The young Colonel Davoust, Duc d'Auerstaedt, rushed forward at the head of his regiment and carried the place. Our engineers immediately commenced an epaulement with sacks of earth, in order to establish a battery. The position of Asnières thus attacked will no longer be able to disturb our *tête de pont* at Neuilly; we have no other object, and still persist in avoiding small actions, until the decisive engagement which shall restore the authority of the law. The event of to-day, executed under a cross fire from Asnières and the ramparts, is nevertheless a remarkable act of skill and energy.

"A. THIERS."

The victorious troops did not at once follow up their successes; and the insurgents, rallied by Dombrowski, endeavored by repeated charges to recover lost ground, but in vain, as they were again driven from Colombes across the river.

The Chief of the Executive Power has had a singular fortune. He attacked the fortifications of Paris which he constructed, and ordered an assault on the Chateau of Bécon, where he passed the whole of the summer of 1835 consecrated to peaceful studies.

"M. Thiers issued to the provincial authorities the following proclamation, in answer to complaints of procrastination made by country journals:

"We persist in our system of temporization for two reasons, which we can avow; first of all, to collect forces so imposing that resistance will be impossible, and therefore not sanguinary; and secondly, to leave misled men the time to return to reason.

"They have been told that the Government desires to destroy the Republic—a statement absolutely false; the sole occupation of the Executive being to put an end to the civil war, to re-establish order, credit, labor, and effect the evacuation of the territory by the fulfilment of the obligations contracted with Prussia.

"Those misguided men have been told that we wish to shoot them all; another falsehood, as the Government pardons all who lay down their arms, as it has done with the 2,000 prisoners it supports at Belle-Isle without exacting any service from them.

"Finally, they have been told that, deprived of the subsidy which enabled them to live, they will be forced to die of hunger—an assertion as untrue as all the rest; for the Government has promised them to continue their pay for some weeks yet, in order to provide them with the means of awaiting the resumption of work which is certain to arrive as soon as order is re-established and submission to the law obtained."

M. Thiers was also seriously embarrassed by the Cabinet of Berlin. The execution of the preliminaries of peace was delayed, and the dissatisfaction of Prince Bismarck was very manifest. Thiers made the same reply to the Germans that he had made to the provinces and the Assembly. He asked them to wait and let him act, otherwise he preferred to resign. Neither the Federal Chancellor nor the Chamber wished to see him leave, as he was necessary for the re-establishment of order. The Prince desired him to remain, and he troubled himself little about the means. He likewise wished him to retain office because the restoration of tranquillity could alone guarantee the debt due to Prussia. The process of re-establishing order concerned the German minister nearly; and had the Versaillais not moved speedily, he would probably have taken the matter into his own hands.

Deputation after deputation continued to arrive at Versailles, mostly emanating from the *Union Republicaine*, for the purpose of inducing the Chief of the Executive Power to treat with the Commune. A considerable movement also took place in several large towns for the same purpose. The Lyons delegation had an interview with M. Thiers; and, in the name of their fellow-citizens, presented considerations in favor of the Communal movement in Paris. The head of the Executive received them kindly, and gave them a safe conduct to the capital, where they had an interview with the Commune; but the result proved that the Commune wanted what Thiers would not concede, viz., power.

The fighting commenced at daybreak on the morning of the 18th, although followed by no important movement of troops. Mont Valérien was never more active.

The regular troops unmasked a new battery in the Park of Neuilly, and from that point and the Chateau of Bécon kept up an incessant discharge on the village of Levallois and the bridge of Asnières, where the insurgents had accumulated extensive works of defence.

A large number of guns had been sent from Paris during the previous day, but they were still lying on the road to Asnières. The insurgent officers appeared not to know what to do with them, and had heaped them up on the banks of the Seine. Six 12-pounders were lying behind a barricade, and numerous others were scattered on the railway embankment. Several iron-clad locomotives were also lying on the line hard by, on one of which a serious accident had just occurred. The gun, a breach-loader, worked by five artillerymen, being overcharged, blew out the movable plug, killing two of the men, and wounding the three others.

The regular troops had iron-clad locomotive batteries on its side also, but they were still kept in reserve.

Numerous accidents were occurring daily near Porte Maillot, at the Ternes and Arc de Triomphe, which were the quarters most exposed to the shots from Neuilly and Rond Point. At No. 11 Rue Bayen a shell entered a room where a woman was seated at table with two children; the mother was killed, and the others wounded. Another fractured both legs of a man who was walking by the side of a cart. A gentleman was crossing the Avenue de l'Impératrice on horseback, and a shell cut off both the horses' forelegs, throwing the man on his face without injuring him in the least.

On the 18th of April, the Republican League published the following address:

"M. Thiers' statements to our delegates afforded us guarantees neither for the maintenance of the Republic nor the establishment of Communal liberty, in fact for none of the things we demanded. That which we predicted has come true—civil war which it depended upon the National Assembly to stop has broken out with fresh fury. On the other hand, the Commune, by putting forward no programme, and by refusing to explain its views with regard to ours, has deprived the defenders of the rights of Paris of the advantages they would possess in having the ground they take up clearly marked out. In the presence of the foreigner, who watches our movements, we hold to the conviction that the only possible issue from the present conflict is to be found in a compromise, of which we have indicated the essential elements. In this position of affairs we have a duty to perform, namely, to maintain the whole of our programme and to take such resolutions as, following the various phases of the struggle, shall appear to us best calculated to ensure the triumph of our principles. We have decided from the present moment to place ourselves in communication with the municipal councils of the principal towns in France, and to make known to them the legitimate wishes of Paris, to which we shall lend a powerful support. Lyons, which has obtained its Commune; Lille, Macon, and other towns which understand that the cause of Paris is the cause of all the Communes of France, have anticipated our appeal. Their intervention is a sign which it would be imprudent in the National Assembly to misunderstand. Let the Assembly comprehend at last that all the great cities of France have resolved to uphold towards and against all, the Republican form of government, and to give it as an unshakable basis, Communal liberties in their integrity."

The Commune finally issued its programme so frequently called for and so long delayed. The document is of such an eccentric character that it well deserves to be reproduced. It was published in the official journal of the Commune, April 19th:

"It is the duty of the Commune to confirm and ascertain the aspirations and wishes of the people of Paris. The precise character of the movement of the 18th of March is misunderstood and unknown, and is calumniated by the politicians at Versailles. At that time Paris still labored and suffered for the whole of France, for whom she had prepared by her battles an intellectual, moral, administrative, and economic regeneration, glory, and prosperity. What does she demand? The recognition and consolidation of the Republic, and the absolute autonomy of the Commune extended at all places in France, thus assuring to each the integrality of its rights, and to every Frenchman the full exercise of his faculties and aptitudes as a man, a citizen, and a producer. The autonomy of the Commune has no other limits but its rights. The autonomy is equal for all Communes who are adherents of the contract, the association of which ought to secure the unity of France. The inherent rights of the Commune are to vote the Communal budget of receipts and expenses, the imposing and alteration of taxes, the direction of local services, the organization of the magistracy, internal police, and education. The administration of the property belonging to the Commune, the choice by election or competition with the responsibility and permanent right of control and revocation of the communal magistrates and officials of all classes, the absolute guarantee of individual liberty and liberty of conscience, the permanent intervention of the citizens in communal affairs by the free manifestation of their ideas and the free defence of their interests; guarantees given to those manifestations by the Commune who alone are charged with securing the free and just exercise of the right of meeting and publicity; the organization of urban defence, and of the National Guard, which elects its chiefs and alone watches over the maintenance of order in the city. Paris wishes nothing more under the head of local guarantees, on the well-understood condition of regaining, in a grand central administration and delegation from the Federal Communes, the realization and practice of those principles; but in favor of her autonomy, and profiting by her liberty of action, she reserves to herself to bring about as may seem good to her administrative and economic reforms. which the people demand, and to create such institutions as may serve to develop and further education. Produce, exchange, and credit have to universalize power and property according to the necessities of the moment, the wishes of those interested, and the data furnished by experience.

"Our enemies deceive themselves, or deceive the country, when they accuse Paris of desiring to impose its will and supremacy upon the rest of the nation, and to aspire to a dictatorship which would be a veritable attempt to overthrow the independence and sovereignty of other Communes. They deceive themselves when they accuse Paris of seeking the destruction of French unity established by the Revolution. The unity which has been imposed upon us up to the present by the Empire, the Monarchy, and the Parliamentary Government, is nothing but centralization, despotic, unintelligent, arbitrary, and onerous. The political unity, as desired by Paris, is a voluntary association of all local initiative, the free and spontaneous co-operation of all individual energies with the common object of the well-being, liberty, and security of all. The Communal revolution, initiated by the people on the 18th of March, inaugurated a new era in politics, experimental, positive, and scientific. It was the end of the old governmental and clerical world, of military supremacy and bureaucracy, of jobbing in monopolies, and privileges to which the proletariat owed its slavery, and the country its misfortunes and disasters. The strife between Paris and Versailles is one of those that cannot be ended by an illusory compromise—the issue should not be doubtful. The victory fought for with such indomitable energy by the Commune will remain with the idea and with the right. We appeal to France, which knows that Paris in arms possesses as much calm as bravery, where order is maintained with as much energy as enthusiasm, which is ready to sacrifice herself with as much reason as energy. Paris is only in arms in consequence of her devotion to liberty, and the glory of all in France ought to cause this bloody conflict to cease.

"It is for France to disarm Versailles by a solemn manifestation of her irresistible will. Summoned to profit by our conquests, she should declare herself identified with our efforts; she should be our ally in the contest which can only end by the triumph of the Communal idea or the ruin of Paris. As for ourselves, citizens of Paris, we have a mission to accomplish, a modern revolution, the greatest and the most fruitful of all those which have illuminated history. It is our duty to fight and conquer."

It might have been alleged that the title of the Commune to rule the country was quite as good as that of the government that preceded it; but well established as was their unscrupulousness, it was amusing to find the men who were daily arresting dozens of harmless citizens talking of their fighting for individual liberty, and after arresting priests wholesale, forcibly closing their churches, and brutally expelling nuns from their convents, having the incredible impudence to describe themselves as the champions of the rights of conscience. The appeal to the people of France to join them against the Assembly at Versailles was too extravagant to be seriously examined. The only thing serious, indeed, in the whole proclamation, was that these men meant to fight to the bitter end, and ruin Paris, unless France acceded to their insane terms.

7*

The fighting was commenced at five o'clock on the morning of the 19th, with great obstinacy. From that hour there was a constant roar of cannon, musketry and mitrailleuses all along the line, from the extreme left to the extreme right. Shells flew through the sky over the doomed quarters to the west of Paris, shrieking like birds of ill-omen, and they fell in scores about the Ternes and the Champ Elysées. Clichy and the northern parts of Levallois were, however, the objective points, and the damage was severe at the right side of the bridge of Asnières, and all about the space between the Versailles railway and the Avenue de Clichy. The insurgents suffered very heavily, for they had a habit of clustering together behind walls, and under what they considered to be the protection of street corners, the consequence of which was, when a shell burst near them it did fearful execution. The heavy fire of musketry was due chiefly to men stationed in the houses and on the house-tops. The walls of every dwelling from whence the bridge and the railway could be commanded were loop-holed with utter disregard to the rights of property; and mattresses, pillows, and even feather beds stuffed into the windows to do duty as sandbags. The insurgents thus intrenched, and further protected by a strong barricade, kept up an incessant musketry fire on Asnières, and the guns at the Porte d'Asnières and the Porte Bineau were each firing in the direction in which the enemy was supposed to be. Of course the shells and bullets must fall somewhere, but as the position of the regular troops was very imperfectly known, and those few that were known could be seen from the walls, the execution they did among the Versailles troops was not very formidable. On the other hand the insurgents occupied a narrow zone outside the walls, and did not even occupy the banks of the river, so that the fierce shelling to which their positions were subjected did great havoc in their ranks. Many, probably, would have run away if they had had a chance; but the fortifications behind them barred the way, and whenever a party came up to the gates, they were rigidly excluded. Numbers, however, congregated all along the covered way behind the glacis, and whenever a party of wounded came in, they made a rush to get inside the city with the convoy.

At Neuilly the firing was quite as heavy as at Asnières and Clichy. In the evening, a body of insurgents made their way through the partition walls of the various houses on the left side of the old Neuilly road, and succeeded in penetrating, unawares, as far as the Rue des Huissiers, within one hundred yards of the bridge of Neuilly, built up a couple of barricades, and armed them with six guns. They immediately opened fire on the Versailles troops in the Avenue de Neuilly, and the movement was executed with great vigor and courage; but it was not likely to be attended with success if large reinforcements could be brought up. The consequence of this manœuvre, brilliant as it was, proved disastrous to the troops of the Commune.

The Versailles forces stormed the barricades with so much impetuosity that the insurgents had no time to get out of the way. Numbers of them were killed, wounded, or taken prisoners. Their six guns were captured and turned against them. They fled in disorder to the gates, volleys of grape being fired into them as they went. The soldiers then made another dash forward, and carried a barricade on the Boulevard Bineau, inflicting serious loss on its defenders. Thereupon the guns on the ramparts began to thunder, their covering parties fired volleys, and an awful din was kept up till daybreak, when the Versailles artillery replied in right earnest, and shelled all the positions, as well as the quarter of the town immediately behind the walls.

This engagement was one of the most sanguinary yet

fought. The 27th, 74th and 76th battalions lost one-third of their effective force.

On the events of the day the official journal of the Commune published the following reports:

"After a sanguinary engagement we have retaken our position. Our troops, the left wing in advance, seized on a store of the enemy's provisions, consisting of sixty-nine casks of hams, cheese and bacon. The combat continues furiously; the enemy's artillery at Courbevoie covers us with projectiles and grape; but in spite of the vivacity of his fire, our right wing is at this moment executing a movement with a view to surrounding the troops of the line who have advanced too far. I require five battalions of fresh men, two thousand at least, because my adversaries are in considerable force.

"DOMBROWSKI."

April 19th, morning.—We were attacked at daybreak by strong columns of the line; and our men, deceived by friendly signals made by the soldiers, were surprised; but I have promptly re-established order.

"DOMBROWSKI."

The Archbishop of Paris having written a letter from his prison to M. Thiers on the subject of pretended cruelties to the Communist prisoners, the chief of the executive power replied through the Paris journals, indignantly denying the charge. He said that the hospitals at Versailles contained a large number of insurgents who are attended to with the greatest kindness; that the sixteen hundred prisoners who had been sent to Belle-Isle or elsewhere were treated with far greater consideration than any of the soldiers would have been if taken by the Communists; and concluded by reiterating his offers of pardon to any of the insurgents who should lay down their arms, and by promising assistance to the necessitous until a revival of commerce should enable them to earn their own living.

The firing was continued on the morning of the 20th on every side, especially between Mont Valérien and Porte Maillot, the insurgents at the latter position sticking to their guns with a daring worthy a better cause. The fire of Valérien was extremely correct, hardly ever missing its object, and probably during the entire bombardment not over fifty shells thrown from that fort passed one hundred feet beyond the gate. The batteries of Courbevoie, the Park of Neuilly, and bridge of Neuilly, were those that did all the damage to the western part of the city. Their guns being directed at the Porte des Ternes or Porte Maillot, and being nearly level with those points, if the shells passed the gates they fell in the vicinity of the Arc de Triomphe or Champs Elysées. Many and loud were the curses during these days from the partisans of law and order in the city at the careless firing from these points; but the firing was not so bad as it seemed to be. When standing at the Arc de Triomphe and looking at the Porte Maillot, it seemed as if the descent to that point was very great, at least ten degrees. This is an optical delusion, for standing at the Porte Maillot, and looking at the Arc, they appear to be on a dead level.

A rather sharp engagement took place during the morning near the bridge of Clichy. A strong reconnaissance of troops from Gennevilliers had advanced to the insurgents' outposts, when the latter commenced firing, and brought on themselves a general discharge which killed some of their men. The insurgents then fell back on their reinforcements, which had arrived on hearing the musketry. The troops continued the fire for about an hour, when they spread out as skirmishers, and retired with some loss. The regulars also made an unsuccessful attempt to seize the bridge of Asnières, and open communications with the right bank. They commenced by bombarding the village for an hour with extraordinary violence from Bécon, Courbevoie, and Neuilly. A strong force occupied the railway station, and a regiment was massed near the bridge, but the insurgents on their sides brought up two mitrailleuses and two iron-clad locomotive batteries, and discharged three volleys at the station, driving out the enemy. An attack by the soldiers of the line against the bridge also failed under the fire of the guns brought up by the insurgents.

In the meantime a shell fell into a powder magazine of the insurgents near the Porte d'Asnières, and blew up a large building occupied by a number of families of working people, and which crumbled to the ground like a house of cards. A large number of men immediately commenced to clear the ruins, and between twenty-five and thirty men, women, and children were got out, many dangerously injured. While this work was going on, the Versailles batteries suspended their fire.

The forts of Vanves, Issy, and Montrouge on the southern side exchanged frequent cannon-shots with the Versailles batteries of Chatillon and Brimborion, whilst the redoubt of Montretout and the battery at Meudon also sent occasional shells on Issy and the lower part of Clamart; but nothing of much importance was done in that direction. Everything, however, presaged a general attack, and the insurgents had received orders to hold themselves ready to march at a moment's notice.

The following official despatches were received from Dombrowski during the day:

"20th, half-past twelve in the day.

"During the night the enemy did not attempt anything against us, and we were merely cannonaded by the batteries at Courbevoie and Valérien. Our troops are fortifying themselves in their positions, and taking a little rest after the great fatigue of the day."

"ASNIERES, 20th, four in the afternoon.

"Colonel Olokowietz has been wounded in the head and arms, and received a contusion in the side. Captain de Gournay was overturned by the colonel when falling, but escaped without hurt. A rumor prevails that three houses have toppled down, and that some men have been taken out dead from under the ruins.

"The store of ammunition placed in one of the cellars is all safe. This morning, in front of the ambulance at Paul Dupont's printing-office, Captain Culot had his head carried away by a shell. The Versailles troops continue their fire on the spot.

"The spirit of the National Guards is excellent. The enemy does not fire much."

"NEUILLY, 20th, half-past four.

"Two barricades abandoned last evening at nightfall were occupied by the enemy, but have been retaken by the federals. The others are intrenched on the left bank of the Seine. The cannonade continues."

The Commune this day searched all the convents and nunneries, and shut up some thirty churches, arresting the priests. A universal feeling of uneasiness pervaded all classes of society, arising from the tone of the ultra journals of the Commune. The following specimen is from the *Montagne*, one of the most rabid of the Socialists' organs:

"In 1848, when Monseigneur Affre was shot, we believed in a divine mission, and fancied that a bishop's cope was of greater value than a workman's blouse. Education has made sceptics of us; the revolution of '71 is atheistic; our Republic wears a bouquet of immortelles in her bosom. We take our dead to their homes and our wives to our hearts without a prayer. Priests, throw aside your frocks, turn up your sleeves, lay your hands upon the plow; for a song to the lark in the morning air is better than a mumbling of psalms; and an ode to sparkling wine is preferable to a chanting of hymns. Our dogs, which used only to growl when a bishop passed, will bite him now; and not a voice will be raised to curse the day which dawns for the sacrifice of the Archbishop of Paris. We owe it to ourselves—we owe it to the world. The Commune has promised us an eye for an eye, and has given us Monseigneur Darboy as a hostage. The justice of the tribunals shall commence, said Danton, when the wrath of the people is appeased—and he was right. Darboy! tremble in your cell, for your day is past; your end is close at hand."

The Communists' writers published such documents as the above, and the masses were harangued by club orators in the following strain: "Down with the proprietors! Let us thank heaven that most of them are gone—having fled like cowards before the gathering anger of the people. Let their property be sequestered for the universal good; let their houses be sold, and the money divided among the working classes. We are poor and hungry. Shall our wives be forced upon the streets, and our brothers driven to robbery for the sake of our starving little ones? No! let us take possession of the palaces that seem to smile at our woe; let us seize the goods of the masters that are away, and even take their wives and children as hostages in case of further need."

The official organ of the Commune published a decree suppressing all night-work in bakeries, also one re-establishing the practice of sending letters by balloon, and organizing a system of civil and military aëronautics.

On the proposition of Citizen Delescluze, the Commune

modified the composition of its Executive Committee, which was to consist in the future of a delegate from each of the nine Commissions. The decree said nothing in regard to the duration of the Committee—declaring that the body was to exercise its powers provisionally. The following were the delegates named:

Delegate of War—Cluseret.
Finance—Jourde.
Subsistence—Viaud.
Exterior Relations—Paschal Grousset.
Labor and Exchange—Franckel.
Justice—Protot.
Public Service—Andrieu.
Information—Valliant.
General Surety—R. Rigault.

The Commune also reminded its members that they were bound to attend the sittings with exactitude. If prevented, they were to send notice to the President, or give a satisfactory explanation on the next occasion.

In addition to the four journals already named as suppressed by the Commune, twelve others were stopped, thus depriving some six or seven thousand persons directly or indirectly connected therewith of their daily bread.

A committee of practical jewelers met to-day at the Ministry of Finance to examine and estimate the value of a number of sapphires and fine pearls found in the cellars of that building. Among other things, there were two pearls as large as pigeons' eggs, and, in the opinion of all present, worth several millions of francs; also an inestimable collection of sapphires, which were to be sold at auction in France or England.

Throughout the whole day of the 21st the cannonade and the rattle of the mitrailleuses continued in the vicinity of Asnières and Neuilly. The musketry, however, was silent, on account of the distance of the barricades from each other. A short engagement occurred in the direction of Levallois, which turned to the advantage of the regulars.

The Versailles troops opened during the day a new battery near the island of the Grande Jatte, and sent some shells to the Porte Bineau, which had been spared until then, although guns were mounted there. From noon to three in the afternoon the district of the Ternes received from two to three shells per minute.

The establishment of insurgent batteries at Levallois and Clichy had placed these villages in an unfortunate situation, as the cannon of the Chateau Bécon and the redoubt of Gennevilliers in returning the fire had crushed them with shells. Some of these projectiles had even reached as far as the ramparts. Most of the inhabitants were obliged to take refuge in the city. An attack was made during the day on the Park of Neuilly, by order of Dombrowski. Two battalions advanced along the road at double-quick, took three barricades by escalade, and planted red flags among the stones, in high delight at their easy victory. Onward they rushed, intoxicated with success, until they arrived at the park wall, when suddenly a murderous fire was poured upon them from the mouths of a row of Gatling guns, which showered such a continuous and merciless hail of bullets upon the unprotected throng as only that terrible engine can inflict. They fled in wild disorder, leaving the road literally piled with dead, only to find at the furthermost barricade a company of their own men, who stood with bayonets fixed to check their flight. Thus driven forward again, they recoiled once more from a renewed volley; and then commenced a panic-stricken rout which no human power could control. They ran from gate to gate clamoring for admittance, which was persistently refused, and at length forced their way over the drawbridge of St. Ouen, which happened to be down at the time.

Numerous omnibuses were requisitioned during the day for the conveyance of the wounded, who appeared to be very numerous. The ambulance service was almost completely disorganized, and the wounded would often lie in the streets and die without receiving any surgical attendance. Many insurgents could be seen lying dead in the gardens at Levallois, or were buried near the spot where they fell. Others were carried into the city, and an eye-witness counted seventeen omnibuses, on the 21st, filled with dead bodies being brought into Paris by the gate of Asnières. Funeral processions, following cars surmounted with the red flag of the Commune, were also passing every moment along the Boulevard de Clichy, on their way to the cemetery of Montmartre. The insurgents began to be somewhat affected at the death of so many of their comrades, and complained that they were not sufficiently supported.

An immense shell entered, on this day, the window of the house of Rev. Dr. Lamson, Pastor of the Episcopal Chapel, and passing through a thick stone wall, dropped on the stairway unexploded; had it burst, the house would have been shattered to atoms. Ten minutes later, a man, woman and two children were killed while passing across the Avenue Josephine. Several other persons in the vicinity threw themselves on their faces at the same time, and were saved. The shells came from the bridge of Neuilly.

On the 23rd of April, the following proclamation appeared in the official journal of the Commune:

"After having conferred with the Executive Commission, and in the strict end of humanity, I authorize a suspension of arms at Neuilly, for the purpose of permitting the old men, women and children to enter Paris—

in a word, all non-combatants surrounded at Neuilly, who are the innocent victims of this struggle.

"General Dombrowski, in accord with Citizens Bonvallet and Stupuy, of the *Union Républicaine des Droits de Paris,* will take the necessary military dispositions, that the suspension of arms and *statu quo* may be strictly maintained. This suspension will take place during the day.

"As soon as a response from Versailles is received, the day and duration of the armistice will be arranged.

"CLUSERET,
"The Delegate of War."

For three weeks the inhabitants of Neuilly had been obliged to live in their cellars, in a starving condition.

On the night of the 22d of April, the movement of the regular troops in the peninsula of Gennevilliers was so marked that all Paris believed a general attack was about to be made from that side. The *rappel* was beaten at the Ternes and Batignolles. The cannon that had been conveyed for the last few days to the ramparts were put in position, and directed on Gennevilliers. The night, however, was calm—more calm than the preceding ones, its silence only being broken by the battery of Asnières, which continued its duel with the Chateau of Bécon.

At seven in the morning the columns of Versailles soldiers took the route along the Seine, in the direction of Clichy and St. Ouen. A bridge of boats had been thrown across the Seine above Clichy, at the narrowest point of the river; and, favored by the fogginess of the morning, the soldiers of the Assembly were advancing on the village. The plan was clear. Clichy taken, Levallois could be surrounded, and the insurgents who remained on the right side of the river, in front of Asnières, were cut off from the rest of the army.

Dombrowski, informed of the movement, hurriedly collected five battalions of his men, and arrived the first at Levallois. The march of the troops was much delayed by the fire of the ramparts, which were armed in this quarter by the largest pieces. The obstinacy was great on both sides. Having placed some flying artillery to counteract the fire from the ramparts, the soldiers of the Assembly, after being shut up in Clichy, attempted twice to pass. They were kept back more by the fire from the bastions than from that of Levallois; but they were obliged to recross the Seine to gain their intrenchments.

This was one of the few operations deliberately sketched for this part of the campaign. It was a plan worthy of success, and did honor to the Versailles generals, as also to Dombrowski, by whose vigilance it was defeated.

The 23d passed without any remarkable engagement, the situation remaining unchanged. Mont Valérien and the batteries of Rond Pont continued to fire on the insurgents' positions at Clichy, Levallois, Porte Maillot, and Ternes. An artillery duel was still kept up between the forts and the Versailles troops at Meudon and Clamart. Soldiers were being moved to different positions round the city, and the general impression was that the decisive moment was approaching.

A proclamation of General Cluseret announced the armistice for the 24th; but the morning dawn left no illusions on that point. Valérien, Courbevoie, and all the Versailles batteries, saluted the rising sun with more than usual noise. Neuilly, the Avenues de l'Impératrice, Friedland, Wagram, and that of the Reine Hortense, were covered with projectiles.

It was supposed that the authorities of Versailles had violated the armistice, or that there was some mistake on their part; it turned out, however, that General Cluseret had only fixed the day without waiting for a reply from the other side.

In the early part of the day a great movement of troops had taken place between St. Ouen and Gennevilliers. Numerous battalions had been massed within the ramparts of Clichy and Batignolles, the artillery-men were at their guns, and mounted orderlies were hurrying through the streets, and calling on the inhabitants to keep their doors and windows closed, and not to venture into the streets. The insurgents waited thus until eight o'clock, when General Dombrowski arrived, and finding the enemy did not attack, sent two battalions in the direction of the Isle des Ravageurs. But in reaching the Seine they were received by a heavy fusillade from the left bank of the river. The troops were concealed in houses at Asnières, and keeping up a musketry fire; but the Federals continued to advance to the island which was then occupied by a small body of soldiers. These latter, however, were dislodged after a sharp engagement.

About one in the afternoon the army opened a fresh battery, which had been put in position on the Courbevoie side of the Chateau Bécon; the one in the mansion was too much exposed, and had suffered considerably from the fire of the guns below the bridge of Asnières. The troops had in consequence removed their guns behind a small ridge about three hundred yards from the Demi-Lune. The commander of the 207th battalion of the insurgents was killed on the bridge of Asnières, but his body lay two days where it fell, and could not be removed, the spot was so exposed to the fire of both parties; and in the midst of the animosity excited by this horrible civil war, no person had an idea of advancing with a flag of truce to bring in the corpse.

The troops had a slight success near the market place at Neuilly; the insurgents were defending a barricade, and as the attack was made without spirit, they imagined they had little to fear from their adversaries, when a part of the soldiers passing through some gardens took them in the rear, and the latter finding themselves between two fires, surrendered to the number of fifty.

The official journal of the Commune printed the following despatches on the events of the day:

"Issy, Headquarters, 24th April.

"The night has been tranquil. Our bombs have disquieted the enemy's workmen. The Versaillese approached to within fifty metres; a discharge of mitrailleuses routed them."

"Neuilly, 4 o'clock, morning.

An attack by the Versaillese repulsed the 27th battalion; we had two killed and seven wounded."

"Afternoon, 4 o'clock.

"The action continues, Versaillese in retreat."

"Asnieres.

"The Versaillese give way; no losses on our side."

The official organ also announced that Citizen Raoul Rigault, Delegate for Public Safety, had resigned and been succeeded by Citizen Cournet. He was, however, appointed a member of the committee at the head of the same service. The cause of this important change was explained in the account published of the last sitting of the Commune, Citizen Rigault, adverting to a decision of that body on the preceding day, when he was absent, that "all members could visit prisoners," declared that for the interests of justice such a course was impossible for persons in secret confinement; unless the vote was annulled, he should be obliged, he added, to give in his resignation. A long and stormy discussion ensued, and at the end of which the former vote was maintained by 24 to 17. In consequence, Citizen Rigault persisted, and his successor was appointed at once.

M. Thiers visited St. Denis on the 24th, and had a long interview with the Crown Prince of Saxony and General Fabrice; he informed them that the Versailles army numbered 150,000 men, and that they would all be thoroughly prepared by the 1st of May.

CHAPTER VII.

The armistice—Unhappy condition of the inhabitants of Neuilly—Sitting of the Commune—Official circular from Versailles—Cannonade of Fort Issy—Reconnaissance on the Boulevard Bineau—Meeting of Freemasons at the Chatelet—English journals—Les Moulineaux captured by the troops—Attack on Neuilly—Reported cruelty of a Versailles captain—Speech of M. Thiers in the Assembly—Combats on the Boulevard du Chateau—Proclamations of General Cluseret—Meeting of Freemasons—Speeches at the Hotel de Ville—Procession to the ramparts—Deputation to Versailles—Evacuation of Fort Issy—Re-occupied by the insurgents—Versailles Circular—Deposition of Cluseret—His arrest—Rossel appointed to the War Department—His history—Issy summoned to surrender—Rossel's reply—Committee of Public Safety—Letter of Rossel—Capture of the Chateau of Issy—Heroic defence of the fort—Cannonade of Fort Vanves—Redoubt of Moulin—Jaquet taken—Fighting at Neuilly—Deputation of the Republican League—Decree of the Committee of Public Safety—Military appointments—Brilliant successes of the troops—The Mont-de-Piété.

ON the morning of the 25th April the suspension of arms took place, in order to permit the inhabitants of Neuilly to leave their houses where they had been hidden in the cellars for weeks. At nine in the morning, a number of vehicles accompanied by some members of the League of the Republican Union, arrived from the Palace of Industry to assist the population in removing their goods. A large number of Paris people took advantage of this opportunity to try and visit the scene of destruction. The armistice nominally commenced at nine; but for several minutes by Paris time shots continued to fall in the vicinity of Porte Maillot, greatly to the indignation of the committee appointed by the Commune to receive the refugees, who thought time should have been given them to reach the gate by nine o'clock.

Idle curiosity-seekers were much disappointed at not being allowed to pass through the Maillot gate. Some who approached too near were compelled to fill sand-bags, and assist the insurgents in repairing the fortification, which they continued to do during the whole day. Notwithstanding this their journals on the following morning were loud in their complaints against the Versailles troops for doing the same.

The armistice was under the surveillance of four members of the Republican League. Two were delegated by the insurgents and two by the army of Versailles. The first were M. Bonvalet, ex-mayor of the third arrondissement, and M. Stupuy, *homme de lettres;* the second were M. Adam and M. Loiseau-Pinson, both former members of the municipality. Their mission was to denounce any movement of troops breaking the essential conditions of the armistice.

The inhabitants of Neuilly, who consisted mostly of women and children, timidly ventured into the outer world, anxiously inquiring if an armistice had really commenced. Most of them knew nothing of what had taken place, not having seen daylight for three weeks, and only venturing out in the night to procure some bread and wine; all were suffering from a fearful state of mental excitement. One day the insurgents were in possession of the houses over their heads, the next day the Versailles troops. Nearly all the ruins were filled with dead insurgent troops, more or less in a state of decomposition; most of them had received bullet-shots through the head, killed in the act of firing over barricades or through loopholes.

The feeling of the troops was one of great irritation against the Parisians.

Scarcely a house in the Grand Armée had escaped, those nearest the ramparts being all in ruins. Beyond the gate the destruction of property was even greater, for in that part the houses were not only damaged, but most of them were literally levelled with the ground.

The troops from Versailles formed a line across the Avenue de Neuilly, at the point which marked the portion of the village they occupied, and beyond which the inhabitants residing in that direction were not allowed to go. On the other hand, those living beyond the line of demarcation could only return to Paris through the lateral streets and the gates of Bineau and Ternes.

At half-past four in the afternoon the insurgents formed a cordon across the Avenue de la Grande Armée, and advancing in the direction of the Arc de Triomphe, pushed before them the crowd, as the armistice was to cease at five. The spectators were reluctant to retire, anxious to hear the first shot announcing the recommencement of hostilities. At eight o'clock the guns of Porte Maillot and Ternes were again heard. The southern forts continued to fire during the day. A reconnaissance made from Fort Vanves discovered that a new battery had been established by the Versailles troops 300 yards below the plateau. Several small engagements occurred on the side of Billancourt, but without any definite result.

The sittings of the Commune were becoming daily more boisterous. The "Citoyen" Régère had given the "Citoyen" Vermorel the lie. The "Citoyen" J. B. Clement had demanded the arrest of Citoyen Felix Pyat, because the latter had threatened to resign. A sharp quarrel had also arisen between Pyat and Vermorel, and hard names were not spared on either side; the epistles interchanged being alike remarkable for their bitterness and diffuseness. The *Cri du Peuple* gave a letter from the last-named member accusing the former of cowardice, and affirming that the failure of the attack on the Hotel-de-Ville the 31st of October, arose solely from his being afraid to come forward and assert his position manfully. After relating several incidents in Pyat's conduct in latter times, the writer said, "Your game is easily divined; you were, on the one hand, endeavoring to preserve your popularity, in case the people should prove victorious; and, on the other, you reserved to yourself a back-door by which to escape prosecution, should Versailles have the superiority."

The letter terminated by declaring that the writer would not abuse his advantage so far as to defy his adversary to place himself at the head of the tenth legion the first time that it went out to fight, but challenged him to appear before a meeting of electors. Pyat, in consequence of the pressure brought to bear upon him, determined to keep his seat.

The following official circular was addressed to the Prefects of the various departments in France:

"VERSAILLES, April 26, 2:50 P. M.

"Active operations were commenced yesterday. Three great lines of batteries opened their fire against Forts Vanves and Issy. The line on the right, having to bear the fire of both Vanves and of Issy, sustained the loss of some lives and some injury to embrasures, but its continuous working was not affected. The line of the centre, which mounted seventeen guns of heavy calibre, had no wounded nor any of its pieces injured, and maintained a formidable cannonade against Fort Issy. From midday its fire assumed a marked superiority over that of Fort Issy, which at five o'clock ceased to send in return more than a few shots at rare intervals. On the left the action was less warm on both sides. The main contest rested with the centre line, and there was every reason to believe that Fort Issy would soon be reduced to silence and rendered powerless. It is for the moment an artillery combat, of which the issue cannot be doubtful, and of the progress of which we will give exact accounts.

"A. THIERS."

The interest of the fighting was once more transferred to the left bank of the Seine. The Versailles batteries had heretofore replied but feebly to the continued provocations of the southern forts, and had remained on the defensive, or fired only to cover the movement of their troops. On the 26th, however, they commenced the offensive, and by a converged fire upon Issy reduced it to silence. The cannonade was kept up from seven batteries—one at Chatillon, three in the woods beyond the railway, and three others around the Palace of Meudon. The insurgents attempted in vain to reply from the station of Clamart, from the Molineaux, and from several of the bastions; the shells continued to rain down on the parapets of the fort, and each explosion could be seen to raise up clouds of dust and smoke. The gunboats on the Seine, however, rendered efficient aid to the insurgents. Six of these vessels were at anchor beneath the arches of the railway viaduct, which almost completely sheltered them from the Versailles artillery. A seventh, the Liberty, smaller than the rest, of a light draught of water, and carrying an enormous cannon, advanced in the direction of Bas-Meudon, discharged its gun, and then retired beneath the viaduct to reload.

The regular forces, during the day, pushed forward their outposts on this side of Bagneux, and below Chatillon to Clamart. On all points were engineers at work, advancing step by step, piercing holes for musketry in the houses and walls, digging trenches, and constructing redoubts. All the previous attacks against the forts were evidently intended only to mask the works of approach. The troops were repairing their batteries, and had now leisure for a serious attack. One important point which they occupied was the Moulin-de-Pierre, where they had put heavy guns in position, within five hundred yards of fort Vanves.

To the west of Paris, the firing became quite sharp during the afternoon, especially between the insurgent batteries at Clichy and the redoubt of Gennevilliers. The troops of the Commune evidently appeared to fear a turning movement towards Argenteuil, and occupied the banks of the Seine opposite the island of St. Ouen.

A most amusing incident occurred on the Boulevard Bineau, while the insurgents were employed in making the reconnaissance of a barricade. A young bugler, fifteen years of age, marched some fifty feet in advance of a company of insurgents. He was full of life and fun, and as he marched would often turn somersets, still playing his fantastic airs. Thinking the barricade deserted, he leaped upon the top, continuing to play, when suddenly he felt himself dragged down by the legs on the other side. He had fallen into an ambuscade of regular soldiers. They immediately wrenched from him his clarion to prevent his giving the alarm to the approaching insurgents; but quick as lightning the young athlete was on top of the barricade, leaving everything but his shirt in the hands of his captors.

"Halt!" he cried to the approaching soldiers, "I am a prisoner!" The troops, finding themselves discovered, opened fire on the advancing victims. The captain, who marched at the head, fell mortally wounded. Several others met with the same relentless fate, while the balls rattled like hail around the young scamp, who sometimes with his head in the air and sometimes his feet, reached an open door in the neighborhood, and disappeared. They had hardly arrived at the door of the house, which was six stories high, when they heard a voice from the roof:

"*Eh! là-bas! mon clairon, s'il vous plait!*" ("Hollo, down there!—my bugle, if you please!")

He had saved the lives of nearly his whole company, and was now disappearing along the roofs like lightning.

The Commune held a secret sitting on the 27th, and the meeting was said to be a most stormy one. The actual situation was under discussion. Several members affirmed that the position was no longer tenable, and that the last elections had superabundantly proved the small amount of confidence inspired by the Commune. Other members manifested a desire to abandon the rude task which they had undertaken, whilst not a few spoke of the disastrous condition of the municipal strong-box, and of the financial embarrassments about to rise.

A meeting of the Freemasons was also held in the Châtelet theatre, and a resolution voted declaring that, as the Government of Versailles had refused to accord the Communal liberties of Paris, the brotherhood would employ every means in its power to obtain them.

The *Temps*, a newspaper appearing at St. Germain, published an excellent series of remarks on the severity of the London journals with respect to the Government of Versailles and the conduct pursued against the Commune. It also explains why so much delay had been absolutely necessary for the success of M. Thiers' plan.

"We were curious," says the writer, "to see how the English journals would judge the Paris insurrection. We have just read them, and that sentiment has been quickly changed into one of disgust. It would be difficult to show more ignorance of facts, more incapacity to comprehend a situation, and, at the same time, more presumption and malevolence of judgment. We could conceive that foreigners should feel embarrassed in presence of a crisis of which the causes have no analogy with the state of any other people; but what we do not understand is the assurance with which the journalists of London explain to us what is taking place in our own country, and point out to us the best means of getting out of the difficulty. The whole, watered with crocodile tears, forms a picture at the same time melancholy and burlesque."

After some sharp comments on the language of several organs published in London, the article proceeds thus:

"We are indebted for this bright school of literature to the military correspondents. A civil war is a war like any other, and so a journal dispatches to Paris or Versailles a man who has perhaps taken out his university degree, who has even travelled on the Continent, but who carries about everywhere with him that thick armor of British notions by means of which he is sure of never entering into real contact with the spirit of the nations he visits. That gentleman displays the most praiseworthy activity; he shrinks from no fatigue, or even danger, to obtain information for the paper which he represents; but he necessarily remains outside the political world; he only sees the external and military side of events, and the same individual who might have been well placed for the siege of Paris by the Germans, is completely bewildered amidst the events now passing on the same theatre. But what is most remarkable in the journals to which we refer, is the absence of sympathy for the party of order and for the Government of France, all having a weakness for the Commune.

"All agree to cover M. Thiers with contempt and ridicule for not having long ago put an end to the insurrection. He should have crushed it in the bud, they say; his weakness and indecision has given strength to the rebellion; all his policy consists in waiting for he knows not what; he has no fixed object in view. M. Thiers has a plan, but one like Trochu's, so profound and so secret, that not the smallest trace of it is ever perceived. The journalists who write thus prove only one thing—that they are ignorant of the very rudiments of the question. The insurrection from the commencement was formidable and irresistible, because from the first it was supported by an armed force, ready organized, namely, the National Guard of Paris; whilst the Government, on its side, had at its command but few troops, and these were of a class which events have proved could not be relied on with entire confidence. For that reason, it became necessary to withdraw to Versailles, weed out the disposable forces, assemble those which the country could spare, await the return of the prisoners from Germany, amalgamate all those elements in new cadres, provide for the equipment and armament of the men, and gradually re-establish discipline and confidence. All this had to be done, and was done, with a rapidity for which it would be unjust not to give the Government credit. The siege of Paris, since the city had to be taken by force, could not be effected with thirty thousand men, nor even with fifty thousand. It is only now, after five weeks of incessant organization, that the army has attained the strength considered necessary, and it is only now that the Government is in a position to strike a decisive blow."

The morning of the 27th opened with a most violent attack on the forts south of Paris, and continued all day without interruption. The cannonade was most terrific from Moulin-de-Pierre, Chatillon, and Meudon; and the bombardment of Montrouge and Issy was commenced with a violence of which the first siege gave but a faint idea. Issy, although dismantled, and, in spite of its escarpes tumbling into the ditch, and its ruined barracks, still fought with desperation, throwing shells on the

Tour-des-Anglais, Clamart, and Meudon. Fort Montrouge, although not yet reduced to silence, was very near that extremity. It was already seriously damaged by the Prussian bombardment, and the batteries of the regular army were completing the ruin. The insurgents, however, continued to hold out, although the position was scarcely tenable, as they knew that its fall would inevitably lead to that of Vanves and Issy.

The Versailles Government had in position on the Terrasse de Meudon, Chatillon, at the station Meudon, Bellevue, and vicinity, 150 guns of large calibre. These different batteries were placed under the charge of General Berckheim, an artillery officer of the first rank, and served by artillerymen of the 2d corps. On the night of the 26th and 27th, while a fearful cannonade was going on, General Faron, with four companies of the 35th infantry and 300 men of the 100th and 110th Marine Fusiliers, carried the station and village of Les Moulineaux in a most brilliant manner. This important position immediately to the west of Issy, and just under the fort, was one of the highest importance; as it stood not over 900 yards distant from the walls and from the Moulineaux, it was possible to reach the Park of Issy, which inclined towards the Seine, and escape the fire of the fort.. The regulars had already occupied Bas Meudon and Bellevue; and from this new position musketry fire could be brought to bear on the garrison of the fort. Hitherto the position had been held by two battalions of insurgents, and with two pieces of field artillery they were able to cause considerable annoyance to the troops.

The insurgents made an abortive attempt during the day on Choisy-le-Roi. They advanced under cover of a fire from Fort Bicêtre, but were received with mitrailleuses and musketry from the soldiers under General Barrail.

The attack on Neuilly was again resumed with increasing violence. A new battery from Mont Valérien opened fire on the ramparts of Maillot and Ternes. The former received about a dozen projectiles, which enlarged considerably the breach in the left bastion. While shots were being continually exchanged between the outposts, laborers were engaged on the additional works of defence in Neuilly and Levallois. The barricades held by the soldiers, however, impeded seriously these counter approaches; and frequent attempts had been made on preceding days to drive the troops beyond the bridge. A still more serious attack was attempted in the afternoon. Ten battalions were engaged, and advanced, six from Les Ternes, and four from Clichy. For three-quarters of an hour the noise of the cannon and fusillade was intense along the whole line of the Seine from the Bois de Boulogne, where the sentinels of the two armies were shooting each other down at fifty paces distance, to the bridge of Clichy, where the insurgents had established a battery. The Communists attacked the barricade boldly; but each time the troops found that they were in danger they retreated into the houses, and then going along the passage made by openings in the walls, reformed two hundred yards in the rear, and with their mitrailleuses rendered the captured barrier untenable. The insurgents at length were, as usual, fatigued with this fruitless struggle, and retired to their former positions. Great concentrations of troops were made in the villages to the west of Paris; and the soldiers finding no longer quarters in the houses, were encamped in the streets and gardens. Further to the north a cannonade was carried on warmly by the iron-clad locomotive batteries on the right bank on the Château of Bécon, and the bastions at the Portes de Clichy and de St. Ouen on Gennevilliers. The Versailles troops, however, only replied from the guns at Bécon, which had for their aim the insurgent batteries at the bridge of Asnières. The projectiles from the Porte de Clichy were directed sometimes to the battery at the junction of the St. Germain and Versailles railways, and sometimes to the neighborhood of the Moulin de la Tour.

The official organ of the Commune published a decree commanding the various railway companies to pay within forty-eight hours two millions of francs, which, according to the Commune, was due the State. An order was also published declaring that in consequence of the gallant conduct of the battery at the Porte Maillot, the delegate of the Commune at the War Department accords to the men composing it thirty revolvers. It was also announced that the gates for the victualling of Paris would be opened at five in the morning, and closed at seven in the evening.

At the sitting of the Commune, Citizen Vésinier read a report from Citizens Langevin, Gambon, and himself, who were all three delegated to Bicêtre to make inquiry about four National Guards of the 185th battalion. He and his two associates went there accompanied by Citizen Raoul Rigault, Procurator for the Commune, and Leo Meillet. They all paid a visit to Scheffer, of the above-mentioned battalion. The man—who was in the sick-ward—declared that on the 25th instant, at Belle-Epine, near Villejuif, he was surprised, with three of his comrades, by some mounted chasseurs, who summoned them to surrender. As resistance was useless, they accordingly threw down their arms, and the soldiers surrounded and took them prisoners without any violence or menace. Only a few moments had elapsed when a captain of chasseurs came up and threw himself upon them, revolver in hand. He fired at one of them without saying a word, and killed him on the spot; he then discharged another barrel at Scheffer, who received a ball in the chest, and fell by the side of his comrade. The two remaining guards recoiled with horror from this assault; but the ferocious captain

COURBET
Commune of Paris
1871

rushed on the prisoners, and killed them with two other shots.

The chasseurs, after these acts, withdrew with their chief, leaving the victims on the plain.

After their departure Scheffer rose, and with a desperate effort succeeded in reaching his battalion, encamped at some distance. His state was such as to warrant hopes of ultimate recovery.

The writers of the report proposed to use reprisals, and to kill all the officers that fell into their hands. After some discussion, the decision was taken to ascertain the number of the regiment to which the officer belonged, and the name of the officer, and publish them in Paris.

Citizen Courbet called on the Commune not to delay the demolition of the column in the Place Vendôme. The pedestal, he thought, could be preserved, as the subject represented there concerned the first Republic. Citizen Clément insisted on the total destruction of the monument. Citizen Andrieu stated that the Executive Committee was occupied with the matter, and the operation of destroying the pillar would commence in a few days.

The charge having been brought against M. Thiers that he wished to destroy the Republic, establishing in its place a monarchy, his remarks in the Chamber on the 27th will be most appropriate in this place:

M. Thiers.—" At the present serious conjuncture, and at the moment when the country is about to elect its Municipal Councils, I think right to briefly describe the situation to this Assembly, its only legitimate and complete representation. Our state is no doubt most painful, as the blood of Frenchmen is flowing, but, in one respect, it is consolatory, as showing that all are doing their duty—the army especially—and thus is foreshadowed a not distant termination of the crisis. (Applause.) Our first task was to create a strongly-organized military force which should be influenced as little as possible by the strange circumstances in which we are placed. We took the men who have shown themselves superior to the hazards of fortune, and who have proved that if they had been well commanded, France would not have been vanquished, but victorious. (Hear, hear.) In accord with my colleagues, I did not hesitate to call to the head of the army that brave Marshal who in our time may be called also the knight without fear and without reproach, and who, even in misfortune, has been able to defy calumny. (Applause.) I should fail in my duty, were I to disclose the plan of the military chiefs who direct the army. I therefore only say that it has been decided on in concert with all the generals who surround our illustrious chief. The investment of Paris occupied the first period; but now that it is complete, active operations have been commenced before Fort Issy. Our artillery, although opposed by the powerful guns abstracted from the country, is continuing its works of approach, and only last night, the brave General Faron, at the head of 100 naval fusileers, 300 soldiers of the 110th Regiment of the Line, and four companies of the 35th, carried the important position of the Moulineaux with such rapidity, that the loss they have suffered was extremely small. (Applause.) I should be rash, were I to try and fix a date for the result at which we aim—the pacification of the country. Whatever may be the means employed, they will be painful; and whether we impede the victualling of the capital, or fire on that Paris which is always so dear to France, our heart will bleed. But we appeal to the judgment of the country: Are we the authors of this cruel war? (No, no.) Even in attacking, we defend the law, public order, and society. (Applause.) Each day the word conciliation is addressed to me, as your representative. Ah! if it only depended on me; if only my pride or my personality was in question, what sacrifices would I not make to put an end to this terrible war! (Here the voice of the speaker faltered with emotion—Sensation.) But to those numerous envoys who come from Paris and other great towns, what reply can we make but this: You wish for liberty; but are we not defending it against an odious despotism, without authority, originating in disorder, and doing evil with a disastrous ignorance. (Applause.) I have said to those men, in the belief that I was expressing your ideas:—You wish for the maintenance of the Republic; in the Assembly there is not at this moment any preconceived decision or mental reservation, and being invested with all the constituent powers, it has respected what it found established. Appointed by electors, the greater part of whom are partisans of the Monarchy, has it made the slightest attempt to change the form of Government? No. It It has had the wisdom to respect what it found; its members are occupied with only one idea—to aid the Government in pursuing its mission, which is, not to constitute, but to organize France. I give to the insurgents the most formal denial when they say that we are plotting against the Republic. There is but one conspiracy against it, that which is at Paris. (Loud applause.) We are also told to be clement! I have said, Let the insurgents lay down their arms, and all chastisement will at once be stayed. The only exception will be for the criminals, happily few in number. (Murmurs on the right.) Am I wrong? Do you regret that the guilty men are not more numerous. (No! no!) Is there not, in our misfortune, reason for satisfaction that such men as those who shed the blood of Generals Clement-Thomas and Lecomte are rare in our country." (Hear, hear!)

A MEMBER.—"And the army?"

M. Thiers.—"I am glad of this interruption, for it allows me to certify a fact. The army is calumniated by those who say that there are many soldiers in the ranks of the insurgents, as the number, we are certain, is very inconsiderable. Certain of the insurgents had found in the warehouses soldiers' uniforms, and dressed up a great number of their own followers in them, so as to lead the world to believe that the number of troops deserting their duty was important, whereas there were few. (Applause.) There are also several foreigners, and many wretches who watched for every opportunity of creating disorder; but they were isolated, and would not, in the end, find any honest man to follow them. I have need to examine myself when forced to give orders, not cruel, but such as are required by a state of war; and I am sometimes obliged to ask if you think with me—(yes, yes!)—and if reason is really on my side. (Noise on the Right.) If any of my colleagues are ill-disposed enough to prevent me from explaining my ideas, let them put forth their own plans—(applause)—and if they think they are surer of success, let them take my place, which I will readily resign. (No, no; speak, speak.) I feel no want of confidence, but I may be allowed to express my affliction, and indicate the cause of it.

"You may, perhaps, imagine that I preside over the horrors of a civil war with *sang-froid*. I do so with a firm resolution, but with a sentiment of grief which equals my determination. As to the matter of right, I believe that we are all agreed on the great principles that we defend. (Assent.) This Assembly is the most liberal one that I have ever seen; it is, I confess, more liberal than I am myself. But what do we see arrayed against us? A few odious dictators who dominate a short-sighted and besotted multitude, and lead it under fire. Yes—the right is with you; and against you there is only a detested usurpation. If we have had different opinions on certain questions, we have sacrificed them to the exigencies of the moment; and as to our opponents, I defy them to say what they want. They are forced to conceal their aims. They require that the Commune should be sovereign; that every town should have its republic, its army, and its general—36,000 republics! This is the most absurd contradiction ever given to the French Revolution and national unity, the work of ten centuries. Our object, on the contrary, should be to conciliate that unity with the greatest share of liberty possible. I repeat that there is no other conspiracy than that which has led to such sanguinary results in Paris. As to those who shall lay down their arms, their lives will be safe; and they who shall be in want of bread will receive it till work can be resumed. If the malcontents have not sense enough to understand my words, we shall accomplish our duty to the end, however bitter may be the task." (Great applause.)

The bombardment of Fort Issy was continued on the 28th with still more severity. A battery of naval guns had been opened at Breteuil, and of 24-pounders near Moulin-de-Pierre. The insurgents had done their best during the night to repair the damage of the previous day, but the fort could reply but feebly. The guns in the Park, however, being well protected, kept up a brisk fire on the positions of the Versailles artillery, which, in its endeavor to reach the battery, concealed by a clump of trees, sent several shells into the village; one unfortunately entered the asylum and killed an old woman in her bed. The fort of Vanves, which was less seriously damaged, also exchanged shots with the plateau of Chatillon, and fired from time to time on the terrace of Meudon. A sharp engagement of outposts took place early in the morning at Clamart, where the insurgents were strongly intrenched around the railway station. A vast barricade armed with several cannon protected the building which commanded the line; smaller defences were raised on each side of the embankment; the walls were pierced for musketry, and all the openings were filled up with mattresses or bags of earth. The centre of combat was, however, at the station. The affair ended without any perceptible results on either side.

The most severe fighting to the west of Paris was on the Boulevard du Château. Three successive combats took place there at six in the morning, and at three and five in the afternoon, but without any positive advantage to either side, only entailing a useless sacrifice of life. The number of victims in these incessant encounters was difficult to ascertain, as the gates were closed so that no fugitives should spread the alarm to the city; the killed and wounded were only removed at night, and the battalions which returned from the villages outside were confined to the barracks, and not allowed to mention what had taken place. The bastions at the gates of Clichy and St. Ouen, continued their fire on Gennevilliers with the object of impeding the movement of the troops. An iron-clad locomotive battery on the railway was also firing at the Château de Bécon.

A barricade was erected on the Boulevard Malesherbes to support the Porte d'Asnières in case of attack. During the whole of the 28th Mont Valérien kept up a fire on the Porte Maillot, sending shells at the rate of two a minute.

Citizen Bergeret, who had been released from prison, was appointed a member of the War Committee as a deputy to Citizen Delescluze.

As General Cluseret's power approached its zenith, so did his orders and proclamations increase. By one he divided the insurgent forces into two chief commands—one extending from St. Ouen to the Point-du-Jour, under

General Dombrowski, who had his headquarters at La-Muette; and the other reaching from the Point-du-Jour to Bercy, and commanded by General Walbrewski, whose headquarters were at Gentilly. The two armies were each subdivided into three sections.

Another, that as constant changes in the officers of the National Guard were most unfavorable to strict discipline, each person regularly elected would be provided with a commission guaranteeing to him his post. Any person wearing an officer's uniform and not provided with such an authority, would be arrested and imprisoned.

Another order said that certain abuses, expensive for the Commune, must be put a stop to. Various officers, thinking of nothing but handsome swords and gold lace, when afterwards rejected by their men, withdraw with their arms, which, however, no longer belong to them. Heads of legions are charged with having such property returned to the central storehouses.

On the evening of the 28th of April a meeting of the Presidents of the Freemason Lodges was held at their usual place of assembling, Rue Cadet, to come to some understanding on the subject of the public demonstration announced for the next morning in favor of the Commune. Thirty-four persons were present, and the great majority decided that the proceedings of certain brothers of the order of the Châtelet were altogether personal, and in direct opposition to the principles of Freemasonry; that, in the absence of any former decision either of the Grand Orient of France or of the Supreme Council, the manifestation fixed for the next day was in like manner irregular, and that the responsibility of the incidents which might occur was completely individual. A notice to the above effect was published by the Presidents in the various journals, as well as a letter from Ernest Hamel, ex-venerable of the Lodge Avenir, expressing his surprise and affliction that any body of Freemasons should have presumed to declare that "Masonry would plant its banner on the ramparts of Paris, and in case of its being pierced by a ball would in a body take part in the struggle." Such a declaration, the writer affirmed, was in entire opposition to the tenets of the order, the mission of which always was to forward conciliation and peace.

The following letter, from the highest dignitary of the Masonic order in the French capital, was sent to several of the journals:

"You have announced that the Supreme Council of Freemasons would hold a meeting on Monday. If you had specified the hour and place, I should have felt that my duty required me to attend. But no convocation having been made, *I, as guardian of the general regulations,* protest against all resolutions taken independently of the Grand Central Lodge of France; and I remind my brothers that *Masons are bound to fight only against a foreign invader.*

"Accept, etc.,

"F. MALAPERT,

"Orator of the Supreme Council."

This document emanated from the sole voice that had a right to be heard, and was a warning to the brotherhood, and a piece of useful information to the public.

Notwithstanding the above, a large number of adherents of the Commune met at the Hotel de Ville on the morning of the 29th, whence it had been announced that the entire body of Freemasons would start on a last pacific demonstration, to plant the banner of that body on the ramparts; and should the Versailles troops dare to fire on it, the whole order would take up arms in defence of the Commune.

At nine o'clock in the morning a cortège with flags and

FELIX PYAT
Commune of Paris
1871

music, led by five delegates of the Commune, left the Hotel de Ville to be joined on their way by the Freemasons, who were to return with them to the seat of government, which had been decorated for a solemn reception. At eleven o'clock the deputation returned with the Freemasons, and made their entrance into the Court of Honor of the Hotel de Ville, prepared in advance to receive them. The insurgent soldiers were formed in lines between which the procession passed. All the members of the Commune were placed at the top of the Escalier d'honneur, before the statue of the Republic. They were decorated with red scarfs, trimmed with gold. The galleries were adorned with trophies, flags, and olive wreaths, whilst the staircases and Court of Honor were fitted out with crimson carpets. The masonic banners were placed upon the stairway, where could be read the different humanitarian mottos. Among others was a large white banner, carried by an artilleryman, with the motto of "*Love one another.*" As soon as the Court was full, immense shouts arose from every side: "*Vive la franc-Maçonnerie!*" "*Vive la Commune!*" "*Vive la République Universelle!*" The Citizen Felix Pyat, member of the Commune, then pronounced, in a strong voice, the following address:

"Brothers, citizens of the great country—of the universal country—faithful to our common principles, Liberty, Equality, and Fraternity, and more logical than the *Ligue des Droits de Paris.* You, Freemasons—you follow your words with actions.

"To-day words mean nothing—acts, everything! Thus, after having posted your manifesto—manifesto of the heart—on the walls of Paris, you go now to plant your banner of humanity on the ramparts of our besieged and bombarded city.

"You go to protest thus against homicidal balls and fratricidal bullets, in the name of right and of universal peace. (Unanimous bravos, and shouts of '*Vive la République!*' '*Vive la Commune!*')

"You go to stretch out to the men of Versailles a disarmed hand—disarmed, but only for the moment—and we, the mandataries of the people and the defenders of its rights; we, the elected by vote—we wish to join ourselves with you—the elected by ordeal in this fraternal act. (New applause: '*Vive la Commune!*' '*Vive la République!*')

"The Commune had decided to choose five of its members who should have the honor to accompany you, and it was proposed that this honor should be drawn for by lot. Five favored names were thus designed to follow you, to accompany you in this glorious, victorious act. (Marks of approbation.)

"Your act, citizens, will remain in the history of France and of humanity.

"Long live the Universal Republic!"

(Loud cries of "*Vive la Commune!*" "*Vive la République!*")

The Citizen Beslay, member of the Commune:—"Citizens, I have associated myself, as you have done, with the words we have just heard, with those fraternal words which have caused all the Freemasons to assemble here.

"Fate was not favorable to me yesterday, when the name of those members of the Commune who should go to receive the Freemasons, were drawn. We wished that the names should be drawn by lot, as from the very beginning the whole Commune of Paris wished to take part in this great manifestation; I had not the honor of being designated, but I asked, nevertheless, to go before you as senior of the Commune of Paris, and also of the Freemasonry of France, of which I have had the honor to be a member during fifty-six years.

"What can I say to you, citizens, after the eloquent words of Felix Pyat? You are about to commit a great act of fraternity in placing your banner upon the ramparts of our city, and in placing yourselves in the ranks against our enemies of Versailles. (Yes, yes!—bravos.)

"Citizens, brothers: Permit me to give to one of you the fraternal embrace."

(The Citizen Beslay embraces one of the Freemasons placed near him. Applause—"*Vive la Commune!*" "*Vive la République!*")

A Freemason, banner in hand:—"I claim the honor of planting the first banner on the ramparts of Paris, the banner of *Perseverance*, which has existed since 1790. (Bravos.)

The music of the battalion played *La Marseillaise.*

Citizen Léo Meillet:—"You have just heard the only music to which we can listen before a definitive peace.

"Here is the red flag which the Commune of Paris offers to the Masonic deputations.

"This flag should accompany your pacific banners; it is the flag of universal peace, the flag of our federative rights, around which we should all group ourselves to prevent, for the future, any hand, however powerful it may be, from throwing us one upon the other, except for an embrace. (Prolonged applause.)

"It is the flag of the Commune of Paris, which the Commune is about to confide to the Freemasons. It will be placed in front of your banners, and before the homicidal balls of Versailles.

"When you bring them back, these banners of Freemasonry, be they torn or intact, the flag of the Commune will not have failed. It will have accompanied them in the midst of the fire—it will be the proof of their inseparable union." (Fresh applause.)

The Citizen Terifocq took the red flag from the hands of Citizen Léo Meillet, and addressed to the assembly the following words:

"Citizens, brothers: I am of the number of those who took the initiative to go and plant the standard of peace on our ramparts, and I have the happiness to see at our head the white banner of the Lodge of Vincennes, on which are inscribed these words: 'Let us love one another.' (Bravos.)

"We will go and present first this banner to our enemies' ranks; we will stretch our hands to them, since Versailles will not hear us!

"Yes, citizens, brothers, we will address ourselves to the soldiers, and we will say: 'Soldiers of the same country, come and fraternize with us; we will have no bullets for you so long as you send us none of yours. Come and embrace us, and let peace be made.' (Prolonged bravos—sensation.)

"And if this peace is accomplished, we will return to Paris convinced that we have gained the most glorious victory—that of humanity!

"If, on the contrary, we are not heard, but are fired upon, we will call every vengeance to our aid. We are certain that we shall be heard, and that the Masonry of all the provinces of France will follow our example. We are sure that in whatever part of the country our brothers see troops directed upon Paris, they will go to meet them and call upon them to fraternize.

"If we fail in our attempt for peace, and if Versailles gives the order not to fire upon us, but to kill only our brothers of the ramparts, then we will mingle with them; we, who until now have taken service in the National Guard only as a service of order; those who have hitherto not belonged to it, as well as those already in its ranks, and all together we will join the companies of war, to take part in the battle, and to encourage by our example the brave and glorious soldiers—defenders of our city." (General adhesion — Applause — "*Vive la Commune!*" "*Vive la Franc-maçonnerie!*")

The Citizen Terifocq, waving the flag of the Commune which he held in his hand, then cried:

"Now, citizens, no more words—to action!"

The deputation of Freemasons, accompanied by the members of the Commune, then left the Hotel de Ville.

While they defiled, the orchestra played *La Marseillaise.*

The procession having made the tour of the boulevards in a pouring rain, advanced to Port Maillot *via* the Champs Elysées and the Avenue de la Grande Armée, and planted their flags on the ramparts. A balloon was sent up at the same time with a proclamation from the Paris Masons to the provincial lodges, after which a body of their delegates, about forty in number, passed through the Porte Maillot, and advanced with a flag of truce to the barricade held by the Versailles troops at the bridge of Courbevoie. There they were met by General Leclerc, who conducted them to General Montaudon, commander of the operations at that point. He received them courteously, but declared that he was only the arm which executed orders given; as he was, he added, a brother of the craft, he had taken it on himself to stop the fire when the Masonic banners were seen; but he could only accord a brief delay. He thought their best plan would be to send forward a deputation to Versailles, and he would himself place a carriage at their disposal. The proposal having been accepted, three of the body immediately set out, and the others returned to the Porte Maillot, where a sort of an assembly was held, after which the Freemasons decided on not returning to Paris, but to remain and guard their flags on the fortifications.

The delegates were received by M. Thiers, who replied: "There will be a few more houses shelled, and a few more men killed, but force must remain to the law." In answer to a communication afterwards sent to him, he declared that he had nothing to add to his previous reply.

They were obliged to return to Paris on foot, owing to the impossibility of procuring fresh horses, and did not reach the gates until six in the morning. After making their report, the Freemasons decided that the banners should remain planted on the ramparts, and, if necessary, that the men who guarded them should fight for the Commune.

On the following day, the Freemasons of all rites were invited to assemble in the Place de la Concorde, at two in the afternoon, in order to go and take away their flags from the ramparts, the fire of the Versailles troops not having shown them any respect.

The army of Versailles followed up its advantage on Fort Issy. At about ten o'clock in the evening of the 29th, the batteries of Meudon, Chatillon and Moulineaux commenced a most terrific converging fire on the fort, with scarcely any reply, as it was then only a mass of ruins. The casemates had been crushed in, and the walls levelled with the ground. Towards one o'clock the Versailles batteries stopped firing, and the regular troops suddenly fell upon the insurgents, who, surprised by the rapidity and fierceness of the attack, immediately fled in wild disorder, abandoning cannon, mitrailleuses and muskets.

The losses on both sides were considerable, according to the insurgents' reports. The 161st battalion was nearly exterminated. At midnight, when the firing had nearly ceased, the Versailles troops were occupying part of the Park of Issy, and the station of Clamart. To the occupants of the fort the momentary respite was of little service, for their commander had disappeared, and all was confusion. Some officers endeavored to give directions for the repair of certain points, but they were not listened to. A few of the insurgents attempted to place sacks of earth in the gaps, but a discharge of chassepots wounded some and forced the rest to retire. It was in this state that the day broke. The whole morning was spent in altercation, some proposing an evacuation—others persisted in holding out to the last.

After a violent altercation, the party advocating the evacuation carried the day. There were about three hundred men in the fort. At ten o'clock another and final council was held in the midst of a shower of shells, and the final resolution was taken at eleven. The sailors spiked the guns, the northern gate was opened, and the insurgents, artillerymen and workmen, set out on their return to Paris.

Some insurgents still remained, it was supposed with the intention of blowing up the fort, as there was an abundance of powder. At half past eleven three superior officers left Paris by the Vaugirard gate, evidently with the intention of reoccupying the fort. The red flag was still flying above the ruins of the barracks. Several battalions of insurgents were now massed in the village of Issy, which lies between the fort and the Vaugirard gate, while fresh barricades were erected. Holes for musketry were pierced in the walls, and passages were made from house to house. The troops, in the mean time, were not inactive. Not venturing to penetrate into the fort, which they knew to be mined, they passed between it and Molineaux to a small wood on the right, while the light batteries were advanced to a spur of the plateau on which the fort is situated, and at three in the afternoon were ready to open fire on the ramparts. The cannonade soon commenced, the guns bearing on the bastions sixty-eight and seventy-two. The inhabitants of Vaugirard, in fearful alarm, were quitting their houses to come into the city.

The following official circular in regard to the affair was immediately telegraphed to the Prefects of the different Departments.

"VERSAILLES, 2:20 P. M.

"The works of approach towards Fort Issy have continued. The Government has received the following despatches, which it hastens to publish:—'Belair, 5:5, A.M.—General de Cissy to the Chief of the Executive.—A *coup de main* has been effected against the farm of Bonney, in front of Châtillon, by a company of the 70th regiment and the light company of the 71st. Two officers on the side of the insurgents were killed or wounded; 71 prisoners were taken, of whom four were officers. On our side two sergeants and two men were killed, and six wounded. Too great praise cannot be awarded to the troops engaged, especially to Captains Dumouchel, of the 70th, and Broissier, of the 71st. Details later.' 'Belair, 6:55 A. M.—Cissy to the Chief of the Executive Power and to MacMahon at Versailles.—I have this moment received from General Faron the following despatch:—Fleury, 6 A. M.—The operations have been very successful. The cemetery, trenches, excavations, and the park of Issy were carried with great spirit by battalions of the brigades under Deroja, Paturel, and Berthe, with the aid of the Marines. We occupy in force positions in close contiguity to the main entrances to the fort. The park is connected with the railway by a trench passing in front of the cemetery. On our side there have been few killed. About 20 wounded. The insurgents, who were very numerous, retired with precipitation, leaving 100 prisoners, 8 pieces of artillery, and 8 horses.' A. THIERS."

The official journal of May 2d announced the astounding intelligence that General Cluseret had been arrested by order of the Executive Committee, and approved by the Commune. The following was the official announcement:

"PARIS, May 1, 1871.

"The negligence and want of precaution shown by the Delegate of the War Department having very nearly compromised our possession of Fort Issy, the Executive Committee determined to propose to the Commune the arrest of Citizen Cluseret. The arrest has been decreed.

"The Commune, in addition, has taken all the measures necessary for maintaining its possession of that stronghold."

General Cluseret was thus dismissed from his command; and that was not all—his arrest was ordered by the Executive Committee and approved of by the Commune. But there was still something more. The public was informed that steps had been taken to appoint some one else in his place, and that measures of *security* had been adopted. That word gave rise to the wildest suppositions. Measures of security did not mean warlike preparations against an assault, but simple precautions against treason.

Many supposed it was Cluseret's intention to betray the Commune; but the real fact no doubt was that the recent failure at Issy demanded a victim, and that that victim should be the Minister of War. On the night of the 30th, when the fort was on the point of surrendering, Mégy, the commandant, was desirous of leaving the mass of ruins to its fate; but General Wroblewski appeared upon the scene in time to relieve Mégy of his command. He was exasperated at what he called an act of treachery, and threatened to resign his command if the important ground of Issy was not confided to trusty hands.

General Eudes was then appointed commandant of the fort, with strict orders not to leave his post, to receive no flag of truce, and to defend himself till death.

It was General Cluseret, however, who first came to the rescue of the abandoned fort. When he heard of the panic he immediately sent forward the "Avengers of Paris" and other battalions which had not seen service for some days. It was too late, however; Generals Dombrowski and Wroblewski both sent in their resignations on account of Cluseret's mismanagement, but on hearing of his arrest withdrew them.

The arrest took place at the Ministry of War at 6 o'clock in the evening. The insurgent soldiers were all posted at the different outlets to the building. Two men without any other insignia than the red scarf entered his cabinet, one being the bearer of a warrant from the Commune. On seeing them the General is reported to have said: "For the last week I have been expecting this step, and am rather surprised that it has not been taken sooner. If I had been guilty of what I am accused, that is to say, treason, I should not have waited for your coming." He was then taken in a carriage to the Conciergerie. His action threw the Commune into the greatest state of perplexity, although the official organ announced the fact without commentary, as dryly as if General Cluseret had not been, during nearly a month, generalissimo of the armies of the Hotel de Ville. Had he been meditating a capitulation? Had he come to an understanding with the chiefs of Versailles? Had he conceived, in fine, a *coup d'etat?* Did he wish to have himself proclaimed Proconsul, Protector, perhaps Emperor? These were questions which helped to agitate the already excited brains of the Parisians for several days. His arrest, however, was in the natural order of things; first M. Lullier, then M. Bergeret, and after the latter M. Cluseret. One more victim, and the list was full.

CLUSERET
Commune of Paris
1871.

The following description of General Cluseret is decidedly true in regard to the feeling of security entertained by all Americans in Paris while he remained in power:

"Cluseret, though, it is said, a naturalized American, is a soldier of a very different type from such as Dombrowski. He has less of the capacity, probably, required by a general on the battle-field handling troops, but in the closet he is immeasurably superior. He is indefatigably active, and of insatiate ambition, greedy of power to such excess that, as was said of Sir Robert Walpole, he has preferred to risk losing it all rather than to sacrifice ever so little of it, and would rather see a too able man among his opponents than among his friends. He has gradually and steadily gathered all power into his own hands, and has made no secret of his resolution to resist and resent all interference on the part of laymen in what he considers the all-absorbing question of the moment—the effectual defence of Paris. He has rare firmness of character and few scruples. A Frenchman, who had the honor the other day of being his prisoner, narrated to me a very characteristic conversation which Cluseret had held with him. The General rather ridiculed the notion of private hostages being wanted by the Commune, when it held such infinitely more valuable hostages as, say, the banks of Paris, and professed his readiness to release all the prisoners, though he took care to guard himself against all suspicion of hesitating to take their lives. 'I don't want to take one life unnecessarily; but if at the last moment I should be called on to kill 10,000 people, I would rather make arrangements for killing 15,000, in order to be on the safe side, than run the risk of not killing the 10,000." He is, in fact, what one calls a thoroughly practical man, somewhat of the shrewd Yankee type; and there is, perhaps, some foundation for the suspicion that at the last moment he would have been as ready to pocket $100,000 by surrendering Paris as to kill 15,000 men in a desperate defence. Many people have for some time been expecting a sort of *coup d'état* on a small scale from him, and to see him for a few days absolute Dictator of Paris, with all our lives and purses at his mercy. He is too sensible a man to have wantonly abused such power, though no doubt he would have used it freely enough for his own private advantages. We foreigners resident in Paris have some reason to regret him, as he has always displayed an extremely liberal policy towards us; and since the war with Germany commenced, foreigners, or at any rate, Englishmen and Americans—about the members of other nations I know less—have never gone about Paris with so little annoyance or fear of arrest—except, indeed, from drunken National Guards, in violation of their duty—as during the last few weeks. With Frenchmen I need scarcely say the case has been reversed, but even they will have some reason to regret Cluseret's fall, except so far as it denotes the decline, through internal dissensions, of the power of the Commune."

General Cluseret's vacant place was given to Colonel Rossel, formerly a captain of engineers, afterwards a commandant in the army of the Loire. He was only twenty-eight years of age, slight figure, pale, with light hair, and, like General Dombrowski, wore spectacles. He was a pupil of the Polytechnic School, and came out second in his class. He served General Cluseret as head of the staff, and was remarked for his activity and great intelligence.

He acted as President of the Court-Martial, and was considered extremely severe.

The following letter, sending his resignation to the Minister of War, only appeared in the Paris journals July 19th, although written on the 19th of March. It throws a new light on the character of the Generalissimo of the Commune, who, during the reign of that body, and long after his capture by the Versailles Government, was considered as a deserter.

"CAMP OF NEVERS, March 19, 1871.

"*À M. le General Ministre de la Guerre à Versailles:*

"GENERAL:—I have the honor to inform you that I am going to Paris to place myself at the disposition of the Government forces which may be constituted there. Instructed by a despatch of Versailles, rendered public to-day, that there are two parties at war in the country, I place myself without hesitation on the side of those who have signed no peace, and who do not count in their ranks generals guilty of capitulation.

"In taking such a grave and sorrowful resolution, I have the regret to leave suspended the engineer service of the Camp of Nevers, confided to me by the Government of the 4th of September. I have placed this service, which consists at present only of orders for expenses and remittances of accounts, in the hands of Mr. Finat, auxiliary commandant of engineering, an honest and experienced man, who remained under my orders by command of General Vergne, in virtue of your despatch of the 5th of present month.

"I inform you summarily, by a letter addressed to the bureau of war-materials, of the state in which I leave the service.

"I have the honor to remain, General, your devoted and obedient servant,

"ROSSEL."

General Rossel received notification of his appointment,

and responded to the Executive Committee in the following letter:

"PARIS, 30th April.

"CITIZENS:—I have the honor to acknowledge the receipt of your letter charging me provisionally with the functions of Head of the War Department.

"I accept the difficult task thus imposed upon me, but I require your most absolute co-operation in order not to succumb under the weight of present circumstances.

"Salutation, and Fraternity,

"ROSSEL."

The new functionary at once issued two orders, one directing General Wroblewski to extend his command to the whole of the left bank of the Seine, both for the troops and the forts from Ivry to Issy; and the other declaring the Citizen Gaillard, sen., was charged with the construction of a second line of barricades immediately inside the fortifications, as well as a third at the Trocadéro, Montmartre, and the Pantheon. New barricades were also to be erected at four points on Place de la Concorde; those at the corner of Rue Royale and Rue Rivoli to be veritable fortresses. Every one was put to work, and Rossel seemed to imbue the waning spirit of Paris with new life.

The following remarkable correspondence was exchanged between the major commanding the trenches of the army of Versailles and Commandant Rossel, and posted on the walls of Paris, May 1st:

"TRENCHES BEFORE FORT ISSY, April 30, 1871.

"In the name of the Marshal commanding in chief, we, Major of the Trenches, call on the head of the insurgents collected in the Fort of Issy to surrender, with all his men, within the space of one quarter of an hour.

"If the said commander declares, in writing, that he

and the rest submit without any other condition than to have their lives spared, and to be allowed to live where they please except in Paris, that favor will be accorded them.

"Should the said commander not reply affirmatively within the time mentioned above, the whole garrison shall be put to the sword.

"E. LEPERCHE,
"Colonel of the Staff, Major of the Trenches."

The insurgents demanded a half-hour to deliberate, at the end of which time they had not yet agreed; a large majority indicating visibly a desire to put down their arms. The close of the day interrupted any further negotiations. The night was occupied by the insurgents in repairing the damage done and occupying the fort with fresh troops.

In the morning the white flag was again hoisted from the fort, and the officers of the staff, in responding, found themselves in the presence of the famous Eudes, who declared that he would continue the resistance to the last—that the Commune did not wish to treat with "assassins." He also forwarded the subjoined mission from the new Minister of War:

PARIS, May 1, 1871.

"*To Citizen Leperche, Major of the Trenches before Fort Issy:*

"MY DEAR COMRADE:—The next time that you venture to send us so insolent a communication as your letter of yesterday, I will have your messenger shot, in conformity with the usages of war.

"Your devoted comrade,
"ROSSEL,
"Delegate of the Commune of Paris."

Rossel and Leperche had served together at Metz. The

official journal of the Commune announced on the 1st of May that a Committee of Public Safety had been organized, composed of five members, who would possess the most extended powers over all commissions, and all the branches of the Government, and that the persons composing it could not be called before any other jurisdiction than that of the Commune.

Citizens Antoine Arnaud, Léo Meillet, Ranvier, Felix Pyat, and Charles Gérardin were appointed on this important commission.

What was to be the duration of this new power, or its particular attributes, was not known. The decree seemed to indicate that it was to replace the Executive Committee. The Delegate Rossel had asked the Commune for its most absolute co-operation as the price of his inestimable services. Doubtless the proof of that assistance was to be found in the creation of a Committee of Public Safety. Such a step was to be expected—first, because at the Hotel de Ville dictatorship was liked; and second, because, fatally vowed to an imitation of 1793, the natural result was that this word, and the thing itself, equally sinister, should be exhumed.

The garrison of Fort Issy was now three times as strong as at the moment of the evacuation. The fire from the fort was, however, very feeble, as only four 24-pounders remained mounted. A barricade at the foot of the slope in front was also armed with two guns, and two American mitrailleuses, but it was of little avail except to defend the access to the village. The officers of the Commune, however, appeared to be so sensible of the weakness of the whole position, that they established three guns on a small eminence outside the gate of Vaugirard. The re-occupation of Issy was only temporary, to enable the insurgents to establish their heavy artillery on the ramparts. In the meantime, two of the insurgent gunboats were cannonading the heights of Meudon and Brimborion.

The new Delegate of War sent the subjoined letter to several Paris journals, the publication of which raised him considerably in the estimation of the populace:

"I read with great regret the complicated fable which you had received relative to the retaking of Fort Issy. General Cluseret first entered it, accompanied by General Cécilia and Colonels Robart and Wetzel, conducting there the 137th battalion, about three hundred strong, and which had lost a dozen men during the march. I must also formally deny the assertion that my predecessor attempted to excite some corps against the Commune. The General, who has always been friendly towards me, was absolutely incapable of doing anything of the sort, or even of thinking of it.

"I feel bound not to make myself, by my silence, an accomplice in the malevolent rumors to which General Cluseret may be exposed in the unfortunate position in which he is placed, until the justice of the Commune has pronounced on his acts.

"Accept, etc., etc.,

"ROSSEL."

The bearer of Rossel's noted reply to the summons to surrender Fort Issy was a young man—an officer in the insurgent forces.

"Do you know what this letter contains?" asked Colonel Leperche.

"No."

"Well, it is an order to have you shot."

"How is that?" exclaimed the other.

"Read. According to Rossel, the bearer of an insolent letter is to be shot, and if ever one merited that qualification, it certainly is this. Therefore—"

The unfortunate officer protested that he was ignorant of the contents; but he was taken to General de Cissy, who, after having read the document, declared that, in fact, he could not help shooting the person who had brought it. The General, however, consented to have the young man sent to Versailles, where the cruel jesting which was to be his punishment was continued for some time. In the end, however, he received a good dinner, of which he stood greatly in need, and was afterwards offered his liberty, which he refused, preferring to remain in Versailles sooner than return to Paris.

The night of the 1st of May was witness to two very important affairs, namely, the capture of the station of Clamart and the Château of Issy by the Versailles troops. The station is an important position, because it completely dominates the fort of Issy.

At 11 o'clock, P. M., the 22d battalion of *chasseurs à pied* of General Berthe's brigade, which had been lying in ambush since 8 o'clock, approached the station in deep silence. "*Qui vive?*" cried the sentinel. "*The 22d battalion of National Guards!*" they replied, and rushed in with fixed bayonets. Two battalions of insurgents, and a company of Francs-Tireurs were in and about the station. The carnage for a short time was dreadful. Nearly two hundred insurgents were left dead on the spot, all killed by the bayonet and sword. Little quarter was given, as there were numerous deserters found among their number.

Almost at the same hour, two battalions of infantry belonging to the brigade of General de la Mariouse retook the Château of Issy. At this point the resistance was much more energetic than at the station of Clamart. The Château was first taken by the troops on the morning of the 30th, but during the negotiations of May 1st the insurgents managed to repossess themselves of it. The Communists defended themselves with the most determined bravery, and succeeded in making two hundred and fifty prisoners. They also prepared to attack a battery situated between the Château of Issy and the fort. The insurgents, with a considerable number of guns, immediately began to shell the station at Clamart and the Château of Issy. In consequence of this movement, which was calculated to inflict much damage on the troops, no time was lost in giving orders that all those batteries which were engaged against the Point du Jour should direct their fire in such a manner as to embarrass the insurgents in their attempt on the station and the Château. General Faron sent forward the engineers, and he was soon able to announce to Marshal de MacMahon that all the new positions were in a state of defence.

On the following morning, at daybreak, a column of three battalions issued from their intrenchments, and advanced against the Versailles outposts. The soldiers being in small numbers, fell back, and the insurgents continued to push forward in the direction of Clamart, turning all the obstacles, and avoiding the mitrailleuses. Reinforcements of the regular troops at length came up, and the insurgents, finding themselves in danger, commenced a retreat, in which they were much hurried by the Government troops. Many of them tried to enter Paris by the Vaugirard gate, but the guard there refused to admit them, as the instructions given were not to allow any National Guard to pass. The fugitives outside threatened to fire on the insurgents at the gate, but did not carry out their menace, and were obliged to disperse in different directions.

The news of this defeat soon becoming known at headquarters, a much more powerful force was directed towards this point, where the resistance shown was truly remarkable, and of incomparable energy. The defenders of the fort used mattresses made of seaweed to resist the bullets which now had become more annoying than the shells. On their side the troops of Versailles having passed the Seine at Sèvre, occupied the Isle of St. Germain, and there established a battery for the purpose of cutting off the retreat of the insurgents from the fort. The fusillade continued the whole night, and the artillery commenced its work of destruction at the break of day.

On the 3d of May Fort Vanves was severely shelled; it being the intention of the Versailles generals to cripple that fort in such a manner as to make it unable to render Issy any protection during the time employed in completing the trenches for its investment.

The shelling of Montrouge continued simultaneously with that of Vanves. The insurgents commenced raising new works in the part of the village near the cemetery which they occupied; and the regulars continued their works of approach, against which the bastions kept up an incessant fire. The proximity of the assailants, and the difficulty of ascertaining the respective positions of the two parties in the houses, prevented, however, the insurgents on the ramparts from rendering efficient aid to their colleagues outside.

The bastions of the Porte de Meudon and of the Point du Jour were also fired on by the Versailles batteries, so that Grenelle and Auteuil were considerably damaged, and all the villas in the neighborhood evacuated.

The two gunboats belonging to the insurgents moored beneath the railway bridge continued to shell the batteries at Meudon, and were replied to by the Versailles batteries, which, however, did more harm to the bridge than to the gunboats.

The line of attack of the regular troops on the insurgent positions became more and more extended to the left—that measure, by rendering combats between the two parties more frequent, appeared to have three objects in view· First, to close on all points the circle of investment which was already so near the forts and ramparts; next, to wear out by an incessant struggle the insurgent battalions, which, with a sensible diminution in their effects, were forced to oppose, day and night, and over a vast front, troops which might be constantly renewed; and, lastly, to open to the army a field of operation so wide that it might choose the most favorable opportunity for a general action, and aid their attack by numerous diversions or demonstrations. In this manner a decisive action might be fought to the greatest advantage.

The insurgents on the south, after having fought the whole of the 2d to resist the successful attacks of the army against the fortified positions on the Vanves road, and in the village of Issy, and, after having to resist a vigorous movement against the outworks of Bicêtre and Issy, passed a very unquiet night. The fort of Issy was now so far surrounded, that reinforcements had to be sent by the gate of Vanves. In fact, after that engagement, the troops, already masters of Moulineaux and the park of Issy, situated to the right of the fort, seized on the left a powerfully armed barricade, which defended the strategical road from the fort of Issy to that of Vanves; then, by a clever flank movement, they advanced from those two points on to the village itself, in which they occupied positions which commanded it completely. The only point which assured the communication of Paris with Issy was the cemetery, still held by the insurgents. Late in the evening there was every expectation that the army of Versailles would be in Paris by daylight next morning. In consequence of something that had transpired, three divisions of the army advanced towards the *enceinte* through the Bois de Boulogne, and an entire army corps was under orders to follow. Marshal de MacMahon, attended by his staff, left Versailles for the advanced posts at eleven o'clock, after an interview with

M. Thiers. Unfortunately, and for reasons not yet fully known, the National Guards of Passy and Auteuil, 38th and 72d battalions, did not make the signals agreed upon, and the affair fell through. This was the second time in ten days that an enterprise of this kind had failed. The non-success of this undertaking was counterbalanced by a great success on the evening of the 3d. The commandant of the 2d corps telegraphed to the Chief of the Executive Power as follows:

"Complete success of our attack on the right.

"The redoubt of Moulin-Saquet has been taken by assault with great gallantry by the troops of General Lacretelle.

"Two hundred dead insurgents remained on the ground. We have carried off three hundred prisoners, eight cannon, and several *fanions*.

"Two of the enemy's cannon, overthrown in the fossé, have been abandoned."

M. Thiers, in his report, said, "This is the victory that the Commune will celebrate to-morrow in its bulletins."

About seven o'clock in the evening of the 3d of May, four companies of the 39th Regiment *de Marche*, supported by the *éclaireurs* of the 41st and 71st Regiments, left the environs of Plessis-Picquet and arrived at the upper Seine by Hay, Chevilly, and Thiasis. There meeting the advanced posts of the 3d cavalry corps, they followed the route from Choisy-le-Roi to Vitry. Then traversing that village in haste, they advanced in silence on the enemy's outposts.

Moulin-Saquet was a position of the utmost importance to take and to *hold;* it was one of those redoubts that, during the former siege, held head against the batteries of Hay and Thiasis, and was situated a little in advance of Bicêtre. Its new works had rendered it very formidable. One account says that the attacking party had obtained the password of the insurgents, and, causing itself to be preceded by a small drove of bullocks conducted by soldiers disguised as peasants, penetrated into the redoubt, the sentinels allowing the supposed convoy to pass without molestation. Another account says that the redoubt fell into the hands of the Versailles troops by means of treason; that the commandant, Gallien, either gave or sold the password; that his disappearance during the combat, and the presence in the Versailles army of all the necessary material for the transport of the captured guns, proved this treachery. Nothing of the kind is mentioned, however, in the official despatches at Versailles, and the inference is, that the men who belonged to the 55th and 120th battalions, having been on the alert the two preceding nights and greatly fatigued and overcome by sleep and strong drink, could offer little resistance. Before they were thoroughly awake, the troops were masters of the redoubt.

Few of the defendants had even time to take up their arms, and the greater part were made prisoners without firing a shot; others, who attempted to resist, were killed, wounded, or captured, and but few of the eight hundred men succeeded in escaping. The soldiers then seized the flags, seven pounders, and mitrailleuses, all of which were carried off.

As soon as Haute-Bruyère and Ivry had received the alarm they commenced firing heavily, and the troops, finding themselves too much exposed to the fire of those forts in addition to that of Bicêtre, abandoned the position, taking with them their prisoners and their trophies. During the following day great discouragement prevailed in the quarter of the Gobelins, to which the surprised battalions belonged. A number of women and children had assembled around the Mairie, crying "Treason!"

The Commune, in its proclamations, boasted of having retaken the redoubt with great dash. They certainly made it untenable, as also the Clamart station, the scene of the other surprise and slaughter. The shells from Fort Vânves inflicted great injury on the regular troops, and Chateau Issy suffered greatly from the splendid firing of the insurgents at the Point-du-Jour. The insurgents about this time seemed to be inflicting as much damage on the regulars as they themselves were suffering.

Colonel Rossel, Delegate of War, in his military report, stated that during the night of the 3d, detachments of Versailles troops presented themselves at Moulin-Saquet as a patrol, and were admitted after giving the correct parole. They then charged the garrison, taking them by surprise, and driving them from the redoubt. The enemy carried off six guns with teams, which had been kept in readiness.

The result of an inquiry was that the commander, Gallien, was accused of having sold the countersign to the enemy, or, at all events, of having publicly divulged it in a café. The redoubt was almost immediately retaken by the 133d battalion.

The insurgents notified the inhabitants of St. Ouen, Clichy, and Levallois, that they must evacuate their homes, as some operations were about to take place.

The official journal of the Commune contains the subjoined report of the last sitting of that body:

"In reply to a demand of M. Courbet, that M. Paschal Grousset, the Minister of Foreign Affairs, should address a manifesto to the European Governments asking for the recognition of the Commune as a belligerent power, M. Paschal Grousset said:

"'The delegation for Foreign Affairs feels that there would be something offensive in having to make

Europe the judge in a civil war, and in soliciting a European verdict, which could not but condemn Frenchmen. It is necessary at any price to avoid foreign intervention, and it would be peurile to demand the character of belligerent when the Commune *de facto* possesses it. The verdict of Europe and the world has been given. No one can reproach the Commune and its defenders with having committed a single act which is not in harmony with the usages of war among civilized nations. We wage war honorably; we do not employ any means which we cannot publicly avow; we do not disguise police agents and gendarmes in the garb of troops of the line; we do not bombard women and children; we do not load our guns with incendiary bombs, or our rifles with steel-pointed balls; we do not summarily execute prisoners."

The members approved of the response of the Minister of Foreign Affairs.

The official journal also published a decree declaring that political and professional oaths should be abolished. Also one appointing Citizen Henry Director of the Organization and Movements of the Ministry of War; and one to Colonel Wetzel, at Issy, as follows:

"CITIZEN:—You have several times addressed applications for reinforcements, either to the military commandant at the Hotel de Ville, or to the commander of the seamen, without sending through your direct chief, the General La Cecilia, or even through the Delegate of War. That mode of acting, altogether irregular, forces me to withdraw from you your command. You will return to Paris, and place yourself at my orders, after taking the directions of your superior officer for giving up your service. "Salutation and Fraternity,

"ROSSEL."

It was currently reported among the adherents of the Commune that there was a growing opposition to the maintenance of Citizen Rossel as Delegate of War.

It was said that Citizen Jourde, Delegate to the Finances, believed himself called upon to resign because, as he said, officials in his position would henceforth be nothing but clerks of the Committee of Public Safety. The Commune, however, refused to accept that resignation. M. Jourde then resumed his mission; but he declared that, in the existing organization at the Hotel de Ville, conflicts appeared to him inevitable between the functionaries at the various ministries and the Committee. These debates did not precisely announce very tranquil days for the men who ruled the capital.

In the meantime the Versailles batteries kept up a regular fire on Issy and the gate of Vaugirard. At the Point du Jour, the gunboats Estoc, Sabre and Perrier cannonaded Meudon, and were replied to by the battery at Brimborion. The bastions. 68 and 69 also took part in the contest.

The fighting at Neuilly was of the same unvarying character, consisting of continual struggles in the streets, houses, and barricades, there being on both sides an incessant noise of cannon or musketry, varied by the rattle of the mitrailleuses. At one moment of the day the insurgents had succeeded in capturing the barricade of the Rue des Huissiers, but on the arrival of reinforcements of troops by the Avenue Sainte-Foy, they abandoned the position, and took refuge in the houses. The guns of Courbevoie were then brought to bear on their retreat, and the insurgents were at length forced to retire behind their own barricades.

Several shells had fallen far down the Champs Elysées, in front of the Palais de l'Industrie, and deaths were numerous on that avenue. Notwithstanding this, it was nearly always crowded. Curiosity is a prominent trait in a Frenchman's character, and he would run to see a dead man if he were positive a second shell would immediately follow the one that caused the accident. Above all, the inevitable individual sprinkling the streets was always at his post, hose in hand, performing his avocation between the shots.

A new deputation from the *Union Républicaine* arrived at Versailles on the 4th, and had an interview with M. Thiers, to propose a new basis of conciliation—the step, however, was not attended with any success. A similar result attended the deputation to the Commune.

The official journal of the insurgents published on May 6th, the following proclamation:

"Paris, May 5, 1871.

"*The Members of the Commune, Delegates of Public Safety:*

"Considering that pending the duration of the war, and as long as the Commune of Paris is obliged to fight the bands of Versailles who besiege it, and shed the blood of the citizens, it is not possible to tolerate the culpable manœuvres of the auxilliaries of the enemy;

"Considering that amongst the number of these manœuvres should be placed in the first rank the calumnious attacks directed by certain journals against the population of Paris and the Commune, and although both one and the other are above such attacks, they are not less a permanent insult to the courage, devotedness, and patriotism of our fellow-citizens;

"That it would be contrary to public morality to let these journals continue to spread defamation and outrage on the defenders of our rights, who are shedding their blood for the safety and liberty of France and the Commune;

"Considering that the Government, seated at Versailles,

interdicts in all parts of France the sale of any journal which defends the principles of the revolution represented by the Commune;

"Considering that the journals the *Petit Moniteur*, the *Bon Sens*, the *Petite Presse*, the *Petit Journal*, the *France* and the *Temps*, excite to civil war in each of their numbers, and that they are the most active auxiliaries of the enemy of Paris and of the Republic,

"IT IS DECREED,

"Art. 1. The journals above mentioned are suppressed.

"Art. 2. Notification of the present decree will be given to each of the journals and their printers, who will be responsible for all further publications. Citizen Le Moussu, Commissaire of the Delegations, is charged with the execution of the present decree.

"F. COURNET,
"The Member of the Commune, Delegate of Public Safety."

"PARIS, 16 Floreal, year 79.

"*Committee of Public Safety:*

"Considering that the House known under the name of *Chapelle Expiatoire* of Louis XVI is a prominent insult to the first revolution, and a perpetual protestation of the reaction against the justice of the people,

"IT IS DECREED,

"Art. 1. That the chapel called Expiatory shall be destroyed.

"Art. 2. The material shall be sold to the public for the profit of the Administration of Public Lands.

"Art. 3. The Director of Public Lands will cause to be executed the present decree within eight days.

"*Ant. Arnaud, Ch. Gerardin, Léo Meillet,*
"*Felix Pyat, Ranvier—The Committee*
"*of Public Safety.*"

Colonel Rossel, Delegate of War, in accordance with the injunctions of the Committee of Public Safety, to allot the military commands as soon as possible, has issued the following orders :

"General Dombrowski will go in person to Neuilly, and take command on the right bank; General La Cecilia will direct the operations between the Seine and the left bank of the Bièvre, and will take the title of General of the Centre; General Wrobleski will remain at the head of the left wing; Generel Bergeret will command the first reserve brigade, and General Eudes the second. Each of the above-named generals will retain headquarters in the interior of the city: 1. Dombrowski at the Place Vendôme; 2. La Cecilia, Ecole Militaire; 3. Wrobleski, Elysée; 4. Eudes, Legion of Honor; and 5. General Bergeret, Legislative Body."

The same functionary published the following circular to the inhabitants of the suburbs :

"CITIZENS:—Since I held the post I now occupy, I have received several letters informing me that inoffensive persons had been struck by fragments of shells in our villages.

"Until the war shall be brought to a close, I will do all in my power to prevent useless suffering; but, in order that I may stop the fire of the batteries directed on such or such a point by individual commanders, I must be informed in time, and in a positive manner, that the enemy does not occupy the spots indicated. On the other hand, it is necessary that I should receive the contrary information when the soldiers are present.

"The communes or hamlets which can offer me such guarantees shall be assured against these regretable and useless cruelties. You see what I ask is not simple neutrality, but a sort of alliance.

"Salutation and fraternity,

"ROSSEL."

On the morning of the fifth considerable skirmishing took place in the Park of Bagneux, and at the entrance to the village. The insurgents, who were only a short distance from that locality, and had barricaded the approach to Montrouge, made a reconnaissance in advance. The army had, however, considerable forces in the neighborhood, and some guns at Chatillon opened fire on the Communists, who were compelled to retreat to their trenches. Issy continued to receive a convergent fire from the batteries of the Orangery, the Tour-aux-Anglais, Val-Fleury, Clamart, and the Moulin-de-Pierre. The insurgents had repaired the fortifications with mattresses of dried seaweed and heaps of stable manure, but the straw had become dried by the wind and sun, and was set on fire by shells. The troops continued their works along the railway embankment, with the object of isolating the Fort of Issy from that of Vanves. About four in the afternoon an engagement, without result, took place before the first houses at the Moulineaux.

A large number of naval gunners arrived from Toulon by express, and were to be sent to new positions recently fortified by the Government. The marine pieces were those which they had been accustomed to work.

The insurgents kept continually losing ground on the west of the city, the regular troops having taken all the houses on the Avenue Neuilly to within three hundred yards of Porte Maillot. The army of Versailles was also working its way along the right bank of the river in the direction of the bridge of Asnières, in order to completely cut off the Communists from the Seine.

The arrival of official information from Versailles was more than acceptable to the large majority of the Parisians, and occasionally an outside journal from Versailles arrived with news which roused their drooping spirits. The subjoined communication from M. Thiers, which was telegraphed to the Prefects of the different departments in France, was the first correct news the law and order party received of this very important affair:

"VERSAILLES, May 6, 7:30 P. M.

"Those who have followed the operations which our army is executing with admirable devotion, in order to preserve social order, which is so gravely menaced by the Parisian insurrection, must have perceived that the object was to reduce Fort Issy by silencing its fire and cutting off its communications both with Fort Vanves and the *enceinte*. These operations are approaching completion, notwithstanding the obstacle which is presented by the batteries of Fort Vanves. At this moment our troops are engaged in forming the trench which will separate Fort Issy from Fort Vanves. The railway, which is crossed by a vaulted passage, is the line which has been disputed for three days. Last night 240 sailors and two companies of the 17th Battalion of Chasseurs à Pied, led by General Paturel, boldly rushed upon the railway and the arched passage. The sailors, being met with a heavy fire, were bravely supported by the two companies of the 17th, and the line of railway, as well as the arched passage, remained in our power. The garrison of Vanves, seeking at that moment to take our soldiers in the rear, were held ready to issue from their positions, when Colonel Vilmette, at the head of the 2d Provisional Battalion, fell upon them, carried the insurgents' trenches, took the Redan in which they were collected, killed and captured a considerable number, and finished the brilliant engagement by a decisive *coup de main*.

"The Redan was immediately turned against the enemy, and a quantity of arms, ammunition, and sacks of provisions abandoned by the Vanves garrison were taken, as also the flag of the 119th Insurgent Battalion.

"Thus it is seen that not a day is being lost; each hour brings us nearer to the moment when the main attack will terminate the anxieties of Paris and of all France.

"We have had several distinguished officers placed *hors de combat* in these operations. Colonel Leperche, Lieutenants Panet and De Broglie have been severely but not dangerously wounded. It is hoped that they will soon be restored.

"A. Thiers."

The first notice the Parisians had of the above combat was at six o'clock on the morning of the 6th of May. About two hundred insurgents, bareheaded, and without arms or equipment, entered Paris in disorder by the gate of Italy, crying out: "The fort of Vanves is taken!" They were in such a state of excitement that for some time no explanation of their panic could be obtained from them. From their confused accounts, the following cause of their retreat was gathered: For three days the fort had been under a constant fire from the batteries of the Tour-aux-Anglais and from the redoubts of Chatillon and Moulin-de-Pierre. Both artillerymen and National Guards were almost worn out with fatigue. They were, moreover, exposed to a fire of riflemen, from trenches constructed by the enemy at a distance of only five hundred yards, and many gunners had been killed or wounded at their pieces. The troops had also obtained possession of the barricade at the point where the railway intersects the military road, and the insurgents were consequently in danger every moment of finding themselves completely isolated.

The evening of the 5th had been comparatively quiet, when about midnight the troops issued from the trenches and made the first sentinels prisoners before these latter could raise the alarm. What followed was not very clear.

According to the insurgents, a party of marines, waving a white flag, advanced up to a trench occupied by the insurgents in front of the fort, crying out "*Vive la Commune!*" and then rushed on the Communists and bayoneted them. It is, however, more probable that this was another well-planned surprise, like that which succeeded at Moulin-Saquet. Many of the insurgents were killed or made prisoners, and the others retreated into the fort. The battery of Chatillon then opened a heavy fire of shell and canister shot, which fell on the parapet like hail.

The panic became general, and the insurgents, believing that a general attack was to be made, and that their retreat might be cut off, fled in confusion.

The fugitives, pursued by the fire of the troops, first endeavored to enter Paris by Porte Vanves, but were refused admission, as well as at several other gates at which they applied. Some attempted to pass by the gap in the fortifications made by the river Bièvre, but there the sentinels, who had strict orders to allow no one to pass, threatened to fire on them. They finally reached the Porte d'Italie, where, after waiting an hour, they were able to enter with the carts of the market-gardeners. The fort was reoccupied early in the morning, but soon became almost untenable, as the soldiers had advanced to within two hundred yards, and formed a semicircle of investment extending from the station of Clamart to the point where the railway intersects the military road, between the forts of Vanves and Montrouge. About fifty of the fugitive insurgents were afterwards disarmed by order of the Delegate of War, Colonel Rossel, and subjected to the military degradation of having the right sleeve of their overcoats cut off.

The official organ of the Commune published a decree declaring that on and after the 12th of May all articles of wearing apparel, linen, books, bedding, and working tools pledged at the *Mont de Piété*, for a sum not exceeding twenty francs, could be taken out without any payment, provided the person who received the money on them could prove his identity. The Delegate for Finance was to arrange with the administration which advanced the money, for the mode of repayment. From a report of the last sitting held by the Commune, the expense of this measure would be about eight million francs.

A notice was issued by the Delegate of War that not more than two men could be admitted together in any fort or redoubt, unless in the case of a troop previously announced and expected. He also visited the Commune, and protested against all orders given directly by the Committee to generals and superior officers under his command, and repudiated all consequences which might result from that course.

CHAPTER VIII.

Concert given at the Tuileries for the benefit of the wounded National Guards—Appeal of M. Thiers to the inhabitants of Paris—Battery of Montretout—Evacuation of Fort Issy—Occupation by the troops—Engagement at Moulin-Saquet—False reports given by the Official Journal—Rossel's report—His letter—His imprisonment and escape—Delescluze appointed Delegate of War—Fort Vanves evacuated—The insurgents again take possession—Differences of the Commune and Central Committee—Government despatch—Decree ordaining the demolition of M. Thiers' house—Camp in the Bois de Boulogne—Procession of troops at Versailles—Sinking of an insurgent gunboat—Capture of Fort Vanves—Villas in the neighborhood of Paris plundered by the insurgents—Threat of the Communists with regard to Paris—Dissensions of the Commune—Fall of the Column Vendôme—Its description—Guns captured at Vanves presented by a deputation to the National Assembly—Marshal de MacMahon's order of the day—Explosion of the cartridge manufactory in the Avenue Rapp—The blame thrown upon the National Assembly by the Commune—Sacrilege at Notre Dame des Victoires—Cluseret tried and set at liberty by the Commune—Arrest of Rochefort at Meaux—His entrance into Versailles.

ON the night of the 7th of May, a grand concert was given at the Tuileries, for the benefit of the families of the insurgents killed or wounded. It took place in the Salle des Maréchaux. That is, it was *announced* to take place there; but it really took place in *several* halls at the same time. While a prima donna was singing Trovatore in one hall, a band was playing the Marseillaise in another. As the halls all opened into one another, the confusion and noise was fearful; but the sight was one never to be forgotten, and well repaid standing in line for more than an hour, as all were obliged to do, before being able to gain admission, although tickets had been engaged in advance. The receipts amounted to over twelve thousand francs. A correspondent gives the following amusing account of the affair:

"In consequence of a large placard posted over the walls of Paris this morning, I passed through the gate of the private garden of the Tuileries, and made my way, in company with a crowd of citizens of all classes, through the apartments occupied but a few months ago by the ex-Emperor and Empress. The printed invitation announced that we might see the rooms in which the 'tyrant' had lived for the modest sum of 50c., but that, should we think proper to take tickets for the concert, 'whereby these saloons might be at length rendered useful to the people,' we should be permitted to enjoy the extra show gratis. I took a ticket, and joined myself to a hot stream of people who belonged to every nationality and rank of life, and whose remarks and criticisms were most edifying. There were shopkeepers and their wives, only too delighted to take advantage of the mildest dissipation; gentlemen whose National Guard trousers were rendered respectable by the gray jacket or blouse of a citizen; humdrum housewives who approved everything, and gaped their admiration of so much gorgeous wall-coloring; there were flaunting ladies in bonnets of the latest fashion and marvellous petticoats, who criticised the curtains and pointed the parasol of scorn at faded draperies; people who felt the heavy hand of the spectre of departed glory, and people who exulted at beholding the hidden recesses of an Imperial mansion laid bare to the jokes and ribaldry of Belleville and La Villette. Every class of Parisian society was represented in the throng that swayed and hustled through the rooms; but the saddest sight of all was the knot or two of decrepit veterans from the Invalides who leant against the balustrade of the grand staircase, and gazed with pinched-up lips and dry eyes at the National Guards on duty, lounging and carousing down below.

"The stairs were littered with bedding and cooking utensils, shirts and stockings hanging to dry over the gilt railings, while in the square at the stairs' foot were ranged benches and boards on trestles, and there the soldiers of the Guard sat in groups picturesque enough, contrasting in the carelessness and dirt of their general appearance with the lavish ornaments of marble and gilt work which served as a background to their figures. Marching orders, more or less thumbed and torn, hung in fragments from the panelled walls; names in pencil and names in ink, and names scrawled with a finger-nail, defaced the doors and staircase wall. A sentry stood at every door to see that the citizens behaved themselves—a precaution by no means unnecessary, the outward aspect of certain members of the crowd being taken into consideration.

"In the Salle de la Paix a number of women were busy uncovering a number of chairs for the promised concert. and in the Salle des Maréchaux beyond, where the concert was to be given, velvet benches were already occupied by old ladies in white caps with baskets in their hands, who presented a stern aspect of endurance, as though they were determined to sit there through the preparations as well as the promised entertainment, and still to continue sitting until turned out by sword and bayonet. The 'Salle des Maréchaux' exists no more except in name, for men on ladders were employed covering up the portraits which decorate the hall with screens of red silk —I suppose lest the past glory of French heroes should pale the brilliancy of the National Guard, just as the bas-reliefs of the Vendôme Column act as an outrage upon the susceptibilities of the Commune. White cloths were being tied over the busts of Napoleon's generals, and everything relating to the past carefully obliterated—a rather foolish proceeding, considering that the bee-spangled Imperial curtains still hang over the doors, and festoons of the same drapery decorate the gallery above. The brocaded panels of the Salle du Trône were objects of much remark among the ladies, as were the tapestries of the Salle des Gobelins; but the bareness and total absence of furniture were commented on freely on all sides. Not a chair or a window-blind, or even a door-plate or handle, is to be seen in any of the rooms, except in those used for the concerts, and the question arose, naturally enough, 'Where is it all gone to?' The same demand was made so often of an elderly bourgeois on duty at the end of the Salle de Diane that he was fairly bewildered, and looked round for help, and, hailing the gold stripes on my cap as a haven of relief, he forthwith seized upon me as a superior officer, and insisted on an explanation. 'You know there were quantities of cases carried off during the time before Sedan,' he said; 'but, with all their cunning, they can't have dismantled a whole palace of this size, can they?' And the crowd stood round endeavoring to account for the nakedness of the land, until a remark that the Commune had been feathering their nests with the chairs and tables dispersed them laughing.

"The Empress's bedroom was a great attraction, Chaplin's charming decorations being subjects of sufficient interest, independent of the absent furniture. The looking-glasses which spring from the walls called down ejaculations of delight from a party of dressmakers, who carefully took notes of the mechanism, 'in order to imitate it, my dear, when Paris becomes itself again.' There was a large placard upon the wall of a kind of library, inviting the attention of the public to the secret arrangements in a recess whereby the Empress obtained her dresses and linen from some manufactory of garments above, and an old lady, after having carefully examined the elaborate details, turned away with a sigh and a shake of the head. 'How foolish of them, after all, not to have done a little for us in order that they might have continued to abide in this paradise!' How different was the Empress's apartment this morning, bare and crowded with the dregs of the Paris population, from the night when I last saw it, the night of her flight, when bed-clothes still littered the floor, and gloves and little odds and ends of female finery told of recent occupation! All was silent then with the stillness of a coming storm; now the walls re-echo with a stir of unhallowed feet, and the spring sunshine streams in at the open window accompanied by whiffs from the garden below, while a distant cry reaches us from the street beyond of '*Le Vengeur,*' '*Le Cri du Peuple,*' '*Le dernier ordre du Comité du Salut Public,*' and we detect curls of smoke about the Arch of Triumph, which remind us that the bombardment still goes on.

"A reflective sentry at the door of the *cabinet de travail* begged me to remark the portraits set round above the doors. 'These are the Empress's favorite ladies,' he informed me; 'are they not *salopines*, one would say, of the period of Montespan? And those were the ladies who were models for the women of our land—no wonder that Paris should have become the Gomorrah that it is!' In the evening the concert was given, and a wonderful bear-garden the Imperial Palace presented. Members of the Commune flitted about in red draperies and tried to find room on the already crowded benches for the struggling mob, who rubbed their hot faces with their unaccustomed white gloves, and used such language to each other as, it is to be hoped, those august walls have seldom heard. Meanwhile the crowd increased in numbers, and by eight o'clock the reception rooms were full, and some 2,000 people still stood in a long string in the garden outside.

They behaved with the wondrous good nature which characterizes a French crowd, laughing over the absurdity of their predicament and waving the tickets, which they would never be able to present, jestingly at one another. In course of time the whole of the *jardin privé* was full of people, who looked up at the lights streaming from the windows, and sat about on chairs quietly smoking their cigars and enjoying the lovely evening, listening to the occasional boom at the other end of the long alley, where a bright flash which bore death upon its wings appeared in the sky from time to time, in mockery of the gas-light chandeliers and feeble attempts at revelry that were going on above our heads."

The construction of barricades in the interior of Paris was now carried on with great activity, the object of the Commune being to establish a series of redoubts in the principal centres of the city. The most considerable were those in the Place de la Concorde, whose deep embankments, with a wide ditch in advance, were raised at the Rue Royale, Rue Rivoli, and at the gate of the Tuileries, facing the Champs Elysées, and at the corner of the quay. These works were constructed chiefly of bags filled with sand, and the angles and faces were carefully finished, so as to resemble masonry work. The barricade at the corner of the Rue de Rivoli reached almost as high as the terrace of the Tuileries, against which it abutted. It was pierced for five pieces of cannon, and a small passage was left open on one side.

The other open places thus defended were the Place Vendôme, Place Peréire, and Hotel de Ville. Similar works had also been commenced on the Trocadéro. Some of the barricades were made in two sections, one behind the other, so as to leave a passage for vehicles between. Works were also raised across the main thoroughfares which lead to the city gates; that in the direction of the

Porte Maillot was before the triumphal arch at the top of the Champs Elysées. The most formidable, however, was that on the Place d'Italie. Those at Montmartre and Belleville had their guns pointed on the interior of the city, instead of being turned to the exterior, showing that in that quarter more fear was entertained of an attack from within than from without.

The Chief of the Executive Power determined, before commencing the finishing stroke for the subjection of the insurgents, to make a final appeal to the Parisians; he caused, therefore, the following proclamation to be circulated:

"PARISIANS:—France, freely consulted, elected a Government which is the only legal one—the only one which can command obedience, if Government be not an empty word. This Government has given to you the same rights which are enjoyed by Lyons, Marseilles, Toulouse, and Bordeaux. Without departing from the principle of equality, you cannot demand greater rights than are possessed by the other cities of the territory. It is the government of the Commune—that is, of the minority—which oppresses you; and, while daring to cover itself with the infamous red flag, claims to impose its will upon France. By its works you can judge of the *régime* which it proposes to inflict upon you; it violates the rights of property, imprisons citizens to use them as hostages, converts your streets and public places into deserts, puts a stop to all work in Paris, paralyzes it throughout all France, arrests the prosperity which was about to revive, retards the evacuation of our territory by the Germans, and exposes you to a renewed attack from them, which they declare they are ready to commence without mercy if we do not contrive by ourselves to put down the insurrection. We have ourselves listened to all the delegations which have been sent to us, and not one but has presented to us as a condition the obedience of the national sovereignty to the revolt—the sacrifice of all liberties and of all interests. We have repeated to these delegations that we would continue to pay the subsidy to necessitous workmen. We promised, and we promise it still, but the insurrection must cease; for it cannot be prolonged without causing the ruin of France. The Government which speaks to you would have preferred that you should liberate yourselves from a few tyrants who are playing with your liberties and your lives; but since you cannot do so, it must itself undertake the duty; and for that purpose it has collected an army beneath your walls—an army which comes, at the price of its blood, not to conquer, but to deliver you. Up to the present time it has confined itself to attacking the outer works. The moment has now arrived when, to abridge your sufferings, it must attack the *enceinte* itself. It will not bombard Paris, as the people of the Commune and Committee of Safety will not fail to tell you it intends. A bombardment threatens a whole city, and renders it uninhabitable, and has for its object to intimidate the citizens, and constrain them to a capitulation. The Government will not fire a cannon except to force one of your gates, and will endeavor to limit to the point attacked the ravages of war of which it is not the author. The Government knows, and would have understood, even if you had not on all hands informed it, that immediately the soldiers shall have entered through the *enceinte* you will rally round the national flag, in order to contribute with our valiant army to the destruction of a sanguinary and cruel tyranny. It depends upon yourselves to prevent disorders which are inseparable from an assault. You are a hundredfold more numerous than the Communist sectarians. Unite, then; open your gates, which they have closed against law, order, your prosperity, and that of France. The gates once opened, the cannon will cease to be heard; order, plenty, peace, will reappear within your walls; the Germans will evacuate our territory, and the traces of our misfortunes will rapidly disappear. But if you do not act, the Government will be obliged to adopt for your deliverance the most energetic means, the most prompt, and the most certain. It is bound to do so for your sakes, and especially for the sake of France, because the cessation of productive labor, which is ruining you, has extended to it, and it has a right to save itself if you know not how to save yourselves. Parisians! think over these things quietly. In a very few days we shall be in Paris. France desires to put an end to this Civil War. She will, she ought, and she can do so. She is marching to deliver you; and you can aid and save yourselves by rendering an assault useless, and by resuming from to-day your place among your fellow-citizens and brothers.

"A. THIERS."

It was on Sunday, the 7th of May, that this document was given to the public. The following day, at ten o'clock in the morning, the great battery of Montretout opened its fire on the bastions between 63 and 72. This battery, which will remain celebrated in the history of the siege of Paris in 1871, was not installed, as most of the other batteries were, behind epaulements of former date. As the Prussians had nothing constructed in this vicinity, it was all entirely new, and had occupied but six days in its formation, viz., from April 29th to May 4th. M. Thiers came every day to watch the progress of the work, which was being executed by 600 *ouvriers* and carpenters, under the direction of M. Hunebelle, well known in Paris for his intelligence and patriotism. In this short space of time 150,000 cubic feet of earth had been moved, the powder magazines, the abri, and the covered communications constructed. It was situated between the railroad from Paris to Versailles and the route from Ville-d'Avray to Mont Valérien. It consisted in reality of a collection of eight distinct batteries, viz., two at the park of Pozzo di Borgo, one on the road to Mont Valérien, the battery of Du Puit, two of the Vignes, one at the Chalet Mathieu, and one at the Maison Vivier, which was used as a powder magazine—the whole covering nearly a mile in extent. The arming of these batteries commenced May 4th, and was terminated on the morning of the 8th. Its material consisted of seventy pieces of large calibre, each piece supplied with 500 shells. Eight were called pieces of *eighty*, on account of the weight of the projectile, eighty kilogrammes, equal to 160 pounds. When these seventy pieces opened fire on the bastions of the city, it remained as if dumb with astonishment, with the exception of bastion 72, which from time to time sent a harmless shell. The bombardment of Point du Jour was perfectly furious, while Valérien kept howling its shower of iron on the Porte Maillot. As to Fort Issy, the incessant bombardment had reduced it to such a deplorable state that, to hold it any longer, became impossible, as the casemates were crushed in, and the men hardly dared to show themselves on the ramparts. The regular troops were masters of the church and a part of the village, and their *tirailleurs* could arrest and destroy the convoys on the route from Vanves to Clamart.

A decision had been come to in the morning to abandon the fort, and the 209th battalion first set the example, and were followed by the 106th and the 261st. This latter from Montmartre had gone out 200 strong the previous morning, and returned 95 only. The companies of engineers were the last to quit, ofter making every preparation for blowing up the fort.

Towards ten o'clock in the morning, the fort being dumb and having the appearance of being evacuated, the *chef de batallion*, Barillon, wishing to know the cause of this strange silence, followed by several sappers of engineers, advanced towards the gate. The drawbridge was down, he entered; the fort was evacuated.

The batteries having ceased to fire, the 38th regiment of the line ran to take possession of the defences which had been so horribly battered for the last eight days, and Lieutenant Biadelli received the recompense due to Commandant Barillon. Contrary to their expectations, the soldiers found in the abandoned fort a considerable quantity of provisions, ammunition, and a large quantity of spirituous liquors. In the greater quantity of the barrels was a strong mixture of tobacco and spirits. This decoction had the effect of exciting the courage and rendering the men what would be called in slang terms "*fighting drunk*," but producing also most fatal results caused by the nicotine. Every man wounded was a man dead. The members of the Committee of Public Safety had but little care for these inevitable accidents, for they professed for human life but a very moderate respect.

The firing from Chatillon and Val Fleury was extremely heavy on Fort Vanves throughout the day, and the shells fell incessantly there and on the ramparts of Vaugirard. About eight in the evening a fire broke out in one of the buildings of the fort, and was blazing till midnight. The cannonade of the Versailles batteries did not, however, cease, and the shells exploded in the midst of the burning mass, raising up clouds of sparks like a firework.

During the day an engagement occurred near the Moulin-Saquet. The insurgents still held the mill, but the regulars occupied some houses near, which a detachment of Communists attempted to take. The combat lasted nearly an hour; the soldiers shot from the windows and from the cellars through air-holes. Eventually the insurgents had to retire, having succeeded in capturing only one of the buildings, which they were obliged to abandon. The position was of some importance, as, being united to the village Thiais by trenches, the soldiers were able to advance to it and annoy the insurgents in the redoubt. The troops made a faint attack during the day on the great barricade of the *Route de Chatillon*, but did not persist in it, and withdrew when reinforcements arrived to the insurgents. About five in the evening a more serious assault was made on the Haute-Bruyères, and the advanced trenches were carried by the troops.

It was generally supposed that the news received by the Paris journals of the results of the fighting going on outside the walls was meagre in the extreme; but the Commune still wished to make it more so. A proposal was consequently brought before that body by Citizen Mortier to the effect that any journal venturing to touch on military matters should be suspended, and its proprietors and printer prosecuted before the tribunals. The examples of military news in the official and other Communal journals were certainly most amusing for their brevity. The subjoined were published the morning after Fort Issy surrendered:

First.—"Night." "Tolerably calm."

Second.—"Day; entirely quiet."

Third.—"Bas-Fontenay attacked the Fort of Montrouge, which replied vigorously, and reduced the Versaillese to silence."

Fourth.—"Morning quiet."

Fifth.—"Night quite calm;" then, "Evening tranquil," etc.

When one had read these announcements, he would say to himself, There is evidently an armistice. So much calm evidently indicates that the situation is quieting down. All at once is heard a most frightful cannonade; fighting is going on everywhere; men are being killed, wounded, and made prisoners, and blazing houses light up the besiegers from a distance. Every one was aware of the fact, except the official organ of the Commune, which knew nothing about it.

According to the official journal, "the citizen who fights, or whose relatives do so, will know at the end of the war whether the combatants are victorious or vanquished."

The Delegate of War, however, occasionally sent a despatch *direct* to the journal, and the astonishment of the Commune can be imagined, when, on the morning of the 10th of May, the following four despatches appeared officially, one under the other:

"Montrouge, Bicêtre.

"Respective positions maintained. Bas-Fontenay continually attacking."

"VANVES, Issy.

"The 'rurals' don't like to advance in this country."

"12:30 P. M.

"The tricolor flag floats on the Fort Issy, abandoned yesterday evening by the garrison.

"ROSSEL,
"The Delegate of War."

"One o'clock.

"General Brunel, Commandant of the Village of Issy, is charged to occupy the position of the Lycée, and to connect it with Fort Vanves.

"ROSSEL,
"The Delegate of War."

These were the last official announcements of Colonel

Rossel, and it would certainly seem, from the style of that one in which he announces the fall of Issy, that he was the conqueror, and not the conquered. He was evidently much annoyed concerning the orders given directly by the Committee of Public Safety, and complained bitterly of the disastrous surprise of Moulin-Saquet, which he attributed to the absence of General Wrobleski, sent to Issy by the Committee of Public Safety. That body denied in the most positive manner, through Felix Pyat, that it had ever sent any despatch to that officer; but the next day the original, signed, strange to say, by Felix Pyat himself, was produced. A discussion, anything but pleasant, then ensued, when Felix Pyat gave in his resignation as member of the Committee.

The next day, when Rossel's despatch was seen posted on the walls of Paris, and published in the official journal, a hurried meeting was held by the members of the Commune, and the following proclamation appeared:

"Paris, May 9, 1871.

"It is by a regrettable error that the announcement has been made, that the Fort of Issy had been taken and occupied by the Versaillese. Nothing of the sort has occurred, happily, and the flag of the Commune still floats on its ramparts!"

This contradiction was ordered to be posted and sent to all the Mairies by Citizen Vésinier, member of the Commune. The official journal, however, never published the contradiction.

"The following morning Colonel Rossel sent the subjoined letter, resigning his position as Delegate of War:

"Paris, May 9th.

"Citizens, members of the Commune:—Being charged by you with the provisional direction of the war-operations, I feel myself incapable of any longer supporting the responsibility of a command where every one deliberates and no one obeys.

"When a necessity existed for organizing the artillery, the Central Committee of that arm discussed but did not order anything. After two months of revolution, the whole service of your cannons was still dependent on the energy of a few volunteers, whose number is insufficient.

"At my arrival at the Ministry, when I desired to facilitate the concentration of arms, the requisition of horses, the pursuit of men evading service, I asked the Commune to turn to useful account the various Municipalities of arrondissement.

"That body deliberated, but came to no resolution.

"Later, the Central Committee of the Federation came and offered, almost imperiously, its assistance in the administration of the war. Consulted by the Committee of Public Safety, I accepted that aid in the clearest manner, and I transferred to the Central Committee all the information I possessed relative to the organization. Since that time that body has been debating, but has not yet acted. During that delay the enemy enveloped the fort of Issy with adventurous and imprudent attacks, which I should punish if I had the smallest military force disposable.

"The garrison, badly commanded, was seized with panic; and the officers, having debated, drove away Captain Dumont, an energetic man who arrived to command them, and while consulting, evacuated their fort, after having foolishly spoken of blowing it up, a thing more impossible for them than to defend it.

"That was not enough. Yesterday, while every one ought to have been at work or under fire, the chiefs of legions deliberated in order to substitute a new system of organization for the one I had adopted, in order to make up for the improvidence of their authority, always uncertain and badly obeyed. The result of their meeting was a project, at the moment when men were wanted, and a declaration of principles, when acts were necessary.

"My indignation brought them back to other thoughts, and they promised me for this day, as their final effort, an organized force of 12,000 men, with which I undertook to march against the enemy. Those men were to assemble at half-past eleven; it is now one, and they are not ready; instead of being 12,000, they are about 7,000, which is not at all the same thing.

"Thus, the nullity of the Committee of Artillery prevented the organization of that arm; the incertitude of the Central Committee arrested the administration; and the petty preoccupation of the chiefs of legions paralyzed the mobilization of the troops.

"I am not a man to recoil before repression, and yesterday, while those officers were deliberating, the execution-company awaited them in the court-yard. But I am unwilling to assume alone the initiative in an energetic manner, to take on me the odium of the executions necessary to extract from their chaos organization, obedience, and victory. Again, if I was protected by the publicity of my acts, I might retain my command. But the Commune has not had the courage to make its proceedings known. Twice already I have given you the necessary information; and on both occasions, in spite of me, you have held a secret committee.

"My predecessor was wrong to struggle in the midst of this absurd situation. Enlightened by his example, and knowing that the strength of a revolutionist consists solely in the precision of his position, I have two lines to choose from—either to crush the obstacle which hinders my action, or to withdraw.

"I shall not do the former, for the obstruction is you and your feebleness; and I am unwilling to make an attack on the public sovereignty.

"I therefore retire, and I have the honor to ask you for a cell at Mazas.

"ROSSEL."

Citizen Rossel, ex-Delegate of War, was arrested the following morning by order of the Committee of Public Safety, and being brought to the Hotel de Ville, was confided to the safe-keeping of Citizen Gérardin, a member of the Commune. At five in the afternoon, Citizen Avriel announced to the Commune that the prisoner had fled, and, strange to say, in company with the citizen appointed to guard him. Warrants were at once issued for the arrest of both fugitives. Citizen Gérardin was, two days back, one of the five members of the Committee of Public Safety. Many were astonished that, after having so proudly demanded "a cell in Mazas," M. Rossel should have fled precisely at the moment when his request was about to be complied with. The ex-Delegate evidently knew wherein his safety lay.

The official journal published the next day, at the head of its columns, an address to the people of Paris from the Committee of Public Safety:

"HOTEL DE VILLE, May 12, 1871.

"*To the People of Paris:*

"CITIZENS: The Commune and the Republic have escaped a mortal peril.

"Treason has glided into our ranks. The reaction, despairing to triumph over Paris by force of arms, has attempted to disorganize the defending body of the capital by corruption and gold. This has been flung about in handfuls, and has found amongst us consciences to purchase.

"The abandonment of the fort of Issy, announced in an impious placard by the wretch who delivered it, was only the first act in the drama. A monarchical insurrection inside, coincident with the delivery of one of our gates, was to follow and plunge us into an abyss. But this time again victory remained with right, and all the threads of this sinister plot are at present in our hands, and most of the guilty parties in custody.

"If their crime has been frightful, their punishment will be exemplary. The court-martial will sit in permanence, and justice will be done.

"CITIZENS—The Revolution cannot and will not be conquered. But it is necessary to show to monarchism that the Commune is prepared for every emergency, rather than see the red flag crushed in its hands. It is necessary that the people should well know that upon the Commune, and it alone, and upon its energy and its vigilance, definite success depends.

"That which the reaction attempted yesterday it will attempt again to-morrow.

"All eyes must watch its actions.

"All arms must be ready to strike the traitors without pity. All the living force of the Revolution must group together for a supreme effort. Then, and then only, will triumph be assured.

"*Ant. Arnaud, E. Eudes, F. Gambon, G. Ranvier—The Committee of Public Safety.*"

There were only four names to this document, Delescluze having been appointed Delegate of War.

Delescluze issued a proclamation addressed to the National Guard, announcing his appointment as Delegate of War. He declared the situation to be extremely grave, and that if he consulted his own strength he would decline the dangerous functions; but that he counted on their assistance to render his task more easy. The question seemed to be no longer one of the municipal franchise of Paris, but of social equality and the enfranchisement of France and the world. Delescluze's first order in the official journal ran thus:

"Every officer coming from the exterior or interior who presents himself at the Ministry of War, or at the *Place* (Place Vendôme), without being the bearer of orders from his hierarchical, will put himself in a position to be immediately arrested.

"DELESCLUZE,
"Civil Delegate of War."

On the 10th of May the firing was continuous along the whole south-west line. The fort of Vanves, however, was the principal point of attack, and shells were thrown on it without cessation. The garrison feebly replied, but preparation was being made to answer the fire from the ramparts. Four guns had already been put in position at No. 76, between the gates of Vaugirard and Montrouge, and three others were waiting to be mounted. Some of the iron-clad locomotives which had been used on the western line opposite Asnières were brought round to this side. The batteries of Montretout still continued to bombard the Point-du-Jour.

Auteuil and Passy suffered considerably, and the inhabitants were moving out in all haste. The headquarters of the insurgents had been removed to the Muette gate, but the soldiers on duty there could scarcely show themselves outside the ramparts.

General Dombrowski had a narrow escape from a shell while passing along the Quay d'Auteuil. One fell at the same time into a manufactory at Grenelle, and went through a boiler of a sixty horse power engine, which was fortunately not in use at the moment.

Courbevoie, Neuilly Bridge, and Valérien continued to fire into Porte Maillot, des Ternes, and St. Ouen, while the insurgents kept up a continual fire on the villages of Asnières and Gennevilliers.

The fort of Vanves was evacuated on the 10th by the insurgents, and remained for several hours completely abandoned. The bombardment of the past week had reduced the works to almost as critical a situation as those of Fort Issy; the garrison was reduced to about two hundred, and the demands for reinforcements had remained unattended to. The stores of provisions and ammunition had become seriously reduced, and could not be replenished, as the fire of the troops covered the only road that remained open. The men were completely discouraged, and were only retained at their post by the energy of their Commander, Durassier, who gave his orders with his revolver in his hand, and who appeared to have no idea of surrendering the place. The garrison seemed to have at length decided on getting rid of this troublesome officer; and an artilleryman had been designated to shoot him with a pistol, when they were spared the crime by a shell from Chatillon, which wounded the intended victim seriously enough to compel him to give up his command. The garrison then prepared to retreat, but the shells continued to fall so heavily that they feared to venture outside. They then hoisted a white flag, and the fire ceased. An officer, followed by a detachment of troops, came out from the trenches to parley, and the insurgents asked to be allowed to march out unmolested. "No conditions can be granted to insurgents—you must surrender," replied the other.

An insurgent then discharged his musket at the officer, but without hurting him; the soldiers returned the fire, and the first rank of the insurgents fell. A few of them succeeded in escaping by the ditch, others returned to the fort, and the rest were made prisoners. The troops did not attempt to occupy the place, believing it to be mined, and in the evening two battalions of insurgents arrived, and again took possession. The place, however, remained quite at their mercy, as it was so far isolated that the only communication open was by a trench between the fort and Petit-Vanves. The village of Vanves itself was entirely occupied by the soldiers, and their outposts were in the first houses of Malakoff at less than musket-shot distance from the ramparts. The progress of the army at Issy was also very apparent, as the insurgents held only the Parc-des-Oiseaux, the barricades at the head of the convent, and the asylum of Petit-Ménages. The insurgent government, however, sent its best troops in that direction, as it expected that the assault would be made there at the same time as at the Point du Jour. Its Zouaves and Turcos, and most devoted battalions, were being concentrated in the houses between the gate of Vaugirard and the outposts. The Fort of Montrouge was completely silent during the day, and the only battery that supported Vanves was bastion No. 73.

The greatest confusion seemed at present to prevail in the intercourse between the Commune and the Central Committee. The conflict which had arisen a short time back between those two powers seemed to have terminated by the triumph of the latter, which was admitted to possess the jurisdiction of the whole National Guard. It was generally thought that the order of the Committee of Public Safety, entrusting to the Central Committee the war administration, had put an end to all competition of authority; but as the co-existence of two such bodies was not only totally irregular, but certain to promote rivalry, a further disagreement was certain to speedily arise.

Accordingly, a new transformation of the War Department, evidently directed against the Central Committee, had just been decreed. The Commune, after having lately consented to all that the other body desired, now brought in the Commission of the War—one of its own creations—and confided to it the task of regulating the relations of the Central Committee with the War Department. On its side the Commission of War interdicted in the most absolute manner the Central Committee from nominating to any employment, and left it only the faculty of presenting candidates.

The bearing of these two decisions, so indicative of antagonism, was clear to every one; and the most superficial observer could at once perceive the great difference that existed between these restrictive measures and the decision of the Committee of Public Safety, confiding the war administration to the Central Committee. Subjoined are the two decrees—the first being from the Commune:

"*The Commune of Paris:*

"Considering that the co-operation of the Central Committee of the National Guard in the War Department established by the Committee of Public Safety, is a measure necessary and useful to the common cause;

"Considering, moreover, that an important point is to have its attributes clearly defined, and that for such purpose the Commission of War shall be called on to fix, in concert with the Delegate of War, the limits of such intervention;

"DECREED:

"*Article Unique.*—We, the Commune, do hereby decree that the said Commission and the War Delegate shall regulate together the relations of the Central Committee with the War Department."

The Commission of War, on its side, carried out the views of the Commune in issuing the following order:

PARIS, May 8.

"*The Commission of War:*

"Whereas the decree which gives to the Central Committee the administration of war contains the following restriction:

"'Under the direct control of the Commission of War;'

"We, the said Commission, ordain that the Central Committee shall not appoint to any place, but shall merely suggest names upon which we will decide.

"Accounts concerning the conduct of each service shall be sent to us regularly every day.

"*Arnold, Avriel, Delescluze, Tridon, Varlin.*"

The Government of Versailles addressed the following despatch to the civil and military authorities throughout France:

"May 9th, 1871, 7 P. M.

"The able direction of our operations, seconded by the bravery of our troops, has to-day obtained a brilliant result. The fort of Issy, after an attack of a week only, was occupied this morning by the 38th regiment of the line. A considerable quantity of artillery and ammunition was found there. We can praise the successful audacity with which our generals conducted the approaches under a cross-fire from Vanves, the ramparts, and Fort Issy itself. A large share of those prompt and decisive results are due to the engineers. Vanves is also in such a state that it cannot hold out long.

"The capture of the fort of Issy is, however, sufficient to ensure the success of the plan of attack now undertaken. Last night General Douai, after a vigorous cannonade from the formidable battery of Montretout, also favored by a dark night, crossed the Seine and took up a position before Boulogne, facing the bastions 67, 66, and 65, forming the Point-du-Jour. Fourteen hundred men from the 18th foot-chasseurs, 26th line, 5th provisional regiment (Gandil's brigade, division of General Berthaut), 26th foot-chasseurs, and 37th marching regiment (Daguerre's brigade, division of General Vergé), opened the trenches about ten in the evening and worked all night till daybreak, when they were forced to suspend their labor. Their right is on the Seine and their left at the extremity of Boulogne. By means of their activity and courage they were at four in the morning sheltered from the enemy's fire. They are now at only three hundred yards from the fortifications of Paris, that is to say, at a distance from which they might, if they pleased, already establish a breaching battery.

"We have now every reason to hope that the hard trials of the well-meaning portion of the population of the capital are drawing to a close, and that the odious reign of the infamous faction which has adopted the red flag for its emblem, will soon cease to oppress and dishonor the capital of France. It is also to be desired that what is now taking place will serve as a lesson to the wretched imitators of the Commune, and prevent them from exposing themselves to the legal severities which await them if they dare to carry any further their criminal and ridiculous enterprise."

The new Committee of Public Safety was evidently much enraged at the above and previous despatch, and signalized its entry into military functions by the following most infamous decree published against the "Sieur Thiers," declaring that his house, situated in Place Saint George, should be razed to the ground:

"Paris, 21 Floreal, An. 79.

"The Committee of Public Safety, considering the posting-bill of Sieur Thiers calling himself Chief of the Government in the French Republic;

"Considering further that the said notice, printed at Versailles, has been posted on the walls of Paris by order of the said Sieur Thiers;

"That in that document he declared that his army is not bombarding Paris, whilst each day women and children are victims of the fratricidal projectiles of the Versailles troops;

"That in it an appeal is made to treason in order to obtain an entrance into the city, he being sensible of the absolute impossibility of overcoming by arms the heroic population of Paris, decrees as follows:

"Art. 1.—The furniture and effects on the properties of Thiers shall be seized by the Administration of Domains;

"Art. 2.—The house of Thiers, situated on Place George, shall be razed to the ground;

"Art. 3.—Citizen Fontaine, Delegate for the Domains, and L. Andrieu, for Public Service, are charged, each in so far as he is concerned, with the *immediate* execution of the present order.

"Arnaud. Eudes, Gambon, Ranvier,—Members of the Committee of Public Safety."

It has been seen that the Committee declared war to the Gregorian calendar and the French dictionary. As will be seen by the text of the decree, the word *Saint* was suppressed from the vocabulary. The Committee were bringing matters back to the peurile and absurd eccentricities of 1793.

M. Thiers' house was situated on Place *Saint* George. The only journal in Paris that supported the above decree was Rochefort's paper, the *Mot d'Ordre,* which contained the subjoined remarks:

"We publicly affirm that the decree of the Commune announcing that M. Thiers' hotel shall be immediately razed to the ground, is a necessary satisfaction given to public opinion. Nothing could be more just than that this old fugitive should see his house fall by such an order, since he has the infamy to knock down ours with his bombshells. We may add that the resolution taken by the Government of Paris will open a new horizon to that chief of bombarders, at the same time that it relieves him from a great weight. The perverse beings who at present compose the population of Paris, in perceiving that hitherto not one projectile has arrived at the Place Saint George, began to suppose that this ferocious but economical inhabitant of Versailles was thinking more especially of sparing his own dwelling."

The official journal of the Commune announced that Citizen Billioray was elected member of the Committee of Public Safety, to fill the vacancy caused by the appointment of Delescluze Delegate of War. The last named citizen proposed to the Commune to place the 128th battalion of the National Guard on the order of the day for gallant conduct, in clearing, under the direction of General Dombrowski, during the night, the park of Sablonville of a party of Versailles troops.

General Bergeret again appeared on the scene, and was ordered by the Commune to place 20,000 earth-sacks at the disposal of Colonel Henry. The latter was ordered to place thirty large mortars on bastions 59, 60, 61 and 62, to bombard Neuilly and Boulogne.

The Commune also received the following letter:

"May 13, '71.

"CITIZENS:—The troops quartered at the village of Issy quitted their positions yesterday during my absence in Paris on an order from the Minister of War, and returned to their homes. As this fact is the result of a succession of causes all more or less connected, and concerning which the public ought to be instructed, I demand to be placed under arrest, and I propose that an investigation be at once opened.

"Receive, etc., etc.,

"COLONEL BRUNEL."

The bombardment of Vânves and Montrouge was exceedingly heavy during the 11th and 12th. About seven on the morning of the 12th, an attack was made by a considerable force of infantry and gendarmes on the former place. Breaches were effected in the walls of some houses occupied by the insurgents, and an assault being made, a hand to hand fight took place, first in the gardens, and then in the houses; but the insurgents were forced to abandon the first line of houses, and a constant fusillade continued throughout the day.

At Montrouge the attack commenced by the advance of some detachments of cavalry, which were received with a sharp fire from the insurgents and forced to retreat. The infantry then advanced in a semicircle, with a mitrailleuse on each flank, so as to attack the position known as the Maison Millaud. The insurgents made several attempts to break through their line, but without success, as the troops were supported by the batteries of Chatillon, which continued to bombard the village of Montrouge. Some shells even fell inside the ramparts. At about ten the insurgents were forced to abandon the barricade and fall back upon Petit-Montrouge. In the afternoon the troops made another advance, and, after some severe fighting, drove the insurgents from their new position; but on the regulars attempting to occupy the houses of Petit-Montrouge, they were fired on from the fort, and were forced to retire.

The cannonade was particularly severe to the west. The great redoubt at Montretout continued to send its shells into Auteuil and Passy, and on to the Point-du-Jour.

They even reached as far as the quay. Others from Meudon fell on the bridge of Grenelle, circulation over which was now suspended. The concentration of troops in the Bois de Boulogne was increased. The army also occupied the village of Boulogne, which, however, was in a most pitiful state, as for two weeks before its evacuation by the insurgents it was bombarded by two batteries in the Park of St. Cloud.

The insurgents having learned by a reconnaissance that a strong barricade had been constructed by the troops at the gate leading into the wood, opened fire in that direction from two field batteries ranged on the bastions at the end of the Avenue de l'Impératrice. Mont Valérien replied, doing considerable damage to the drawbridge and railway station.

A new battery, constructed under Fort Issy, and between that position and Meudon, assisted in the attack against the Point-du-Jour and the position of the bastions between it and Vaugirard.

The insurgents commenced to build up a direct communication between Fort Vânves and the *enceinte*, with the object of facilitating the retreat of the garrison, in case the fort should be taken by the troops.

The regulars now commenced to arm the bastions of Fort Issy with ship-guns for the purpose of directing them against the insurgents. They also continued to push forward their parallels in the Bois de Boulogne, thousands of men being at work on them. Perhaps a more imposing camp never was seen than that on the Bois. It positively realized the idea of the poet, an army encamped and waiting for battle. All visitors to Paris know what a magnificent park that is stretching from the Allée de Boulogne, at one extremity of the Bois to Bagatelle near the other, the river forming the boundary, the whole surrounded by a beautiful background of rich and luxurious foliage. Here were to be seen thousands of white tents in semicircular rows, the headquarters at the Longchamps race-course; the troops seen marching, and going through drill, had the appearance of a magnificent review, such as took place nearly two months later on the same spot, when 150,000 conquerors were reviewed before the same civil and military chiefs who now directed the active operations of the siege. The air, however, was rent by shrieking shells, and the ear pained with the continual sound of mitrailleuses and chassepots, and dreadful events were drawing near.

About the time at which the ex-Delegate of War disappeared from the scene, after having bade the Commune adieu in such a singular manner, a patriotic fête took place at Versailles, of which the entire population were spectators.

A cortège, composed of delegations from the different branches of the service which had assisted at the operations under Fort Issy, passed through the town. Their muskets, drums, and twenty-eight of the 109 cannon taken at Issy, were covered with flowers and foliage. The flags of the 5th, 99th, 94th, and 115th insurgent battalions were also carried in the procession.

At three o'clock the column arrived at the hotel of the Prefecture, clarions sounding and drums beating. The Chief of the Executive Power, accompanied by the General-in-Chief, received the deputation of chiefs on the steps of the hotel, and felicitated them on their great success. The troops responded by shouts for M. Thiers and Marshal de MacMahon. The cortège proceeded to the palace, where the soldiers were addressed by M. Leon de Malleville, Vice-President of the National Assembly, who warmly thanked them, in the name of France and her representatives. Marshal de MacMahon also issued the following order of the day to the army:

"HEADQUARTERS, VERSAILLES, May 12.

"SOLDIERS:—You have responded to the confidence which France has placed in you. By your bravery and energy you have overcome obstacles opposed to you by an insurrection disposing of all the means prepared by us against the foreigner.

"You have successively carried the positions of Meudon, Sèvres, Rueil, Courbevoie, Bécon, Asnières, Moulineaux, and Moulin-Saquet, and, finally, you have entered the fort of Issy. In these different combats, more than 3,000 prisoners and 150 pieces of cannon have remained in your hands.

"The country applauds your success, and sees in it the presage of the end of a struggle which we all deplore.

"Paris calls us to deliver it from the pretended government which oppresses it; and before long we shall plant the national flag on the ramparts, and obtain the re-establishment of order, so imperatively called for by France and the whole of Europe.

"Soldiers, you have deserved the gratitude of the country.

"DUKE DE MACMAHON,
"Commander-in-Chief."

The insurgent gunboats on the Seine had for several days been causing considerable annoyance to the Government batteries at Meudon; and as they remained partly concealed under the arches of the Viaduct, they presented only a small point of aim for the Versailles guns. The shells which fell in the water around them were, of course, quite harmless. The regulars, however, established a battery of 7-inch guns on Fort Issy, which crosses its fire with that of Montretout de Breteuil and Brimborion, in cannonading the Point-du-Jour. From this new position a cannonade was opened on the 13th with such effect on the gunboats, that one, the *Estoc,* was pierced through the hull by shells in three places, and went down. The Commune gives the following report of the occurrence:

"On Friday morning early, shells began to fall around our gunboats, which replied with great courage. The fire continued at intervals during the day, and, towards five in the evening, the fort of Issy, the battery on the Isle Saint-Germain, suddenly unmasked, and another of mortars, directed a terrible fire on the boats. These latter, after a horrible cannonade, were obliged, by the precision of the enemy's aim, to abandon the dangerous post which they had occupied for more than a month, but did not move, until one of them, the *Estoc*, got almost split open by the Versailles shells, and foundered gloriously, to the cry of the sailors, '*Vive la Commune!*' All the equipage was received on board a smaller vessel, which was in attendance. We have to deplore one man severely wounded and several contusioned. The citizen delegated to the naval force places on the order of the day all the brave seamen of the flotilla who, during the space of a month, supported at the viaduct of the Point-du-Jour the deadly fire of the adverse party."

The insurgents immediately constructed a strong barricade on the Quay de Passy, at the angle of the Rue Guillon, mounted with guns to command the river.

On the morning of the 14th the Versailles troops attacked simultaneously the insurgents entrenched between the forts of Issy and Vânves. The Communists, surprised by a heavy fire of musketry and mitrailleuses, abandoned their posts, and fled to Paris. Those who occupied the college remained firm. The troops then advanced and took possession of the houses, from which, during the rest of the day, they kept up a constant fire upon the insurgents on the ramparts.

At Montmartre the cannon on the Butte commenced

firing on the evening of the 13th, and continued until four o'clock next morning, keeping the population in that district in the greatest state of alarm. The aim there seems to have been very bad, as many of the shells, instead of reaching the Chateau de Bécon and Gennevilliers, at which points they were aimed, fell at Clichy, and other places occupied by the insurgents, who suffered many casualties from their own men. The railway station at Asnières was also burnt by the insurgent shells.

The following is the official announcement of the affair of the 12th:

"VERSAILLES, May 13, 4:30.

"While our troops undertook, in the Bois-de-Boulogne, to open trenches of great length, and the formidable artillery of Montretout protected the works of approach, the 2d corps (General Cissey) accomplished, on the side of Issy, a most brilliant feat of arms.

"Yesterday, at noon, the soldiers of General Osmont occupied the houses situated at the point where the strategical road meets that from Chatillon to Montrouge. This operation, which was executed by a body of marines, a company of the 4th battalion of foot-chasseurs, and a detachment of the 113th regiment of the line, had for result to cut off all communication between the forts of Vânves and Montrouge.

"A few hours later, Commandant de Pontécoulant, with a battalion of the 46th of the line (brigade Boçher), carried with the bayonet the Couvent-des-Oiseaux at Issy.

"In that attack, executed in the most admirable manner, the men displayed wonderful dash and spirit. The losses of the enemy are considerable. We took eight pieces of cannon, several flags, and some prisoners.

"After that affair, the insurgents, comprehending that they could not any longer maintain themselves outside the ramparts, abandoned successively all the parts of the village which they still held, again leaving in our hands a large number of prisoners.

"The occupation of the college of Vânves, effected last night, brings our troops to within a few hundred metres from the fortifications.

"Thus, on all sides, we are approaching the final term of our operations and the deliverance of Paris.

"THIERS."

The demolition of M. Thiers' residence was commenced on the 13th; by the evening the roof was off, and the workmen had attacked the tops of the walls with their pickaxes.

The house originally belonged to Madame Dosne, mother-in-law of M. Thiers, and now deceased. It was left in equal shares to her two daughters, Madame Thiers and Mademoiselle Félicie Dosne, and was therefore the property of two women, eminently respectable, and entirely strangers to political affairs. Moreover, Madame Thiers has no children, and Mademoiselle Dosne employs a handsome fortune in works of charity; so that the poor would have been the greatest losers by this unjustifiable act, had not the National Assembly decreed to replace the mansion.

On the afternoon of Sunday, May 14th, the Minister of the Interior received at Versailles a telegram announcing that the fort of Vânves had been captured at half-past twelve. Since the morning the investment had been complete, but the operation had been attended with serious loss. Amongst others, Captains Rosheim and Durand de Villers had been killed. The insurgents evacuated the fort through the quarries and underground passages which communicated with the Porte de Montrouge and the military road inside the fortifications, between the gates of Vânves and Vaugirard. Some of the insurgents appear to have lost their way, and to have wandered about the catacombs with which the caves were connected, until they found an issue. Several remained under ground for twenty-four hours, and there were probably others still lost in the labyrinth of arched ways which extend an immense distance to the south of the city. The men who arrived by those galleries were in a miserable condition, being covered with dirt and worn out with fatigue. It was this incident that probably gave rise to the rumor that a number of gendarmes, disguised as National Guards, had attempted to enter Paris by the sewers. The army of Versailles occupied the fort during the afternoon, and at once opened trenches to cut off all communications with the interior, and prevent a surprise.

The cannonade during the day from Montretout and Mont Valérien on the Point-du-Jour was fearful. The insurgents were compelled to abandon entirely the bastions, at the ramparts, and they could only now await the assault. The shells continued to fall on the quay at Passy and around the Pont de Grenelle, making fearful havoc among the houses. The villas there were besides pillaged in a most barefaced manner by bands of individuals, many wearing the uniforms of National Guards. They were accompanied by women, and trucks, in which they carried off everything portable.

On the night of the 14th the regular troops succeeded in throwing a bridge across the Seine below Asnières; in this work they were lighted by the glare from two houses which were burning near the river. The insurgents attempted to oppose their passage, but were driven back to the ramparts by the fire from Bécon and the redoubt of Gennevilliers. The soldiers then spread to the right and left along the banks of the river. Exchanging shots with the insurgents, they finally advanced to the gate of Clichy and surrounded the village. Later in the day a strong force of insurgents was concentrated on the Asnières road, and an attempt was made to drive back the troops; but fresh regiments crossed the river, and the attack of the insurgents was repulsed.

A decree was passed by the Commune ordering each person in the city to carry a card of identity, which any insurgent National Guard could demand to see whenever he thought fit. This decree was turned into ridicule by most of the Paris journals; in fact, those in favor of the Commune reprehended the order most seriously. All the male inhabitants were now National Guards; the result was that everybody had a right to arrest everybody else. However good, charitable, and peaceful a man may be, he has always one or more enemies about, who, in this case, could stop him at any street corner, and if perchance he had forgotten his card, carry him away to prison.

Another decree immolated a large number of journals—the *National*, *Siècle*, *Discussion*, *Corsaire*, *Avenir National*, and *Journal de Paris*. It was only journals like the *Cri du Peuple* that could survive in the atmosphere of Paris. That journal published on the 15th the following mysterious article, which at the time was much derided. The said article hinted very strongly at the cherished project of blowing up the capital, which eventually turned out but too true; had the Versailles Government given the Commune three more days, half the city would have been in ruins.

"We received some days since information of the greatest gravity, and of the correctness of which we are now completely certain. Every measure has been taken to prevent the entry into Paris of any soldier of the enemy. The forts may be taken one after the other; the ramparts may fall. *Not a man will penetrate into the city. If M. Thiers is a chemist, he will comprehend us!!!"*

A delegation was sent from the Hotel de Ville to the banking establishment of the Société Générale to examine the books of that immense establishment. Those containing the private accounts of the pretended enemies of the Commune received especial attention. The amounts standing to the credits of those persons were added up, and the sum demanded to be paid immediately.

The sub-director protested against this act of brigandage, but the only reply made was, the Commune wanted money, and could not do better than take it from its adversaries. At one moment the delegates demanded all the shares, inscriptions of *rente*, and other securities deposited in the strong room. The money claimed was paid under protest, which made but little difference to them.

Paschal Grousset published in the official organ an address to the great towns of France, assuring them that, after two months' contest, Paris was neither wearied out nor weakened, and calling on them to come to its assistance. He specially appealed to Lyons, Marseilles, Bordeaux, Toulouse, Nantes, and Lisle.

There was also an order from Delescluze forbidding all officers of the National Guard to appear in their battalions with a musket in hand, as for the pleasure of firing on the Versailles troops they neglected their command. The Delegate also published the following note:

"We point out to public indignation the conduct of the colonel commanding the 39th of the line. When the Versailles troops took possession of the Park of Neuilly, that infamous butcher ordered eighteen federal prisoners to be shot, swearing that he would do the same with every man from Paris that fell into his hands. Let him beware on his side of falling into theirs."

There was also an order from Citizen Fontaine, Director-General of Domains, directing that in reply to the tears and menaces of Thiers, the "bombarder," and to the laws passed by the *rural* Assembly, his accomplices, all the objects of art and valuable books found in his hotel should be sent to the national museums and libraries. The furniture was to be sold by auction, and the proceeds distributed amongst the families of the National Guards killed defending Paris. A similar destination was assigned to the moneys arising from the sale of the house materials. This, with numerous other decrees of a similar character, created considerable dissensions among the members of the Commune. The minority, or more respectable portion of that body, resolved at the sitting that was to take place the following day, to read a declaration intending to put an end to the misunderstandings existing; but the absence of the majority prevented the transaction of any business. In consequence, they published the following manifesto:

"By a special and precise vote the Commune of Paris abdicated its power into the hands of a dictatorship, to which it has given the name of 'Committee of Public Safety.'

"The majority, by its vote, declared itself irresponsible, and abandoned all care of our situation to the new body.

"The minority, to which we belong, asserts, on the contrary, that the Commune owes to the political and social revolutionary movement the duty of accepting every responsibility and not declining any, however worthy may be the hands to which they might be confided.

"As for ourselves, we desire, like the majority, the accomplishment of the political and social renovation; but, contrary to its idea, we claim, in the name of the suffrages we represent, the right to answer ourselves to our electors for our acts, without sheltering ourselves behind a supreme dictatorship which our mandate does not permit us to recognize.

"We shall not, therefore, again appear in the Assembly until the day when it shall constitute itself into a court of justice to try one of its members.

"Devoted to our great Communal cause, for which so many citizens die every day, we shall withdraw to our arrondissements, which have perhaps been too much neglected.

"Convinced, morever, that the question of war at this moment takes precedence of all others, the time left us from our municipal functions we shall go and pass in the midst of our brothers of the National Guard, and we shall take our part in this decisive struggle, sustained in the name of the people's rights.

"There still, we shall usefully serve our convictions; and we shall avoid creating in the Commune those dissensions which we all censure; for we are persuaded that, majority or minority, notwithstanding our political divergences, we shall pursue the same object—

"Political liberty; and emancipation of the working classes.

"*Vive la République Sociale! Vive la Commune!*"

"*Charles Beslay, Jourde, Theisz, Lefrançais, Eugene, Gérardin, Andrieux, Vermorel, Clémence, Serrailler, Longuet, Arthur Arnould, V. Clement, Avrial, Ostyn, Franckel, Pindy, Arnold, Vallés, Tridon, Varlin, G. Courbet.*"

The day following the publication of the above manifesto there was a stormy sitting of the Commune, at which sixty-six members were present, including the

A. ARNOULD
Commune of Paris
1871

greater number of the seceders, who had come to defend their conduct. Citizens Pyat, Miot, Amouroux, and Grousset strongly condemned the manifesto published, the majority blaming the minority in the harshest terms. Citizen Urbain proposed that, in consequence of the conduct pursued by the Versailles troops in shooting a vivandière, five hostages should be at once shot in Paris. After a long discussion, the following order of the day was proposed and voted: "The Commune referring to its decree of the 7th April, 1871" (concerning hostages) "calls for its immediate execution, and passes to the order of the day."

The advance of the Versailles forces on the morning of the 16th was more and more apparent, although the insurgents kept up a strong fire from Bicètre and the Haute-Bruyères, on Bagneux and Thiais. The bastions 70 to 74 still continued to harass the works of the regular engineers at Issy. The college there was almost entirely destroyed, but the fort was opening new batteries daily, and was, on the 16th, cannonading the ramparts at Grenelle and the Point-du-Jour, from three different positions. On the west the insurgents had again the rash idea of erecting a battery on the Trocadéro. During the morning it opened a fire on Mont Valérien, and, as before, provoked from that fortress such a shower of projectiles that the guns had to be abandoned, while the houses around suffered severely. Montmartre once more opened fire on Gennevilliers, this time with more success; but, as at Trocadéro, it resulted in drawing a fearful bombardment from the Versailles batteries.

In the interior of Paris, the Commune meanwhile was preparing to amuse its adherents by an entirely new spectacle.

The decree had gone forth—the column must fall. The monument erected to glorify the deeds of the Grand Army was declared incompatible with the era of peace and good-will, which was to date from the victory of Communal doctrines. As though France had not need of all her souvenirs of military glory; as though her humiliation and defeat of the preceding months had not been complete; as though the remembrance of former victories did not raise a Frenchman's hopes, proving what his country might yet be, by comparison with what she had been; as though the very Communists themselves were not proving, each moment, by arbitrary arrests, cruel executions, and fratricidal war, their utter want of anything resembling fraternity or good-will—proving, in fact, the utter falsehood of their lying doctrine—the column was condemned.

On Monday, May 15th, a large crowd assembled in the Rue de la Paix and Place de l'Opera, to see, some their hopes, others their fears, realized. Faint protests had been raised in several of the Parisian journals against this act of vandalism, but the Commune had established too firmly its iron yoke upon the neck of the people to fear much opposition in carrying out its projects. For many days men had been working hard, sawing through the base of the column, and loosening the bronze that coiled around it. The grand ceremony of its overthrow was announced for Monday. The crowd in the streets was dense; one could have walked upon the heads of the multitude, so close did they stand; the balconies of the Rue de la Paix were filled with ladies, and all the windows, mirrors, etc., of the houses, were pasted with paper to neutralize the expected concussion. A long, narrow bed of dung, sand, and branches, had been spread on the square to deaden the shock of the falling mass. Three ropes were fastened around the top of the column, just beneath the statue, which communicated with a windlass and anchor placed in the centre of the road at the entrance of the Rue Neuve des Capucines. The excitement was intense. Fears were entertained that old houses in the neighborhood might be overthrown by the shock, that balconies would fall, slates tumble from the roofs, or that the rushing mass would crash through the vaulted arch into the sewers beneath the road. At four in the afternoon a cordon of National Guards pushed back the crowd as far as the Rue Neuve St. Augustin, leaving an empty space along the Rue de la Paix. This was watered in true Parisian style, and all prepared themselves for the great event. Movements were distinguishable on the small balcony running round the top of the column; two men were busily engaged in tying something to the hand of the great Emperor. Impossible to understand their occupation, when a breath of wind unfurled the *tricolor*, many murmurs were to be heard in the crowd; people, whose hatred of the author of Sedan had extended backwards to his great ancestor, were yet loth to see their glorious flag brought low. The intended insult of the Commune was the most overwhelming tribute to the great man's memory; a thrill of joy shot through many hearts at his association with the flag. A prayer rose to heaven, "O God, let their fall be as great and as complete," and the prayer was answered in God's own time.

As the windlass was about to be turned, and when the moments of the column seemed numbered, a gust of wind overthrew the flag. Unwilling to be foiled in its malicious design, the Commune, owing to the lateness of the hour, and the time required to re-erect the flag, postponed the ceremony to the following day.

On Tuesday morning the *Officiel* announced the ceremony for that day at two P. M., and the concourse was greater than ever. The arrangements were all so bad that hopes were entertained that this second attempt would also prove a failure. The ropes attached to the column were very slender, while two beams, one on either side, were to give it the proper inclination as it fell. The column had always leant a little towards the Ministère des Cultes, and many feared it would take the wrong direction, and were uncertain where to place themselves for safety. It was expected, also, that the bronze Emperor would become detached from his base, and be shot into the air to a great distance, carrying terror and danger in his track. The members of the Commune were seated on the balcony of the Ministry of Justice, to witness the spectacle. At half-past three General Bergeret arrived on horseback with his staff, and passing through the crowd, stationed himself, with his escort, in front of the spot where the column was to fall. At a given signal several bands struck up a medley of patriotic airs, the men at the windlass began to move, and all eyes were anxiously turned towards the column's height, when one of the ropes snapped suddenly, overthrowing, in its whirl, several men at the windlass. Two or three of these were seriously hurt, and succumbed to their wounds on the following day.

The attempt had failed, and it was hoped that the Commune had abandoned its project; but no—more ropes and apparatus were sent for, the bands continued to play, horsemen galloped round the square, while the great figure still looked down on the life and turmoil below, smiling on his baffled enemies.

It was long after four o'clock before the new ropes arrived, and some time passed before they were finally hoisted to their places. They were not attached to the capstan like the others, but were held on each side of the road by sailors, fifty at each rope. As the windlass turned, these ropes were to be alternately jerked. These preparations were regarded with great contempt, and it was with difficulty that the crowd could be kept out of the way of immediate danger. Suddenly a cry of horror burst from the multitude—all hearts stood still—the great mass tottered and fell, breaking, as it reached the ground, into

ROUSSELLE
Commune of Paris
1871.

numberless fragments. A cloud of dust rose for a moment and obscured the scene. When it melted away, red banners were seen floating from the base where once had stood the mighty monument. The bands struck up the *Marseillaise,* and the crowds rushed towards the square. Many succeeded in effecting their entrance, and mounted on the ruins of the column. A company of marines, drawn up across the Rue de la Paix, soon succeeded, however, in checking the mass.

Bergeret, meanwhile, decorated with his red scarf and tassels, mounted on the pedestal, and thus addressed the crowd:

"CITIZENS:—The 26th of Floréal will be memorable in our history. Thus we triumph over military despotism—that bloody negation of the rights of man. The first Empire placed the collar of servitude about our necks—it began and ended in carnage, and left us a legacy of a second Empire, which was finally to end in the disgrace of Sedan."

The Emperor's statue was separated from the column, and had fallen a little beyond the heap. It lay a wreck, with the head severed from the body, and one arm broken.

The equestrian statue of Louis XIV once stood on the site of the column, but was overturned by the *sans-culottes.* The spot remained vacant until 1806, when Napoleon determined to consecrate it to the glories of the Austerlitz campaign. The first stone was laid on the 18th of August. The foundations were the same that served for Louis XIV's statue. The bas-reliefs were cast by Launay. The column was of Doric order, built of stone, coated with four hundred and twenty-five plaques of bronze, moulded in bas-reliefs, which wound round the shaft from pedestal to lantern. These bas-reliefs represented the history of the campaign of 1805.

We cannot do better than to quote here a well-known description of the column and the history it represents:

"The inscription was by Visconti, and ran as follows:

"'*Neapolio . Imp. Aug.*
"'*Monumentum . Belli . Germanici.*
"'*Anno . MDCCCV.*
"'*Trimestri . Spatio . Ductu . Suo . Profligati.*
"'*Ex . Ære . Capto.*
"'*Gloriæ . Exercitus . Maximi . Dicavit.*'

"The bas-reliefs were three feet eight inches high, and circled the column 22 times, making a spiral 840 feet long. They were a series of tableaux, 76 in number, having for their subjects the principal incidents of the Austerlitz campaign. These were selected by the Emperor himself, and the inscriptions which accompanied them, and were engraved on a cordon under the bas-reliefs, were written by 'le savant Denon' and the Prince of Wagram.

"Napoleon's first intention was that the statue upon the lantern of the column should be, not his own, but Charlemagne's. After Jena, Eylau, and Friedland, however, he changed his mind, or allowed his flatterers to change it for him, and a statue of himself by Chaudet was placed upon the column. This gave way, in 1844, to another by Seurre, in which the great Emperor was represented standing on a heap of cannon-balls, dressed in his '*costume de bataille.*' The hat, the epaulettes, the boots, the '*redingote à revers,*' the lorgnette, and the sword worn at Austerlitz, were copied exactly. The statue was cast in gun-metal taken from the enemy, 'under the Empire, let it be well understood,' adds the writer of the year, 'for if we make war now-a-days we do not take cannon.' The present figure succeeded M. Seurre's, and is one of Napoleon III's tributes to the memory of his uncle.

"The bas-reliefs begin with the breaking up of the Camp de Boulogne. The first represents the troops in review, and the Havre flotilla rounding Cape d'Alpreck. The commentator construes the appearance of the ships while Napoleon was inspecting his army into a desire on the part of Ocean to pay also its tribute to the Emperor. Then we have the departure of the various corps from Boulogne, Brest, Utrecht, and Hanover on the great converging march, which, until last year, was perhaps the finest campaign opening ever planned. The troops are represented taking farewell of the sailors who were to have ferried them over to a battle of Dorking; we see them on the march, crossing rivers, entering towns, etc., and in their various arms of artillery, cavalry, and infantry. In the sixth tableaux the Emperor appears before his servile Senators at Paris, and informs them that the war against the third coalition has begun. The will of the eternal enemies of Europe is accomplished (said the Emperor on that occasion), the peace I hoped would continue is broken; blood will flow, but the French name will win a new lustre. A few words like these were quite enough to cover the demand for 80,000 men of the next year's conscription. The tableaux continue; the soldiers are still on their road, crossing the Rhine at Mayence, Mannheim, Spires, Dourlach, Strasburg—no less than five different places. Then comes the Emperor himself, riding over the bridge of Kehl, with his headquarter staff, on the 1st of October, exactly one month after the breaking up of the camp. The submissive Electors of Baden and Würtemberg, who were rewarded with crowns after Austerlitz, receive their benefactor; and in the 15th tableau the first blow is struck at Donowerth by the 4th corps, thirty-six days from Boulogne. Then we have Murat clearing the road to Augsburg and Ulm by the combat at Wertingen, and the passage of the Danube at Neuburg by the 2d and 3d corps. The plot thickens, Augsburg is entered, and the Emperor harangues the troops, 'after the manner of the Roman Emperors,' upon the position of the enemy, and the imminence of a great battle. The 24th tableau depicts Soult's success at Menningen; a spirited relief and a long inscription told how Ney forced the bridge of Elchingen, which gave him his title of Duc; the enemy are driven back on their intrenchments before Ulm, and the Emperor arrives at headquarters on the 15th of October. Two days afterwards (31st tableau) Berthier, surrounded by his staff, receives General Mack's capitulation. The panorama continues; the garrison of Ulm file out and lay down their arms; the Emperor receives General Mack, in tableau 33, and then came what the legend calls 'a superb and ingenious allegory, dedicated to the glory of the Emperor Napoleon.' The allegory is as simple as it is superb, for it is nothing more nor less than Victory writing on a shield the words, 'Capitulation d'Ulm.' This is, or was, succeeded by the entries into Munich and Brannan, the key of Austria, and by passages of the Inn and Traun; a little further on the 76th regiment regain the colors lost in a former campaign, and now found in the captured arsenal of Innspruck. A few more scenes, among which is the desperate fight at Krems, near Durnstein (where Frenchmen met Russians in a narrow defile and were so crowded together that they could not use their muskets and fought with unfixed bayonets), brought the spectator to the quarters at Schönbrunn, the entry into Vienna, and the surrender of the keys of the capital. A deputation from Paris arrive with felicitations, and then the Emperor is seen quitting Vienna with many of his Generals for Braun. The great blow is impending; a reconnaissance is pushed as far as Olmutz; Presburg is entered; a strong position is taken up, and the heights of Sauton are occupied by the artillery. On the night of the 1st of

December the Emperor, wrapped in his cloak, visits the advanced posts; it is the anniversary of his coronation, and the soldiers light pine torches till the whole camp is illuminated.

"High up the column began the series of bas-reliefs in which its climbing glories culminated. The sun of Austerlitz rises, and the Emperor was to be seen seated on horseback giving orders to the Marshals and Generals. A furious cavalry charge breaks a column of the enemy's infantry, captive Generals surrender their swords and Oudinot's footguards drive a body of Russians into the icy lake of Augerd. In the next scene the battle is won, the Emperor of Austria has craved an interview, and is asking his *bon frère* to grant an armistice. Further on still French soldiers carry off cannon and other arms from the Vienna Arsenal. Talleyrand arrives at Presburg to negotiate the treaty, which is signed by Napoleon the day after Christmas-day. St. Mark's Lion and some richly-decorated gondolas denote the cession of the Venetian States, the Electors of Bavaria and Würtemberg receive their Crowns, the Imperial Guard enter France bearing captured standards, the Emperor returns to Paris, and passes under the Arc de Triomphe, a car laden with spoils of war follows, and, last of all, hundred-voiced Fame proclaims the high deeds of the campaign of 1805, while old Seine, reclining on his flood, listens to the story of so many glorious battles."

At the same time the insurgents were committing the insensate and odious crime of overthrowing the Vendôme Column, another public fête was taking place in Versailles similar to the preceding one. The cannon captured at Vânves were being presented to the National Assembly. The President, M. Grévy, harangued the soldiers. Marshal de MacMahon complimented the engineers, and issued the following order of the day in regard to the Vendôme Column:

"SOLDIERS:—The Vendôme Column has just fallen; the foreigner had respected it. Persons who call themselves Frenchmen have dared to throw down before the eyes of the Germans, who are watching us, that testimony of the victories of our fathers over combined Europe.

"Did they hope, the miserable authors of the outrage on the nation's glory, to efface the memory of the military virtues of which that monument was the glorious symbol?

"Soldiers! if the recollections which the Column brought to mind are no longer engraven on bronze, they will nevertheless remain living in your hearts; and taking our inspiration from them, we shall know how to give to France a fresh pledge of bravery, devotedness, and patriotism.

"MARSHAL DE MACMAHON,
"Duke de Magenta."

M. Thiers was exceedingly moved when he heard of the fall of the Column, and exclaimed in the Assembly, "*Now I am ashamed of being a Frenchman!*" but his cry of grief was soon drowned in a concert of patriotic outcries; and on the 22d of May the National Assembly, by a unanimous vote, decreed the following law:

"The Column of Place Vendôme shall be rebuilt at the expense of the State, and surmounted by a statue of France."

The following day, and as if to punish Paris for its crime, a horrible explosion was heard about six o'clock in the evening, which struck terror and dismay into the hearts of the inhabitants. Several hundreds of women and children were victims to this terrible calamity.

The cartridge factory, situated between the Champs-de-Mars and the Avenue Rapp, blew up. The concussion was felt over nearly the whole of the city, but in the immediate vicinity the effect was lamentable in the extreme. As soon as the first dreadful detonation had been heard, it was followed in the space of a few seconds by thousands of smaller ones in every direction, arising from the combustion of cartridges—many millions of which were stored on the premises—and of boxes of grape-shot, which burst in the air, and descended in a perfect storm of blackened lead. An immense column of smoke rose over the spot in majestic form, and floated slowly away towards the southwest. Its disappearance was, unfortunately, followed by another mass, which rose more rapidly, and which, by its crimson reflections, showed that a conflagration had arisen. Such was in fact the case, as the wooden huts in the Champs-de-Mars were burning fiercely.

The agitation in the quarter was indescribable—men, women, and children rushing about in the wildest disorder in search of parents or relatives, absent at the moment from their homes. Their terror was increased by the fact that at first no one knew what had occurred, every one believing that a bombshell had fallen in his own house. Nor was the alarm by any means allayed, when the real nature of the accident became known, as the rumor spread rapidly that all danger was not over, and fears were entertained that a store of shells near the building destroyed might also blow up. In fact the insurgents, who hastened to the spot as soon as possible to maintain order, told all the inhabitants to retire to their own houses, and even recommended them to seek temporary shelter in their cellars. Happily, that second horror was spared the district; and after a short time the people began to reappear, and turned their attention to assisting the wounded, large numbers of whom might be seen being transported through the streets, many bleeding profusely, principally from cuts received by fragments of glass, almost every window within a considerable radius having been demolished. In many houses the sashes, frames, and doors were blown out, and iron-shutters twisted into the strangest forms. In some places the morsels of glass were lying on the pavement to the depth of more than an inch.

The hospital of Gros-Caillou was seriously injured on its roof, through which a large shot had fallen. The patients rushed out in the greatest alarm, those able to walk hurrying off with the first garments they could lay hold of—many of them with only a dressing-gown on, and with bare feet. They were all sent to the Hotel-des-Invalides, as well as their companions, who had to be removed in vehicles.

Ordinarily about 800 women were employed at the establishment; but fortunately they had left at five instead of seven o'clock, their usual hour.

The population at first believed that the disaster was the work of an incendiary, and the report spread that it had been caused by an agent of the Versailles Government. Numerous persons were arrested as being implicated in the matter. The general idea, however, prevailed that it was either caused by an accident or the fall of a shell. The insurgents wished to convey the idea that it was caused by the Government; and the official organ of the Commune published the following note, throwing on the authorities of Versailles the odium of this terrible explosion:

"PARIS, 27 Floreal, an. 79.

"The Government of Versailles has just disgraced itself with a fresh crime, the most frightful and the most dastardly of all.

"Its agents set fire to the cartridge manufactory on the Avenue Rapp, and produced a frightful catastrophe.

"The number of victims is estimated at more than a hundred. Women were blown to pieces as well as a child at the breast.

"Four of the criminals are in custody."

The official journal also says: "Certain officers of the staff of the National Guards who failed in their service in order to indulge in an orgie at Peter's Restaurant with women of light character, were arrested yesterday by order of the Committee of Public Safety. They have been sent to Fort Bicêtre with shovels and pickaxes for service in the trenches, and the women sent to *St. Lazare,* to make earth-bags."

The *Commune,* one of the organs of the insurgents, had been for some days sneering at the action of the authorities at the Hotel de Ville, becoming more and more indignant at their decrees. It said, on the morning of the 18th:

"Have they lost their heads at the Hotel de Ville? Are they going to play at parliamentarism? What! the intelligent minority is withdrawing, not to Mount Aventine, but under the tent of inaction. It is abandoning the citadel to the ignorant, material, and grotesque element, to the brawlers of the clubs, the mountebanks of 1793, the popes and canons of fusionism, to the believers in Robespierre and the Père Toureuil, to ghosts and reverends, and to the carnival of the revolution! What remains of the Commune? The upright Gambon and the stoical Delescluze; with Diogènes-Pyat seeking in vain at noon with his lantern for an honest man, and in the evening, having become a rag-gatherer, turning over the heaps of rubbish to find some useful scraps. To-morrow he will blow out his candle, convinced of the perfect uselessness of his search. What so unusual has then taken place? The pedants, hair-brained men, and ambitious nullities, without science or knowledge, are in a majority. And that result is in no way extraordinary. Considering the state of our early instruction, education, and prejudices, and our infatuation especially, for every one intelligent man to be found, there are a hundred idiots."

The devout and religious portion of Paris attributed the fearful explosion on the Avenue Rapp to a judgment on the insurgents for their sacrilegious violation of the Church of Notre-Dame des Victoires. This church, situated in the Place des Petits Pères, was founded in 1629 by Louis XIII. It was used during the Revolution of 1789 as an exchange, and was, on the 17th of May, about five o'clock, or one hour before the explosion, entered by a *Commissaire de Police* by the name of Le Moussu, at the head of the 159th battalion of National Guards (insurgents), belonging to the Belleville Quarter. The priests were about finishing the service of the "*Mois de Marie*" when they were expelled in the most brutal manner, and with much difficulty, the worshippers protesting in the loudest manner; the women fled to the Chapel of the Virgin. The Abbé Delacroix saved the consecrated articles, which he conveyed to the Church of St. Roch. The Citizen Le Moussu, after having arrested two vicars of the parish, the Abbés du Courroy and Amodru, and two members of the Council, gave the order to sack the church. A rage truly infernal was exhibited in this Communal orgie. The tabernacles were torn up, the altars demolished, the confessionals overturned, the marble slabs of the temple broken. The body of Saint Aurelia, which reposed under the altar of the Virgin, and that of the venerable Des Genettes, former curate of the parish, and founder of the Archi-Confrerie, buried at the foot of the same altar, were profaned. The vaults enclosing the dried remains of the Augustines, who died in the old convent, were violated.

BILLIORAY
Commune of Paris
1871

At the same time the contribution boxes were robbed, the church was despoiled of all its ornaments, without exception, and the fury of the miserable creatures only ended when the sanctuary presented an aspect of complete ruin.

Then commenced an orgie not less revolting than the other. The money found in the church was divided between these pillaging heroes, and served to pay the expense of a bacchanalian feast, at which the *cantinières* and other women of doubtful habits took part. Then returning to the revolutionary habits of '93, they clothed themselves in the sacred vestments of the church, and went through the religious ceremonies, such as administering the sacrament, etc. This saturnalia only ended when, overpowered with drunkenness and fatigue, they fell asleep on the floor of the sacred edifice.

The next day they made an exhibition of the remains found in the vaults, showing from a distance, to the people in the Place, a wax head of St. Aurelia, covered with hair, which they pretended was the head of a young girl lately murdered by the priests, and, to complete the hideous spectacle, they administered the communion to one another, using the bread not consecrated found in the sacristy, and scattering the rest to the winds.

An arrangement had been entered into between the Government at Versailles and four members of the Commune, viz., Billioray, Cerisier, Mortier, and Pilotell, to open the gate at the Point-du-Jour, for which service they secured 25,000 francs each. These honest Communists were to appear at the gate at half-past one o'clock at night, disguised as National Guards; but, in the meantime, Cerisier took fright and refused to act, and when the troops appeared, they were forced to beat a precipitate retreat under a murderous fire from mitrailleuses.

The cannonading raged along the whole line on the evening of the 18th with a violence hitherto unequalled since the commencement of the siege. The fusillade was also continuous in the Bois de Boulogne, while in the south the greatest alarm prevailed during the whole day. Two batteries were unmasked on the north front of the fort of Vânves, one to take the village of Montrouge obliquely, the other to attack the gate of the ramparts leading to Issy. The heavy cannonade was supposed to be the prelude to an assault, and several battalions were under arms in the Avenue d'Orleans, to be sent to reinforce any point on which the attack might be made. No attempt was however made, and the terrible cannonade of the whole day and night left both parties in the same positions.

The insurgents attempted a sortie during the day, but were repulsed with great loss. Various battalions returned to Paris apparently much dispirited. They attacked the regulars with a force 6,000 strong, and at first were successful; but reinforcements coming up, they were attacked in turn, and defeated with frightful slaughter.

The insurgents continued to carry out the conscription with increased vigor, death being threatened to those who refused to serve.

The decrees of the Commune became more and more severe as their hour approached. The Committee declared its intention to blow up Paris sooner than capitulate. A decree arrested all prostitutes and drunkards; another suppressed nine more journals; another, from the Central Committee, stated that all inhabitants of Paris must return to their homes within forty-eight hours, after that time the claims in the Rentes standing in their names in the state funds would be destroyed.

Cluseret was tried by the Commune and set at liberty on the 20th. The command of the important post at Montmartre was also given him.

The court-martial presided over by Colonel Gois also

tried the Lieutenant-Colonel, Daviot, and Commandant Vanostat of the 115th battalion of the National Guard, for having, without any superior orders, abandoned their posts at the Convent of Issy, thereby allowing the position to be occupied by the enemy. It appeared that the battalion was seized with a panic and took to flight towards Paris; it had lost twenty-six men the night before in an attack badly conducted, and had become sadly disorganized. The two prisoners attempted to stop the men, but without effect; and, finding that they could not induce them to return, had at last yielded to the current, and proceeded themselves towards the gates of the city. Several witnesses deposed to the general good conduct and courage of the prisoners, but the court condemned Daviot to fifteen years, and Vanostat to ten years imprisonment; further, it ordered that the 115th battalion be struck off the list, and the men drafted into other bodies of the same force.

A proclamation was published announcing that the Central Committee had, on the proposition of the Committee of Public Safety, and with the approval of the Commune, undertaken the Administration of War since the 19th.

M. Mortier, a member of the Commune, proposed the abolition of religious worship in all churches, and expressed the wish that they might be only opened for lecturing on Atheism and annihilating old prejudices.

Reports were spread throughout the city on the evening of the 20th that Fort Montrouge had been evacuated. The Central Committee ordered larger numbers of troops and quantities of *matériel* to be dispatched to the threatened points. Several members of the Commune had also left for the advanced posts among the troops. There was something in the air which presaged immediate danger.

While the Commune of Paris was excited by a foreboding of evil, Versailles was excited by great good news. On the evening of the 20th M. Thiers issued a circular, dated noon of the same day, in which he said:

"Several prefects have demanded that news should be published; the following answer has been sent them:—Those persons who are uneasy are greatly mistaken. Our troops are working at the approaches, and at the moment of writing the breaching batteries continue their fire upon the walls. Never have we been so near the end. The members of the Commune are busy making their escape. Henri Rochefort has been arrested at Meaux!"

Rochefort arrested! the demagogue, the falsifier, and coward arrested with the lie in his mouth! arrested escaping from Paris on the *20th of May!* It seems some few days before a letter, written by him to his mistress in Arcachon, had fallen into the hands of the Prefect of Bordeaux, who sent it to M. Thiers. In this letter, he said, "*Leave at once for Brussels, and engage the same apartment as before; I will meet you there on the 20th.*" The *Gaulois* of Versailles published this letter, which Rochefort repudiated in the most indignant manner; and in his journal, the *Mot d'Ordre*, of date the 20th of May, printed on the 19th, the last number published, he said: "I would not have condescended to notice this contemptible invention, but several journals have reproduced it. I have only at Arcachon my sister, my daughter, and little boy, who came to see me when I was sick. I wrote them some days since, not to invite them to retain an apartment at Brussels, but to *join me at Paris*, where I have but little fear of the entry of the Versaillese. The only dread the publication of this note gave me was that my letter had fallen into the hands of the Prefect of Bordeaux, because it contained a check addressed to my family to pay their expenses from Arcachon to Paris; and

Hy ROCHEFORT
Rr of Mot d'Ordre.

1871.

it is possible that, faithful to the traditions of the Empire, that functionary has at the same time kept my letter and pocketed my money."

As soon as the Minister of the Interior had read Rochefort's denial in the *Mot d'Ordre,* he supposed with reason that the ex-president of barricades would leave for Brussels the same day. The Minister immediately sent telegraphic despatches to all the departments, ordering the surveillance to be doubled. At two o'clock in the morning he received a despatch from Meaux stating that Rochefort had been arrested in the act of getting into the railroad train. He had left Paris in a carriage accompanied by his secretary, Mouriot, and was travelling under the name of Le Comte de Saint Luce, a respectable souvenir of his true name—Comte Henri de Rochefort Luçay.

Previous to Rochefort's departure from Paris, and to hide his flight, which must have been discovered the following day if his journal ceased to appear without notice, the following letter was sent to the editor of the *Politique :*

"MONSIEUR LE REDACTEUR:—I would be much obliged if you would announce to your readers that in presence of the situation of the press the *Mot d'Ordre* believes it in keeping with its dignity to cease to appear." The *dignity* of a "Lanterne."

Rochefort was brought into Versailles in an omnibus drawn by two horses, escorted by a squadron of gendarmes and Chasseurs d'Afrique. He was accompanied by his secretary, Mouriot, and four policemen in plain clothes. He had had his moustache cut off before leaving Paris.

When the cortège entered the Rue Reservoirs every one ran into the street, and shouts of execration were raised on every side. Citizens of all classes joined in the demonstration. "*A bas l'assassin; à pied le brigand; à mort!*" The people were indignant that he was riding in an omnibus, and it was with difficulty the cavalry prevented them from dragging him out and inflicting summary execution. He was, however, safely lodged in jail, and but for the precaution taken by the Government, the world would have been spared the infliction of his name having been brought again before it. The coward had continually poured oil on the smouldering mass, and when it flamed he fled.

Madame Tussaud, hearing of his arrest, sent an agent immediately to Versailles, and made a very liberal offer to the Government for his clothes.

CHAPTER IX.

Porte St. Cloud—Communication of M. Ducatel—Entrance of the troops into Paris—Fourth Army Corps—Army of Reserve—General Ladmirault at the gates of Passy and Auteuil—Entrance of General de Cissy—Arrest of Assi—Entrance of the troops long unknown in the city—Plan of attack—March of the different corps—Occupation of the Park Monceaux—Confusion at the Hotel de Ville—Erection of barricades—Violent proclamations—Melancholy appearance of the city—Deputations to the Hotel de Ville—Orders given by Delescluze—Evacuation of the Palais de l'Industrie and Ministry of the Interior—Fighting in the Faubourg St. Honoré—At the Rue d'Anjou—In the Boulevard Haussman—Investment of Montmartre—Left bank of the Seine—Barricades constructed—Manifestation in favor of the Government.

ON Sunday the 21st of May, the troops between the gates of St. Cloud and Auteuil were actively engaged at the works of approach, endeavoring to render a breach practicable for an assault. The fire from the ramparts had been gradually decreasing, and finally ceased entirely. The commandant, Trèves, who was overseeing the work in the trenches at St. Cloud, determined to reconnoitre to discover the cause of this silence. He advanced to the drawbridge, the chain of which had been broken a few days before by a cannon-ball, when a civilian appeared at the bastion on the left, and raised a white flag, making violent gesticulations, and shouting something which, owing to the cannonade of Montretout and Breteuil, it was difficult to understand, but which seemed to be "Come, there is nobody." Commandant Trèves immediately jumped into the trench, and, followed by Sergeant Constant of the 3d battalion, 91st regiment, ran toward the bastion, crossed the drawbridge, of which only a small beam remained, and joined his interlocutor, who said: "My name is Ducatel—a former officer of the infantry of the Marine. You can have confidence in me. Paris is yours, if you wish to take it. Bring in your troops immediately, as you see everything is abandoned." In fact, no troops were visible in any direction, and the bastions on the right and left were entirely evacuated.

M. Ducatel was invited to leave Paris by the commandant, to render an account of the situation to the General-in-Chief. The following despatch was sent immediately to the Generals Douay and Vergé at Villeneuve l'Etang, and Sèvres, dated from the trench:

"I have just entered Paris with M. Ducatel by the Porte St. Cloud. Everything is abandoned. I have ordered the torpedo wires to be cut."

Half an hour afterwards the firing had ceased along the entire line. Commandant Trèves, accompanied by M. Ducatel and Captain Garnier, with a body of engineers, returned to Paris. The commanders of the 37th and 91st battalions followed with their troops to secure the position against an offensive return of the insurgents. It was then half-past four in the afternoon.

Immediately after the reception of the above despatch, General Douay, commanding the Fourth Army Corps, advanced his troops, and occupied strongly the Porte St. Cloud and the Rue du Rempart. He was followed by General Vinoy, commanding the reserve, who entered the same gate, and took possession of the important position of Trocadéro.

In the meantime, General Ladmirault (First Army Corps), entering by the gates of Passy and Auteuil, continued along the ramparts, and surprised the insurgents at the Porte de la Muette, where he took five or six hun-

ASSI
Commune of Paris
1871

dred prisoners. Advancing along the Avenue de la Grande Armée, he took possession of the barricades, driving the insurgents before him, and thus became master of the Arc de Triomphe, where the tricolor was first displayed inside the walls.

Finally, General de Cissey, commanding the Third Army Corps, entered during the night by the gates of Vaugirard and Montrouge, and thus the whole line of ramparts, from Vaugirard to the Porte Dauphine, was in the power of the Versaillese. General de Cissey proceeded with his troops in the direction of the Champs de Mars, where an energetic resistance was expected; but the whole movement had been so sudden that time was wanted to organize the defence. The Ecole-Militaire was taken possession of without opposition, the staff of the National Guard having quitted the building, in a precipitate if not undignified manner.

In the meantime, an important arrest had taken place. Towards midnight Citizen Assi made his appearance in the neighborhood of the Point-du-Jour. His carriage was escorted by half a dozen cavaliers with red vests and caps.

A sentinel called:

"Who goes there?"

"Staff officer," replied Assi.

"Advance in order."

Assi leaned forward to reply, when seeing the uniform of the sentinel, he threw himself back in the carriage, exclaiming:

"The line! We are lost!"

His escort was already secured, and a quarter of an hour later, Citizen Assi was rolling along the road to Versailles.

Notwithstanding the ringing of the tocsin, and the beating of the *générale* in the occupied quarters, the entrance of the troops was not known throughout Paris until late on Monday. During the previous evening an immense crowd promenaded the boulevards, and filled the cafés until long after midnight. Delescluze himself, to whom the news was brought at four in the morning, refused to credit it, and even when convinced of the truth of the statement, issued the following proclamation:

"The observatory of the Arc de Triomphe denies the entrance of the Versaillese; at least, nothing has been seen which resembles it.

"The Commandant Renard, of that section, has just left my cabinet, and he affirms that there has only been a panic, and that the gate of Auteuil has not been forced; that if the Versaillese presented themselves, they were repulsed.

"I have sent eleven battalions of reinforcements by as many officers of the staff, who will not leave them until they have conducted them to the posts they are to occupy.

"DELESCLUZE."

At about four o'clock Monday morning the vast movement for the occupation of Paris really began. This great and difficult strategic combination, conducted with as much energy as ability, and with unhesitating unity of action, was but the continuation of the plan followed from the beginning of this horrible civil war. Outside, the insurgents, from Asnières to Montrouge, had been made to recede step by step toward the ramparts—their principal positions had been successively taken from them. The fortifications once passed, the same operation was continued on a concentric line, almost parallel with the outer line of investment.

The troops marched always in advance, enclosing the Communists in an immense semicircle, which gradually narrowed, until the insurgents were thrown back on their last places of refuge—on the left bank towards the Gobelins and the Salpêtrière, and on the right toward the heights of Menilmontant, of Charonne, and the upper end of the Faubourg St. Antoine.

This attack, directed and constantly overseen by Marshal de MacMahon, whose headquarters were established first at Trocadéro, and afterwards at the Ministry of Foreign Affairs, enclosed the city from the southwest to the northwest in advancing to the northeast and southeast.

But while continuing the exterior movement, the operation within the city produced new and serious obstacles owing to the multiplicity of the transversal streets, which at one time discovered the march of the army to the insurgents, and at another suddenly separated the different corps, and by interrupting their communications, rendered it difficult for them to make their attacks in concert.

The army of France numbered from 90,000 to 100,000 men, commanded in chief under the orders of Marshal de MacMahon, by Generals Ladmirault, Douay, De Cissey, De Clinchant, Du Barail, and by General Vinoy at the head of the army of reserve. General de Cissey specially conducted the operations on the left bank, where he was seconded by General du Barail, who took with his cavalry the forts of Montrouge, Bicêtre, and Ivry.

The movements on the right bank were developed under the directions of Generals Ladmirault, Clinchant, Vinoy, and Douay, the first two acting at the beginning of the attack in the northern quarters (Batignolles and Montmartre), while the other two occupied the Champs Elyseés and its neighborhood. According to the necessities of the action, they supported each other reciprocally.

This investment, by successive zones, was executed with so much precision, that as the army advanced from one zone to attack another, the one just quitted was cleansed of every element of insurrection. The inhabitants could circulate freely without meeting a single Federal uniform, and without incurring any danger but from spent projectiles, which sometimes passed beyond the line of battle. During the seven days which the taking of Paris occupied—from Sunday the 21st, to Sunday the 28th—there was not a single offensive return or any attack made in the rear of the assailants by the National Guards. Nothing more clearly proves the excellence of the plan.

In the beginning of the day, Generals Ladmirault and Clinchant solidly established the base of their operations by the occupation of Passy and La Muette. General Ladmirault then advanced towards the Arc de Triomphe, as already described, and carrying the barricade in front of the monument, planted the tricolor on its summit. From that moment bombs, directed by the insurgents from Montmartre, endeavored vainly to overthrow the flag.

Meanwhile the 5th corps, under General Clinchant, entering by the gates of Auteuil and Maillot, continued along the ramparts as far as the Place Pereire, taking possession of the Ternes and the gate of Asnières, and then descended the Faubourg St. Honoré.

General Montaudon, commanding the third division of the 1st corps, followed this movement outside the walls, taking Neuilly, Levallois, Perret, and Clichy, and carrying the gate of St. Ouen, where he took 105 cannon from the insurgents.

The Arc de Triomphe being taken, the troops descended simultaneously to the Place de la Concorde, and towards the New Opera, by the Avenue Friedland and the Boulevard Haussmann.

At Neuilly, Levallois, the Ternes, and Courcelles, the National Guards were very much surprised to find that, though they had no serious combats the night before, many of their men were wounded by balls coming from the Bois de Boulogne, the gate of Neuilly and its neighborhood. These balls were fired by sharpshooters, who had spread along the ramparts and taken possession of the gates abandoned by the Federals.

The evacuation was immediately decided, and all the battalions hastened to enter Paris by the gates of Bineau, Asnières, and Clichy. They were closely followed by the regular troops along the Boulevards Neuilly and Malesherbes, and were obliged to turn many times during the retreat and discharge their pieces to check the heat of the pursuit.

The ardor of the Versaillese, however, was not to be restrained; balls whistled in every direction, losing themselves at the extremities of the great avenues in the very heart of Paris. Men and women ran about distractedly, and in a few moments the streets were deserted by all but the combatants.

The regular troops advanced thus as far as the Park Monceau, of which they took definitive possession, while the retreat of the Federals became more and more accelerated.

On his side, General Vinoy held the heights of Trocadéro, and the troops of General de Cissey extended from the dépôt of Montparnasse to Grenelle, occupying the Champs de Mars, the Ecole Militaire, and the Invalides.

Meanwhile, at the Hotel de Ville, orders had been issued by the Committee of Public Safety, which was sitting there *en permanence*, to erect barricades in every direction, and the injunction was most faithfully and extensively executed. Along the Boulevards from the Madeleine to the Chateau-d'Eau barricades cropped up on every side, and every passer-by was forced to give his aid and place a stone; indeed, as the troops advanced and the danger became more imminent, many unfortunate individuals were pressed into the service, and obliged to work for several hours, finally to have a rifle forced into their hands, with orders to defend the barricade which they had only helped to erect *à contre-cœur.* Women and children worked just as actively as the National Guards themselves, and formidable barriers were soon to be seen at the Rue de la Chausée-d'Antin, the Rue Richelieu, the Rue Drouot, and the Porte St. Martin. The neighborhood of the Hotel de Ville was defended by immense constructions, and the Rues St. Denis, St. Martin, and many of the side-streets were strongly fortified. The same was the case in the neighborhood of Montmartre, and on the left bank of the river in the Faubourg St. Germain, Rues du Bac and des Saints-Pères, along the quays, and at the entrances of the different bridges.

The members of the Commune withdrew to their several arrondissements to organize the defence and to encourage their men to a desperate resistance. The unexpected and easy entrance effected by the Versaillese had at first greatly demoralized the Federal troops. The old cry, "*Nous sommes trahis!*" was raised, and numberless stories were told of gates which had been opened by traitors within the walls.

A few hours, however, gave the Communists time to recover themselves, and by nightfall a complete change had come over the spirit of the scene. The large number of extempore barricades which had at first sprung up too quickly to be worth much, had been made strong enough to be really formidable, and the men in charge of them seemed not only pretty cool, but even in good spirits, with little about them of the air of beaten troops whose last hope has gone.

When the members of the Commune departed for the various arrondissements, Delescluze, the Delegate of War, the Military Commission, and the Committee of Public Safety, remained at the Hotel de Ville. As to the Central Committee, no one could say what had become of the persons composing it, and at the final struggle they had entirely disappeared. The Committee of Public Safety chiefly employed its time in issuing a variety of proclamations. The following appeal was made to the National Guards:

"PARIS, May 22, 1871.

"Rise up, patriotic citizens!

"To the barricades! The enemy is within our walls! No hesitation!

"Forward, for the Republic, the Commune, and Liberty!

"To arms!

"*Ant. Arnaud, Billioray, Eudes, Gambon, Ranvier—Committee of Public Safety.*"

To the assailants, the following was addressed:

"PARIS, May 22.

"*Soldiers of the Army of Versailles:*

"The people of Paris can never believe that you will direct your arms against them, when their breasts touch yours. On the contrary, your arms will shrink from such an act, which would be positive fratricide.

"Like us, you are proletaires; and like us, you have an interest in not allowing to the conspiring monarchists the right to drink your blood as they profit by the sweat of your brow.

"The course which you followed on the 18th of March you will repeat once more, and the people will not have the affliction of fighting against men whom they regard as brothers, and whom they would be only too delighted to behold seated with themselves at the civic banquet of Liberty and Equality.

"Come to us, therefore, brothers! Come to us! Our embrace is ready for you!

"*Ant. Arnaud, Billioray, Eudes, Gambon, Ranvier—Committee of Public Safety.*"

To the inhabitants of Paris it issued the following:

"PARIS, May 22.

"The Porte de Saint Cloud, attacked from four sides at the same time, by the fire of Mont Valérien, the Butte-Mortemart, Les Moulineaux and the fort of Issy, has been forced by the Versailles troops, who have now spread themselves over a portion of the territory of Paris.

"That misadventure, far from depressing us, ought to be an energetic stimulant. The people that dethrones kings and destroys Bastilles—the people of '89 and '93—cannot lose in a single day the benefit arising from the emancipation of March 18th.

"*To arms, then!* Let Paris be covered with barricades, and from behind those defences let it shout to the assailants its war-cry, its defiance, and its promise of victory, for Paris with barricades is impregnable! Let all the streets be torn up, and the paving-stones be carried to the balconies of the houses.

"Let the city do its duty! The Commune and the Committee of Public Safety will do the same!

"*Ant. Arnaud, Billioray, Eudes, Gambon, Ranvier—Committee of Public Safety.*"

In the meantime, Cluseret, who had been acquitted at the sitting of the Commune and released from prison the previous day, was nominated commander of the forces at Montmartre, and the command at Belleville and La Villette was given to Dombrowski.

While these preliminaries of the great struggle were taking place, the appearance of Paris was most melancholy. Everywhere the shops were closed, the cafés and restaurants shut, and in many cases the persiennes drawn to, as though all inhabitants had departed. Later, shots having been fired at the National Guards from a house on the Boulevard Rochechouart, strict orders were given for

JULES VALLÈS
Commune of Paris
1871.

all window shutters to be opened, and, in many cases, the agents of the Commune had the doors of apartments forced and the shutters thrown back. No vehicles were to be seen, with the exception of ammunition and ambulance wagons, which clattered along making fearful echoes in the vacant streets, and sending a thrill through the terrified hearts of the inhabitants. Few persons ventured out, and wherever the circulation existed, the passers-by were forced by the National Guards to contribute to the construction of the barricades. It has already been stated that in this work the energy of the women exceeded that of the men. The Hotel de Ville was continually invaded by deputations of these *citoyennes exaltées,* who wished to take their part in the defence.

At one time thirty women came with a demand for a mitrailleuse to arm the barricade in the Place du Palais-Royal. They all wore a band of crape round the left arm; each one had lost a husband, a lover, a son, or a brother, whom she had sworn to avenge. Horses being at this time scarce in the service of the Commune, they harnessed themselves to the enormous machine, and dragged it off, fastening their skirts round their waists lest they should prove an impediment to their march. Others followed, bearing the caissons filled with munitions. The last carried the flag.

Citizen Vallès, a delegate of the Commune, delivered to them the mitrailleuse and the flag, together with an order written and signed by Delescluze, commissioning the above mentioned *citoyennes* to aid in the defence of Paris. One of them received the embrace of Citizen Vallès in the name of all, and they then departed, bearing with them the engine of destruction.

They were immediately followed by another deputation of women, mistresses of the schools of primary instruction established by the Commune in place of the religious houses in which children were formerly educated. These women offered to employ the children under their charge in making linen bags necessary for the barricades, that they also might have their glorious part in the defence of Paris.

A commission was signed authorizing the citizens to transform their schools into workshops. The little girls, assimilated with the Federal soldiers, were to receive rations of food and wine. The young boys were ordered to aid in the erection of the barricades.

Towards evening, an order was placarded giving the National Guards full permission to enter private apartments, and take possession of any objects likely to aid in the defence. This authorization caused great alarm to the wealthy inhabitants, as it opened the door to every kind of pillage; but the rapid advance of the Versailles troops rendered it, fortunately, of little avail.

The following is one of many orders of the same purport given by Delescluze:

" *Commune of Paris:*

"The Citizen Jacquet is authorized to requisition all inhabitants, and all objects necessary to him, in the construction of the barricades in the Rue du Chateau-d'Eau and of the Rue Alhouy.

"Wine and whiskey alone are and remain excepted.

"All citizens, men or women, who refuse their aid, shall be immediately shot.

"The citizen chiefs commanding the barricades are charged to assure the security of the different quarters.

"Domiciliary visits are to be made to suspected houses, and, during the perquisition, all doors and windows must be opened.

"All window-shutters must be open; all windows closed.

"The gratings of the cellars must be guarded with particular care.

"No lights are to be allowed in any quarter attacked.

"Suspected houses are to be set on fire at the first signal.

"DELESCLUZE,
"Chief of the Legion of the X Arrondissement.
"BRUNEL."

While the Commune was thus devoting all its energies in exciting the people to a strenuous resistance, the Versailles troops were steadily advancing. Batteries were established at the Arc de Triomphe, which fired on the Champs Elysées, Place de la Concorde, and Tuileries Gardens. Other batteries, placed on the terrace of the Tuileries by the insurgents, replied from time to time to this fire.

The Palace of Industry, becoming untenable, was abandoned to the Government troops.

While the soldiers of General Douay were thus keeping the insurgents at the Place de la Concorde and the Tuileries in check, a portion of the troops under General Clinchant, advancing down the Faubourg St. Honoré, found the Ministry of the Interior, Place Beauveau, and the Palace of the Elysée abandoned by the Federals. These last had retreated at five in the morning to the Mairie of the Arrondissement Rue d'Anjou. One man, left on guard at the corner of the Rue Duras, hastened at the sound of the approaching chassepots to implore a civilian's dress from the inhabitants, which was accorded him from pity.

The troops were received with loud acclamations and every manifestation of joy, by the people whom they had delivered from the hated rule of the Commune. The red flag which dishonored the Ministry was torn away by a boy, and presented to a *lignard* amidst the applause of the crowd.

The fighting in the neighborhood was believed to be ended. The inhabitants were professedly anti-Communists, but, unfortunately, the quarter had been occupied two days previously by three battalions from Belleville, charged with executing the famous *ordres formels*, or the chase after refractory National Guards.

These battalions erected three barricades, one in the Faubourg St. Honoré, at the corner of the Rue d'Anjou, and two in the Rue de Suresnes; one at the corner of the Rue d'Anjou, and the other at the corner of the Rue Boissy-d'Anglas; behind which they were now entrenched.

The soldiers, masters of the Elysée and the Rue des Saussaies, *immediately opened* their fire. Sharp-shooters mounted on the roof of the Elysée, and reported to the spectators below the success of their shots.

Several officers, standing at the gates of the Palace, borrowed arms from their men, giving them an example of address and self-possession—courage they did not lack. The attack was not at first pushed very rapidly, as the time for the movements in the Rue Royale and Place de la Concorde had not arrived; but at about five o'clock in the afternoon two detachments of infantry entered a house in the Rue Aguesseau, separated from the Mairie by a slight partition, forced the wall, and thus gained possession of the building, where they took numerous prisoners. These were all decorated with the armlet of the Geneva Convention, which they had probably stolen from the ambulance next door. At the same time the two barricades in the Rue d'Anjou were taken. Meanwhile, in the Boulevard Haussmann the troops had carried the Caserne Pépinière, and advanced on the Gare St. Lazare; while General Ladmirault, advancing from the Park Monceau along the exterior boulevards, carried successively the defences of Batignolles, thus opening the way to the cemetery of Montmartre, already reached by the division under General Montaudon, who had followed the same route outside the walls as far as St. Ouen. The object on the right was to attack Montmartre by its most accessible side. Here the insurgents had gained their victory of the 18th of March. The place was now strongly fortified, and regarded by them as the citadel of the town. To attack it in front would have been folly. It was necessary to envelope it, rapidly to concentrate great masses of troops, and to scale the heights at the mouth of the cannon; these, happily, could not do much to annoy the invaders, owing to the steepness of the hill, which prevented their being employed on assailants passing close to the base.

While Montmartre was thus being surrounded preparatory to the attack on the morrow, the troops of General de Cissey, on the left bank of the river, were equally successful.

Early on Monday morning, a body of troops was sent to occupy the Gare Montparnasse, which they succeeded in doing, after carrying several strong barricades in the quarter of Plaisance. Several companies penetrated into the depôt by the entrance at the junction of the streets Armorique and Cotentin. At their approach, the National Guards who occupied this important post, and who were entirely unprepared for so sudden an attack, hurriedly evacuated the spot. It was immediately placed in a state of defence, and occupied by the troops in great numbers.

The insurgents meanwhile hastened to construct two strong barricades in the Rue de Rennes, at the corners of the Rue du Vieux-Colombier and the Place St. Germain-des-Prés. These barricades were armed with cannon, to reply to the fire from the depôt, and to prevent the troops from descending towards the Seine by the Rue Bonaparte. They were supported by barricades in the latter street, also by those in the Rue du Four and Du Vieux-Colombier, which protected the Place St. Sulpice. On the other side of the depôt was the formidable barricade of the Croix Rouge, protecting the streets of Grenelle, Sèvres, and Cherche-Midi.

Finally, to complete this system of defence, and entirely cover the Luxembourg, two barricades were erected in the Rue Vaugirard, near the Rue Madame and the Rue Bonaparte, and a third was established in the Rue Fleurus.

All these ramparts were defended by artillery. Less important obstacles, accumulated in the side-streets, permitted the Federals to establish posts of observation, and facilitated the communications between the different centres of operation. At about eleven in the morning the soldiers, sheltered by a stone balustrade in front of the depôt, opened a violent fire of musketry on the barricades in the Rue de Rennes; and bombs from cannon, established at the corner of the Place, were sent whistling through the air every ten minutes during the entire day and most of the ensuing night.

Meanwhile, a manifestation in favor of the Government troops had taken place in the Rue du Bac. At three o'clock in the morning, the news of the entrance of the Versaillese having reached this quarter, seven National Guards of the 16th battalion, among whom were M. Duronchoux, colonel of a legion, and two officers, advanced sword in hand to the corner of the streets of Grenelle and Du Bac, where the Federals, headed by M. Sicard, member of the Commune, were erecting a barricade. While M. Duronchoux cried "Down with the Commune!" an officer tore down the red flag, and stamped it under foot. At the same time the tricolor was planted at the corner of the Rues du Bac and Varennes amidst shouts of "*Vive la*

République!" Next penetrating into the Rue de Grenelle, the Party of Order were fired upon by the insurgents, and the Colonel Duronchoux severely wounded.

The example thus given was followed by all the National Guards hostile to the Commune, who, grouping around their comrades, preserved this quarter from the occupation of the insurrection. A barricade was erected for this purpose on the corner of the Rue Babylone, where the Order Party entrenched themselves until they were joined, at about one o'clock, by the 39th of the line.

The soldiers were received with clapping of hands and shouts from all the windows of *"Vive la ligne!"* Many Communists were taken prisoners, among others a commandant of artillery and a staff officer, who were taken to the Babylone Barrack and immediately shot.

The troops of General Vinoy had meanwhile descended along the banks of the Seine, and taken possession of the Ministry of Foreign Affairs.

It was known that on the 21st of May, the day of the entrance of the troops, the Citizen Bergeret had passed the night at the palace of the Presidency of the Corps Legislatif. M. de Lanzières de Thémines, officer of the 2d regiment of the Infantry of Marine, received an order to go and arrest him.

His means of resistance were not known, but it was expected that he would sell his life and liberty dearly. The young officer took with him twenty men, passed by the Ministry of Foreign Affairs, broke the gates of the Hotel of the Presidency, and entered the court. It was deserted. They then entered the apartments.

Bergeret had slept in the bed of the President, after having passed the great part of the night in an orgie, the remains of which were scattered round the room. Many arms were found, besides many papers and portraits which the General had not had time to destroy. As for finding "himself," all search was vain. He had prudently decamped at the approach of the marines.

M. Hottot, chief surgeon of the ambulance of the Corps Legislatif, lent his aid to the officer and soldiers in making the necessary perquisition.

Among the different papers discovered we will insert two letters from members of the Commune who have rendered themselves particularly conspicuous. The first is written by Paschal Grousset, and addressed to Bergeret personally. We here find the buffoon-like coating with which the Delegate of Foreign Affairs surrounded all his acts.

"FOREIGN AFFAIRS. *Delegation.*	"LIBERTY, EQUALITY, FRATERNITY. *Commune of Paris.*

"MY DEAR BERGERET:—I beg you to give a certain parade in sending a mission to the Commandant-in-Chief of the 3d Prussian Army Corps.

"It is necessary to know *officially* at what date the Germans will evacuate the forts on the right bank, so as not to let them fall into the hands of the Versaillese.

"The despatch should be delivered by a staff officer sent *en parlementaire*, and followed at least by a large guard.

"*Salut et Egalité.*

"PASCHAL GROUSSET,
"Delegate of Foreign Affairs."

The other letter is from Raoul Rigault:

PREFECTURE OF POLICE.
Cabinet of the Prefect.

"PARIS, 23d March 1871.

"MY DEAR BERGERET:—I send you Bouillon, who is an intelligent and energetic fellow.

"He was Commissary of Police from September until the 31st of October, when he was discharged. For this reason I have named him Commissary to the Staff. This position exists, and while rendering you other services, his title will permit him to execute any arrest or summons which might be useful to you.

"I press your hand.

"RAOUL RIGAULT."

Other letters were from Lullier, Lefrançais, and Bergeret himself.

It has been seen that in all the fighting throughout the day, the National Guards were in every instance forced back, and to such an extent that they repeated their usual declaration of being betrayed and abandoned by their officers. Nevertheless, they enjoyed extraordinary advantages over their opponents in the struggle, who were obliged to attack without any protection, while they fought behind solid barricades.

In the centre of the city shells fell without any intermission during the entire day, rendering circulation almost impossible, and doing a great deal of damage.

CHAPTER X.

Attack on the Place Clichy—The Rue Lepic—Manner of attack—Assault of the Moulin-de-la-Galette—Volunteers of the Seine—Capture of Montmartre—The barricades of the exterior boulevards taken—Boulevard Magenta—Death and burial of Dombrowski—Place de la Concorde—Chapelle Expiatoire carried by the troops—Fighting in the Boulevard Malesherbes—Places de la Madeleine and Concorde taken—Conflagration in the Rue Royale—Persons smothered in the flames—Ministry of Marine—Ministry of Finances—Conflagration of the Tuileries—The Louvre saved—Barricade of the Place de l'Opéra—Church of the Trinity—Chaussée d'Antin—Place Vendôme taken—The Bourse saved—Bank of France bravely defended—Cruelty of the insurgents—Combat at Montparnasse and in the Rue de Rennes—Defeat of the insurgents—The Croix Rouge taken—Place Saint-Sulpice—Conflagrations on the left bank—Montrouge—Frightful slaughter at the Church of Saint Pierre—Government circular—The Expiatory Chapel—Barricades erected during the night—Assassination of Chaudey—His funeral—Attempt made by several Communists to escape.

AT early dawn on Tuesday, the troops attacking the 9th Arrondissement were directed against the New Opera, the Rue de la Chausée-d'Antin, the Place de la Trinité, and the barricade at the Place Clichy, driving towards these different points the Federals who had not yet taken refuge there.

The attack of the barricade of the Place Clichy was the first serious movement of the day. Early in the morning a violent combat of artillery was begun between the Parc Moriceaux and Montmartre, while the batteries placed in front of the barricade defended the approach by the Place de l'Europe. But the patriotic energy of the soldiers triumphed over these obstacles. Towards seven o'clock a part of the corps of General Clinchant, headed by the 3d regiment of the line, Colonel Bréard, crossed with their cannon the Place de l'Europe, and established a barricade under the enemy's fire, which soon silenced the guns of their opponents. Soon, by a combined movement, these troops, with those established in the College Chaptal, rushed on the barricade and carried it rapidly amidst a perfect rain of bullets and bombs.

The Federals then retreated towards the barricade at the junction of the Avenues Clichy and Saint Ouen, but the soldiers by a rapid detour, stopped them on the way and took many prisoners, while the others escaped into the side-streets leading towards the cemetery of Montmartre.

A little before this successful attack, another column had taken possession, at about nine in the morning, of the Mairie of Batignolles, which had been abandoned by M. Malon, member of the Commune. He had taken refuge at Montmartre, directing all the munitions to the same place.

It was now that the investing march on Montmartre was begun which, by the promptitude and ability with which it was executed, saved the city from so much misery.

During the attack of the Place Clichy, a column skirting the streets Cardinet and Balagny executed a flank movement, taking Montmartre in the rear, while the troops of General Ladmirault attacked the barricade of the Rue Lepic and the boulevard de Clichy.

This was one of the most formidable of all the barricades, both from its position and the manner in which it was constructed. It was composed of two lines at right angles, one crossing the Boulevard de Clichy, and the other the entrance to the Rue Lepic (formerly Rue de l'Empereur), which mounts to the Heights of Montmartre. Five 12-pounders defend the latter, which alone remained in the power of the insurgents, raking with their fire the

Rue Blanche, the Rue Fontaine, and theRue de Bruxelles, which open on the Boulevard de Clichy.

During the imperial rule large avenues had been opened in every part of Paris, which, in a military point of view, were considered favorable to the suppression of any insurrection, always on the hypothesis that the troops alone would be possessed of artillery. Unfortunately in this case the insurgents possessed cannon—indeed, a great many cannon—together with mitrailleuses of every size and description. It, consequently, became very difficult to take barricades thus defended without an enormous loss of life. Long cannonades and numberless flank movements were the result.

The attack was ordinarily begun by two guns firing alternately at the barricade from the corner of the nearest street. The cannon being charged, was pushed rapidly forward, with the mouth a little beyond the angle of the wall, quickly pointed and discharged, and then withdrawn by means of cords into its former sheltered position. Solid shot was generally employed, it being more efficacious in making a breach in a wall of paving-stones. Bombs and grape-shot were only used by the artillery in the large squares and avenues.

When a sufficient breach was made, the soldiers ran one by one along the sides of the streets, stopping in the doors to fire, and then advancing as before. Others entered the houses, and fired from the windows. The insurgents executed the same manœuvres, hiding in the windows and alleys. These skirmishes often lasted very long, but an assault was rarely necessary; for the insurgents, seeing themselves about to be surrounded, generally abandoned the barricade. One hundred insurgents defended the barricade in the Rue Lepic, while others occupied the houses on the corner, and fired from the windows on the troops. From the manner in which the Federals fought, it was very difficult to put many of them *hors de combat.* It was necessary that a ball should just graze the top of the barricade in order to strike one of them. Their bodies being protected by a thick wall of stone, they were only to be touched on the forehead or the hands, which they were obliged to leave unprotected.

The cannonade and musketry fire lasted from nine o'clock till twelve, when four soldiers of the line, crawling across the boulevard, in spite of the bullets and the menacing mouths of the cannon, rose suddenly in front of the barricade, and fired upon the terrified insurgents, who, believing themselves assailed by an entire regiment, fled in every direction. At the same time two columns advanced from the Rue Blanche and the Rue de Bruxelles, and the tricolor was planted on the barricade.

The red flag of the Commune, pierced with balls, had been transported by one of the insurgents to the barricade in the Place Pigalle, the attack of which was immediately begun.

The rôles were now changed. The troops entrenched behind the barricade of the Rue Lepic opened fire on the insurgents, but the contest was very unequal. Although the Federals had been unable to carry with them but one of their guns, those remaining were rendered useless by the want of artillerymen and ammunition, the attacking column being entirely composed of soldiers of the line. The combat had lasted two hours, when a body of troops suddenly appeared in the Rue Houdon, opposite the barricade, and the Federals hastily retreated.

Amongst the number of their dead, the body of a poor baker-boy was found, who had been forced by them to aid in the defence of the barricade.

The quarter being thus entirely conquered, a search for arms was immediately instituted, when a woman, leading an officer into a cellar—where, she said, several guns were hidden—suddenly drew a revolver, and shot him through the head. The woman was immediately arrested, and the body of the officer was carried to the cemetery of Montmartre.

Meanwhile, after the capture of the Place Clichy, a second column had penetrated into the Rue des Carrières, where another barricade had been raised. Here the insurgents held out until the troops, masters of Saint Ouen, had turned the cemetery, and placed the Rue des Carrières between two fires.

A dozen National Guards remained alone on the barricade, and refused to surrender. They were taken, and immediately shot.

The troops now advanced to the assault of the Moulin de la Galette, the highest point of the Buttes Montmartre. After an active engagement of twenty-five minutes, the 72d and 51st regiments, aided by the Volunteers of the Seine, carried the place, and planted the tricolor on the heights.

The Volunteers of the Seine, who took so active a part in the capture of Montmartre, belonged to the brigade of General Pradier, in the 1st army corps. This battalion consisted of 300 officers who had volunteered their services to the Assembly at the outbreak of the insurrection, and who heroically fulfilled their engagements. Out of the three hundred, sixty-two were killed or wounded.

One of these, the Commandant Durrieu, rendered himself particularly remarkable for his courage.

The 1st corps advanced toward Montmartre. The fire from the barricade in the Rue Marcadet troubled the march of the column. Twenty-five volunteers, with a company of soldiers, carried the position. Durrieu proposed immediately to assault the heights:

"*Allons-y!*" replied the captain, simply.

Before advancing, officers and men, heated by the march, took a glass of wine at a café in the avenue.

"The cross was given me a few days ago," said Durrieu, "but I do not wear it, because I have not received the embrace. I feel that if I had it on my breast, it would bring me good fortune," and he drew from his pocket a cross which a friend had given him.

A captain, who was decorated, immediately advanced, fastened on the cross, and gave him the embrace. Tears of joy stood in the eyes of the brave Durrieu, when, suddenly, his face grew clouded, and taking a pencil, he wrote on the shutter of the house these words:

"In case of accident, carry Durrieu, 21 Rue de Torcy."

The assault was commanded, and the height captured. A barricade in the Rue Fontenelle was also carried. Durrieu was left with seven men to guard it, while the plateau of Moulin-de-la-Galette was attacked and taken; when his comrades returned, Durrieu was dead. He was thirty-five years of age.

Meanwhile, another column, skirting the Rue du Rempart, mounted the heights by the Rue Fontaine-du-But, on the opposite side, and took possession of the Chateau Rouge.

The two columns met on the top, where they found the guns still loaded as they were abandoned by the Federals.

During this time all had been confusion at Montmartre. Early in the morning the Federals were informed by their General that they had been betrayed; that ammunition and reinforcements had been refused them, and that the gates of Saint-Ouen and Clignancourt had been opened to the Versailles troops.

The movement executed by the soldiers along the Rue du Rempart had led the insurgents to suppose that they had entered those gates.

The heights were soon almost abandoned, and the troops met with but a slight resistance. The different columns having united at Montmartre, a part descended the hill and attacked the Mairie of the 11th Arrondissement, from the windows of which, as well as from the surrounding houses, the insurgents kept up a quick musketry fire. The combat, however, was not of long duration; many of the insurgents made good their retreat, while a great number were taken, or surrendered themselves prisoners, leaving without defenders the barricades in the Rues-Germain-Pilon and Houdon.

The latent opposition to the Commune which had reigned in the greater part of the Parisian population soon made itself manifest, even at Montmartre. As soon as the people discovered that the regulars had occupied definitively all the important positions, they hastened to applaud the soldiers. The search for arms immediately began, and, after laying their guns and bayonets on the pavements, the inhabitants threw from the windows cartridge-boxes, uniforms, and every war-like accoutrement.

At the capture of Montmartre the Government gained possession of 150 cannon and mitrailleuses. The batteries menacing Paris were removed, while others were established above the Chateau Rouge to command the heights of the Buttes Chaumont and Père-Lachaise, where it was foreseen the insurgents would entrench themselves strongly.

The taking of Montmartre was the principal event of the day, and indeed we might add, of the occupation of Paris. It was universally believed that the insurrection would here make its strongest resistance. In the eyes of the defenders of the Commune it possessed a certain prestige, for here the movement of the 18th of March had had its origin and decisive success. Montmartre, supported by the Buttes Chaumont and Père-Lachaise, assured to the defenders a position most dangerous for the rest of Paris, which the heights entirely dominated, particularly the richer quarters. From the disasters which everywhere marked the retreat of the Federals, it is not to be doubted that, had they remained in possession of the heights, the portion of the city lying on the right bank of the Seine would have been one mass of ruins.

This bombardment was foreseen, and had excited most cruel apprehensions in the central quarters. If it did not take place, no honor is due to the conscientious scruples of the chiefs of the Commune, who have sufficiently proved their utter want of any feelings of humanity. This important success was chiefly due to the divisions, uncertainty and divergency of action, which were manifest in all the military operations of the Commune, and also to the sudden entry of the army into Paris, it being expected that the troops would be kept in check a long time at the ramparts.

Montmartre taken, and the quarters below it occupied, the barricades of the exterior boulevard retained little power of resistance. That of the Place Blanche, attacked by the Rue Vintimille and the boulevard, was abandoned as soon as its defenders recognized the regular troops in the interior of Montmartre. They retreated to the Place Pigalle, where a desperate struggle took place, lasting three hours, at the end of which time the troops became masters of the barricade.

When the army had thus taken Montmartre and several other important points of the same zone, it remained necessary to gain possession of Belleville, Père-Lachaise, the Buttes Chaumont, and Menilmontant. To invest these points, which were all strongly occupied by the insurgents, it was necessary first to take the Boulevard Magenta, and next the Place du Chateau-d'Eau, a strategic position of first importance, commanding, as it does, the Bastille, Belleville, the Faubourg Saint Antoine, the Boulevard Prince-Eugène, and the Place du Trône.

The Boulevard Magenta, about a mile and a quarter in length, was defended by four formidable barricades established across the avenue, and by about twenty others built in its transversal streets.

These four barricades were situated at the entry of the Boulevard Ornano, at the corner of the Rue Rochechouart, before the church of Saint-Laurent, and the last at the junction of the streets Magnan, Dieu, and Chateau d'Eau.

The corps of General Ladmirault, advancing along the Boulevard Rochechouart and the Avenue Trudaine, met with a stubborn resistance at the Collège Rollin. After gaining possession of this building, an attack was made on the barricade of the Boulevard Ornano, which was carried after a long and severe effort. The capture of this barricade was of great importance in enabling the army to make use of the artillery of the insurgents, and with it to attack the other defences of the Boulevard Magenta.

The barricades Rochechouart and Saint-Laurent fell in their turn, and the attack was immediately directed against the fourth barricade, which was the key of the position. Here, however, the insurgents held good until Friday at noon.

It was during the attack on the Boulevard Ornano that Dombrowski, commander-in-chief of the army of the Commune, received his death-wound.

Dombrowski did not escape the fate of all those whom the Commune exalted to eminent positions, who were applauded one day, imprisoned the next. Accused of treason in abandoning Neuilly, his arrest was decided upon Monday evening, and immediately executed.

Military events demanding a supreme effort on the part of the Commune, he was set at liberty, when he replied to

DOMBROWSKI

Commune of Paris.

1871

their suspicions by courageously confronting the enemy at the Boulevard Ornano.

On Tuesday afternoon, during the attack, he arrived at the barricade. He was on horseback, followed by several aides-de-camp. He had hardly been five minutes on the scene of battle when a ball struck him in the abdomen, inflicting a mortal wound.

Placed on a litter, he was carried by four insurgents to the hospital of Lariboisière, where every effort was made to save him by Dr. Cusco, the surgeon-in-chief. An hour after, he expired amidst most horrible sufferings. His last words were these: "Kill me at once, I suffer too much."

This was at about seven o'clock Tuesday evening. At half-past eight, the regular troops being still advancing, Dombrowski's chief of the staff, Commandant Brioncel, arrived at the hospital followed by the escort of the General.

"Is the General dead?" asked Brioncel.

"Yes, sir," replied the attendant.

"Then give me his body."

The corpse of Dombrowski was placed in a cab and delivered to his staff.

At this moment the Director of Lariboisière arrived.

"Why are you taking away this body?" he asked from the soldiers of the Commune.

"It is our General; we don't wish the Versaillese to have this corpse," they replied, in giving the order "To the Hotel de Ville."

As the carriage started, an artilleryman threw himself precipitately from his horse, and approaching Dombrowski, kissed him on the forehead and said, "General, I will avenge you!"

He then withdrew, but, as he mounted his horse, a ball struck him in the forehead, killing him on the spot. The carriage left immediately for the Hotel de Ville.

In the court of the Hotel, Dombrowski's remains were taken from the carriage and carried into the building, where they were exposed until midnight. His portrait was taken in crayon by Pilotell. At midnight the body was transported to Père Lachaise, under the direction of Brigadier Chéron, of the 254th battalion, where it remained unburied until Thursday morning, forgotten by the Commune in the confusion and terror of that time. On Thursday morning, however, one of the members, accompanied by the Colonel, brother of the General, and several officers, repaired to the cemetery.

The body was exposed on a litter, dressed in a Polish jacket, with the limbs enveloped in linen. An oaken coffin had been prepared; the blankets of two National Guards present were folded in the bottom of the coffin, and the body placed upon them wrapped in a red flag.

Commandant Brunereau then called in the artillerymen, marines, and all who were on guard in the cemetery. Each kissed in turn the forehead of the General, and the coffin was closed.

It was then carried to an empty vault, in which it was placed, after the brother of Dombrowski had written a few words in pencil on the lid.

Citizen Vermorel then delivered an address, in which he expressed himself with great rage, not against the regular army, but against the horde of drunkards and cowards who had deserted their chief, leaving him to die alone on the barricade.

While the corps of Generals Ladmirault and Clinchant were engaged in taking Montmartre, the Place de la Concorde had been the scene of a strange struggle. The Versailles troops were in possession of the Palais de l'Industrie, and of the Palais Bourbon, seat of the Corps Legislatif, which stands on the other side of the river, facing the Ministry of the Marine, which was held by the insurgents. The latter were also strongly fortified in the Tuileries Gardens.

A contest was conducted for hours across the four sides of this square, and had the insurgents retained possession of Montmartre, the position would have been untenable for the troops. As it was, they were for some time little able to do more than hold their own. The enthroned cities of France suffered severely in this artillery battle, Lille being entirely destroyed, and all the others receiving some damage. The Egyptian obelisk, though attained by several shells, remained uninjured, while the ruins of stone balustrades and beautiful fountains of bronze covered the ground.

In the Boulevard Haussmann an attack was begun early in the morning on the Expiatory Chapel, held by the insurgents, which lasted with more or less intensity until four in the afternoon, when an order was given to the troops to advance down the Boulevard and force the position.

This was effected most gallantly, and the insurgents fled.

In the Faubourg St. Honoré, the attack on the barricade of the Rue Boissy d'Anglas was commenced at an early hour. At five in the afternoon an advance was made, and the position carried. The barricade of the Rue Royàle was thus taken in the rear.

In the Boulevard Malesherbes the contest was most violent, and lasted many hours. The troops, having gained possession of the barricade in the Rue Ville l'Evèque, attacked from there the Rue de l'Arcade, where the insurgents were in great force, both behind the barricade and in the houses. The traces left by the battle were numberless. Trees were cut down, and houses riddled with bullets and shells, while the columns and steps of the Madeleine were covered with many scars.

Late in the afternoon the defences of the insurgents were carried, and the terrace of the Tuileries succumbed, at the same time leaving the Place de la Concorde and the Place de la Madeleine in the possession of the troops.

The insurgents, in retreating, spread fire and desolation in their path. In the Rue Royale, the houses were forcibly entered by the Communists, petroleum was flung on all the furniture and woodwork, and in some cases thrown on the upper stories by means of fire-engines, so that in a short time the whole range of buildings from the Faubourg St. Honoré to the church (on the left, looking toward the Madeleine), was a mass of ruins. In the Faubourg, several houses were totally destroyed, and others greatly injured, while on the opposite side of the Rue Royale, on the corner of the Rue St. Honoré, two or three houses were also made a prey to the flames.

Any attempt to extinguish the conflagration was punished by the insurgents with instant death, and many persons who had taken refuge in their cellars, to escape the dangers of shot and shell, were smothered by the smoke.

In No. 1 Faubourg St. Honoré, seven persons thus became the victims of death, and their bodies were afterwards taken from beneath the ruins. This building was entered early in the morning by several National Guards, who informed the proprietor, M. Aurelly, that they were about to set fire to his house, but that, as he had been always kind to them, they would allow him to escape. He begged leave to inform his servants and some friends who had taken refuge in his cellars, but was told that if he did so he should be burned with them, and he was forced to leave the unhappy victims to their fate.

The story of two of these, man and wife, was very sad. Early in the morning, their son, a lad of eighteen, being wounded by the bursting of a shell, was carried to an ambulance in the Faubourg St. Honoré. He called so incessantly for his parents that they were finally sent for.

They set out immediately to join him, accompanied by their daughter, a young girl of twenty. The bullets were falling like rain. The young girl was shot through the heart, and the agonized parents were obliged to hasten on, leaving the dead body of their daughter in the streets. At the Rue Royale, it seemed madness to proceed, and the poor people took refuge in the cellar of No. 1, until the firing should have somewhat abated. Here Death overtook his prey, while the son called wildly for the parents who would never answer.

Among the victims were three young men who had hidden here to prevent being forced to join the forces of the Commune.

The design of the insurgents had been to fire the whole quarter, but time was wanting; and when the troops forced the barricades near the church, the incendiaries were obliged to take flight.

It is not to be doubted that the immense building on the Place de la Concorde, the Ministry of Marine, had also been doomed by the insurgents to destruction. The following order was addressed to the Commandant Brunel, who was lodged in the Ministry:

In a quarter of an hour the Tuileries will be on fire. Remove the wounded from the Ministry and blow it up.

"*I like that,*" said Brunel.

The inner court was filled with materials to aid in the defence of the adjoining barricades, large cases filled with cartridges and shells, together with eight barrels of gunpowder and two large carboys of petroleum.

The barricades on the Place de la Concorde and the Rue de Rivoli having been defended to the last extremity, the Federals began their retreat and the Marine was evacuated.

14

Orders were given to one of the men to empty, as soon as all had gone, the vessels of petroleum near the ammunition. The man was fortunately somewhat the worse for drink, and while seeking for some rope or tow to communicate the fire to the combustible material, he was accosted by the superintendent-in-chief of the hotel, who, partly by argument and partly by threats, induced him to abandon his undertaking.

In the Rue St. Florentin, a *cantinière* while requisitioning linen, sugar, and wine from the concierge of one of the houses, said to him on leaving, "Take care of yourself, for all this quarter is to be burnt to ashes." This proved too true with regard to the Ministry of Finance, which was set on fire in the morning. All day long pieces of blackened paper, *débris* from the archives of the city, were wafted through the air, showering down in the streets, and in many cases falling far out in the country.

The following order was found on the body of an insurgent killed fighting in the Rue Castiglione:

MINISTÈRE
de la Guerre.

Paris, le 18

CABINET
du ministre.

Cabinet du Ministre
de la Guerre.

Au citoyen Lucas

Faites de suite flamber Finances et venez nous retrouver.

Timbre:
Ministere
DE LA GUERRE.

4 Prairial, an. 79.

TH. FERRÉ.

This was not the worst disaster. At about nine in the evening a strong volume of fire rose high in the air, revealing to the stupefied inhabitants the pavilion of the Tuileries in flames. The fire spread fast and soon embraced the entire building, while every possibility of checking the flames had been prevented by the Commune, they having smeared the principal parts of the structure with petroleum. This, added to the dryness of the weather, which had rendered the timber-work dry and inflammable, caused a most terrible conflagration. Had a breath of air been stirring, the whole of the beautiful Rue de Rivoli would have been in flames.

Meanwhile every effort had been made to save the Louvre. On Monday night all the guardians of the Louvre had been taken prisoners and kept as hostages at the mayoralty of Saint-Germain-l'Auxerrois, where they were several times on the point of being shot.

All day Tuesday, numerous carriages charged with powder passed through the court of the Louvre on their way to the Tuileries. In the evening the guardians who had been taken prisoners were allowed to return to their homes exhausted with fatigue.

In the night a terrible explosion was heard, and the Louvre shook to its foundations. The central portion of the Tuileries, where the combustible matter had been accumulated, had just blown up. Soon the palace was but an immense furnace, the flames colored here and there in a fantastic manner according to the mineral oils and ingredients which were burned.

What souvenirs and riches lost!

The evening before, eleven wagons, bearing a portion of the collections of M. Thiers, had been brought here, and all were consumed.

The flames were approaching with rapidity the Library

of the Louvre, and it was time that every effort should be made to save it.

M. Barbet de Jouy caused the delegates of the Artistic Federation then in the Louvre to be seized. Iron chains were placed across the gates to prevent the entrance of the Federals into the court, they having already stolen the keys.

Unhappily the flames attacked the Library, where, notwithstanding the efforts of the guardians, the fire was not extinguished until after the arrival of the Division Vergé, when the firemen, aided by a company of engineers, finally mastered the conflagration.

Thus, with the exception of the Library, the rich collections contained in the Louvre have been saved. The building itself has suffered some damage from shells, all of which, however, can be easily repaired. The fire in the Tuileries continued to smoulder for several days.

After gaining possession of the barricade of the Rue Royale, a portion of the troops of General Douay advanced along the Boulevard de la Madeleine, where they took possession of the barricade in the Rue Luxembourg after four hours' hard fighting. The Maison Giroux was occupied in force, and the surrounding houses suffered severely in consequence. Over sixty dead were left upon the ground after this engagement.

While this success was being achieved by the soldiers of General Douay, the troops on the Boulevards Haussmann and Malesherbes advanced to attack the strong barricades on the Place de l'Opera and Chaussée d'Antin, preparatory to an assault on the Place Vendôme.

The first of these barricades, which commanded the Boulevard des Capucines, and the Rues Auber and Halévy, was guarded by the 117th battalion of National Guards. The attack was begun about noon, and conducted on both sides with great fury, the click of the musket and the roar of the cannon never ceasing for a moment.

The barricade was defended valiantly, and during several hours the troops were unable to make the assault. They first gained possession of all the streets opening on the boulevards, and at the corners of those on the northern side soldiers were posted, who aided the attack in the Rues Auber and Halévy, where it was chiefly conducted.

At about five o'clock the troops penetrated into the New Opera. The doors were forced, and Lieutenant Ziegler, who commanded the first detachment of the attack, entered the building and summoned the insurgents to surrender, under penalty of being instantly shot.

He was answered by shouts of defiance; and an officer, who appeared to be the chief of the band, instantly drew his revolver and aimed it at his head. The lieutenant, however, was too quick for him, and in the act of firing he fell dead upon the ground. The remaining insurgents were thrown into confusion, and soon surrendered their guns.

Several soldiers then mounted to the roof, where one, half enveloped in a huge tricolor, crawled cautiously up the balustrade and planted the flag on an angle of the building. The most difficult part of his task, however, had yet to be accomplished. On the 15th of May, the day on which the first attempt was made to overthrow the Column Vendôme, the red flag of the Commune had been planted above the great bronze statue of Apollo, who stands on the highest pinnacle of the Opera, holding his gilt lyre above his head. The red banner had to be removed from the lyre, by no means an easy task, the figure being thirty feet high, and within direct range of the insurgents below.

Several attempts were made by the soldiers to shoot it down with their chassepots; but this, though repeated many times, proved a failure. One man, more daring than the rest, began the ascent of the gigantic figure, and climbing from limb to limb, reached the top in safety. He tore down with his two hands the blood-red banner, while bullets whistled round him, striking every moment the pedestal of the statue, but leaving him untouched.

The Opera House being taken, the position was fast becoming untenable for the insurgents, when a column of the line debouched along the boulevard from the Rue Drouot, and advanced in the direction of the Place de l'Opera, thus taking the barricade in the rear.

The insurgents hastened to make good their retreat by the neighboring streets. Two officers of the 117th battalion, not wishing to leave their cannon and ammunition in the possession of the army, harnessed themselves, with several of their men, to the gun and the artillery caisson, and dragged them away, notwithstanding a perfect shower of bullets and shells. One of the officers carried in one hand the red flag, while with the other he helped to draw the cannon.

Meanwhile a neighboring street, the Rue de la Chaussée d'Antin, had also been the scene of a long conflict.

Early in the morning of Tuesday, the troops, who had become masters of the Dépôt St. Lazare the night before, advanced to the assault of the Church of the Trinity, feebly defended by barricades at the foot of the Rues Blanche and Clichy.

Two or three hundred insurgents had established themselves in the church, and were not dislodged without a violent effort. Cannon were brought to bear upon them, and after a valiant assault on the part of the soldiers, they were obliged to surrender. The prisoners were marched out in file surrounded by soldiers, and nothing could be more wretched than their appearance.

At the head marched a delegate of the Commune, well dressed, and with a resolute air, but the remainder was a pell-mell of individuals with every kind of costume. They all seemed ready to drop with fatigue.

A large crowd collected as they passed, manifesting the most profound indignation, when an incident occurred which shows with what regretable facility the Parisian population will pass from one extreme to another.

As the prisoners advanced, two gendarmes were seen approaching in an opposite direction, and were received with loud acclamations by the crowd. One of them remarked, philosophically, "Three days ago these same people would have helped to cut us to pieces." In fact, the whole body of gendarmes had been the object of the most violent vituperation and the greatest cruelty during the reign of the Commune, and woe to the unfortunate member who fell into his enemies' hands. He was shown no mercy.

The Church of the Trinity being taken, a violent contest ensued for the possession of the barricade at the end of the Rue de la Chausée d'Antin. Cannon were placed on the porch of the church, which commanded the street, and were fired during the entire afternoon without intermission. The insurgents replied with a cannon and mitrailleuses, considerably damaging the church and neighboring houses. One shell pierced the steeple; another penetrated through the dome into the interior; while a third left its mark just below the gilt face of the clock. By a chance which seems almost miraculous, not one of the three beautiful statues which decorate the staircase leading down to the square, was touched.

While the combatants were thus cannonading each other with violence, several companies of the Line, advancing along the roofs of the houses from the Rue St. Lazare to the Rue de la Victoire, and from there to the Rue de Provence, approached the barricade, and firing down upon the insurgents, obliged them finally to retreat.

During the previous night an attempt had been made to erect a barricade at the corner of the Rues de la Victoire and Taitbout, but this was not seriously defended, and soon fell into the hands of the troops.

At six o'clock the fighting near the Chaussée d'Antin was entirely finished, and a crowd was soon collected in the streets, eagerly looking for traces of the combat.

The soldiers were everywhere cheered with the greatest enthusiasm. Refreshments and wine in abundance were pressed upon them, the inhabitants seeming unable sufficiently to show their great joy at their deliverance.

After a short period of rest, following the successes in the Chaussée d'Antin, the troops prepared to attack the Place Vendôme. Batteries were established on the Place de l'Opera, which fired at regular intervals during the night, doing considerable damage to the houses in the Rue de la Paix. Towards morning, finding their fire unanswered, they dashed forward, and mounting the barricade, found the Place Vendôme almost entirely abandoned.

An advance was also made toward the Bourse, by the Rue du 4 Septembre, in order to flank the Hotel de Ville on the right. Artillery was brought to bear on the barricade which guarded the end of the street opening on the square, and toward morning the barricade was carried by assault.

The following order was found on the body of an insurgent killed a few days later. He was, happily, unable to carry it into effect:

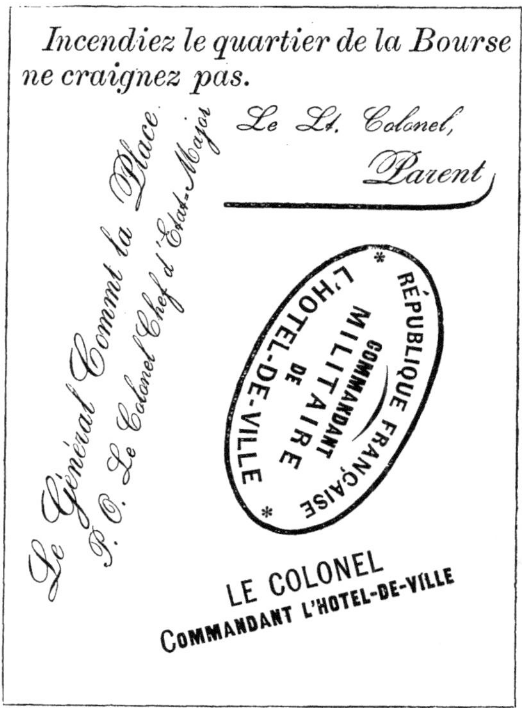

Incendiez le quartier de la Bourse ne craignez pas.

Le Lt. Colonel,
Parent

Le Général Commt la Place
P. O. Le Colonel Chef d'Etat-Major

RÉPUBLIQUE FRANÇAISE
COMMANDANT MILITAIRE DE L'HOTEL-DE-VILLE

LE COLONEL
COMMANDANT L'HOTEL-DE-VILLE

The Bank of France had also happily escaped its designed destruction.

About a month before the entrance of the troops, the Bank was surrounded by National Guards, and M. Beslay, member of the Commune and delegate to the Bank, took up his residence in the apartments of M. Rouland. The latter, Governor of the Bank under the Assembly, had quitted Paris immediately after the nomination of this delegate by the Commune. Later, several amicable attempts were made by the Guards, under various pretexts, to enter the court of the Bank with their arms, but this was invariably opposed by the 12th battalion, consisting of five hundred men, who, since the 18th of March, had not left the building. Each day half of this number was on guard, while the other reposed.

The Federals also made several attempts to gain possession of the post at the corner of the Rues La Vrillière and Radzirvill, but they always failed before the energetic attitude of those by whom it was occupied.

The defenders of the Bank were kept always on the alert. They could rarely go to their homes to sleep, and frequently were unable to go out for their meals. The shutters were crenelated, and every man had his place assigned him in advance in case of combat.

Happily they were not reduced to this extremity, which would have been fatal to the employees of the Bank, who would have been burned, not attacked. General Douay arrived in time to prevent this disaster. The Place Vendôme, which was considered an impregnable fortress, being taken with but little difficulty, the troops were able to cross directly from the New Opera to the Bank.

The Federal battalions cantoned in the Rue d'Aboukir had received orders to set fire that day to the four corners of the building, and the guards within would have been powerless to prevent them from accomplishing their infamous design.

It is due to M. Beslay, the delegate of the Commune, to state that he opposed, by every means in his power, the exactions of the Federals; and it is generally believed that he effected his escape from Paris only because he was unmolested by the Government.

Meanwhile General Clinchant advanced his troops to

attack the barricades in the Rues Chateaudun, Notre-Dame-de-Lorette, and Drouot, whence the soldiers pushed forward to the Place Cadet by the Rue Lafayette and the Faubourg Montmartre. The barricade erected in the Rue Montmartre was carried the same night, as well as another built at the intersection of the Rues d'Aboukir and Petit-Carreau. Here the engagement was long and violent, and all the energy of the soldiers was required to carry the position. At the Place Cadet the resistance of the insurgents was equally desperate.

The battle was gradually approaching the headquarters of the insurgents; their despair and hatred increased as their hopes of success became diminished, and every day the contest assumed a more bloody and revengeful aspect.

At Montmartre, on the previous day, twelve unfortunate soldiers, who had been made prisoners and conducted there, had their two hands cut off at the wrists, when they were set at liberty.

Similar acts of cruelty were of frequent occurrence during the death-struggle of the Commune, which ended in exciting greatly the passions of the soldiers, and rendering them more cruel in their retaliation.

To non-combatants, however, they were lamb-like in their demeanor, being evidently well pleased with the joy and enthusiasm their arrival had created.

"*On est content de nous voir, eh? les Parisiens?*" a *lignard* would ask jocosely, too confident of what he would be answered to await any reply. While on the right bank of the river the troops were everywhere successful, the movements of General de Cissey were marked by equal energy and success.

The night between Monday and Tuesday had been relatively calm, but at eight in the morning two furious combats had begun at different points, which lasted throughout the entire day.

The first took place at the Dépôt Montparnasse. The insurgents, repulsed the previous evening, profited by the darkness to arm with cannon the barricade in the Rue de Rennes at its intersection with the Rues Cassette and Du Vieux-Colombier. From this position they bombarded, at a distance of 860 yards, the depôt which stood opposite. Shot and shell rained upon the building, rendering it soon a mass of ruins, while the surrounding houses were horribly maltreated.

While the battery of the barricade was thus bombarding the depôt, six battalions of Federals advanced to attack. The firing of musketry and the rattling of the mitrailleuse was then added to the already horrible din, and for five hours the troops within sustained this violent attack with energy and sang-froid.

Two detachments of the Chasseurs d'Afrique then advanced, one to the right and one to the left of the Rue de Rennes, turning the insurgents, who, assailed in front and on two sides, beat a retreat and rapidly disbanded. They were furiously pursued by the troops, and obliged to abandon their dead and wounded by hundreds.

An attack had been made meanwhile on the formidable barricades at the Croix Rouge. This place is formed by the intersection of six roads—Rues du Dragon, Du Four, Du Vieux-Colombier, Du Cherche-Midi, De Sèvres, and De Grenelle, and had been formed into a veritable entrenched camp.

The barricade of the Rue de Grenelle being forced, the troops by whom they were carried divided into two columns—one leaning towards the left continued to operate in the Rue du Bac, while the other pushed directly forward. They were received near the Rue des Saints-Pères by a violent fire of musketry from the Croix Rouge, and turned to shelter themselves in that street; but hardly had they appeared, when they were again assailed by a fire from the barricade Saints-Pères-Taranne.

Fired upon on every side, and not wishing to fall back, the soldiers forced the doors of the houses on the left side of the street, and advanced through the interior courts to the foot of the barricade, which they carried at the point of the bayonet. The barricade in the Rue St. Dominique was taken at the same time. Continuing the same movement through the houses of the Rue du Dragon, the soldiers gained possession of the Croix Rouge, while the National Guards hastily retreated through the streets Gozlin and Bonaparte.

The troops then advanced by the Rues Jacob, De l'Abbaye, and Gozlin to the Place de l'Abbaye, which they found defended by a solidly-constructed barricade. Here the combat, which was commenced at half-past ten, threatened to last an indefinite time, when the marines were informed that the position might be turned by passing through the garden of the abbey which stood on the Place. A small framework in the wall built above a well permitted an entrance into the narrow passage of the Petite-Boucherie.

The 2d fusiliers of the Marine effected this perilous entrance, and penetrating into one of the houses, fired from the windows on the insurgents, who fell back quickly to the barricades in the Rue de Seine. These, however, were but slightly defended, as the marines followed up their success, and the quarter was soon delivered from the presence of the Federals.

As soon as the inhabitants perceived the soldiers, the doors were all opened, and they hastened to offer them bread and wine. Domiciliary visits were immediately made, and, among other captures, that of a Federal named Gilbain was effected, who the day before had traversed the quarter threatening to blow it up. Barrels of powder had been placed in the sewers connected by wires, to which, at the proper time, the electric spark was to be communicated. After a short interrogatory, in which Gilbain plainly avowed his participation in the insurrection, he was led out and shot, together with eighteen other National Guards taken with arms in their hands. A few days later his wife, who had been left at liberty, was discovered throwing petroleum on a house in the neighborhood, and was immediately led a prisoner to Versailles.

The successive occupation of the barricades De Buci, Saint-André-des-Arts, and the Rue Christine, against which it was necessary to employ cannon, led the troops as far as the Boulevard Saint Michel. The Place Saint-Sulpice was taken at the same time; and here we may mention a curious incident. The officers of the Marine having installed themselves in the telegraphic bureau of the Mairie, sent a despatch to the Hotel de Ville, leading the Federals to believe that they were still in possession of the quarter. Having asked what they should do if the Versailles troops continued to advance, they received the following laconic answer:

"*Faites sauter la boîte.*"

One of the delegates of the arrondissement was instantly shot.

The streets in the neighborhood of the Seine had also their part in the combat. Early in the morning the Federals had fortified themselves in the passage Sainte-Marie, and had occupied the neighboring houses. Towards noon, two regiments of the line, supported by three pieces of artillery, appeared before their defences. These pieces, placed in position, kept up during the afternoon a vigorous cannonade, directed against the passage Sainte-Marie, which, added to the fire of the infantry, rendered towards evening the position untenable for the insurgents. At the close of the 23d of May the army was mistress of all the portion of the left bank bounded by the Seine, the Boulevard Saint Michel, as far as the School of Medicine, and back of this by the Rue Bonaparte, including the Place Saint-Sulpice and the Rue de Rennes, to the Depôt Montparnasse.

All the quarters in the centre of this large zone had suffered severe damage from heavy projectiles, but this did not satisfy the fury of the insurgents. While their accomplices on the right bank were setting fire to the Tuileries and the Palais-Royal, they, from a pure spirit of vengeance, lighted a conflagration in the streets of Lille, Verneuil, Du Bac, and on the Quai d'Orsay.

Many private hotels, and the vast and beautiful edifices of the Legion of Honor, the Conseil d'Etat, and the Caisse des Depôts et Consignations, became during the evening a prey to the flames. The second great scene of battle on the left bank was at Montrouge, before the church of St. Pierre, and in the Avenue d'Orléans, before the barricade at the corner of the Rue Brézin. A frightful struggle of four hours took place at each of these barricades before they were captured.

At the barricade in front of the church, cannon were at first used to make a breach. This was followed by a rapid musketry fire, which lasted two hours. Finally, it was charged with the bayonet.

Entrenched behind the houses, and even in the steeple of the church, the insurgents made frightful ravages in the ranks of the troops, who stood entirely unprotected in the centre of the square formed by the intersection of the Avenues d'Orléans and Du Maine. Their attack was truly heroic, and their impassibility under the balls which rained upon them from the steeple, the barricade, and the surrounding houses, was more heroic still.

After three hours combat, the colonel of the 114th regiment, placing himself at the head of his men, called:

"*En avant!*" Officers and soldiers threw themselves on the insurgents who defended the barricade, and, after a frightful slaughter, carried the position.

The movement of attack was so precipitate, that the insurgents in the steeple began ringing the tocsin for aid; hardly had the last sound been heard, when the barricade was carried. The insurgents who had fired on the troops from above, were forced to descend, and instantly shot. In this action the army made four hundred prisoners. The dead and wounded were to be counted by hundreds.

The attack on the barricade of the Rue Brézin, carried at three o'clock in the afternoon, was as bloody as that on the barricade of the church. In one, as in the other, several dramatic things occurred.

At the barricade of the Rue Brézin, a soldier of the line, calling to an insurgent who was aiming at him to surrender, avoided the ball, and while on the point of returning the fire, recognized his father. Two artillerymen and a marine who pointed the pieces placed in battery on the barricade of the church, were recognized as deserters and killed beside their guns.

One of the most furious defenders of this barricade was a woman dressed in the uniform of a National Guard. She was killed during the action, and in clearing away the bodies her sex was discovered. A hair-dresser, who had fired from the interior of his house upon the troops, was shot before his own door.

At four o'clock the tri-colored flag floated from the Mairie of Montrouge, and the people received with acclamations the soldiers of France, whose presence in their midst filled them with joy. The 114th regiment was everywhere feasted by the inhabitants, who looked upon them as their deliverers. From this moment the insurrection in the 14th Arrondissement was ended.

The following despatch relating to the military events of the day was forwarded by M. Thiers to the Prefects of the several Departments:

"VERSAILLES, May 23, 2 P.M.

"The course which events are taking justify our expectations. We have now 90,000 men in Paris.

"General De Cissey has taken up his position from the railway-station at Montparnesse to the Ecole Militaire, and is proceeding along the left bank toward the Tuileries.

"Generals Douay and Vinoy are enclosing the Tuileries, the Louvre, and the Place Vendôme, in order subsequently to advance on the Hotel de Ville.

"General Clinchant having made himself master of the Opera, the St. Lazare Railway Station, and the Batignolles, has carried the barricades at Clichy.

"General Ladmirault is approaching the foot of Montmartre with two divisions.

"General Montaudon, following the movement of General Ladmirault, has taken Neuilly, Levallois-Perret, and Clichy, and is attacking St. Ouen. He has taken 105 guns and a quantity of prisoners.

"The resistance of the insurgents is gradually declining, and there is every ground for hoping that if the struggle is not finished to-day it will be over by to-morrow at the very latest, and for a long time.

"With respect to the killed and wounded it is impossible to fix the numbers, but they are considerable. The army, on the contrary, has suffered but very slight loss.

"A. THIERS."

Later in the afternoon a second circular was issued:

"3:30 P.M.

"The tri-colored flag waves over the Buttes Montmartre

and the Northern Railway Station. These decisive points were carried by the troops of Generals Ladmirault and Clinchant, who captured between 2,000 and 3,000 prisoners. General Douay has taken the Church of the Trinity, and is marching upon the Mairie in the Rue Drouot.

"Generals de Cissey and Vinoy are advancing towards the Hotel de Ville and Tuileries.

"A. THIERS."

Although later events did not justify M. Thiers' expectations with regard to the length of the struggle, the army had every reason to be proud of its achievements throughout the day. Its arrival had saved, among many other objects of value, the Chapelle Expiatoire.

This building, erected at the Restoration to the memory of Louis XVI. and Marie Antoinette, had been doomed to destruction by a decree of the Commune. The fulfilment of this decree, which appeared at about the same time as that ordaining the destruction of the Column Vendôme, and which was peremptory, like all the decrees of the Commune, was unaccountably postponed.

Immediately after the publication of this decree in the *Journal Officiel*, M. Libmann, a gentleman to whom many members of religious communities pursued by the Commune owed their safety, presented himself to M. Fontaine, Communal Director of Domains, and proposed to buy the sacred vessels, linen, and all the objects used in divine service belonging to the chapel.

The estimable delegate of the Commune fixed, after a great deal of bargaining, on the price of 5,000 francs, which M. Libmann paid from his own pocket, and for which he received the following receipt:

"PARIS, May 18, 1871.

"Received from Citizen Libmann, 12 Rue Lavoisier, the sum of five thousand francs, amount of the sale, for the benefit of the Commune, of the following objects:

2 boxes (church-silver).
1 " (silver-gilt).
1 pyx "
1 censer, holy-water sprinkler, etc. (silver).

All ornaments of the church, such as albs, chasubles, in a word, all the linen, missals, and crosses.

For the Director of Domains.

(Signed) LABORDE.

This was not all. The material was saved, but there remained the monument. M. Libmann did not hesitate, but opened immediately new negotiations, to which the Citizen Fontaine, enticed by the five thousand francs already paid, lent himself with all the good grace of which he was capable.

The following estimate was the result of these negotiations:

CHAPELLE EXPIATOIRE OF LOUIS XVI.

Estimate of the Value of Materials.

	fr.	c.
Masonry	813,480	20
Granite	39,702	00
Marble	16,480	00
Metals (copper, lead)	12,403	10
Woodwork	2,830	00
Iron	32,900	00
Sculpture on the building	15,000	00
Artistic sculpture (2 groups, bas-relief)	150,000	00
Two stands for holy water	1,000	00
Two altars	1,500	00
Furniture of the church	50,000	00
Chasublery	15,000	00
Sacred vessels	50,000	00
	1,200,295	30

This amount was more difficult to realize than the former. M. Libmann accepted in principle, but reclaimed valuation after valuation, for to gain time was everything. The attack on Paris came to interrupt the negotiations, and proved that the foresight of the courageous defender of the monument had been correct.

The building is to-day intact, with the exception of a little damage received during the attack made against it by the troops.

The night of the 23d passed with a sinister tranquillity, scarcely troubled by the works of defence, which were being actively continued, or by an occasional report of a distant cannon.

The time, however, was not lost by the insurgents. Federal officers, passing in the Rues Saint-Jacques, Gay-Lussac, and the Boulevard Saint-Michel, gave orders for a new disposition of barricades, and, following their indications, several squads of barricade-makers set immediately to work. Women were there in great numbers, calling, with threats and imprecations, on all the citizens, male and female, to aid in pulling up the paving-stones, in digging the ditches.

The barricade of the Rue Royer-Collard was composed of three defensive works: one at its entrance into the Boulevard Saint-Michel; another at its intersection with the Rue Gay-Lussac; and a third in the middle of the Rue Royer-Collard itself.

Meanwhile, at the prison of Sainte-Pélagie, was perpetrated the first of the many horrible murders which leave such a stain on the memory of the Commune.

M. Gustave Chaudey, one of the editors of the *Siècle*, had been arrested in the middle of April, at the instigation of Citizen Vermesch, editor of a scurrilous paper called the *Père Duchesne*. M. Chaudey was accused of having, while adjoint to the Mayor of Paris, ordered the repression, by force of arms, of the riot of the 22d of January, which was the sequence of the 31st of October.

After inquiry upon inquiry, Citizen Protot, grand judge, himself acknowledged that there was no ground for continuing the prosecution.

As Chaudey was still, however, retained in confinement, M. Rousse, advocate, took the necessary steps to obtain his release.

"No formal requisitions will be made against Gustave Chaudey," said Citizen Protot; "only, what would you have? Raoul Rigault is *fort monté contre lui*, and wishes absolutely to have him shot. But no. Leave him in prison and nothing shall be done to him."

Having first been confined in the Mazas Prison, he was later removed to Sainte-Pélagie, where, on Tuesday night, May 23d, at eleven o'clock, his cell was brusquely entered by Raoul Rigault, who said:

"Well, you are to be shot to-day ... now ... instantly!"

After the first moment of surprise, Chaudey replied:

"You know that I have only done my duty. You come to kill me without any mandate, any judgment. It is not an execution but an assassination."

Raoul Rigault, however, interrupted him with imprecations, and Chaudey was dragged outside.

There, while awaiting a platoon of Federals, for whom Rigault had been obliged to send, the National Guards in the prison having refused to execute the odious work demanded of them, a few more words were exchanged between the butcher and his victim. Chaudey remembered that he was both husband and a father.

"Rigault," said he, "I have a wife and child; you know it."

These words producing no effect upon his enemy, Chaudey had nothing to do but resign himself manfully to his fate. He was then led out to a road near the chapel, where, in a corner, by the light of a lantern fastened to the wall, and another carried by the overseer Berthier, the procession halted.

Either by design or hazard, the old employees of the prison, who were regarded with suspicion, and themselves destined to a near execution, were absent on that evening. Rigault only had with him the trusty followers of the Commune, the jailor Clement, Brigadier Gentil, and a friend, Préau de Vedel, a volunteer for the assassination; also the platoon for execution.

Vermesch, who had denounced Chaudey, and Pilotell, who had robbed and arrested him, were not at the rendezvous.

The Federals seeming to hesitate, Rigault drew his sword, and commanded them, with threats, to fire. The men aimed at first too high, and Chaudey was only wounded in the arm. Clement then fired two shots, when he fell, crying "*Vive la République!*"

"I will give you enough of a Republic!" cried Gentil; and rushing forward, he fired, breaking his jaw in fragments. Préau de Vedel then advanced and shot him through the head.

Gustave Chaudey was an advocate of talent, and possessed of ardent democratic sentiments. He had been formerly proscribed, was the executor of P. J. Proudhon, the advocate of G. Courbet, and the defender of the *Courrier Français;* and had thus given sufficient pledges to the cause of the revolution, and of such a nature, as it would seem would have obliged it to spare him. "But the revolution," says Rivarol, "kills above all those who wish to serve it."

The body of Chaudey was found shortly after the entry of the Versailles troops, and his funeral attended by all the eminent journalists and chief notables of Paris. The following address was delivered by M. Etienne Arago,

Mayor of Paris, after the 4th of September, to whom M. Chaudey was adjoint:

"MY DEAR CHAUDEY,—After the admirable remarks we have just heard, I will restrict myself to addressing a few words to the friend.

"In times of revolution, every one does his duty according to his courage and his faith. Fortune decides the event, often fatal to the men most worthy. Chaudey, of this you are the proof—you, whose tragic end honors your great heart.

"When I called you to the Hotel de Ville as my adjoint, you did not hesitate, although the horizon was already dark, and you saw that the perils were growing greater; but you were both patriot and republican, and no danger caused you to stop.

"The task which fell to your share at the Hotel de Ville was principally that of humanity. Yours, the subsistence of the poor, the ambulances, and all services of charity and fraternal zeal.

"Of all the heads which our discords could menace, yours, it would seem, should have been most protected by the remembrance of so many services, of so much affectionate devotedness.

"And yet you have succumbed—victim of an atrocious vengeance—which erred in striking you. Who can be a better witness than I, who was present at your side from the very beginning of the discussion which took place between you and a representative of the insurrection about to break forth. You had certainly the right to reply to the shots from the Place by shots from the Hotel de Ville; but—I declare it on my honor—the just repression came from other than your orders. History will attest it, as she will also tell of your family virtues, your sincerity, and your constancy in friendship; she will not forget the force of examination which you brought to bear upon our laws, nor your recent studies to reform them according to the republican idea.

"Shall I speak of your genius? Before this tomb it is no time to praise the ingenuity, amenity, and originality of the French mind.

"A higher thought impresses itself upon my heart. It is of a duty accomplished, of a martyrdom generously suffered for principle; it is of your heroism that I ought to speak.

"Defender of the law, you have perished for her; and against her was struck a blow of premeditated fury in assassinating you!

"Adieu, my friend; adieu, Chaudey."

Chaudey's death is believed to have been caused at the instance of Delescluze, Delegate of War. The latter had in his youth committed a theft on a M. Denormandie, which he had been obliged to avow. He knew that the written proof of his fault was in the hands of M. Chaudey; and this explains the fury with which he pursued the man whose revelations he feared.

While this frightful crime was being perpetrated in one portion of the city, in another several members of the Commune, wishing to save their heads, had determined to attempt an extreme means of escape.

A carriage arrived at about ten o'clock in the evening in the neighborhood of a gas manufactory, situated on the Boulevard de Vincennes, and orders were given to inflate a balloon which was in readiness there.

The National Guards established in the neighborhood were rather surprised at these preparations, but they were informed that the balloon was to be sent with proclamations from the Commune to the provinces.

At two in the morning, the balloon was ready to leave.

Four carriages, filled with people, arrived at the gas-works.

The National Guards, who did not even recognize the persons wishing to make their escape, opposed their departure, menacing to make holes in the balloon with their bullets if the gas was not immediately discharged. One National Guard even added, "You have brought us to the pit, and you must remain in it with us."

Seeing that flight was impossible, the members of the Commune, with the four carriages, retook the road to the Hotel de Ville.

Although, as has already been stated, M. Thiers, in his proclamation, outstripped in his desires the course of events, still it is certain that the day of the 23d was decisive. In a moral relation, it showed on all the points of attack the energetic decision of the troops, their strong discipline regained more firmly than before, and now unchangeable in all contacts with an insurrectional population. Advances and fraternal proclamations had as little influence upon them as the abuse which, for the last two months, the Commune of Paris had showered upon the army of investment—upon that army of France which, as Marshal de MacMahon so well said, was now penetrated with a sentiment of its duty and its national mission.

In a strategic point of view, the consequences were not less important. The army was master of all the great arteries which penetrate to the heart of the capital; the communications had been strongly established, and were perfectly secure; and, finally, the position of Montmartre was in possession of the Government, the occupation of which delivered Paris from a most menacing danger, while at the same time it was able to concur, in a most efficacious manner, in the succeeding operations of the army.

Also, the uncertainties which had been conceived, not with regard to the result of the struggle, but as to its length, and the dangerous turns of fortune which it might present, were entirely set at rest; and seeing the precision and connection of the movements of the army of occupation, the moment of definitive success was generally regarded as very near—a matter, at most, of one or two days.

CHAPTER XI.

Paris on the morning of the 24th—Incendiary orders—Proclamation to the soldiers—M. Thiers' speech in the Assembly—Porte St. Denis—The Theatre of the Porte St. Martin set on fire—Massacre of women and children—The hostages transferred to La Roquette—Massacre of the Archbishop and five other persons—Monseigneur Darboy—M. Duguerry—President Bonjean—Visit to the Archbishop—Progress on the right bank—Saint Eustache—The Palais Royal in flames—Occupation of the Faubourg Saint Germain—The Pantheon taken—Explosion of a powder magazine—Arrest and execution of Raoul Rigault—His character—His extravagance—Cannonade from Montmartre—Night of the 24th—Conflagration of the Palace of Justice—The prisoners of the Conciergerie.

ON the morning of the 24th, the districts delivered by the army on the previous day had the appearance usual on some grand fête. Tricolored flags floated from almost every house, while the streets were filled with the curious, anxious to see the results of the terrible struggle which had kept them prisoners so long.

The Boulevards des Capucines and Malesherbes were particularly frequented. The latter, from the church Saint Augustin to the Madeleine, gave strong evidence of the desperation with which the struggle had been here conducted. The shops had particularly suffered. The heavy iron shutters of one had been pushed up, and projected outward at least two feet by the force of a shell. The windows of most of the houses were broken. The pretty little newspaper *kiosques* that line, here and there, the boulevard, had been broken to fragments; while branches of trees strewed the ground, dipping and staining their bright green foliage in a dark liquid, recognized with a shudder to be human blood.

The Boulevard des Capucines presented a similar appearance; but it was at the aspect of the Rue Royale that a cry of horror burst from every lip. Here the fire still smouldered sulkily, notwithstanding all the efforts made to extinguish it, and now and then some blackened wall would totter and fall with a dull thud to the ground. The fire had, in many houses, shown strange caprices. In one, hanging on the inner wall, which alone remained standing, in the fifth story, was a woman's dress and an umbrella, not even scorched by the flames; while on a mantlepiece, high in the air, in another house, stood a pretty little clock, firm on its resting-place, although the surrounding walls had entirely disappeared. The mirror above it also stood intact, covered with strips of paper such as the Parisians had pasted on all their shop windows, thinking to save their being broken by the concussion caused in firing. The poor little mirror remained, but the home was gone.

Several houses which were not burned had their fronts entirely knocked away by shells, and presented very much the appearance of a scene in a theatre when the stage is divided into two compartments, a different representation going on in each.

Of one house, the entresol alone remained; and that stood entirely open, the front wall being knocked away. The furniture was intact; the bed, ornamented with green curtains, trimmed with guipure and caught back by bands of the same; in the centre of the room stood a chair placed as though some one had just risen from it, while over the back a shawl was carelessly thrown. All this was inexpressibly sad to look upon; but horrible as it was, it might have been worse. The city was everywhere mined and ready to be blown up by the demons of the Commune. But a merciful Providence spared the French this crowning disaster, which, coming after a year of such utter misery and misfortune, might have proved a finishing blow.

The burning of Paris had been long premeditated by the Commune as a last resource, and every preparation had been made to ensure its success. The incendiaries were regularly enrolled, and were mostly women. These infamous creatures had for mission, to throw petroleum and matches through the gratings of the cellars into the windows, particularly of public buildings; and anywhere, in fact, where a conflagration could be lighted.

They went mostly alone, modestly but not poorly dressed, gliding along the sides of the houses, and looking very much like housekeepers going to market.

Those who were furnished with incendiary matches carried them in their hands, and without either stooping or stopping, threw them quickly into any openings which they passed. Those who carried petroleum, hid the bottle which contained it in the folds of their skirts, and operated in the same manner.

Later, when the suspicions and vigilance of the inhabitants were strongly excited, the petroleum was carried in a milk-can and in this way they were enabled to continue their odious mission for some time undiscovered.

If detected, however, they expected and received no mercy, and were mostly executed on the spot. On the morning of the 24th, thirteen of these *pétroleuses,* the name given them by the population, who had been discovered in the act, were shot on the Place Vendôme, now occupied by the soldiers.

In the Rue du 4 Septembre, in the short distance comprised between the New Opera and the Bourse, ten *pétroleuses* were arrested, some of them children between ten and fifteen years of age.

To add to these horrors, many of the water-pipes had been cut, so that a fire, once ignited, was with difficulty extinguished; the inhabitants were obliged to form a chain, and every passer-by was requisitioned and obliged to work for two hours.

At the Place de la Concorde, a regiment of the line was stationed; many of them were sleeping under the shade of the Tuileries terrace, which had been bought the night before with the blood of their comrades. Their rest, however, did not remain undisturbed, for shells fell rapidly on the Place, and often burst far up the Champs Elysées, coming from the batteries at the Hotel de Ville.

This firing became more violent as the day advanced, shells being sent also from the Federal batteries at the Buttes Chaumont and Père-Lachaise.

The following order was sent by General Eudes to the commandant of the battery at Père-Lachaise:

"REPUBLIC OF FRANCE.

"COMMITTEE OF PUBLIC SAFETY,
"PARIS, May —, 1871.

"*Commune of Paris:*

"Fire on the Bourse, the Bank, the Posts, the Place des Victoires, the Place Vendôme, the Garden of the Tuileries, and the Babylone Barracks. We leave the Hotel de Ville under the command of Pindy. The Delegate of War, the Committee of Public Safety, and the members of the Commune now present, will transport themselves to the Mairie of the 11th Arrondissement, where we shall establish ourselves. It is there that we shall organize the defence of the popular quarters.

"We will send you the artillery and munitions of the Park Basfroi.

"We shall hold to the end and *quand même.*

"E. EUDES."

The following incendiary order had also been given:

"PARIS, 3 Prairial, year 79.

"The Citizen Millière, at the head of 150 men, with fusees, will burn the suspected houses and public monuments on the left bank.

"Citizen Dereure, with 100 men, is charged with the 1st and 2d Arrondissements.

"Citizen Billioray, with 100 men, is charged with the 9th, 10th, and 20th Arrondissements.

"Citizen Vésinier, with 50 men, is specially charged with the boulevards from the Madeleine to the Bastille.

"These citizens will arrange with the chiefs of the barricades in a manner to insure the execution of these orders.

"*Delescluze, Régère, Ranvier, Johannard, Vésinier, Brunel, Dombrowski.*"

A final attempt had been made to influence the soldiers in their favor, and the following notice was pasted on the walls of that part of the city still in possession of the Commune. It was the last ever issued by that body:

"COMMUNE OF PARIS.

"CENTRAL COMMITTEE, 3 Prairial, year 79.

"*Federation of the National Guard:*

"SOLDIERS OF THE ARMY OF VERSAILLES:—We are fathers of families.

"We are fighting to prevent our children from being, one day, like you, under a military despotism.

"You will be one day fathers of families. If you draw on the people to-day, your sons will curse you, as we curse the soldiers who tore the entrails of the people in June, 1848, and in December, 1851.

"Two months ago, on the 18th of March, your brothers of the army of Paris, their hearts infuriated against the cowards who had sold France, fraternized with the people; imitate them.

"Soldiers, our children and our brothers, listen well to this, and let your consciences decide.

"When the watchword is infamous, disobedience is a duty!

"THE CENTRAL COMMITTEE."

This proclamation, it is needless to say, had not the slightest effect on the minds of the soldiers, who were becoming every hour more incensed against "their brothers," and the atrocities they committed.

The Bourse had been occupied early in the morning by the soldiers of the line. In the Place Vendôme a body of cavalry, and a large number of troops who had taken part in the attack of the preceding night, were stationed, while from the Ministry of Justice and on the pedestal of the fallen column floated the tricolored flag.

The re-erection of the Column Vendôme had already been voted by the National Assembly during Monday's sitting.

After voting unanimously the following proposition, "The National Assembly declares that the land and sea forces and the Head of the Executive Power have merited well of their country," the following bill was presented by M. Jules Simon:

"Art. 1. The Column of the Place Vendôme shall be reconstructed. (*Loud applause.*)

"Art. 2. It shall be surmounted with a statue of France.

"Art. 3. An inscription shall mark the date of the destruction and that of the re-erection.

"Art. 4. The expiatory monument raised to the memory of Louis XVI. shall be immediately repaired." (*Loud applause on the Right.*)

On the Place de l'Opera the damage done was considerable, although the Opera itself had escaped almost uninjured, notwithstanding the numerous shells sent against it from Père Lachaise. These fell very thickly during the afternoon, both in the Place and along the boulevards. Several persons were killed in front of the Théatre des Variétés and in the Rue de la Paix, and the crowds that in the morning had filled the streets gradually diminished and finally disappeared altogether.

The fears of explosions and petroleum had become universal. The inhabitants had stopped up every chink into which anything could be thrown; cellar-lights, ventilators, and gratings, had all disappeared from view. Some were covered with sand-bags, others were built up with paving-stones like miniature barricades, while the majority were plastered with sand and mortar.

Every woman walking in the streets was regarded with suspicion by her neighbors, and many innocent persons narrowly escaped becoming the victims of an angry mob whose fury had been roused by some jealous individual who had seen evidences of guilt where none existed.

As an excuse for the mob it may be said that the very persons the least calculated to excite their suspicions were invariably the ones who committed these atrocious crimes; and as discovery followed discovery their terror reached such a height that they distrusted all mankind. In the Rue Royale where the *pompiers* were energetically employed in extinguishing the fire, it was discovered that several of them, instead of pumping water, were actually throwing petroleum into the flames, and so adding to their fury. The guilty firemen were immediately surrounded by a body of cavalry, conducted into the Parc Monceaux, and there shot.

About eleven o'clock in the morning, M. Thiers and M. Jules Simon entered Paris escorted by a strong body of cavalry. They proceeded at once to the Ministry of Foreign Affairs, where Marshal de MacMahon had established his headquarters. He gave them every information concerning the situation. The headquarters of General Vinoy were at the Corps Legislatif.

After a visit of two hours, the two members of the Government returned to Versailles to assist at the sitting of the National Assembly. Here M. Thiers was interpellated by M. Calmar de Lafayette, who, while expressing the greatest confidence in the Head of the Government, wished to inquire what measures he intended to take with regard to the Prefecture of the Seine.

M. Thiers, Head of the Executive Power:—"I am quite ready to give every explanation. I went to Paris this morning, and saw much there, and had everything explained to me. I return quite inconsolable, and I do not attempt to give you any comfort. (*Agitation on all the benches.*) The insurrection is certainly vanquished, and the tri-colored flag floats from most of the public monuments of Paris. But the last acts of the insurgents are abominable—are, in fact, the reprisals of despair. Last evening we succeeded in occupying the Place de l'Opera, and all the neighborhood. After forty-eight hours of combat a night's rest was evidently required by the troops, and the generals were unanimous in thinking that such a period of repose was indispensable. The insurgents took advantage of the respite afforded them to set fire to the Tuileries, the Court of Accounts, and the Conseil d'Etat. It was utterly impossible to prevent them, as their entrenchments were unassailable owing to a numerous artillery, and they employed petroleum to ensure their frightful conflagration. (*Movement.*) Early this morning we took the Place de la Concorde, the Place Vendôme, and the Tuileries, but that palace was only a heap of ruins. (*Explosion of horror.*) Fortunately, owing to the energy of General Douay, and the exertions of the men under him, the flames were prevented from reaching the Louvre; such, at least, is what I gather from a hurried despatch just received from that brave officer, so that this additional severe trial will, I trust, be spared us. But that is not all; at the present moment the Hotel de Ville is on fire. (*Great agitation.*) However that may be, the Communists are surrounded; they are all endeavoring to withdraw, so that this evening the rebellion will be completely vanquished. Unfortunately it has remained, even after its military defeat, in possession of our monuments, and has not been satisfied with using petroleum for their destruction, but has sent shells prepared with that same substance against our soldiers, fourteen of whom have been struck by such missiles. (*Loud marks of reprobation.*)

"Our first duty in opposing this insurrection is to preserve our coolness of judgment and remain united, as otherwise we shall not be able to succeed. We shall, first of all, have to terminate our victory, which result will be arrived at to-morrow; and next we must beware of consenting to anything that could at this moment weaken the army and the Government. (*Applause.*) After what I have already done, no one can doubt of that which I shall still accomplish. The criminals shall be punished according to law, but implacably, as is called for by public feeling. (*Hear, hear.*) As to the exercise of the right of indulgence or pardon, I propose that that privilege shall be vested in the hands of the National Assembly. (*Movement.*) Therefore, as soon as the military operations have terminated, justice will pursue her rigid course. (*Hear, hear.*) I now enter on the question of the National Guard, which, according to public rumor, is to be re-armed. The truth is, that during the last few weeks we have been frequently told that the orderly portion of that body were most anxious to take up arms against the insurrection; and when the 16th Arrondissement (Passy) was evacuated, officers entirely devoted to the Assembly repaired at once to that district, and, without authorization, proceeded to arm the battalions which remained faithful to us. But, after my orders, that movement has been at once arrested, as arms cannot be left in the hands of any National Guards. (*Applause.*) As to the Prefecture of the Seine, a misstatement has been made in what concerns M. Ferry; the real facts being these: When I arrived at power the said situation was vacant, and I offered the post to several men, some of them the most respected of our time; but they all declined it. It was then that M. Ferry, although he had resigned, consented still to support the burden until some one was named to succeed him. He is an active, determined man, who from that moment has taken part in the councils of the Government. At the present moment, when no authority exists in Paris, Marshal de MacMahon urges us to proceeed at once to the installation of an administrative authority; but I ask you to whom am I to address myself. The mayors and the police are both wanting in the capital, and M. Ferry is not Prefect of the Seine, but simply a *locum tenens*, who has consented to again collect together in that city the various threads of the administration so long suspended. But the first point of all is to disarm Paris (*loud cheers*), and a resolution to that effect will be immediately presented to you. (*Repeated cheers.*) As to the mayors, we are anxious to name them, and shall, in that case, make use of the right which the law confers upon us. Before that is done, however, the insurrection must be put down completely. At the present moment I have more difficulties before me than prior to the victory, and I shall not now, or for some time to come, have the slightest repose. Do not, therefore, add to the present trouble, but leave us all our calm for action." (*Applause and agitation.*)

The military operations, meanwhile, were being conducted with the usual vigor.

The barricades in the Rues Lafayette and St. Vincent de Paul were successively forced by the soldiers. The barracks of the Faubourg Poissonière was the scene of a most desperate struggle, as was also the barricade at the Porte St. Denis; but both were finally carried.

A battery was then established on the Boulevard Montmartre, near the Rue Drouot, to bombard the barricades of the Porte St. Martin.

The insurgents had begun to erect these barricades on Monday morning, crossing the boulevard from the Rue de Bondy to the Faubourg Saint Martin. They were not finished until Tuesday, and even then free circulation was allowed, as the attack was yet far distant. The barricades were guarded by the 143d and 131st regiments of the Federals, who chiefly spent their time in eating and drinking. They obtained their supplies from the wine-shops in the neighborhood, kept open "*au nom de la Commune,*" the owners being paid by *bons* on that body.

On Wednesday morning the bombardment of the barricades began, and was conducted with great fury, the Federals replying with their muskets and cannon through the entire day.

In the evening the few inhabitants who were not yet in their cellars, saw the first faint glimmers of the fire in the theatre of the Porte Saint Martin, lighted by the insurgents. The flames were spreading fast, when M. Andoche, a manufacturer of fire-engines in the Rue de Bondy, placed all his machines at the disposal of the inhabitants, who rivalled each other in their endeavors to extinguish the conflagration.

This was the more praiseworthy, as to the danger incurred from the fire were added those of shot and shell, which fell almost without intermission in the Rue de Bondy and the Boulevard Saint Martin.

The Federals also, by an ambush at the corner of the Rue Bonchardon, fired on any one who entered or left the building in endeavoring to save it.

Every effort was made to prevent the fire from catching on the opposite side of the Rue de Bondy, but about two in the morning this fear was realized, and the buildings being of light construction, the flames made rapid progress.

An appeal was made to all the inhabitants, who hastened—men, women, and children—to the pumps and chain. A passing band of firemen were hailed as deliverers, and entreated to aid in subduing the flames; they, however, replied in the most brutal and abusive manner to all such requests, and hastened onward to continue a very different task. These were the men, disguised as firemen, who were employed by the Commune to penetrate everywhere, and set fire to the entire city.

Notwithstanding all efforts, the theatre of the Porte St. Martin was entirely destroyed, while a great portion of the Rue de Bondy became a prey to the flames.

The block of houses situated between the above mentioned theatre and that of the Ambigu-Comique was also invaded by a band of insurgents. The Restaurant Deffieux was first entered, and the cellars pillaged, when the invaders announced their intention of occupying every story, and firing from the windows on the Versailles troops. The inhabitants of the house, mostly women and children, begged them on their knees to abandon this intention. The commanding officer seemed softened by their appeal, and retired, saying that he would establish an ambulance in the house.

A short time after, the same man returned, but with an increased force, and then began a regular pillage. Every article of furniture was thrown from the windows, under pretence that it was needed for making barricades. The tenants were loud in their complaints and indignation. One young man, unable to control his feelings, struck an insurgent in the face.

That act was fatal to the unfortunate people, who were pursued from room to room, and massacred by the Federals without mercy. Men, women, and children all shared the same fate. Fire was then set to the houses, and they were entirely consumed. Meanwhile, in another part of Paris a scene was enacted exceeding even this in horror.

This was the murder of the hostages.

The following order had been given by the Commune on the 22d of May; and we have already seen the manner in which it was employed by Raoul Rigault, with reference to the unfortunate Chaudey:

"COMMUNE OF PARIS.

"DIRECTION OF GENERAL SECURITY,
"PARIS, 2 Prairial, year 79.

"The Citizen Raoul Rigault is charged, together with the Citizen Régère, with the execution of the decree of the Commune of Paris relative to the hostages.

"*Delescluze, Billioray.*"

These hostages, mostly priests, had been arrested at different periods during the reign of the Commune; and their execution, threatened at first as a means of intimidation, was finally decided upon.

The chiefs of the Commune felt that they were in possession of a magnificent prey, and that the assassination of such eminent persons would be for them a triumph. The writers of the Commune who had shown the most fanaticism in pushing the orgies of the people were those who first demanded the execution of the heads of the Parisian clergy. Rochefort, in his *Mot d'Ordre*, and Vermesch, in the *Père Duchesne*, both called loudly for their assassination.

As the checks experienced by the battalions of the Commune became more frequent, these threats increased in violence; and on Monday, the day after the entry of the troops into Paris, about forty of the hostages were conveyed from the Mazas prison to that of the Roquette. Among these were Monseigneur Darboy, Archbishop of Paris, and M. Bonjean, President of the Court of Cassation. On Tuesday fifteen more were removed to the same place. Out of the fifty-five persons transferred from one prison to another during the two days, not more than ten belonged to the laity. All the others belonged to the regular or secular clergy—Jesuit Fathers, the Fathers of Picpus, missionaries, vicars and curés of the parishes of Paris, and functionaries of the archbishopric.

The transfer from one prison to another was effected in the middle of the day, in an open wagon, which was followed by an infuriated multitude, calling "*A mort!*" "*A mort!*" These menaces produced little effect on victims who were prepared for anything.

The fate reserved for them was only too evident from the appearance of the cells into which they were thrust. Neither tables nor chairs, mattresses, nor sheets, but a simple bed of straw, with a blanket for covering. It was quite sufficient, they were told, for the short stay they would make there.

Forty-three of the prisoners were placed in the fourth

division of the prison—division from henceforth celebrated; for from here were taken the illustrious "victims of a political furnace."

Here they passed two quiet days, allowed to take their recreation—two hours daily—together, and treated with every kindness possible by the jailers, who belonged mostly to the old administration.

On Wednesday morning, the 24th, the corridor of the division was suddenly invaded by a strong detachment of Federals; many of them were boys hardly able to carry their guns and equipments. One of them held a list of names in his hands; and, passing from cell to cell, called out six of the hostages, exactly as in the revolution of '93. They were the following:

The Archbishop of Paris.

M. Bonjean, President of the Court of Cassation.

Abbé Duguerry, Curé of the Madeleine.

Father Ducoudray, Superior of the College of Jesuits in the Rue Des Postes.

Father Clercq, Professor in the same college.

Abbé Allard, Chaplain to the Ambulances.

As their names were pronounced, each of the prisoners was led out into the gallery, and descended by a winding-staircase, near the chapel, into the court which serves as a promenade for the prisoners. On each side as they passed stood the National Guards, who insulted them with every epithet their coarse tongues could utter. In the court was a platoon of execution. Monseigneur Darboy advanced and addressed a few words of pardon to his assassins. Two of these men approached, and, in presence of their comrades, knelt, and implored his forgiveness. The other Federals immediately threw themselves upon them, kicked them to one side with insulting language, while they addressed new words of outrage to their victims.

Their conduct and language became finally so violent

that their commandant himself was scandalized, and silenced them with a horrible oath, saying, "You are here to shoot these men, not to insult them."

The arms were then charged, and the prisoners placed against the wall. Father Allard was the first victim, then Monseigneur Darboy fell, and each of the others was shot in turn, all showing the greatest courage and fortitude.

After this tragical execution, which was attended only by a few bandits, the bodies of the unhappy victims were placed, dressed as they were, in a carriage of the Company of Lyon, which had been requisitioned for the purpose, and conveyed to the Cemetery of Père-Lachaise. Here they were placed in the common trench, one beside the other, not even covered with earth, and here they remained until the cemetery was captured by the Versailles troops, when the bodies were removed to receive funeral honors.

Monseigneur Darboy was fifty-eight years of age. He was born in a village of the Upper Marne, at Fayl-Billot, the 16th of January, 1813.

George Darboy was educated at the Seminary of Langres, where he passed most brilliant examinations. In 1836 he was ordained priest, and sent as Vicar to Saint-Dizier, near Vassy. A little later he was recalled to the Seminary of Langres, where he was given the Professorship of Philosophy, and afterwards that of Dogmatic Theology. In two years' time he came to Paris, where the death of one of his predecessors, Monseigneur Affre—victim, like himself, to revolutionary fury—caused him to be named Almoner to the Lyceum Henri IV, and later, Honorary Canon of the Metropolis.

He was called by Monseigneur Sibour to the direction of the *Moniteur Catholique*. He then became first almoner of the Lyceum and honorary Vicar General, with mission for inspecting the religious instruction of the lyceums of the diocese.

In 1854, during a voyage which he made to Rome with the Archbishop, the Pope conferred on him the title of Apostolic Prothonotary. Finally, after being named Titular Vicar-General of Paris, he became, in 1859, Bishop of Nancy.

A decree of the 10th of January, 1863, designed him for the archi-episcopal seat of Paris, where he was precognized the 16th of March, and installed the 21st of April of the same year.

On January 8th, 1864, he became Grand Almoner of the Emperor, and a decree of the following October called him to the Senate. He was a member of the Council of Public Instruction, and grand-officer of the Legion of Honor in 1868.

The moderate and conciliatory political *rôle* which Monseigneur Darboy endeavored to fill after his elevation to the archi-episcopacy, did not always succeed. The persistent refusal of the Pope to accord a cardinal's hat to the Archbishop of Paris was for a long time considered as a sign of a misunderstanding between them. Monseigneur Darboy, however, protested against the existence of anything of the kind in a pastoral letter, written on the fiftieth anniversary of the priesthood of Pius IX.

It is interesting to recall, *à propos* of the death of Monseigneur Darboy, what has been the fate of his predecessors who succeeded each other after the revolution of '89 to the Archi-episcopal Palace in Paris.

In 1793, Monseigneur de Juigué died on the scaffold

In 1815, Cardinal Maury was obliged to take refuge in Rome.

In 1830, Monseigneur de Quelen was hunted by the populace, the Archi-episcopal Palace sacked, and afterwards entirely destroyed. The persecution of this prelate lasted several years.

His successor, Monseigneur Affre, fell on the barricade of the Faubourg Saint-Antoine, June 24th, 1848.

Monseigneur Sibour, who succeeded him, was assassinated by Verger in 1857.

Finally, after the untroubled episcopate of Cardinal Morlot, Monseigneur Darboy was arrested as a hostage and murdered by the insurrection.

Thus, in the same century, one single sovereign has died on his regal bed, and only three out of all the archbishops have died a natural death.

Monseigneur Duguerry, curé of the Madeleine, was struck by two balls; one entered the cheek under the right eye, the other passed through the lungs and came out behind the right shoulder.

The Abbé Duguerry was born in Lyons in 1797, and was the son of a wood merchant. At his death he was seventy-four years of age.

After having commenced his studies at the seminary of his native city, he went to finish them at the College of Villefranche, but he was not ordained priest by dispensation until 1820.

During four years he was professor of philosophy, theology, and eloquence, and finally became preacher.

In 1824 he preached at Lyons; in 1825 and 1826 at Paris. The following year he was named almoner of the 6th regiment of the Royal Guard by Charles X. He followed his regiment to Orleans, to Rouen, and Paris, until 1830.

In 1828, he pronounced at Orleans a discourse in eulogy of Joan of Arc, which twenty-eight years later (1856) he was called upon to repeat.

From 1830 to 1839 he continued exclusively his course of predication. In 1840 he made a voyage to Rome. On his return, M. Duguerry became canon of Notre-Dame, and in 1844, archpriest. The following year he was made curé of Saint Eustache, and in 1849 curé of the Madeleine.

In the month of June, 1861, he was called to the bishopric of Marseilles, but he declined with thanks, saying—"*Je suis à la Madeleine, j'y resterai, j'y mourrai, et j'y serai enterré.*"

He was replaced by M. Cruice.

In 1868 he was charged with the religious instruction of the Prince Imperial.

Decorated in May, 1846, he was made officer of the Legion of Honor in 1853, and commander 8th of May, 1868. M. Duguerry was the author of many religious works.

The following anecdote was related some two years ago by the Abbé Duguerry in person, and will show how the faith of this good man in the Parisian people was later rewarded.

Speaking of the month of June, 1848, he said:

"I shall always remember that month and that year, for it is only since that time that I have known the worth of the people of Paris, of whom so much evil has been said.

"The insurrection was thundering throughout the capital. The Faubourg Saint-Antoine was covered with barricades, and the Faubourg du Temple was being fortified. Even the centre of Paris was assuming a similar aspect, and everything gave evidence of the near outbreak of a popular storm.

"I was alone in the sacristy with my vicars, who, in the fear of danger, had thought it necessary to close the doors of the church (Saint Eustache). We were anxious. We waited and listened.

"Suddenly we heard a distant sound of musketry, followed by the rolling of carriages taking flight, and the noise made in closing the shutters of the shops around us.

"This tumult was succeeded by a profound and fearful silence, which lasted only a few moments. In about ten minutes a few cries were raised, succeeded by a frightful clamor, which seemed entirely to surround the church.

"We still remained seated, without uttering a sound.

"The noise outside continued increasing, and I felt instinctively that danger menaced us. I was not mistaken. A stone, breaking through one of the windows, fell at our feet; while the noise made by the hammering of the butts of muskets upon the door, echoed through the aisles of the church.

"The rioters wished to enter Saint Eustache. They intended to force the doors.

"A few priests could make no head against thousands of madmen. It was evident that we were lost. Nothing remained but to die worthily.

"By a common accord, and without saying a word to each other, we put on our church vestments, determined to deliver ourselves up, and save, if possible, the violation of the sanctuary.

"The assault made by the rioters was already breaking the doors, when I ordered that they should be opened.

"The last bolt had hardly been withdrawn when they gave way with a frightful noise, and we perceived the streets and steps of the church black with a compact and armed crowd.

"I made the sign of the cross, and advanced with my vicars.

"Then was accomplished a fact which I shall never forget during my life. This howling crowd, uttering cries of death, became suddenly silent, and I saw faces which a moment before had been disfigured with fury, now regarding us with stupefaction.

"We advanced several steps, and the front rank of insurgents stopped. I then said: 'What do you wish with me, my children?'

"Not one replied. A sort of retrograde movement made itself manifest, and one of the deluded men who stood near to me said: 'It is well, Monsieur le Curé—it is well; we will defend your church.'

"Then the crowd retired peaceably, and seemingly rather ashamed. Those who had entered the building bowed to me and went out. The church was saved."

Unfortunately, in 1871 there were more free-thinkers than in 1848, and consequently they understood better how to go to work to kill an old man and a priest.

It would be impossible to give at length the history of all the worthy men murdered by the Commune. They were mostly persons of eminence, well chosen, in view of their exalted positions and the irreparable loss inflicted on the country by their deaths, to satisfy amply the lust for vengeance of which that body gave evidence throughout. The following letter, written by President Bonjean from the Mazas prison, is a touching example of the writer's self-sacrifice in the path of duty:

"MAZAS, April 30th, 1871.

"You ask me, my dear Guasco, why twice, on the 8th of September and 20th of March, I returned to Paris, when dwelling in that city presented such serious dangers. You are, above all, astonished that I did not profit by the armistice of the 28th of January to go to Bayeux and embrace my wife and children, for whom you know my extreme tenderness, and from whom I have been separated so long.

"If, instead of fighting bravely at Villiers, and having yourself mutilated by a Prussian shell on the Plateau of Avron, you had come to talk sometimes with your old friend, you would have known that, given the incontestable principle that above all in days of danger a functionary should be at his post, I could not act otherwise than I have done. I answer your three questions.

"1st Question.—The Court of Appeal, over which I preside, being in vacation from September 1 to November 3, I could have, without doubt, very regularly, and without incurring any reproach, remained in Normandy with my family, and awaited the end of a siege which nobody then believed would last more than a few weeks. But, on the other hand, as the result of the departure of M. Devienne, it was on me, being senior of the presidents of the chamber, that the duties of first president devolved, that is to say, of the highest magistrature of the country. I thought it therefore my duty to return to Paris when the siege became imminent, and I entered on the 8th, leaving in Normandy my wife and children in tears.

"My sentiment was shared by all my colleagues; when, a few days later, M. Cremieux, keeper of the seals, consulted us on the expediency of transporting the Court of Cassation to Poitiers, the twenty-four members in Paris did not hesitate to reply by a large majority that this removal was not necessary to the welfare of the service. It was also unanimously decided that it was 'more worthy for the highest judiciary body to associate itself with the perils of the Parisian population.' (See the *Officiel* of September 18.) I continued, therefore, during the siege, to exercise the functions of first president added to those of president of appeals. I attempted to contribute even more actively in the defence of Paris, and had myself inscribed as a volunteer in the National Guard; but this service was beyond my strength, and I was obliged to renounce it.

"2d Question.—Why, after the capitulation of January 28, did I not profit by the cessation of the investment to rejoin, if only for a few days, my well-beloved family at Bayeux? This is the reason:

"The capitulation left unsettled a question full of peril—that of the entry of the Prussians into Paris. Had they persisted in traversing the city triumphantly, an attempt against the life of the King of Prussia was to be foreseen. This attempt might lead to a horrible massacre. I did not think it was permissible for the highest representative of French justice (and I was that *par interim*) to be absent from his post on the eve of such terrible events, in which his rank might furnish him an occasion of being useful, and I resisted the legitimate longing which drew me towards Bayeux.

"3d Question.—Why did I return on the 20th of March?

"It was only when the question of the entry of the Prussians into Paris had been more happily decided than I had at first hoped, that the duties of my charge permitted me to leave, and I started for Bayeux. I was obliged to stop at Orgeville (Eure), to endeavor to organize the cultivation of our domain, which the farmer had abandoned at the invasion of the Germans, leaving the ground uncultivated. I did not become aware of this until February 18th. I was at Orgeville on the 14th of March, and having arranged my affairs was about to continue my route to Bayeux, when late on Sunday the 19th I learned the events of the preceding day: the retreat of the Government to Versailles, and the establishment at the Hotel de Ville of a rival power; the whole with the exaggerations common under such circumstances.

"It was no time for hesitation. I wrote to my dear and worthy wife not to expect me for several days, and very late on the night of the 19th I entered Paris. Monday was consecrated to reading the papers, which I had not seen since the 13th, in order to form an idea of the character, still very obscure, of the movement of the 18th of March. On Tuesday, the 21st, I presided as usual at the *chambre des requêtes*. At half past three, as I returned to my house, I was arrested, conducted to the Prefecture of Police, then to the dépôt, and later to Mazas, without being able to discover the motives which caused my arrest. To-day even, after forty-one days of detention, thirty-seven of them *au secret*, I know no more than on the first day, except from the vague information that I am held as a hostage.

"These, my dear Charles, in all their simplicity, are the facts which you wished to know. I abstain from all reflections which might be considered by my jailer as an obstacle to the departure of this letter.

"Well, my dear child—your age and your almost filial devotion authorize me to give you this title—what I have done I would do again, no matter what may be the unhappy results for my beloved family. In doing one's duty there is an interior satisfaction that permits one to bear with patience, and even with a certain suavity, the most bitter sufferings. It is the quotation of the Sermon on the Mount, of which I never before so well understood the sublime philosophy, 'Blessed are they which are persecuted for righteousness' sake: for theirs is the kingdom of heaven.'

"It is the same thought expressed by Sydney under another form, when beginning to laugh, while descending the steps of the Tower on his way to the scaffold, he replied to his friends, astonished at his gayety in such a moment, 'that one must do his duty and remain gay on the scaffold inclusively!'

"Far from discouraging you, let my example aid you to do your duty, no matter what may follow; for I can affirm to you, upon my honour, that, except the terrible anxiety I feel for the health of my noble and holy companion, never has my soul felt such calm and serenity as since I have lost even my name to become No. 14 of the 6th division. But this No. 14 loves you very dearly, and blesses you as though you were one of his own children.

"I do not need to add, for your friend has most likely told you, that in announcing my arrest to my brave George, I added a most energetic prohibition against his coming to Paris to attempt anything in my favor.

"I told him that his post was by the side of his dying mother, near the two young brothers of whom he may become one day the solitary protector. I added that his presence in Paris would cause me a veritable despair, for I should have to fear either that they would retain him here also as hostage, or that he would be obliged to serve in this horrible civil war; and that either of these events would certainly be a mortal blow to his poor mother.

"Thank God, my brave child had a heart sufficiently elevated to understand this language, and I am proud as well as grateful for the conquest which that generous nature has made over itself to accomplish the duty imposed upon it by my paternal authority; my heart blesses him with the tenderest affection.

"BONJEAN."

Such were the men murdered by the Communists. Among the hostages remaining in prison was Father Guerrin, of the Foreign Missions, who occupied the cell No. 22. This cell communicated with No. 21, where one of the hostages belonging to the laity was confined—a married man and father of a family.

After having given every consolation and encouragement to his companion which could be prompted by the most loving charity, Father Guerrin, on the night of the assassination of the Archbishop and the five other victims, remarked to his neighbor that the call of the condemned had been made, and would probably be made again, without any attempt to prove their identity; that consequently a substitution of persons was an easy thing, and that if they proceeded by squads, the last survivors would have some chance of being rescued in time by the deliverers whom it was still permitted to expect.

At the moment of his arrest, Father Guerrin had chanced to be dressed in civilian's clothes; since his entrance into prison he had allowed his beard and mustaches to grow, and there was nothing in his exterior to indicate a member of the clergy. Under these circumstances, "*heureusement réunies*," as he said with touching simplicity. Father Guerrin offered his neighbor to reply for him and take his place, if, at the next call, the name of this father of a family should be called before his own. "You are married," he said; "you have a wife, a child, for whom you ought to save yourself, if possible. Those are ties which it would be too painful to break, and our sacrifice is much less difficult than yours. For me, a priest, a missionary, the martyrdom which I sought in China without finding it, *eh bien!* I shall find it here. It little matters whether it is to-day instead of to-morrow; above all, if I can render my death useful, and make it contribute in saving your life."

This heroic act of abnegation could not have been proposed more simply or more as a matter of course, and it was only after a violent debate, and an absolute and reiterated refusal to profit by any substitution, that the companion of the holy father could induce him to abandon his design. What commentaries can be made on such an act! While no country is cursed with such a large body of atheists and free-thinkers as France, in no other is to be found a clergy excelling the French in their loving charity and perfect performance of duty towards God and mankind.

Happily the army arrived in time to prevent either No. 21 or No. 22 from answering to the fatal call upon which Father Guerrin had insisted with such generous self-sacrifice.

During the incarceration of the hostages, every effort was made by their friends to alleviate their sufferings. The following account is given by M. Rousse, staff-man of the order of advocates, and the same who attempted to obtain the liberation of Chaudey, of the steps taken by him in favor of the imprisoned priests:

"I directed myself, at hazard, towards the dependencies of the Court of Assizes by the entrance of the advocates, while a guard on duty allowed me to pass without opposition. Not an usher, not a servant, not a sound; an abandoned house. I opened discreetly two doors; no one. In passing before the chamber of council I mechanically turned the handle and pushed open the door. To my great surprise I found myself in the presence of seven or eight individuals sitting, without any order, round the room, and discussing. One alone was standing before the table; he was a small man, about thirty years of age, dark. wearing a full beard, with a very energetic air. His button-hole was ornamented with a large red ribbon, fringed with gold. I was about to withdraw when this individual raised his head and called to me in a most brutal tone:

"'What do you want?'

"At this unusual reception, instead of leaving, I closed the door, and made a step in advance, saying—

"'I was told that I should find here the Procurator of the Commune.'

"'Ah! and so *on vient comme ça vous causer*?*

"'Oh! permit me,' I replied, coolly. 'If I entered here it was because I found neither servant nor usher. I am perfectly well acquainted with the usages of the Palace. I am an advocate and staffman of the order.'

"This reply instantly changed the situation.

"'What do you wish, citizen?'

"'To speak to the Procurator of the Commune.'

"'He is before you.'

"And excusing himself to his colleagues, the fierce Procurator made me pass before him, and enter his cabinet. He then seated himself, and said—

"'I beg your pardon, citizen, for having received you in this manner, but every day I am disturbed for the most absolutely useless objects. Would you believe it, there are people who come here to ask for passports?'

"I told him the object of my visit. He made not the slightest objection, and immediately began to write the permit I requested. While he wrote, I asked—

"'Do you think that these affairs will soon be brought before a jury? I have been told that the trials would take place on Monday.'

"'Oh, no! I will bring them on later. I do not wish them to be judged at present. Since we are alone, I will tell you that we have commenced negotiations with the Versaillese for an exchange of prisoners, and I hope that we shall succeed.'

"'But,' said I, 'this negotiation was attempted some time ago, and failed.'

"'Yes, because it was badly conducted; but we are now upon another ground.'

"'So much the better; it would be the solution most to be desired.'

"Profiting by the familiarity with which this high functionary seemed inclined to treat me, I added—

"'How many priests have you arrested?'

"'I don't know, but *not enough*,' he replied, in shaking his head. '*I wanted to arrest a great many more*, but I was prevented.'

"'Ah! then we will talk no more of that, for we should not agree.'

"'Oh, I know that very well,' he answered, with a smile of benevolent pity.

"'But,' I said, 'there is something that frightens me more than your jury; it is the perspective of a popular movement against the priests, and a massacre such as took place in '92.'

"'Oh, don't be afraid of that, we are *perfectly the masters;* and at any rate you are acquainted with Mazas. People cannot enter there as they choose. The prisoners are in safety there; and it is for that reason that I did not have them transferred to *Pélagie*. Pélagie is an open house, and would be less secure.'

"While we were talking, I was endeavoring to find a means of making him add to the permission for seeing the Archbishop and Abbé Duguerry, another for the Père Canbert, a Jesuit, admission to whom I had demanded uselessly for the last fifteen days at the Prefecture of Police.

"'Ah! I forgot; I have here another letter from a prisoner who wishes to see me. I will be much obliged if you will add his name to the other two—M. Canbert."'

"'Is it another priest?'

"'Yes.'

"The worthy citizen hesitated a moment, but added the name, and handed me the official paper almost as graciously as a functionary of the reaction could have done.

"'Then,' said I, as we left the cabinet, 'I can count that these affairs will not come on for several days?'

"'No, I am not in any hurry . . . unless the prisoners demand a judgment.'

"'But,' I added, in leaving him, 'are you not afraid of having your hand forced by an interpellation from your colleague, Urbain, of the Commune?'

"Citizen Rigault smiled with the air of a man sure of his superiority.

"'Urbain,' he answered me with a gesture of disdain; 'I am not at all afraid of his interpellations; *I fear no interpellation.* The affair shall only come on *when you give me the sign.*'

"After this information, little academical, but entirely Parisian, I took leave of my redoubtable interlocutor, and I thanked him, promising not 'to give him a sign' so very soon.

"In leaving the palace, I entered my carriage and was conducted immediately to Mazas. I asked to see the Archbishop in his cell, and not in the parlor of the advocates. My request was accorded with a good grace.

"'He is quite ill,' the chief guardian told me.

"On entering the cell of the poor Archbishop, I was struck, in fact, by his air of suffering and depression. Thanks to the doctor of the establishment, the regulation hammock of the prisoners had been replaced by a bed. On this he was lying dressed, his beard and mustaches long, and on his head a small black skull-cap. He was dressed in a rather worn cassock, from beneath which fell the ends of a violet sash. His features were much changed, and his face very pale. The noise I made in entering caused him to turn his head. Without knowing me, he imagined who I was, and extended his hand with a sad and sweet smile, which was at the same time of penetrating finesse.

"'You are ill, monseigneur, and I disturb you. Had I not better come some other day?'

"'Oh, no; I thank you so much for coming. I am ill, quite ill. I have suffered for some time from an affection of the heart, which is aggravated by want of air and diet of the prison. I wish in the first place that you could put off my affair, since they wish to judge me. I am utterly unable to go before their tribunal. If they wish to shoot me, let them shoot me here. I am not a hero, but it is as well to die that way as another.'

"I hastened to interrupt him.

"'Monseigneur,' I said, 'we have not reached that point *yet;*' and I related, insisting on all the points that could reassure him, the conversation which I had just had with Rigault. By talking thus, Monseigneur Darboy became animated and almost gay. He developed in a few words the ideas which he judged most useful for his defence.

"'I do not know,' he said, 'what causes their animosity against me. I have incurred, on account of my ideas on certain subjects, the disfavor of the Court of Rome. When, in 1863, I was called to the Archbishopric of Paris, I explained to the Emperor my views regarding the separation of Church and State. I begged him to occupy himself with the clergy as little as possible, and since, I have always avoided speaking in my public acts of the Emperor and his government. After my arrest I was subjected to the most ridiculous interrogatories. This Rigault or Ferré told me that I had taken possession of the people's property.'

"'What property?' I asked.

"'Parbleu, the churches, the vases, the ornaments.'

"'But,' I replied, 'you don't know of what you are talking. The vases, the ornaments, everything which serve in the religious worship, belong to persons called *fabriques,* who have the right to possess them; and if you had taken them, you would expose yourself to penalties written in the laws.'

"The Archbishop then spoke to me of the visits he had

received from Mr. Washburne, Minister of the United States, and of the negotiations which had been made for the exchange of prisoners between the Government and the Commune. I then recalled to him the allusion made by Raoul Rigault to new negotiations. He told me that he knew about them, and that Mr. Washburne had been conducting them with great zeal.

"He then returned to the subject of his defence, of the necessity for delay, and of the composition of the jury. He spoke with great sweetness, with perfect freedom of mind, and sometimes with an irony without bitterness. He told me that for some time they had allowed him to walk in the yard, in company with either the Abbé Duguerry or President Bonjean.

"'The President,' he added, 'proposed to defend me, but I told him that he would have quite enough to do in defending himself.'

"The Archbishop then spoke of his sister, who had been arrested with him and afterwards released. I asked him if I could render him any service; if he had any letters to be transmitted; if he had need of anything.

"'Nothing,' he said; 'I have need of nothing, unless it is to be left here; let them come here to shoot me if they wish, but I could not go to the trial; the doctor must have told them so.'

"After half an hour's conversation, I offered him my hand, and pressed his with emotion. More than once I had felt the tears coming. He bade me good-by with effusion, thanking me warmly for my *charity*. My visit, the assurance I gave him that the judgment would not take place immediately, the promise that I made to come and see him often, had evidently raised his spirits. When I rose, he threw off the rough woolen blanket that half covered him, and, holding my hand in his, conducted me to the door.

"'You will come again soon, will you not?'

"'Tuesday, monseigneur.'

"And I went out. His cell was No. 62.

"A few doors further on was the cell of M. Duguerry. When I entered he was seated between the bed and the table on the only chair the room possessed. On the table were several books, newspapers, and a small copper crucifix, like those worn by the nuns. Without rising, the poor curé held out his arms and gave me a long embrace. He then forced me to take his chair.

"'Ah! I have plenty of time to be there,' he said, and he seated himself near me on the foot of the bed. I did not find him much changed, only thinner. His white beard and mustaches displayed themselves against his florid complexion and large features, which were framed by the remains of a plentiful head of hair. The good curé immediately began to repeat to me the burlesque remarks made to him by Rigault and his secretary Dacosta.

"'What is this trade of yours?'

"'It is not a trade, it is a vocation, a moral ministry, which we undertake for the amelioration of souls.'

"'Ah, that is all *blagues*. We want to know what stories you tell the people.'

"'We teach them the religion of our Lord Jesus Christ.'

"'There are no more Lords; we don't know any Lords.'

"The director of the prison said to the good Abbé in a moment of confidence: 'I, too, have religious ideas. I wished to be a Moravian brother; afterwards I had an idea of belonging to the Brotherhood of Chartreux; but I think I had sooner become a Mormon.'

"The Abbé Duguerry added that he had need of nothing; that his domestic had everything passed to him for which he asked. I saw, in fact, on the table several oranges, chocolate, and some bottles.

"'We receive the papers,' he said. 'Ah! I wish you would bring me the *Grandeur et la Décadence des Romains*, by Montesquieu.'

"'Willingly, *Monsieur le Curé;* I will bring it Tuesday when I return to see you.'

"'You *can* return?'

"'Assuredly; as often as I wish. My permission is not limited.'

"'Ah! I am very happy to hear it, very happy. How I thank you!' and tears stood in his eyes.

"I had risen. In taking the few steps that separated us from the door, he held my hand. Arrived at the end, he said:

"'*Allons*, dear friend, take my regards to your mother. *You will tell her that I cried*,' and he embraced me, sobbing.

"He recovered himself in a moment, and said:

"'*Allons, allons*, until Tuesday. Don't forget my book.'"

Notwithstanding the violences of which the insurrectional government had proved itself capable, no one believed that they would go so far as to assassinate the hostages. Assassination it must be called, for there is no other name with which to qualify executions made without any motive of accusation, without judgment, without even an interrogatory. There is, however, a state of furious exaltation which, passing a certain degree, becomes delirium, a bloody frenzy. When this exaltation, mingled with emphatic phrases, with words of right, of emancipation, and of social enfranchisement repeated far beyond their true signification, gains an ignorant crowd, spoiled by vanity and envy, then indeed the worst results are to be anticipated; then the conscience becomes mute, all notions of equity are effaced, and the passions have full sway without any curb to restrain them.

It would seem as though the army had a presentiment of these catastrophes from the ardor with which they carried the different positions, and the rapidity with which they advanced as far as the security of the general plan would allow.

During the day of Wednesday, the 24th, the troops divided on the right bank into three principal columns, advanced through the 1st, 2d, 3d, and 10th Arrondissements. In this last they had taken possession of the church of Saint-Vincent-de-Paul, of the Northern and Eastern Railway Stations, and commanded the Boulevard Magenta; in the centre they had invaded the old boulevards, and had carried the barricades of the Portes St. Denis and St. Martin. In abandoning the latter the Federals had set fire to the Theatre of the Porte St. Martin, and to all the block of buildings beyond as far as the entrance of the Faubourg; towards the Seine, after a long and furious combat, they had become masters of the wheat-market, the central-market, of Saint-Eustache, and the insurgents, everywhere driven back, retired precipitately by the Rues Turbigo and Rambuteau to concentrate at the grand fortress of the Chateau-d'Eau and at the Bastille.

The insurgents in withdrawing set fire to the Church of Saint-Eustache, but the flames were fortunately extinguished before they could do much damage. The spire was demolished during the bombardment.

Finally, the soldiers conquered, step by step, after a series of fierce engagements, the Louvre, the Place Saint-Germain-l'Auxerrois, and the streets Saint-Honoré and Rivoli as far as the Pont-Neuf. Most of the houses in these large thoroughfares bear the traces of bullets and shells; many indeed were entirely destroyed. Arrived at the Rue des Halles and the Pont-Neuf, the assailants were joined in the Cité by one of the divisions of General de Cissey.

At the attack of the barricade of the Théatre Français, which was made by the Rue Montpensier, the Rue Richelieu, and the Rue Saint-Honoré, many of the National Guards refused to surrender and were immediately shot.

In the afternoon, at about three, the Palais Royal was set on fire by the insurgents. A merchant in the building, believing the fire to be an accident, hastened to offer his services, but was roughly received by a captain of the National Guard, who threatened to fire upon him if he did not immediately withdraw. He added that the quarter was to be blown up, and that everything must burn. Nevertheless, notwithstanding his menaces, two pumps were placed in action by the inhabitants of the neighborhood. It was then four o'clock. No water was to be had in the Court des Fontaines, and it was necessary to make a chain in the passage conducting to the Court of Honor.

A ladder was placed against the wall in order to reach the terrace of the Rue de Valois, but the menaces of the insurgents to fire were so precise that the attempt to save the pavilion from that side was abandoned.

The fire and smoke poured forth from three windows above the terrace No. 17, where the flames were successfully extinguished in the midst of shots fired from the barricade of the Rue de Rivoli.

At five o'clock a pump was established in the Court of Honor, and a large quantity of paintings, precious marbles, furniture, etc., was saved.

The chains were formed, but unfortunately the most difficult thing to obtain was water, the insurgents having cut all the pipes to insure the destruction of the palace. At seven o'clock several members of the Paris Fire Company arrived, but by that time pavilion No. 1 was entirely consumed.

On the arrival of the firemen, they began immediately

to combat the fire in pavilion No. 2, to prevent its gaining the apartments of the Princess Clotilde. The furniture of the chapel, and all the church ornaments were saved.

Finally, at eight o'clock, the troops of the line arrived. They were received with cries of "*Vive la ligne!*" "*Vive la France!*"

The work was then continued with more calm, and a means was sought for attacking the fire from above—that is, from the second story or from the roofs. The great danger was from the theatre, which the flames were rapidly approaching. If this was reached, it was to be feared that the whole quarter would be destroyed.

The idea was then formed of attacking the fire from the theatre itself, and of arresting the flames by means of its pipes. M. Le Saché placed himself at the head of this movement. Mounting on the roof with the head machinist, he was obliged to hide himself, to avoid the balls fired by the Communists from the top of the Hotel du Louvre. Braving the danger, the roof was mined; the water finally arrived; and it was time.

At ten o'clock, a body of thirty firemen appeared, and succeeded in rendering themselves masters of the flames. An hour sooner, the whole could have been saved.

The resistance in the neighborhood of the Hotel de Ville was most obstinate, and before the defences surrounding the building had been entirely captured by the troops, it was evacuated and set on fire by the insurgents.

Strategically a considerable advance had been made during the day. The line of investment had been greatly narrowed, thus enabling the different corps to render each other more assistance; while the Federals, on the contrary, commenced to be discouraged, and were deprived of all unity of commandment, and of almost all combined direction, dating from the 24th. They were isolated in two distinct combats on the right and left banks, where they accumulated uselessly at certain preferred points.

As regarded the action, however, the most perilous portion of their task was yet to be achieved by the troops. They were approaching the traditional ground of the insurrection, where the remembrance of former popular combats still heated the ardor of the insurgents, where narrow and winding streets succeed each other rapidly, still existing in great numbers beyond the Faubourg Poissonière, the Rue Montorgueil, and the Rue St. Denis, notwithstanding the large avenues which have been made through these populous quarters to the Place de la Bastille.

They were penetrating, in fact, upon the theatre of the terrible days of June, 1848, which at that time seemed to those who witnessed them the end of all attempts at insurrection in Paris, but whose scenes, reproduced with even more violence in the last days of the insurrection of 1871, have seemed but slight episodes in this horrible street battle.

The object of the army had been fully determined when it began its march on the morning of the 24th. On the right bank, their course has been already described; their advance on the Hotel de Ville, in order to gain the Bastille by the Rue Saint Antoine; the taking of the Central Market and the Rue Turbigo, opening the way to the Chateau d'Eau. In the centre, the march of General Douay's corps along the old boulevards also approaching the Chateau d'Eau, and in the north, the occupation of the Rue Lafayette as far as the Northern Railway Station and the Boulevard Magenta, in order to second either the attack on the Chateau d'Eau and the Bastille or that of La Villette and the Buttes Chaumont.

On the left bank it was necessary to gain possession of the Pantheon before pushing on towards the Gobelins, and to reach the Orleans Railway Station by taking possession of the quays, concurring on the way in the occupation of the Cité and the Hotel de Ville.

Early on the morning of the 24th, the troops took possession of the barricade at the Barrière d'Enfer, after a violent combat. A large number of prisoners were taken. Among them was a staff captain, his breast covered with medals—the Crimean, Italian, Chinese, and Mexican, together with three medals of salvage. This man, with a large face, full chest and bull neck, was dragged along pale and trembling, begging for mercy, telling of his devotion to his fellow-creatures, of his wife and child who were expecting him at Charenton, and swearing that he had been taken by force to the barricades—which was sufficiently disproved by the grade he bore.

The chasseur who had taken him prisoner, and torn from his hand the flag of the Commune, had been twice fired upon by this wretch. In direct contrast with this cowardice was the attitude of an old sergeant, at least sixty years of age, who stood firm and impassible amidst the shouts and execrations of the populace.

The 24th, in the morning, the occupation of the Faubourg Saint Germain was assured; and at about eleven o'clock a portion of the troops of General de Cissey began the attack of the Pantheon, in combining a double movement of approach by the Place Medicis and the Rue Soufflot, and by the Rues Gay-Lussac, Royer-Collard, and Ulm. At all these points the combat was exceedingly violent.

A brigade, formed in three columns, opened the action by rushing on the Luxembourg through the gates of the garden, which open on the Rue d'Assas and the Rue de Vaugirard, while the column on the right carried the Ecole des Mines, and extended its sharp-shooters the length of the railing in the Rue de Médicis.

At the same time a battalion of chasseurs crossed the garden at a quickstep, and arrived at the gate of the Rue Soufflot, where, under a rain of bullets and shells thrown from the Pantheon, from the Rue Soufflot and its barricades, they broke down the gate, and carried the barricade which stood opposite, gaining possession of two mitrailleuses. They then invaded the Boulevard Saint Michel, and established their guns on the barricades of the Rues Cujas and Mallebranche.

The insurgents who had taken refuge behind the barricades of the Boulevard Saint Michel were able to command these positions, and rendered them very dangerous for the troops who remained, during an hour, exposed to a most terrible fire, which did not however succeed in making them fall back.

At this moment, the General Paturel who directed the attack was struck in the leg by a ball. He had remained with the most remarkable *sang-froid* at the head of the Boulevard Saint Michel, notwithstanding the terrible fire, giving his orders with the greatest calm, causing the points which seemed to him most important to be occupied, and going from barricade to barricade encouraging the troops by his presence.

At the same time, another column, under the orders of General Bocher, carried, with equal intrepidity, the barricades erected in the Rues Royer-Collard and Gay-Lussac, and advanced on the Pantheon by the Rues du Faubourg-Saint-Jacques and d'Ulm.

The efforts on the side of the Place Saint-Michel were then redoubled. The fire of the National Guards being answered vigorously by the troops, gradually decreased in intensity, when the soldiers, advancing by the Rues Soufflot, Cujas, and Mallebranche, attacked the barricades in front, and finally carried them, rejoining the column which issued from the Rue d'Ulm at the same moment.

After a last attack with the bayonet, the insurgents were entirely routed, and fled towards the Gobelins and the Barrière d'Italie. The Pantheon was taken. It was time; without the rapidity of the action, which had thrown trouble and disorder among the Federals, this monument would have been broken to fragments by a horrible explosion. The order had been given to blow up the Pantheon; barrels of powder, and vats filled with petroleum, placed in the cellars, only awaited the electric spark.

There, as in many other places, time had failed the insurgents, and prevented them from giving free course to their terrible designs.

These designs were not due, as one would like to believe, to the sudden inspiration of madmen, drunk with whiskey, powder and despair. No! It is certain, unhappily for the honor of human nature, that these projects of destruction, dictated by a true sentiment of social hatred, formed a part of the plan of resistance of the Commune and the Central Committee, and were, above all, entertained by the members of the Committee of Public Safety.

The burning of so many public monuments, of so much private property, is a sufficient proof of this design; and yet all these conflagrations were, thanks to the promptitude of the military operations, but partial incidents in a general system conceived for the ruin of Paris.

Discoveries have been made in most of the quarters of quantities of powder and petroleum placed in the sewers, in the depths of cellars, in the different stories of houses, in the interior of public edifices, placed in such a manner as to blow up or set on fire entire streets.

Finally, written orders have been found on the different chiefs of the insurrection, denoting how carefully the horrible combination had been carried out.

Those ordering the formation of four companies under

the orders of Millière, Dereure, Billioray, and Vésinier, for the purpose of setting fire to the different quarters of Paris, have been already given in this work.

On the 24th of May, at nine in the evening, the following notice was placarded on the walls of the 11th Arrondissement:

"COMMUNE OF PARIS.

"*Order.*

"4 Prairial, year 79, 9 P. M.

"Any house from the windows of which a shot is fired on the National Guards will be immediately destroyed; and all the inhabitants who do not deliver or themselves execute the author of such a crime, will be immediately shot.

"THE COMMISSION OF WAR."

The following order was found on an insurgent killed at the barricade of the Croix Rouge:

"The bearer of this order is authorized to destroy by fire or mine any public or private establishment prejudicial to the defence of the Commune."

At the moment when the attack on the Pantheon was in full progress, the fighting was suspended on both sides for several moments by a terrible detonation which shook the quarter of the Luxembourg to its very foundations.

A powder magazine situated in the back of the garden, near the Rue de l'Ouest, had been exploded by the insurgents, who had communicated a spark to the powder by means of an electric wire. The noise was frightful; a great number of houses in the Rue de l'Ouest, in the Boulevard Saint-Michel near the Observatory, were much injured; also those in the Rues d'Enfer, D'Assas, De Vaugirard, De Madame, De Fleurus, etc. In the Place de Medicis, and the neighboring portion of the Boulevard Saint-Michel, the fronts of the shops had been literally torn

RAOUL RIGAULT
Commune of Paris
1871

away. Throughout the whole quarter, all the windows were broken into thousands of pieces.

This secondary injury was happily the only one sustained by the Palace of the Luxembourg, so near the scene of the explosion.

Clouds of dust obscured the light of the sun; the inhabitants everywhere rushed out into the courts and streets, fearing every moment to be crushed beneath their falling houses; remains of furniture, of glass, of timber, of marble, were thrown far and wide, covering the ground in every direction. While the terror was at its height, the battle recommenced; and it became all the more difficult to escape disaster, as, fleeing from the rain of falling fragments, the unhappy inhabitants were often reached by the balls of the combatants. It was during this same day of the 24th that Raoul Rigault, Procurator of the Commune, was shot.

He came at about three in the afternoon, to give instructions regarding the defence to the Federals of the 5th Arrondissement. He then went to the Rue Gay-Lussac, where he had hired a hotel under the name of Varcla, which hotel was inhabited by an actress of one of the smaller Parisian theatres.

As he placed his hand upon the door-bell, the soldiers of the line made their appearance by the Rue des Feuillantines. At the sight of Raoul Rigault, who wore the uniform of a chief, they fired without reaching him.

The door opened at the same instant, and Rigault entered, closely followed by the soldiers. They first seized upon the proprietor of the house, who was in shirt-sleeves, taking him for the man they sought, on account of his black beard, which resembled that worn by Rigault. A surgeon who inhabited the house hastened to inform them that they had seized a peaceful man, entirely stranger to all political quarrels.

The soldiers then began to search the house, and soon laid their hands upon Rigault, who, having given his name, followed them quietly.

They then descended the Rue Gay-Lussac, leading their prisoner to the Luxembourg. When at the Rue Royer-Collard they met a colonel of the staff, who asked his name. Rigault replied with a shout of "*Vive la Commune! à bas les assassins!*"

He was forthwith placed against the wall and shot. His body lay abandoned at the entrance of the street for twenty-four hours, and presented a frightful spectacle. His head, surrounded by hair and beard, glued with blood, was horrible to see. The left side of the face was entirely crushed, and formed an undistinguishable mass, while the right eye, which alone remained, stood open, fixed and haggard in its expression.

Early in life Raoul Rigault had felt himself made for a double vocation, that of forming conspiracies and of doing the police on a large scale. These two specialties would seem at first sight to exclude each other, but he managed to conciliate two things apparently so hostile. Friend and disciple of L. A. Blanqui, he is believed to have derived his strange tastes from the French Mazzini. In his youth he had entered several schools, attempted a little of everything without any success, particularly the preparation for the Polytechnic School; and from these different failures at his examinations he had drawn a feeling of envy and hatred of others which prompted him to destroy everything. One is tempted to believe that the defeats which he had undergone counted for something in the extravagance of his radicalism.

His old father—a most honorable man—and his brother, a young man, sensible and well-bred, had both attempted at different times to bring back this prodigal son to his family, but always without success. He was entirely absorbed in politics and the police. In writing for different papers, he always had in view this double work. In 1870, at the time of the process of Blois, when he had to reply in regard to facts touching the conspiracy, he had for an advocate M. Lachaud, to whom he confided the vivacity of his instincts.

During the Commune this advocate had need of a permit of circulation, of which the delegate to the police was so avaricious. He asked and obtained it, remarking at the same time to his former client that he must have reached the height of his desires, since he was at the same time member of the government and chief of the police. "Without doubt," replied Rigault, "only it must last."

After the revolution of the 4th of September, he had found means of introducing himself to M. Kératry, and had placed his hands on all that was most mysterious or most intricate in the Rue de Jerusalem. When M. Kératry ceded his functions to M. Edmond Adam, the young conspirator was obliged to retire also. In leaving the Prefecture of Police, he carried with him a large quantity of documents relative to the secret police; and afterwards published a list of the ex-democrats who had been paid during the Empire to denounce the proceedings of the party to which they had belonged. Fifteen or twenty persons had thus their proceedings laid bare, but they were for the most part illiterate men, drunkards, or laborers without work, whom M. Ernest Picard calls with reason the "low demagogy."

By constantly frequenting the clubs from the beginning of the siege, Raoul Rigault gained a certain popularity which caused him to be named chief of one of the battalions of the 5th Arrondissement.

This title, and the embroideries it enabled him to wear, helped him to become initiated in the Republican Confederation, presided over by the ex-Count du Bisson, general under the Commune. At the revolution of the 18th of March, the monomaniac had only to present himself at the Prefecture of Police in order to take possession. From that day he reigned there, not as master, but as tyrant.

Rigid in his attitude, hard and brief in his words, listening only to the passion which dominated him, to such an extent that he would hear neither his friends nor his equals, he spread over Paris an immense web, entangling in its threads all persons hostile to the Communal movement; and, as is well known, their number was not few.

In the derisive elections made on the 26th of March, he was elected member of the Commune by a small majority, and in the sittings of that body he supported with all his power the necessity of imitating the movement of '92 in every proceeding. To this was added the arrest of hostages—a practice which had been renewed by the Prussians.

Before him the priests first appeared after their arrest. Monseigneur Darboy having been conducted to his anteroom, entered, saying mildly to those present, "What do you wish, my children?"

"Citizen," replied Raoul Rigault, roughly, "leave off that wheedling and familiar manner of speaking. Do not forget that you are in the presence of a magistrate," and he showed his scarf of Prefecture of Police.

From the moment he became member of the Commune he dreamed only of uniting his functions of Delegate of Police with those of Procurator-General. He had thus gained one quality more, and a new pretext for meddling in public affairs. His ideal was to himself sue those whom he had arrested; and twice during the sittings of court-martial he demanded, without any hesitation, sentences of death.

It is not to be wondered at that, from the beginning of April, his very name caused a certain terror; men ordinarily full of courage avoided going where they were in the habit of meeting him; a single sign of his hand being sufficient to cause any one's arrest, while no one knew what might become of his prisoners.

From the day of his entrance into power, Rigault had taken as associate a third-class artist called Pilotell, whom he employed in seizing his victims. One of these, M. Polo, director of the *Eclipse*, was imprisoned for having sent copies of his paper to Versailles, and plundered at the same time of 3,000 francs. His real offence consisted in not having accepted for his satirical sheets all the caricatures presented by Pilotell. He was afterwards set at liberty through the efforts of his friends, but his three thousand francs were not returned.

Pilotell was later employed in making a domiciliary visit at the house of Gustave Chaudey. Having taken possession of all the papers on which he could lay his hands, he discovered in the bottom of a drawer 815 francs in gold, which he pocketed, saying to Madame Chaudey, who was present, "Who knows? There is perhaps blood on this gold."

The following curious conversation, which was held by Raoul Rigault and M. Cochinat, who went to demand the liberation of M. Balathier de Bragelone, editor of the *Petite Presse*, arrested without any plausible motive, will explain the object of many of his public acts:

Rigault having at first refused, without giving any reason, to grant the demand of M. Cochinat, the latter remarked that he was making very free with the *liberty of the press.*

"The liberty of the press!" replied Rigault; "*connais pas!*"

"What! you know nothing about it! Why, you demanded it every day in the *Marseillaise*, of which you were one of the editors!"

"Ah! not I; the others! At all events, that was in the time of Badinguet. As for me, I always declared loudly that we would not suffer hostile papers *when we were the strongest*. As we are the strongest now, we can't have any."

"But will you always be the strongest?"

"Certainly; Paris is impregnable, and Versailles must finally yield."

"And the provinces?"

"The provinces!" he replied, laughingly; "much we care for the provinces!"

To that there was no reply, but M. Cochinat used other arguments, which finally induced Rigault to give an order to Dacosta, his private secretary, for the liberation of M. Balathier.

M. Cochinat then asked Rigault if he did not think it peurile and absurd to arrest journalists so moderate in their language as M. Balathier and others? to which Rigault replied that he quite agreed with him; above all, as the arrests gave him a great deal of work.

"Then why," said he, "do you do these things if you yourself think them absurd?"

"Ah," he replied, with a careless air, "because it keeps up '*une petite terreur*' in the city."

Such were the individuals for whom thousands of unhappy creatures lost their lives or liberty.

Although the Commune ostensibly allowed but six thousand francs a year to its highest functionaries, they managed to lead *la vie douce* in it fullest signification. The following bills of fare of two breakfasts taken at the restaurant of the Frères-Provençaux by Raoul Rigault and his secretary Dacosta, show at least that they were connoisseurs in matters of the table:

Breakfast of May 10th.

	Frs.	C.
Nuits	15	
Clos-Vougeot	12	
Bread		50
Hors-d'œuvre	3	
Sole	3	
Chateaubriand aux truffes	8	
Chicken	12	
Salad	1	50
Cheese		75
Oranges	2	
Coffee, liqueurs	4	
Cigars-Cazadorès	13	50
Total	75	25

Breakfast of May 15th.

	Frs.	C.
Pomard	5	
Nuits	10	
Clicquot	13	
Bread		50
Hors-d'œuvre	1	60
Mackerel	3	
Côte provençale	3	75
Chicken	12	
Salad	1	50
Cheese		50
Ices	3	
Coffee, liqueurs	3	
Cigars	6	
Total	62	85

At this restaurant Rigault was in the habit of taking most of his repasts.

After his dinner, Rigault's evenings were mostly spent in drinking and smoking in front of the cafés in the Boulevard Saint-Michel. One night, sitting before the café Soufflot, the man of pleasure becoming for an instant effaced by the fanatic, he exclaimed, in striking his glass against that of his neighbor, that he "should like to place a bouquet of 300,000 decapitated heads around the feet of the statue of Liberty."

During the day of the 24th, the service of artillery had been reorganized at Montmartre, and about half past seven in the evening a furious cannonade was begun. The batteries of Montmartre thundered against La Chapelle, La Villette, and the Buttes Chaumont, while those of the Pantheon covered with shells the neighborhood of the Place de la Bastille.

At ten o'clock the fire became most intense, and those who heard those detonations will never forget the terrible uproar. It was no longer roaring cannons exchanging regularly their projectiles, but a continual rolling of shot upon shot, coming from an army of batteries placed in every direction. The Seine itself took part in the struggle, and the gunboats moored beneath the bridges poured forth fire like so many volcanoes. The musketry fire was so rapid that the sound resembled the whistling rush of a mighty wind, now and then deadened by the sharp rattle of the mitrailleuse.

The battle was everywhere going on: at La Villette, on the boulevards, at the Hotel de Ville, the Luxembourg, and the Pont Neuf. Paris was entirely lost in a cloud of smoke, lighted now and then by the flashes of the cannon, and reddened by the flames of burning buildings. From La Villette and the Buttes Chaumont, shells were thrown to every portion of the right bank. No quarter was spared. Incendiary projectiles fell in quantities in the Rue de la Monnaie, on the Place Saint-Germain-l'Auxerrois, in the Central Markets, the Rue Montmartre, Place de la Bourse, the Rue Neuve des Petits-Champs, the Place

Ventadour, the Marché Saint-Honoré, on the Boulevard des Italiens, Rue de la Chaussée-d'Antin, Rue Blanche, Rue Pigalle, and all the streets extending from there to the Faubourg Saint-Martin.

Had Montmartre been able to add its fire to that of the two formidable positions still held by the insurgents, half of Paris would have been reduced to ashes. As it was, the destruction was enormous; and though most of the inhabitants had the precaution to take refuge in the cellars, the number of victims to this bombardment was very great.

No! Paris will never forget the night of the 24th of May, to which history can find no parallel unless perhaps the 24th of August, 1572—all fanaticisms, whether religious or revolutionary, resembling each other in their blind transports of fury. To find anything truly similar to the burning of Paris we must remount to the celebrated night on which Nero treated himself to the spectacle of Rome in flames. What was done by the Roman Emperor from a mere whim of ferocious curiosity, the Commune did not hesitate to do incited by a furious desire for revenge; uniting thus in their hatred of the future, modern demagogy with the most hateful of the tyrannies of ancient Rome.

Nothing can express the cruel impression produced during the night as each new fire broke forth, extending along the line of the horizon from the Hotel de Ville to the Place de la Concorde. As each new light appeared, people questioned each other with anxiety as to what building it might be on which the work of destruction was being completed.

In the evening, a little before nightfall, thick clouds of smoke had announced the points at which the fire had declared itself; but the gravity of the situation was not realized until darkness fell upon the city. Then the flames became more distinct, reddening the sky in every direction, and rendering it more easy to judge of the extent of the disaster.

The conflagration of the upper portions of the pavilions of the Tuileries presented the most terrible spectacle that can well be imagined. The flames could be plainly perceived, and every instant immense columns of sparks rose high in the air, falling like a volcanic eruption on the surrounding quarters. From the neighborhood of Montmartre the fire could be distinctly seen, extending and reaching the gallery which connects the Pavilion Maison with the Louvre; and at that terrible moment it seemed inevitable that the depôt of such immense and wonderful treasures, once lost never to be replaced, would also become a prey to the flames. The conflagration of the Palais-Royal confounded its light with that of the Tuileries gallery.

Looking towards the right in the directio of the Place-de-la-Concorde, a long line of fire denoted the position of the Ministry of Finance, which had continued since Monday to pour forth columns of reddened smoke. In the obscurity this immense furnace, from which gigantic flames leaped forth, mingled with bright sparks from the masses of burning paper, presented a terrible picture, contrasting with the dark clouds that hung like a pall over the doomed houses of the Rue Royale. On the left, towards Saint-Germain-l'Auxerrois, the Palace of Justice, the Central Markets, and the Hotel de Ville, were all in flames.

Soon this immense zone, from the Place-de-la-Concorde to the Hotel de Ville, was veiled in smoke, from which jets of flame shot forth here and there, indicating the situation of the different conflagrations.

Beyond this first line, new columns of fire might be seen rising from the left bank of the Seine, announcing continually new disasters. The *Conseil d'Etat*, the Palace of the *Légion d'Honneur*, and the *Caisse des Depôts et Consignations*, were also in flames.

This terrible spectacle, less frightful during the day, gave to the nights of the 23d and 24th an aspect of which the horror cannot be described, but such as can never be effaced from the memory of all who witnessed it.

As early as Monday morning the Palace of Justice had been covered with petroleum by order of Raoul Rigault. In order that this infernal work should not be deranged, a battalion of Federals was placed on guard around the Palace, and two men were sent by the Commissary of Police to Wurtz (Rigault's substitute) with the following recommendation:

"COMMISSARIAT DE POLICE, DU PALAIS DE JUSTICE.

CITOYEN:—Prenez ces deux citoyens qui sont deux bons bougres à poil.

"BREUILLE."

These men accomplished their task conscientiously, and the building was set on fire.

The Prefecture of Police had been taken possession of on the 18th of March by Raoul Rigault, who had immediately installed himself as Prefect. The employés left him and his band masters of the establishment, and took their departure for Versailles. They were easily replaced, however, by Rigault, who recruited among his friends and acquaintances a collection of individuals who had never before been guilty of holding a situation.

The new employés of the Prefecture passed their time most delightfully, drinking innumerable jugs of beer, and smoking endless pipes. The chest of the administration paid for all these libations, and finally two of these individuals, Riel and Leballeur, were imprisoned for drawing too liberally upon it.

On Tuesday, the 23d, Th. Ferré, who was Prefect at

the time of the entrance of the Government troops, ordered the walls of the building to be covered with petroleum. The concierge Charlet, wishing to oppose this criminal act, was immediately imprisoned.

That same evening Ferré gave a grand banquet to twenty-eight of his friends and accomplices. Their orgies lasted until the following morning, when they fired the building at eleven different points, and immediately took their departure.

At the Conciergerie, meanwhile, the prisoners had been set at liberty. At eleven on the morning of the 24th, Raoul Rigault made his appearance in the prison, and gave the order for their liberation, and they were forthwith released, one hundred and fifty in number.

Hardly had they left the prison when they found themselves everywhere surrounded by barricades, which they were ordered by the Federals to defend under pain of death. They all refused emphatically to make use of the arms presented to them against the troops. A young girl of fifteen, wearing a red sash across her shoulders, was particularly violent in calling upon the prisoners to defend the barricades.

The prisoners then took to flight amidst a rain of bullets sent against them by the Federals, and, sooner than draw upon the regular army, they took refuge in the Prefecture, in the midst of a court which the fire had transformed into a veritable furnace.

There they remained until five o'clock, when they were rescued by Lieutenant Berger, at the head of a detachment of the 79th of the line.

Among the prisoners who found themselves in this terrible position were the Prince Galitzin and M. Andréoli, director of the *Observateur*.

CHAPTER XII.

Government circular—Capture of the Butte-aux-Cailles—The Gobelins taken, but in flames—Fall of the forts Bicêtre and Ivry—Massacre of Dominicans—Death of Millière—Of Vallés—General de Cissey—His brilliant career—Capture of the Hotel de Ville—The building in ruins—Advance on the Place de la Bastille—Attack on the Austerlitz bridge—The Mazas prisoners released—Their death—Citizen Vincent—The Grenier d'Abondance in flames—Despatch of Ferré to Delescluze—The Chateau d'Eau—Artifices of the Commune—The Boulevard Magenta—Capture of the Chateau d'Eau—Death of Delescluze—Papers found on his person—Large number of prisoners taken—Preparations for blowing up the neighborhood—Place du Trône—More victims at La Roquette—The remaining prisoners erect barricades within the building—Some of them leave the prison and are murdered—Announcement made by the Minister of War in the National Assembly—Circular of M. Jules Favre to French Representatives at Foreign Courts—Answer to the Belgian and Spanish Governments—Protest of M. Victor Hugo—He is ejected from Belgium—Conflagration of the docks of La Villette—Offers of firemen made by the English and Belgian Governments.

THE terrible cannonade kept up during the night obliged the insurgents to evacuate the central portion of the city, and take refuge in the northwestern quarter, leaving only near the Halles and the Palais Royal a few battalions sacrificed in advance. Protected by their sharpshooters, and by the conflagrations they had lighted, they hoped sufficiently to cover their retreat.

It is thought that they intended, under the protection of the cannon of the Buttes Chaumont, to retake the exterior boulevards, and thus cut off the French army; but they were then too utterly demoralized to attempt anything of the sort. Fleeing in disorder, and thrown back upon their last entrenchments, what could they do? Sally out by the northeast and abandon the place? It was not to be thought of; the Prussians were there, barring the passage to the people they had taken such pleasure in seeing *at work.*

The Communists were caged; nothing remained but to sell their lives as dearly as possible, and to fight to the last. "Better death than Cayenne" was on every tongue; all felt that no mercy could be accorded to such as they, and nerved themselves with the energy of despair.

On Thursday, the 25th of May, at seven in the morning, the following despatch was sent by M. Thiers to the different Prefects

"We are masters of Paris, with the exception of a small portion, which will probably be occupied this morning. The Tuileries is in ashes; the Louvre is saved. The portion of the Ministry of Finance which fronts on the Rue de Rivoli has been destroyed. The palace of the Quai d'Orsay, in which the Conseil-d'Etat and the Cour des Comptes held their sittings, has also been burned. This is the state in which Paris is delivered to us by the wretches who oppressed and dishonored it. They have left in our hands 12,000 prisoners, and we shall probably have at the end from 18,000 to 20,000. The soil of Paris is strewed with their dead bodies. This horrible spectacle will serve, it is to be hoped, as a lesson to the insurgents who dared to declare themselves partisans of the Commune. Justice, however, will soon satisfy the human conscience, outraged by the monstrous acts of which France and the world have been the witness.

"The army has been admirable. We are happy to be able to announce in the midst of our misfortunes that, owing to the wisdom of our generals, the loss among the troops is very slight."

At nine o'clock fifty-five minutes, General de Cissey sent the following despatch from the Luxembourg:

"The fort of Montrouge and that of Hautes-Bruyères are ours. . . . We are masters of the Pantheon, of the Halle aux Vins, and all the neighborhood. The Barrière-d'Italie only remains for us to take. I shall close and occupy all the gates as far as the Seine. Advance your troops and occupy Choisy-le-Roi, l'Hay, and neighborhood. Strengthen the investment; let no one leave the city."

The soldiers had, in fact, after a few hours' repose, necessitated by the terrible struggle of the previous day, continued their advance at an early hour.

After the capture of the Barrière d'Enfer and Montrouge by the troops on the previous day, the insurgents had established themselves in force (from 7,000 to 8,000) on a height called the Butte-aux-Cailles. Their artillery commanded the quarter of Montrouge, which they covered with shells, while their sharp-shooters, descending into the valley, made an offensive demonstration against the regular troops, who found themselves thus arrested in their movement. They held good, however, during the evening and throughout the night. On Thursday morning they were reinforced, and a battery was established behind the Sceaux Railway, which covered the Butte-aux-Cailles with its fire; at the same time the soldiers advanced to the attack in front, and, after a most deadly struggle, carried the position.

The operations were then continued in the direction of the Gobelins, the troops advancing through the streets of the Faubourg Saint-Marceau. The resistance was prolonged during several hours, though without much energy on the part of the insurrection. The population in this quarter, composed in great part of rag-pickers, especially in the Rue Mouffetard, had, forming a curious exception, little sympathy with Communist ideas, either from a sort of philosophical indifference often to be observed among the followers of this trade, or rather perhaps from the decline which the reign of the Commune had brought upon this industry, not so wretched a one as is generally imagined. It was, in fact, to be remarked during the first siege of Paris, and after the 18th of March, that there was quite a scarcity of rags on the Parisian pavements, and the rag-pickers, always enemies of chimeras and declamations, had doubtless borne a grudge against the Commune.

Be that as it may, the barricades of the Rue Mouffetard were feebly defended, and the Gobelins carried without too vigorous an effort. But the insurgents, in abandoning this magnificent establishment of so national a character, delivered it as a prey to the flames. In a few moments the tapestry and looms of the work-shops were destroyed, and the saloon of designs and sculptures, and the precious collection of the most remarkable tapestries executed from the seventeenth century down to our time, were reduced to ashes. This act, as well as the burning of the docks, was a direct outrage on labor, whose intelligent workmanship had been so directly manifested in these magnificent productions.

The regular forces advanced without interruption, pushing back the National Guards to the Barrière d'Italie, where they dispersed on all sides, leaving numerous prisoners. The troops then re-descended the boulevard to the Austerlitz Bridge, rejoining the left wing of General de Cissey's corps, which had advanced along the quays of the left bank of the Seine, and had, after a succession of vigorous engagements, taken possession of the Bridges des Saints-Pères, Pont Neuf, Saint-Michel, and Notre Dame. They then established themselves at the Jardin des Plantes and the Orleans Railway Station, having left sufficient force behind to secure their rear and to co-operate in the taking of the Hotel de Ville.

The fall of the position of the insurgents at the Butte-aux-Cailles had hastened that of the Forts Bicêtre and Ivry, both taken by an assault of the cavalry of General du Barrail. A shell having fallen in the powder-magazine of the latter fort caused a terrible explosion. Profiting by the confusion which ensued, the dragoons rushed to the assault, and gained possession of the fort, Wrobleski surrendering himself prisoner with 6,000 insurgents.

Meanwhile another horrible massacre of hostages had taken place; more victims to the insatiable revenge of the Commune had been added to the lists of horrors with which that body intended to startle the world.

On Friday, May 19th, two battalions of Federals, the 101st and 120th, appeared at Arcueil, led by Commandant Quesnot and Citizen Millière. Entering the College of Dominican Friars, they carried off as hostages six of the Fathers who were in the college, together with several professors and domestics, in all twenty-four persons, and conducted them to the Fort Bicêtre.

Twelve sisters of Saint-Marc, charged with the ambulance of Arcueil, who had been employed during the whole of the preceding night in picking up the wounded National Guards, and giving them every care, were also torn away from Arcueil and conducted to the prison of Saint-Lazare. From that day they have not been heard of.

The Father Captier, Superior of the Dominican College, and his twenty-three companions in captivity, were taken to Bicêtre. Here, having been robbed of their money, and thoroughly searched, they were shut up in a casemate, where they remained during eight days, their only bed being a little straw, and their nourishment bread and water, which the Federals neglected to give them during the last two days. They were made to pass through a semblance of an interrogatory, after which they were told that, though recognized innocent, they would be retained as hostages.

On Thursday, May 25th, the Federals evacuated Bicêtre. A Belgian and an Italian domestic belonging to the College d'Arcueil were released while the others were led away prisoners, the Federals telling them that as soon as they arrived at the Barrière Fontainebleau they should be set free.

In leaving the fort, a few shots, fired through carelessness, caused a panic among the Federals, in consequence of which one of the fathers, the Père Rousselin, succeeded in making his escape.

During the transfer the unhappy Dominicans were continually outraged and insulted by the people in that quarter. Arrived at the Mairie of the Route d'Italie, they were placed in a court where shells were perpetually falling; they were then taken to the 9th section and again interrogated.

At half-past two a man in a red shirt arrived, calling, "We want workmen for the barricades. What are these cassocks doing here. Bring them along, it is just what we want."

The prisoners were then conducted to a barricade where the balls fell with such rapidity that the insurgents could not retain possession, and they were led back again to the section by order of Colonel Cerisier.

At four o'clock a new order arrived from the same personage brought by a red shirt; the Dominicans were placed in file two by two, and told to go out, that they were free. Understanding the sinister meaning of those words, Father Captier advanced, saying, "*Allons, mes amis, pour le bon Dieu!*"

Hardly had he advanced a few steps when he was struck by several balls, and instantly killed. Twenty-one out of the twenty-four were successively shot; five

Dominicans, Fathers Captier, Cothereau, Bourard, Delhorme, Châtaigneraie; two civil professors, MM. Volant and Gauquelin; and several domestics, three of whom were fathers of families, whose wives had been taken as prisoners to Saint Lazare.

Having fired upon their victims, the Federals finished the terrible work with their bayonets, or with blows from the butts of their muskets; the bodies were so terribly mutilated that it was afterwards impossible to recognize their identity.

On Thursday morning the insurgents had commenced the pillage of the College of Arcueil, but were interrupted by the arrival of the Versailles troops. In this college, early in September, an ambulance had been established which remained open during the siege, although situated at the very outposts, and exposed to Prussian shells and balls. This hospitable house was well known to the soldiers, and the only one that remained open in the midst of the abandoned and deserted villages.

There was no one who, more than Father Captier, joined to the Christian faith an ardent feeling of patriotism, together with all the qualities which make a great citizen, too worthy, alas! to draw down the hatred of those who proved themselves enemies to all country, all liberty, and all religion.

Retribution, however, had overtaken during the day several members of the Commune.

Millière had taken refuge at the house of his father-in-law, No. 38 Rue d'Ulm. On Thursday morning a sergeant of the line, breakfasting at a small café in the neighborhood, overheard a woman who was speaking of the Commune, say, "Ah! there is a good capture to be made, but the individual is in safety in the Rue d'Ulm." The sergeant shortly after took his departure, and, joined by several of his comrades, searched carefully the Rue d'Ulm. Arrived at No. 38, the apartment of M. Fourès, father-in-law of Millière, was searched with particular care. No one was discovered, but a soldier watching at the door saw the ex-deputy in the act of escape. Seeing all hope impossible, he drew his revolver and fired six times, but without wounding any one.

He was immediately conducted before General de Cissey, where he replied with firmness to the questions made to him. He was then directed towards the Pantheon. As he mounted the steps of the peristyle, an officer pointed out to him the traces of balls. It was there that, two days before, thirty National Guards were shot by his orders for having refused to defend the barricades.

Arrived at the top of the steps he stood facing the soldiers, when an officer obliged him to turn his face towards the door of the church, with his back to the troops; but by counter-order of a superior officer, he was again made to resume his former position, at the same time being forced to kneel.

Millière uncovered his breast, and, lifting his right arm, cried in a loud tone, "*Vive la République! . . . Vive le Peuple! . . . Vive l'Humanité! . . . Vive——.*" A discharge of chassepots interrupted his last words, and he fell leaning towards his left side.

His shirt was pierced with balls near the heart, over which a large stain of blood appeared. One ball had struck him in the right eye. An officer then approached, and, placing his revolver at his ear, fired, giving him the *coup de grâce.* Millière's wife had been killed on the previous day fighting at a barricade.

On the same day another of Millière's associates met the just reward of his crimes. This was Jules Vallès, the man who, in writing of defending Paris, said that the Commune would defend it by every means, and added: "If M. Thiers is a chemist, he will understand us."

MILLIERE
Commune of Paris
1871

Vallès was led out from the theatre of the Chatelet at six o'clock on Thursday evening by the platoon charged with his execution. He was dressed in a black coat and light trousers of a yellowish tinge. He wore no hat, and his beard, which had been shaved off a short time before, was very short and turning gray.

In entering the street where his sentence was to be executed, a feeling of self-preservation restored to him the energy which had previously abandoned him. He wished to flee; but being held by the soldiers, he became horribly infuriated, calling, "*A l'assassin!*" twisting himself, seizing his executioners by the throat, biting them, in fact opposing a despairing resistance.

The soldiers commenced to be embarrassed and somewhat moved by this terrible struggle for life, when one of them passing behind him gave him a furious blow on the back with his musket, and the wretched man fell with a dull groan to the ground.

His spine was doubtless fractured; several shots were then fired upon him, and he received also two or three bayonet thrusts. As he still breathed, one of the soldiers advanced and discharged his chassepot in his ear. His body was then abandoned until it should be carried away by those charged, during those bloody days, with that commission.

On Thursday night the left bank of the Seine was completely freed from every element of insurrection. General de Cissey, who conducted all the military operations in that portion of Paris, and who has since been nominated Minister of War, is one of the most brilliant of the French officers. Rarely has any military career presented a finer list of services rendered, all his grades having been gained in campaign and on the field of battle. The army which he has been called to reorganize, and to whom he will restore its former military glory, feels with satisfaction that there is a soldier at its head.

Ernest-Louis-Octave Courtot de Cissey, born in Paris December 23d, 1810, is now sixty-one years of age. He belongs to a noble family of Burgundy; his grandfather was a lieutenant-colonel in the dragoons of Segur, and chevalier of Saint-Louis. His father, also a chevalier of Saint-Louis, served in the same regiment with the rank of captain.

The first part of the career of General de Cissey was passed exclusively in Africa.

Admitted to Saint-Cyr December 2d, 1830, he left a member of the staff in 1832, and made his first campaign in Africa from 1836 to 1838. Remarkable from the first for his intrepidity and presence of mind, he received his first citation in the order of the army after the two expeditions of Constantine. Captain on the 27th February, 1839, serving in turn as aide-de-camp the Generals Dejean, Rumigny, and Tarlé, he continued to take part in different expeditions, and his name is continually to be found in the reports of the Governor-General and in the order of the day of the army.

On the 28th of May, 1840, particularly, he distinguished himself in the expedition of Médéah; June 5th, at Tegdempt and Mascara; May 3d, at Milianah, where he had a horse killed under him, after having slain with his own hand several Arabs. Captain de Cissey became major of cavalry July 19th, 1845; lieutenant-colonel June 14th, 1850; colonel May 10th, 1853; employed at the headquarters of the staff at Algiers from 1840 to 1850; he was successively aide-de-camp of General Pélissier, governor par interim of Algeria, and then sous-chef of the staff of the army of Africa. It was at this time that he married in Algiers the daughter of Rear-Admiral Rigodit, commanding the marine.

In this second period of ten years passed in Africa, M. de Cissey signalized himself by new exploits. He took part in the expeditions of 1843, and both at Dellys and at Onarezedin charged in the first rank at the head of his cavalry. He was also, on the 14th of August, at the battle of Isly, where he was cited by Marshal Bugeaud as one of the officers who had behaved themselves most remarkably. In 1850 he took part in one of the first expeditions of Kabylie, commanded by Colonel de Lourmel, and distinguished himself on May 21st in the combat with the Beni-Ymel.

When the Crimean war broke out, Colonel de Cissey was asked for by General Bosquet, as chief of the staff of the 2d division of infantry in the army of the East. General of Brigade March 17th, 1854, after Inkermann, his name is found in the order of the day of the army at the taking of the redoubts before Sebastopol.

After leaving the Crimea he returned to Africa, where, February 27th, 1856, he was made chief of the staff in the southwestern divisions.

At the creation of a ministry for Algeria and the colonies, he was called to the direction of military and maritime affairs. Although the ministry of Algeria was but of short duration, General de Cissey found time to give proof of great aptitude in the direction of affairs, of a profound knowledge of the different branches of military art, of administrative details, and of a remarkable genius for organization. The remembrance of this direction of a few months has not been one of the least titles of the General to his appointment as Minister of War.

In 1869, General de Cissey commanded the 1st division of infantry at the camp of Châlons, and in 1870 he was Inspector-General of the Military Schools.

When war was declared against Prussia, the General was at Rennes, at the head of the 16th military division.

It was expected that he would be placed at the head of the staff of the Army of the Rhine, his rare military talents designing him for this difficult post; but he received the command of a division in the 4th corps of General Ladmirault, and assisted at Borny, at Resonville, and at the bloody battle of Saint-Privat. The 16th of August, he succeeded in completely breaking the left wing of the Prussians; at Saint-Privat he had two horses killed under him.

On the 22d of October, when Marshal Bazaine announced to the generals under his command his intention to capitulate, General de Cissey proposed energetically that the army should attempt to force a passage through the Prussian lines. His plan consisted in reuniting hastily all the resources of which the city and the army still disposed, to give to each soldier one hundred and eighty cartridges and four days' provisions, to requisition in the city and its surroundings all available horses, to harness them to the guns, and to fall with a supreme and energetic effort upon the investing army.

This plan was not adopted, and the French army marched out from Metz as prisoners.

General de Cissey was sent to Hombourg. To the patriotic grief which filled his soul, another affliction was soon added. Madame de Cissey was dying at Rennes, of a long and painful malady which neither the aid of science nor the tender care of her mother had been able to alleviate.

The General hoped that Prussia would at least allow him the liberty of shutting the eyes of her who had been the loving companion of his rude soldier's life, but this satisfaction was refused him, and he was not able to return to Rennes until after the signature of the peace preliminaries.

His name was persistently called upon at Versailles for

some time before he could tear himself away from the tomb so prematurely opened.

Charged with the command of the 2d army corps under Paris, the active part he took in the operations of the siege is already known, and also how much his care in re-establishing discipline, his wise measures and his energy, hastened the end of that painful and redoubtable enterprise. His campaign, opened at the forts of Issy and Vanves, whose capture was owing to him, ended at his entrance into the Luxembourg, where his sudden apparition surprised the insurrection preparing the conflagration of all the monuments as well as private houses of the left bank.

The Faubourg Saint Germain owes to him its preservation.

The General de Cissey, who counts no less than forty years of service, thirteen citations in the order of the day—who has been successively in Africa, the Crimea, at Metz and under Paris—has had the rare good fortune never to receive a single wound. Chevalier of the Legion d'Honneur in 1868, he has been made recently grand-croix, April 20th, 1871. He is besides decorated with the orders of Medjidié, of the Bath, and with the medal of military valor of Sardinia.

The present Minister of War is of middle height, and has a fine military deportment. On his face, with grave and regular features, firmness and loyalty are easily read.

The General talks but little; but when a service is to be rendered, he is seen to act. He has an upright soul, working always for good. At the same time a man of action and a studious man, his great integrity makes him anxious to render an account of everything for himself; thus in his different commands he was oftener to be found in the neighborhood of the trenches than at his headquarters.

Public opinion has greatly applauded his elevation to

the Ministry of War, believing with reason that with the portfolio in such able hands, nothing will be neglected for the reorganization of the noble army of France.

On the right bank of the Seine the military operations, which had been interrupted by the approach of night, were recommenced with vigor on the morning of the 25th, and the Hotel de Ville was taken by an ingenious combination. While it was attacked on one side by the Rue de Rivoli, and watched from the left bank by General de Cissey, the column which marched along the boulevards to the Porte Saint-Martin had been divided, and a strong body had gained by a rapid turning movement the Place des Vosges, penetrated into the Rue Saint-Antoine in the rear of the Hotel de Ville, and thus gained possession of the building, The Commune had already abandoned the place, and taken refuge in the Mairie of the 11th Arrondissement, leaving behind only a heap of blackened ruins.

Nevertheless, the moral effect was considerable. Three-fourths of Paris belonged henceforth to the regular army. Montmartre and the Hotel de Ville were in the hands of the troops, and from that time the Communal insurrection could be considered as vanquished. All hope of success, if the insurgents had ever entertained any, had entirely vanished. There remained still facing the troops nothing but a riot—formidable, no doubt, but without any chance of an offensive return. The Federals, notwithstanding the strong positions they occupied, were defending an absolutely desperate cause, which good sense and patriotism should have advised them to renounce.

The tricolored flag floated above nearly all the monuments in the city, replacing the *drapeau rouge.* From the Châtelet Theatre to the Hotel de Ville the Communists had left a smoking trail. The houses were nearly all badly injured, and many entirely consumed. The Hotel de Ville presented a most painful spectacle, its destruction being more complete than that of any other building. As a ruin, however, the beautiful but defaced remnants, still standing, present an unusually touching and imposing appearance.

Immediately after the capture of the Hotel de Ville, the army of reserve, under General Vinoy, advanced upon the Place de la Bastille.

Early in the morning the division Bruat, charged with turning by the east the Faubourgs Saint-Antoine and Belleville, had taken possession of the Jardin des Plantes and the Orleans Railway Station.

They then attacked vigorously the bridge of Austerlitz, supported on the left bank by the brigade Derroja, and on the right by the brigade De la Mariouse, both belonging to the division Faron; also on the Seine by the flotilla of gunboats recently organized.

The defences of the bridge were formidable; but towards four in the afternoon the position was carried. This success hastened the fall of the Lyons Railway Station, the Mazas prison, and the viaduct of the Vincennes Railway.

In the Mazas prison, early on the morning of the 25th, a bomb had fallen in the 2d division, shortly followed by another, which had caused considerable injury. The keepers were seized with terror; and causing the prisoners to leave their cells, they conducted them into the patrol path between the outer and inner walls. At seven o'clock a superior officer of the Federals arrived, and ordered the prisoners—five hundred in number—to be set at liberty. Only five ecclesiastics remained among this number.

Hardly outside the prison, they all found themselves surrounded by barricades, where the insurgents endeavored to force them to take part in the struggle. Most of them refused and were shot, while others succeeded in escaping from the midst of such terrible perils.

One of the prisoners, M. Bacon, foreseeing the fate

reserved for those to whom liberty was given in such a moment, remained in the prison, where one of the keepers, a compatriot, protected him.

On the morning after the departure of the prisoners, the Citizen Gareau, director of Mazas, came to inform the keepers that, by order of the Commune, the prison was to to be set on fire, and that all the administration must immediately withdraw.

M. Bacon then learned that the evening before the keeper Collin had buried in the garden the barrels of powder which had been placed in the sewers of the prison. By his advice the brigadier keeper was prevailed on to close the gates to prevent the director from leaving the building, and to await events, confident as they were that the prison could not be blown up.

The Director Gareau was, in fact, kept as hostage, and notwithstanding the incessant shots directed by the insurgents from without, through the crenelated openings in the walls, the place was held until nine in the morning, when the 35th of the line, which had crossed the Seine at Bercy, arrived and took possession of the prison.

The Director Gareau, creature of the Commune, was placed in a cell by order of the commandant, and all the buildings were occupied by the troops.

In the Rue de Bercy the troops had met with a most obstinate resistance, but had conquered here as elsewhere, and had then marched to the relief of Mazas. It was in the Rue de Bercy that Vincent, delegate to the Committee of the Rue d'Aligre, had been arrested. Vincent had formerly been concierge in the Hotel de la Dordogne, situated in the Rue de Bercy. Having been dismissed by the proprietor, M. Conderc, he resolved to be revenged.

On Thursday morning M. Conderc was standing in the midst of a group in the Avenue Millaud, when a ball whistled by, and struck a National Guard a few feet off.

Vincent, who commanded the barricades, denounced M. Conderc to a commissary of the Commune, who instantly arrested the unhappy man accused of having fired upon the Federals. M. Cassié was also arrested.

They were both immediately conducted to the guardhouse of the Marché Noir, and about to be shot, when a spectator obtained a delay of the execution, and hastening to the Committee of the Rue d'Aligre, affirmed the innocence of the prisoners, and demanded an order for their release.

He was answered that "moments were precious, the situation grave, and that they had no time to occupy themselves with such an affair."

By force of persistence, however, he finally obtained an order for the release of the two prisoners.

Vincent did not consider himself beaten. He remained at the barricade of the Rue de Bercy, and, aided by his wife, excited the insurgents, distributed cartridges, and fired himself upon the troops from behind the barricade.

When the barricade was carried, he succeeded in making his escape, ran to his home, dressed himself in civilian's clothes, and descending into the street walked straight up to an officer of the line and denounced M. Conderc as having fought until the last moment.

The officer immediately ordered the arrest of M. Conderc, and that of a poor young man about thirty-four years of age, beside whom an insurgent in escaping had thrown his gun, still hot from the last discharge. The wretched man was shot without being able to prove his innocence.

As for M. Conderc, he was about to suffer the same fate, when his wife, throwing herself at the feet of the officer, related the scene which had taken place that morning.

Vincent was instantly apprehended; a perquisition made at his abode proved his identity as delegate and combatant.

He was led immediately to the Rue de Bercy, in the court of the municipal dépôt of paving stones, and shot forthwith.

Before his execution he boasted of having caused thirty refractory National Guards to be shot, and of having himself drowned the agent Vincentini in the previous month of March.

While the Divisions Faron and Bruat were attacking the Austerlitz Bridge, the Division Vergé (3d of the army of reserve) advanced by the Rues Saint-Paul, Charles V., De la Cerisaie, and proceeding through the houses of the Rue Saint Antoine, carried the barricade of the Rue Castex and debouched on the Place de la Bastille. There they encountered a most violent resistance, rendered still more serious by the conflagration of the Grenier d'Abondance and of the houses situated around the Place.

The following concise document was afterwards found in one of the mairies of Paris:

"RÉPUBLIQUE FRANÇAISE.
"*Liberty, Equality, Fraternity.*

"VILLE DE PARIS,
"MAIRIE OF THE XI ARRONDISSEMENT.

"*I have set fire to the Grenier d'Abondance.*
"Artillery magnificent.
"Resistance good.

"C. ULRIC,
"Chief of the 13th Legion.

"MAY 25, 1871."

Beside this document we may place another of equal chronological interest. It is the last despatch addressed to the Citizen Delescluze by his colleague Ferré, of the Prefecture of Police:

"PARIS, May 25, 1871—9.30 A.M.

"*Secretary-General of War:*

"A man belonging to the 1st regiment of Federals informs me that since four o'clock this morning Montmartre is ours no longer. I have seen the Place de la Bastille well defended, but the Versaillese are in the church of the Rue Saint-Antoine, and are doing their utmost to take the Place de la Bastille. I saw personally four shells fall in the Rue de la Roquette, one of which entered No. 49 of said street. If Montmartre is still ours, *they* must be ordered to regulate their aim."

Montmartre had been taken at twelve on Tuesday, and there was nothing to rectify.

The troops engaged in the old boulevards had fought throughout the day in the quarters of Saint-Denis, Saint-Martin, the Boulevard Sebastopol, and the Rambuteau quarter.

The army had gained possession of the Conservatoire des Arts-et-Metiers, where several pieces of artillery were established, and fired on the boulevards.

During the day the city was transformed into an immense camp. The Rue de Grammont was filled with artillery; the Theatre of the Opéra-Comique was turned into an ambulance, and was surrounded by immense material of war. The streets were everywhere filled with soldiers, and, wherever the cessation of the battle would allow, with civilians looking eagerly for the traces of the struggle. Every few moments large crowds would gather to see the convoys of prisoners, sometimes amounting to several hundred, which were led off to Versailles. Many of these were women. Persons caught setting fire to the houses were generally taken to the guard-houses, and the proofs of their guilt being established, they were shot forthwith. In many cases, however, the enraged population took the punishment of such criminals into their hands and tore them almost to pieces in their fury. Too much cannot be said in praise of the demeanor of the soldiers, who showed throughout extraordinary control over passions which the insurgents had certainly done everything to excite. A soldier falling a prisoner into the hands of the insurgents could expect no mercy. Several were burned to death; among others, M. de Segoyer, commandant of the 26th battalion of *chasseurs à pied,* was made prisoner by the insurgents at the Place de la Bastille, and having been covered with petroleum was burned alive.

The Federals now held but one strong position, but it was more important than any that had yet been wrested from them. This was the Chateau d'Eau, protected by the Buttes Chaumont, Belleville, and Père-Lachaise. It is true that Chaumont and Belleville were under the fire of Montmartre, but that did not prevent the Federal artillery, installed there, from covering the quarters Saint-Denis and Bonne-Nouvelle with shells.

Seven avenues or boulevards open on the Place du Chateau-d'Eau: Rue de Turbigo, Boulevard Saint-Martin, Boulevard Magenta, Rue du Faubourg-du-Temple, Boulevard des Amandiers, Boulevard du Prince-Eugène (now Boulevard Voltaire), and Boulevard du Temple. At the entrance of each of these streets on the Place, a barricade had been constructed.

General Clinchant advanced by the Boulevards Magenta, Saint Denis and St. Martin; General Douay, by the Conservatoire des Arts-et-Métiers, the Rues de Turbigo and Du Temple; General Ladmirault by La Chapelle and Villette; and General Vinoy by the Bastille.

As may be seen, the different army corps continued to follow their first strategy, the great merit of which was its simplicity. Marshal de MacMahon was, doubtless, inspired by the geometrical axiom—a straight line is the shortest distance from one point to another—being sure that his soldiers would know how to vanquish every obstacle that rose in their path.

The troops who had taken possession of the Central Market had advanced during the day through the Rue Turbigo, sustaining at almost every step a violent combat, and had commenced towards evening, in concert with the troops who had taken the line of the boulevards, the attack on the Chateau d'Eau.

The insurgents, established in the vast buildings of the Magasins-Réunis and the barracks of the Prince Eugène, defended with all the energy of despair the barricade which covered their stronghold in the 11th Arrondissement, and the access toBelleville and Père Lachaise. Nevertheless, the troops had succeeded in reaching the Buttes Chaumont by the upper quarters of La Villette, and had immediately proceeded to their investment.

During the last hours of Thursday the 25th, the line of battle extended, in making a large curve, from the Bastille to the Buttes Chaumont, passing by the Boulevards Beaumarchais, Des Filles-du-Calvaire, and Du Temple, by the Chateau-d'Eau, the Rue de la Douane, the Entrepôt and the canal, ending in turning round the hospital of Saint-Louis at the foot of the Buttes.

The army of France, since the evening of the 21st of May, the date at which it entered Paris, had accomplished an enormous task, marching in advance without interruption, surmounting valiantly every obstacle, and marking each day by important successes.

Paris, emerging from the terrified stupor into which it had been plunged by the reign of the Commune, regained the consciousness of its existence. The insurrection was evidently vanquished, and yet three days were still occupied by violent combats before the bloody struggle could be entirely terminated. During Friday, Saturday and

Sunday, the Federals never ceased to oppose to the indefatigable ardor of the soldiers the most furious zeal, which was sustained until the last hour, and which those will understand who have witnessed the great insurrections in France during the last forty years, and who are acquainted with the extreme tenacity of the Parisian workman, once he has taken a gun and entered into revolt for an idea. However false this idea may be, he will defend it with passion, without being even willing to reflect upon its worth.

For the last two months the word Commune had been repeatedly dinned into the ears of the Parisian workmen; they had adopted it, without examination, as the mysterious Sesame which would open a new era of universal happiness, and they could not or would not believe in the crumbling of their bright dreams, although everything, from moment to moment, announced an irremediable defeat.

Moreover, up to the last moment, the chiefs of the Commune did everything in their power to delude their adherents concerning the gravity of the situation. For this they resorted to the most miserable subterfuges. Thus, while the fighting was going on at the Chateau-d'Eau, tricolored flags were shown, with cries of victory, to the National Guards assembled in the Mairie of the 11th Arrondissement. These the members of the Commune pretended to have captured from the army of Versailles, and marching in procession to the Place Voltaire, the trophies were solemnly burned at the feet of that writer's statue. These flags, some of which still bore the imperial eagle, had been taken from the store-rooms of the Mairie, where they were kept for public festivals.

On the following day they resorted to another artifice. About a thousand soldiers of the line, who had been imprisoned at La Roquette since the 18th of March, were taken from prison and led to the Mairie of the 20th Arrondissement as a detachment of the regular troops which had deserted to the cause of the Commune. These sad trickeries succeeded but partially, and instead of raising the confidence of the National Guards, helped to weaken it.

But the Federals at the same time drew the obstinacy of a desperate resistance from the bitter knowledge of their utter ruin, and from the perils which everywhere surrounded them. In this they were encouraged by a number of strangers—refuse of all the nations in Europe—of whom the Communal cause had made shameful auxiliaries. These men, convicts and exiles, had nothing to fear, because they had nothing to hope. They sought only to drag down with them in a common ruin those whose conduct, guilty as it was, could yet find some excuse.

On his side, Marshal de MacMahon, assured as he was of success, did not wish to hazard anything by hastening his operations; and he desired, at the same time, to save the blood of his soldiers by moderating their action.

These different causes prolonged the struggle until the afternoon of Sunday, the 28th, without, however, its being interrupted for a moment; the positions still to be carried presenting so many difficulties.

The defences of the Boulevard Magenta have been already described, together with the capture of three out of four of its barricades by the regular troops. The fourth, which was the key of the position, was situated a few yards back of No. 6, of which the insurgents retained possession, and through which they communicated with the Passage du Wauxhall, where they had their reserves, and also with the Rue des Marais-Saint-Martin, which conducts to the barracks, the Rues Magnan, Dieu, and De l'Entrepot.

When the action was about commencing, the insurgents informed the inhabitants of this house of their intentions, and of the necessity under which they might find themselves of destroying everything for the execution of their plans. The latter decided unanimously that they would remain in the house, notwithstanding the danger, aud that they would live for the time together and watch for the safety of all.

On Wednesday morning Citizen Gambon, member of the Committee of Public Safety, arrived at the house, after having inspected the defences, and informed the inhabitants that the commandant of the barricade had over them the right of life and death; that he would use this right according to the necessities of the defence, and that their furniture would be sacrificed if it was judged useful.

The Versailles troops, having occupied the Boulevard Ornano, opened at long range a quick and well-directed artillery fire against the barricade, whose defenders were decimated during two days and nights, but whose guns never ceased for an instant to reply.

On the 25th, early in the morning, the troops advanced, and continued during several hours to cover with their fire the barricade and the insurgents who still defended it. The ground around was covered with muskets, grape-shot, and pieces of shell.

Finally, on Friday, the 26th, at noon, the soldiers left Saint-Laurent, the Mairie of the 10th Arrondissement, and, advancing in single file, gun in hand, along the houses of the Rue du Chateau-d'Eau, they concentrated in the Grand Café Parisien. At the end of a few moments they approached the barricade, opening a rapid and efficacious musketry fire on the insurgents. Two hours later they carried the position, and hastened to plant the tricolor in the centre of the fortification—a sight which filled with joy the entire population.

The brave soldiers then attacked the Place du Chateau-

DELESCLUZE
Commune of Paris
1871.

d'Eau with a courage, animation, and intelligence which were admirable; they entered the houses and fired from the windows on the barracks of the Chateau-d'Eau, the Magasins Réunis, and the six barricades of the Place.

After fifteen hours effort, the barricade yielded before the energetic attack of the troops; the cannon ended by opening a breach, and the soldiers rushing on the Barrack Prince Eugène and the Magasins Réunis, carried them at the point of the bayonet.

Most of the houses of the Place du Chateau-d'Eau attest the violence of this rude engagement; their fronts are riddled with bullets and shells, while many are entirely consumed by fire.

It was near the barricades of the Chateau-d'Eau that the Delegate of War, Citizen Delescluze, faithful to his promise, came to seek his death by the side of those whom he had encouraged in this horrible revolt.

Judging the cause lost, Delescluze left, about noon, his colleagues, who had taken refuge in the Mairie of the 11th Arrondissement, and directed himself with the calm appearance of an indifferent pedestrian towards the scene of combat, passing through the Boulevard Voltaire. On the way he met several National Guards soldiers and officers, whose hands he silently pressed. As he advanced, he was told of the dangers which menaced him in that direction from the falling shells. Without any reply to this warning he continued to advance, and a few moments later he was struck by three balls and mortally wounded. He paid with his life the "*trop coupable*" agitation of which he had been one of the most ardent promoters.

The body of Delescluze was found on Friday afternoon surrounded by twenty-eight corpses. It was recognized by the architect Lenormand.

Delescluze was in civil dress; black coat and gray trousers, with a silk hat and patent-leather boots. By his side lay a cane which he had carried for ten years, and which first led to his recognition.

After the discovery of his body he was immediately searched. He had with him his nomination as Delegate of War, his passport as member of the Commune, and letters from La Cecilia, Lisbonne, and other chiefs of the band.

Among the remaining papers there were several both mysterious and interesting:

"PARIS, May 16, 1871, (Tuesday, 7 P. M).

"CITIZEN DELESCLUZE:—A *citoyenne* who is entirely devoted to you, has a most serious communication to make you; only as she wishes to make it to you alone, she begs you to keep absolutely secret the reception of these few lines, and also to find yourself to-morrow (Wednesday, 17th) in the Rue Neuve-des-Petits-Champs, at No. 48, under the entrance to the Ventadour Baths. You must appear to be strolling, and no one will pay you any attention; be there at four o'clock; you may have to wait five or six minutes at the most. A carriage will stop before you, and you must enter.

"Be without fear; the person who wishes to speak to you will be alone. Put a flower of some kind in your left button-hole, so that the coachman may distinguish you at once.

"Above all, discretion. Not a word of this to those surrounding you.

"Yours with all my heart,

"JEANNE LACASSIÈRE.

"P. S.—Burn this."

The second letter is still more interesting, and shows with what confidence these people inspired each other:

"MONSIEUR DELESCLUZE:—A vast conspiracy is being

organized against you among your colleagues, and even among those whom you think your friends. If steel cannot act, poison will be employed. Above all, distrust Vermorel.

"A DEVOTED FRIEND."

Among the other letters were several orders for the service, which prove the desperation of the situation of the insurgents.

The following is a sample:

"MINISTRY OF WAR.
Cabinet of the Minister.

"PARIS, May 21, 1871.

"CITIZEN DELESCLUZE:—Send immediately, artillerymen, wagons, and harness for the transport of munitions. The ramparts are no longer tenable if I do not receive artillerymen. It is impossible for me, with the National Guards and free-shooters furnished by the volunteers, to perform the service of the artillery. I cannot hold out any longer.

"COLONEL LISBONNE."

At the Magasins Réunis more than two thousand insurgents were taken prisoners.

In the Rue du Temple, where a barricade had just been carried by the troops, a large number of prisoners were also taken, and led to the Rue Notre-Dame-de-Nazareth, opposite the Café Dodar. Among them was a child about fifteen.

The contest had been violent, and the soldiers were in all the exaltation which follows an action so important. The prisoners had not capitulated; they had been taken with arms in their hands, and ought to die according to the laws of war, especially the law accorded to insurgents.

The turn of the child arrived.

He was pushed against the wall to be quickly dispatched. He asked to speak to the captain, who advanced and demanded what he wanted.

"I should like," said the child, drawing a watch from his pocket, "to carry this to the concierge who lives opposite; he would know to whom to give it."

The captain, who, even in the fever caused by powder, sees but a child in the insurgent, divines the artless subterfuge of the poor fellow.

"Well, go! and hurry yourself!" he said, roughly.

The platoon of execution understood also, when, suddenly, running as though for an urgent affair, the child re-appeared, placed himself before the soldiers, with his back to the wall, and said, "*Me voilà!*"

The captain looked at his men, and the men at their captain; everybody was confounded.

But the captain had his own idea; he advanced furiously to the child, and, taking him by the shoulders, gave him a violent kick, saying, "Get out of the way, you wretched little imp."

Meanwhile the Generals Vinoy and Douay gained possession, after a shorter but no less violent attack than that of the Chateau-d'Eau, of the Place de la Bastille. Here the houses suffered, as everywhere else in Paris, as much from the flames spread by petroleum as from artillery projectiles. Immense buildings recently constructed at the head of the Rue Saint-Antoine were entirely consumed.

The troops next precipitated themselves into the Faubourg Saint-Antoine, through which the principal retreat of the Federals had been managed, and occupied it in a few hours, notwithstanding the formidable defences with which the Faubourg was covered as far as the Place du Trône. The laboring population of this former birthplace of all revolutionary agitations, had associated but feebly in the resistance, which was due almost exclusively to Federals from other quarters who had taken refuge in the old faubourg.

The streets surrounding the Place de la Bastille were all obstructed by barricades, which were successively carried by the troops. At the corner of the Rues Rampon and Valmy, where Canal Saint-Martin opens, a number of insurgents were found drowned.

On the 24th, the Federals had conducted under the vaults of the canal to the middle of the Boulevard Richard Lenoir, almost opposite the Rues du Chemin-Vert and Des Amandiers, several barges which had been moored at the quay of the Boulevard Bourdon. One of these was filled with barrels of powder and casks of petroleum; the others were filled with inflammable materials, planks, and shavings, over which petroleum had been scattered.

All the gratings and air-openings communicating with the canal had been stopped up.

The barges charged with powder and petroleum had been first conducted to the spot where it was intended to commit the crime. The boat which was to be used for firing the others was taken last. It was set on fire under the Place de la Bastille. From there the incendiaries evidently intended to drag it towards the others; but the smoke occasioned by the fire was so thick that, being unable to escape through the air-openings, it prevented the flames from rising. The matter all burned away without flaming, which rendered the smoke denser and denser, and which ended by smothering the Federals—victims to the very act which was intended to bring so much misery and ruin upon others.

It is only too evident that the charming revolutionaries of the Commune had the intention of destroying all the public monuments of Paris. Time only failed them.

On the Place du Trône works had been commenced to overthrow the stone columns which have decorated this place since 1788, and which the devastators of '93 had subsequently respected.

Ten or twelve bandits had first mounted on the pedestal of the column which supports the statue of Philip-Augustus, had broken with hammers the figures with which the pedestal was ornamented, and then began to cut away a portion of the base of the monument, thinking probably that it would fall by its own weight.

But this mode of proceeding appearing either too long or too dangerous, they soon renounced it and had recourse to mining, after having cut an opening of ten centimètres in one side.

They then dug on the opposite side several holes, which were to receive enormous charges of powder, and had almost reached the required depth, when the inhabitants of the neighborhood, encouraged by the successes of the regular troops, who had already occupied a portion of Paris, informed these wretches that the fall of a column could do their cause no good, and finally succeeded in driving them away.

The Place du Trône being occupied by the soldiers of the line, a portion remained to watch the elements of disorder which might still exist in the upper streets of the Faubourg between the Place and Bercy, while by the remainder the insurgents were thrown back on Charonne and Ménilmontant.

By an almost simultaneous movement, the forces which had so intrepidly gained the position of the Chateau-d'Eau, having assured its possession, and that of the boulevards, as far as the Bastille, divided into two columns. One mounted the Boulevards Voltaire and Richard-Lenoir, enveloping the prison of La Roquette, of which the troops gained possession on Saturday morning, and approaching at the same time the cemetery of Père-Lachaise; the other column, by the Rue de la Douane and the borders of the canal, approached the Buttes Chaumont to complete their investment.

The circle had constantly and regularly narrowed; it compressed, indeed it strangled, this prodigious insurrection, thrown back in a definitive manner on to its last intrenchments.

In reality, it no longer existed; there remained only a few desperate bands, whose energy, however, never failed for a moment as long as there was a gun left to be fired.

During this supreme effort, Paris, almost entirely restored to law and order, was traversed by long files of prisoners, wearing on their faces an expression of fierce energy, and in many cases pride of their cause even in disaster; they marched bareheaded between two lines of cavalry, who rode gun in hand. They were all divested of their uniform of the National Guard, and were dressed in blouses, working-jackets, or coats.

Among the prisoners were a large number of women, who had taken an active part in the struggle, engaging, if possible, with even more fury than the men. Many had defended alone the barricades, firing resolutely upon the troops, fighting with a kind of pitiless rage, and, when they found themselves vanquished, throwing themselves recklessly upon the bayonets.

Many had worked actively in the construction of barricades, and a large number had aided in igniting the conflagrations, carrying everywhere, with inconceivable eagerness, explosive materials, petroleum, and incendiary bombs. With dishevelled hair, garments in disorder, they retained, amidst the soldiers who conducted them, a bearing of furious passion, venting itself occasionally by violent imprecations and wild cries.

Meanwhile, in the Prison de la Roquette, more victims were added to the insatiable rage of the Commune. On Thursday but one execution took place, that of the banker Jecker, who was called from his cell in the morning, and who has never been heard of since.

On Friday, 26th, the noise of the battle, which approached the quarter of La Roquette, and the news which reached them from without, gave the prisoners a little hope, although all had resolutely offered the sacrifice of their lives, and prepared themselves for death in a Christian manner, the laity being sustained and encouraged by the clergy.

On account of the bad weather, the daily recreation had been taken in the hall on which the cells opened, and had been extended in the afternoon far beyond the usual hour. It was about five o'clock, when, in the midst of the recreation, one of the keepers appeared, a list in hand, and the sinister call began. Fifteen prisoners, among whom were ten members of the clergy and five of the laity, were called, ranged in order, counted, and led off just as they were found, many of them bareheaded. They were led out of the prison, and probably taken to Père-Lachaise, or behind some barricades, where they were shot. Not one has reappeared.

Among the victims were the Père Olivaint, superior of the Jesuits of the Rue de Sèvres, and former pupil of the Ecole Normale. At La Roquette he met one of his school companions, a hostage like himself, whom he had not seen for thirty-four years.

Another prisoner was a young seminarist of Saint-Sulpice, about twenty years of age, named Seigneret, son of the inspector of the Academy of the Jura. His truly angelic face, and his extreme youth, had moved all his companions of captivity, and no one believed that he could be executed. His only crime was having demanded a passport at the Prefecture of Police in order to return to his family. Immediately arrested by the insurgents, he was first thrown into the Conciergerie, transferred to Mazas, and then to La Roquette, where he fell a victim to the common fate.

"My poor father! my poor parents!" said he to one of his companions in misfortune; "what despair for them! However, I pay for the position of my father, happy if my death can save a fellow-creature, and give some remorse to my executioners."

All the condemned believed that their last hour had come, and that their slow agony would that evening be ended. The last farewells were exchanged and the last prayers said, and each one took the necessary dispositions to send to their parents and friends the sad relics or last wishes which they left behind them.

Nevertheless the evening, the night passed without any new incident, in the midst of a horrible expectation, and an anxiety a thousand times more cruel than death itself. In the morning the noise of the firing approached sensibly the neighborhood of the prison and the Mairie of the 11th Arrondissement, where the last remnants of the Commune were sitting.

The prisoners had mostly to fear the final crisis; the defeat of the insurrection might be the signal for a general massacre. The bandits who surrounded and occupied the prison were not likely to abandon their prey without attempting to avenge themselves by butchering the remainder of the hostages. This design they attempted, in fact, to execute in the afternoon after the capture of the Mairie, when they beat a retreat in the direction of Père-Lachaise.

Ferré, Delegate of General Safety and member of the Commune, made his appearance at the prison, and calling for all the criminals condemned to the galleys who were detained in the prison until the time of their transportation arrived, restored them at once to liberty. Arms and ammunition were given to these bandits, who immediately commenced a massacre of a large number of prisoners, among whom were sixty-eight gendarmes.

Five gendarmes, who were then in the infirmary, alone escaped.

The honorable resistance of most of the keepers, who, aided by the prisoners themselves, barricaded the doors and halls, saved the lives of the hostages.

Towards four o'clock the horde thus held in check had a panic, and took to flight, crying that the Versailles troops were upon them. In an instant the prison was freed from its assailants, and the prisoners of every category were at liberty to flee or to await the arrival of the troops, which was near at hand.

Many of the hostages, fearing the return of some of these madmen, drunk with wine and blood, or the execution of the horrible menaces of fire which had been made for several days, resolved to make their escape and gain the outposts of the army of Versailles.

Some of them had the good fortune to succeed, while others, not knowing the quarter, betrayed rather than protected by incomplete disguises, or failing in coolness and presence of mind, were massacred in the neighborhood of the prison by rioters who were prowling with arms around La Roquette, and who were truly fiendish in their chasing of priests.

Four of the unhappy clergy perished thus at the corner of the prison Des Jeunes-Détenus; their bodies, mutilated in the most horrible manner, and hardly conserving the human form, were thrust on the spot into the same hole, where they remained until Sunday morning.

Among them, the only one who could be identified was the curé of Bonne-Nouvelle, whose church, like that of Notre-Dame-des-Victoires, was one of the most devastated. Most of the objects employed in the exercise of divine service had been carried off or destroyed.

A few days after the arrest of the unfortunate M. Bécourt, curate of Bonne-Nouvelle, a band of Federals arrived at his house with several furniture wagons which they had requisitioned, and began to load them with the furniture of the prisoner. At the same time, they searched the domestic, and took from him a sum of 120 francs.

The indignant neighbors succeeded in obliging the robbers to release a portion of the furniture, but nothing would induce them to surrender the money, which they regarded as only their rightful profit.

On Friday, the 26th, the following announcement was made by the Minister of War in the National Assembly:

"MESSIEURS:—The situation in Paris becomes better and better. The troops meet with an energetic resistance, but their courage and devotedness exceed the opposition they encounter. They advance slowly but surely. We are masters of all that portion of Paris situated on the left bank. On the right bank, our attack has extended to the Place de la Bastille, which is now in the possession of the army.

"General Vinoy is manœuvring at this moment for the capture of the Barrière du Trône. Nearly all the boulevards are in the power of the army. The Place du Chateau-d'Eau, the barracks of the Prince Eugène, the Magasins-Réunis—all that portion of Paris is in our hands.

"All the forts on the left bank, Bicêtre and Ivry included, are in our power. Bicêtre and Ivry were carried by the cavalry.

"There remain at this hour only the Buttes Chaumont, and the portion which extends on that side—that is, Belleville, La Villette, La Chapelle. But the troops advance methodically and regularly on these last points. To-morrow, I hope, they will be able to conquer this last citadel of the insurrection, and the great satisfaction will be given to the Government of announcing to the Assembly, that the army, thanks to the devotedness of its soldiers and the ability of its chiefs, has become completely mistress of Paris."

On the same day, the Minister of Foreign Affairs sent by telegram the following note to the diplomatic representatives of France in foreign countries:

"VERSAILLES, May 26th.

"SIR:—The abominable work of the odious criminals who are now perishing under the heroic efforts of our army, cannot be confounded with a political act. It constitutes a series of crimes, provided for and punished by the laws of every civilized country. Murder, robbery and incendiarism, systematically ordered, and prepared with an infernal skill, cannot permit to the persons engaged in them any other refuge than that of expiation by the law.

"No nation can cover them with immunity, and their presence on the soil of any would be a shame and a peril. If, therefore, you learn that any individual, compromised in the crimes at Paris, has crossed the frontier of the country to which you are accredited, I request you at once to solicit from the local authorities his immediate arrest, and to inform me of what you have done, in order that I may apply for his extradition.

"Receive, etc., JULES FAVRE."

The French Government immediately learned, in answer, that the Belgian Cabinet would not consider as political refugees any of the men concerned in the crimes of Paris, but would deliver them up at once; while the Spanish Consul at Marseilles announced that he would permit all vessels of his country in that port to be searched, and that the authorities of Madrid had decided that all French criminals who crossed the frontier would be seized and given up.

M. Victor Hugo, who had been called to Belgium by a recent bereavement, where he prudently remained during the reign of the Commune, addressed the following letter to the editor of the *Indépendence Belge* of Brussels, expressing his disapproval of the conduct of the Belgian Government:

"BRUSSELS, May 26th, 1871.

"SIR:—I protest against the declaration of the Belgian Government relative to the vanquished of Paris.

"Whatever may be said or done, these vanquished are political men.

"I was not with them.

"I accept the principle of the Commune. I do not accept the men.

"I have protested against their acts: law of hostages, reprisals, arbitrary arrests, violation of liberties, suppression of newspapers, spoliations, confiscations, demolitions, destruction of the Column, attacks on the law, attacks on the people.

"Their violences have rendered me indignant, as to-day the violence of the opposite party will do the same.

"The destruction of the Column is an act of treason against the nation. The destruction of the Louvre would have been a crime—treason against civilization.

"But savage acts, done in ignorance, are not villainous acts. Madness is a disease, not an offence. Ignorance is not the crime of the ignorant.

"The Column destroyed was a sad hour for France. The Louvre destroyed would have been for all people an eternal mourning.

"But the Column will be raised, and the Louvre is saved.

"To-day, Paris is retaken. The Assembly has vanquished the Commune. Who made the 18th of March?

Which is the true culprit, the Assembly or the Commune? History will tell.

"The burning of Paris was a monstrous act; but are there not two incendiaries? Let us wait before judging.

"I never understood Billioray, and Rigault astonished me to indignation; but to shoot Billioray is a crime—to shoot Rigault is a crime.

"Those of the Commune, Johannard and La Cecilia, who cause a child of fifteen to be shot, are criminals; those of the Assembly, who cause Jules Vallès, Bosquet, Parisel, Amouroux, Lefrançais, Brunet and Dombrowski to be shot, are criminals.

"Don't let us pour forth our indignation upon one side only. Here the crime is as much in the Assembly as in the Commune, and the crime is evident.

"First, for all civilized men, the punishment of death is abominable; secondly, execution without judgment is infamous. One is no longer a part of the law, the other never has been.

"Judge first, then condemn, then execute. I could blame, but I could not dishonor.

"You are under the law.

"If you kill without judgment, you assassinate.

"I return to the Belgian Government.

"It does wrong to refuse an asylum.

"The law permits this refusal, the right forbids it.

"I, who write you these lines, have a maxim: *Pro jure contra legem.*

"The asylum is an ancient right.

"It is the sacred right of the unhappy.

"In the middle ages the Church accorded this asylum even to parricides.

"As for me, I declare that:

"This asylum, which the Belgian Government refuses to the vanquished, I offer.

"Where?

"In Belgium.

"I do Belgium that honor.

"I offer an asylum in Brussels.

"I offer an asylum, Place des Barricades, No. 4.

"If a vanquished of Paris; if a man of the reunion called Commune, which was very little elected by Paris, and which, for my part, I never approved—if one of these men, were he my personal enemy, above all if he is my personal enemy, knocks at my door, I open. He is in my house. He is inviolable.

"Am I, perhaps, a stranger in Belgium? I think not. I feel myself the brother of all men and the guest of all people.

"In any case, a fugitive of the Commune in my house will be a vanquished at the home of a proscribed man; the vanquished of to-day with the proscribed of yesterday.

"I do not hesitate to say, two venerable things.

"One weakness protecting another.

"If a man is beyond the pale of the law, let him enter my house. I defy any one to tear him away.

"I am speaking of political men.

"If any one comes to my house to take a fugitive of the Commune, they will take me also. If he is given up, I will follow him. I will share his seat. And for the defence of right, by the side of the man of the Commune, vanquished by the Assembly of Versailles, will be seen the man of the Republic, proscribed by Bonaparte.

"I will do my duty. Above all, principles.

"One word more.

"What can certainly be affirmed is, that England will not deliver up the refugees of the Commune.

"Why place Belgium below England?

"The glory of Belgium is to be an asylum. Do not take from her that glory.

"In defending France, I defend Belgium.

"The Belgian Government will be against me, but the Belgian people will be with me.

"In any case, I will have my conscience.

"Receive, sir, the assurance of my distinguished sentiments,

VICTOR HUGO."

Although M. Victor Hugo was not mistaken in the first portion of his declaration that "the Belgian Government will be against me, but the Belgian people will be with me," he certainly was in the latter.

The night following the publication of his letter, a mob gathered in front of his house and greeted him with anything but friendly demonstrations. He was first wakened by a ring at the door-bell, which, coming at about two in the morning, rather surprised him. Putting his head out of the window to ask who was there, he was answered, "*C'est Dombrowski.*" Rather doubting the truth of this assertion, as Dombrowski had been reported killed, he was hesitating what to do, when a large stone crashed through the window directly above his head, quickly followed by a shower of others. At the same time, shouts were raised of "*A mort! à mort!*" Others facetiously informed him that the Commune had come to ask an asylum. Many called "*A bas Jean Valjean!*" showing at least an acquaintance with his works. Efforts were made to break open the door, which, happily for the "friend of the people," resisted these attempts. Not a window-pane in the front of the house remained intact, the front rooms were uninhabitable, and but for the timely break of day, M. Hugo might not now be alive to tell the tale.

On the following day, Victor Hugo having been invited by the Belgian Government to leave the country, and having refused, an order was issued for his ejection. It was to be supposed that this great genius, outraged by the terrible misfortunes which had been accumulated upon his country by the men of the Commune, would have flashed forth a superb denunciation, such as forms the power and glory of a poet; but no! Paris destroyed, the conflagration spreading with ardent flames from street to street, the archbishop assassinated in a cowardly manner, could not console the author of *Les Châtiments* for the death of Billioray, and of Rigault, the assassin of Chaudey.

The poet saw with an indifferent eye both victims and ruins, and kept all his pity for the assassins and incendiaries.

Happily, the Belgian Government had different views respecting them, and cordially responded to the appeal of France.

At the very moment in which M. Hugo was writing in exculpation of the odious Commune, another conflagration had been ignited, and the flames rose high to heaven as witnesses against such criminals. This fire was at the bonding warehouses of La Villette and the magazines of M. Trotrot, containing immense supplies of coal, wood, wine, provisions, and other articles of merchandise. Here twenty millions worth of property had been wantonly destroyed, no possibility existing of saving the smallest portion.

Offers were made by both the English and Belgian Governments to send their firemen, in order to aid in extinguishing the conflagration in Paris. These offers were thankfully accepted, and were announced to the National Assembly by General Le Flô (War) in the following manner:

"The losses of our troops are infinitely less considerable than might have been feared, and the wounded are most carefully attended to in the various hospitals. Bodies of firemen have hurried in from every part of France (*hear,*

hear), and the Lord Mayor of London has asked us for permission to send a number of those belonging to the English capital to co-operate in the task of saving Paris. (*Loud applause.*) The French Government at once replied that it accepted that assistance, and at the present moment a body of the London firemen are, with their apparatus, on the way to Paris. (*Renewed marks of approbation.*) Belgium, likewise, was unwilling to remain behindhand, and the Government of that country has made us the same offers of aid. The steam fire-engines of Antwerp have also left for France." (*Long continued cheers.*)

The burning of the docks of La Villette was the signal for another defeat of the insurgents.

In fact, during this same day, General Ladmirault executed at La Villette a movement similar to that of General Vinoy on Charonne. The two army corps took their positions simultaneously in the rear of Père-Lachaise, and in the rear of the Buttes Chaumont.

The troops advanced on the Place de la Rotonde, which is the central position of La Villette by the Rue de Lafayette and the Boulevard de la Chapelle.

In the Rue de Lafayette they encountered a vigorous resistance at the Strasbourg Railway Station and in the Boulevard de la Chapelle, at the barricades of the Rue d'Aubervilliers.

These positions being taken, the barricades were attacked vigorously, both in front and flank, and were unable to hold out, although their principal position, the Douane-Centrale, was a veritable bastion. It was then that the docks were set on fire.

The army was then allowed a few hours repose before making a supreme effort, which was to crush entirely the insurrection.

CHAPTER XIII.

The line of battle—Boulevard Richard Lenoir—Capture of the Buttes Chaumont—Resistance at Père-Lachaise—Appearance of the cemetery—Taking of La Villette—Government circular—Hostile attitude of Belleville—Rage of the insurgents—Belleville conquered—Circular issued by M. Thiers—Proclamations of Marshal de MacMahon—Vicar Lamazon's letter—Military decrees—Arms taken from the insurgents—Paris divided into four military departments—Aspect of the city—The Louvre—The Tuileries—The Palais-Royal—The Hotel de Ville—Escape of the Archives—The Bank of France—The Palais de Justice—The Legion of Honor—The Conseil d'Etat and the Cour des Comptes—Cost of the Commune to the city of Paris—Strangers of the Commune.

On Saturday, May 27th, the silence which had reigned throughout the night was broken at an early hour. The last desperate struggle began.

The Federals were being pushed upon Belleville, and were confined in a semicircle, always narrowing, the two extremities of which rested on the ramparts, the intermediate part following the boulevards from the Bastille to the Chateau-d'Eau, and skirting the canal from the Faubourg du Temple to the Place de la Villette. Three-quarters of the army were there massed, in order to finish at a single blow.

The aspect of the line of battle was lugubrious; the sky was gray with clouds, and rain fell from time to time, settling down in the afternoon to a steady pour.

On the left stood the Butte Chaumont; on the summit, at the foot of a tree which dominated the platform, were the pieces of the insurgents, pointed from behind a wooden balustrade in the direction of Montmartre; the artillerymen, few in number, on account of the shells which rained upon the Butte, were in their shirt-sleeves. Just below the heights, on the declining ground, could be seen the church of Belleville, with its high and pointed steeples. Still further down is the quarter of Ménilmontant, distinguished by the steeple of Saint Ambroise. From this point the ground rises rapidly, and to the right appears a vast line of verdure; this is the cemetery of Père-Lachaise. The detonations of artillery sounded here frequently, from the foot of a long obelisk, monumental ornament of a tomb.

The line of the Federals bordered the canal by La Roquette, the Boulevard Richard-Lenoir, and the Boulevard de la Villette, but they fell back incessantly as the attack progressed.

General Douay, master of the barracks of the Chateau-d'Eau, advanced by the Faubourg du Temple, which resisted with fury. The barricade established beyond the canal, at the corner of the Rue Fontaine-au-Roi, fired without interruption upon the barracks. But the troops advanced on the left, and, carrying the barricade of the Rue Grange-aux-Belles, occupied the hospital of Saint Louis.

Towards the east, General Clinchant attacked by the Boulevard Prince-Eugène, by the Rue d'Angoulême, and by the extremity of the Boulevard Richard-Lenoir, the barricades which defended the approaches of the canal. The resistance in the Rue des Trois-Bornes was particularly vigorous, the fire from the barricade being aided by that of insurgents in the surrounding houses, the windows of which had been stuffed with mattresses for their protection.

At the intersection of the Boulevard Richard-Lenoir and the Boulevard du Prince-Eugène, stood a barricade sixty yards in length, with ditches and embrasures; the exterior parapet was made of bags of paper to deaden the force of the shells. This obstacle was unapproachable in front; it was supported on the sides by barricades in all the streets running down towards the canal. The troops, however, advanced by the Bastille, attacking the secondary obstacles, such as the barricade of the Chemin-Vert, and succeeded in placing between two fires the great fortification at the bifurcation of the two avenues. The Federals were forced to abandon it, leaving the neighborhood in ruins. Clothes with large red stains; corpses black with powder; horses horribly mutilated, and broken arms and caissons, were lying everywhere upon the ground, which seemed perfectly saturated with blood.

During the entire afternoon shells fell like rain upon Belleville, the Buttes-Chaumont, and Père-Lachaise, enveloping the horizon in enormous clouds of smoke, and forced the musketry fire to descend gradually from the heights and take refuge in the lower quarter of Belleville, between the Chateau-d'Eau and the Buttes-Chaumont, where it continued to roll with diabolical rage.

The Buttes-Chaumont, bombarded for three days by the battery established at Montmartre, surrounded and strongly attacked on Friday night, was not definitively taken until Saturday evening. Numerous traces of projectiles in the neighborhood of the Buttes attest the efficacy of the artillery fire directed against them. A height situated at the extremity of the park of which the Federals had formed an advanced redoubt armed with cannon, was first taken by the troops; the assault was then given on the interior hillocks, which were carried after a violent combat. The insurgents resisted to the very last moment, only a few shells remaining in their possession when the soldiers penetrated into their entrenchments, where they were surrounded and taken prisoners to the number of 7,000 or 8,000 men.

The investment of Père-Lachaise was conducted at the same time by the combined action of the troops under General Vinoy, who, from the Place du Trône, had gained the cemetery by the exterior boulevards and Charonne, and of the column which advanced along the Boulevard Richard-Lenoir.

The Père-Lachaise had been occupied for several days by the Federals; they had easily appreciated all the importance of this commanding position. Consequently, without respect for this place of eternal repose, without fear of calling the tumult and trouble of battle amidst these tombs—last testimonies of affection and regret, which contain the remains of so many men illustrious in politics, in letters, in the sciences, and in the arts—they had made of the cemetery a sort of entrenched camp, all the better defended as each of its narrow pathways, each of its funereal monuments, offered from step to step a refuge to the combatants. On the elevation surmounted by the well-known pyramid consecrated to the family of Beauséjour, the insurgents had installed a battery of large calibre, whose shells burst during three days over all the habitations of the right bank. In the beginning, the Père-Lachaise had received a garrison of from 7,000 to 8,000 National Guards, but as circumstances became more menacing, the ranks gradually thinned; the men profited by the night to make their escape, and on Saturday morning the cemetery contained only from 3,000 to 4,000 combatants.

In the evening, towards nine o'clock, the Federals were seized with a general panic at the alarming news of the capture of the barricades at the Chateau-d'Eau and the Boulevard Richard-Lenoir, and of the approach, more and more imminent, of the regular troops. The National Guards withdrew in great haste, scaling the walls of the cemetery, and commenced a retreat which greatly resembled a disordered flight. The chiefs, however, succeeded in rallying a portion of their forces, made them return to the cemetery and continue the service of the batteries which they had abandoned so precipitately.

But this return of resistance was not of long duration. The insurgents, seeing themselves attacked on three sides at the same time, understood that soon all retreat would be impossible, and most of them fled in great haste, after having spiked their pieces. It was time; three regiments of the line crossed at the same moment the boundary of Père-Lachaise. The determined men who had persisted in retaining this position, opened upon the soldiers a violent fire of musketry, sheltering themselves behind the tombs, among which they slowly retreated. It was a useless effort; soon forced to yield before the firmness of the attack, the troops were quickly in possession of the disputed ground, making its defenders prisoners.

The cemetery, garnished with cannon, with loopholes pierced in its walls, dug up in different parts for the establishment of entrenchments, presented a singular spectacle, the disorder contrasting sadly with its solemn and peaceful intention.

Near the tomb of the Duke de Morny were several pieces of artillery, while in the vault itself the ammunition was stored. On the left of the tomb were two guns, and a few steps to the right five more. Near the chapel, which probably served as headquarters of the staff, were two more pieces. This position was, in fact, well chosen for the end the insurgents had in view. The eye from here embraces, in their smallest details, the large avenues of the capital, and the quarters which had suffered so terribly from the conflagration.

Many of the tombs were badly injured, particularly in the 37th division, Chemin du Bourget. In one a shell pierced the outer wall of the tomb and lodged in the bottom of the sepulchre without exploding. Others had their inscriptions entirely destroyed, or their monuments much defaced.

Meanwhile, General Ladmirault had continued his movement on La Villette, and taken possession of the Abattoir and the Cattle Market. He then advanced towards the Buttes Chaumont, attacking this position in the rear, and aiding in its capture as already described.

The entire quarter of La Villette at the end of the struggle bore strong evidence of the fury and violence with which it had been conducted. The houses of the boulevard were riddled with bullets and shells from the roof to the ground. The insurgents had not been contented with firing from behind the barricades; it had been necessary to dislodge them from the windows, and nearly every house had become in turn the scene of a violent struggle.

The benches were torn from the sides of the streets; the trees, twisted, broken, and notched, literally covered the ground with their fragments. Broken lamp-posts were strewn around, and the wooden huts erected during the siege to shelter the Mobiles were knocked down, burned, pierced with bullets, or cut in pieces. Most of these shelters were filled with the bodies of the insurgents killed in battle, lying one upon another. The faces smeared with mud and blood, or gashed with horrible wounds, were terrible to look upon. Behind the barricade of the Place de la Rotonde, although the dead had been carried away, their number was proved by the quantities of blood which ran in streams through the gutters. Cannons with broken carriages, guns lying in heaps, and stained with blood, horses stretched dead upon the ground mingled with boxes of preserves and portions of bread—such were the sights which might be seen behind every barricade in the quarter.

In the Rue de Puebla sixty insurgents were killed

behind one barricade; they felt their cause to be infallibly lost, and thought only to sell their lives as dearly as possible.

One of the insurgents taken during the combat had with him his two children, one eight and the other ten years of age.

After the death of their father, these two young orphans remained in the midst of the soldiers, who treated them with the greatest kindness.

A few days later, the colonel of the regiment, perceiving these poor little creatures eating out of the same dish with a squad of soldiers, asked their names and how they came there.

A corporal replied that they were the sons of an insurgent condemned to death by court-martial; he added that the two orphans had neither family nor friends to charge themselves with their fate.

Moved by this recital, the colonel proposed to the officers and soldiers to adopt these orphans, and to admit them amongst the children of the troop. His proposition was received with enthusiasm. The children were clothed in military dress, and will be henceforth sons of the 29th of the line.

The following circular was issued by M. Thiers relative to Saturday's military proceedings:

"VERSAILLES, May 27—7 P.M.

"Our troops have not ceased to follow up the insurgents step by step. They have carried daily the most important positions, making 25,000 prisoners, besides the killed and wounded. In this ably-calculated march, our generals and their illustrious chief have been desirous of sparing as much as possible our brave soldiers, who were only too anxious to overcome rapidly the obstacles opposed to them.

"While General du Barrail with his cavalry was capturing Forts Montrouge, Bicêtre, and Ivry, General de Cissey was executing brilliant operations, which have had the effect of procuring us the whole of the left bank of the Seine.

"General Vinoy, following the course of the river, marched towards the Bastille, which bristled with formidable entrenchments. He carried this position with General Vergé's division; and subsequently, with the aid of divisions under Generals Bruat and Faron, he obtained possession of the Faubourg Saint-Antoine as far as the Place du Trône.

"Our flotilla has afforded General Vinoy brilliant and efficacious assistance. The latter's troops carried to-day a formidable barricade at the corner of the Avenue Philippe Auguste, and one at Montreuil. They have thus taken up a position to the east, at the foot of the heights of Belleville, the last refuge of this insurrection, whose leaders in their flight resort to incendiarism as the monstrous revenge for their defeat.

"In the centre, General Douay has followed the lines of the boulevards, resting his right on the Bastille and his left on the Cirque Napoleon.

"General Clinchant, who joined General Ladmirault in the west, has had to overcome a desperate resistance at the Magasins-Réunis, which, however, he has valiantly subdued.

"Lastly, General Ladmirault, after vigorously carrying the Northern and Eastern Railways, has taken the direction of La Villette, and occupied a position at the foot of the Buttes Chaumont.

"Thus two-thirds of the army, after having conquered the whole of the ground on the right bank, are now ranged at the foot of the Belleville heights, which they are to attack to-morrow morning.

"During six days there has been constant fighting, and our energetic and indefatigable soldiers have really achieved wonders. The merit of those who have had to attack barricades is far different from that of those who have defended them. The officers in command of troops have shown themselves worthy of leading such men, and have fully justified the vote of thanks passed by the Assembly.

"After the few hours' repose which they are now enjoying, they will to-morrow morning bring to an end the glorious campaign which they have undertaken against the most odious demagogues and criminals the world has ever seen. They will thereby deserve the eternal gratitude of France and humanity.

"Our troops have suffered painful losses. General Leroy de Dais is dead. Commandant Segoyer was made prisoner by the insurgents in the Place de la Bastille, and his captors, without respect for the laws of war, shot him at once. This act is what we might have expected from men who set fire to our cities, and who have even collected a quantity of venomous liquid wherewith to poison the soldiers, and cause almost instantaneous death."

The Staff of the Army of Versailles issued the following report:

"After having captured the slaughter-houses and cattle-market of La Villette with the division of General Grenier, and the large barricade armed with cannon at the Rond Point of the Boulevard de la Villette with the aid of General Montaudon's division, General Ladmirault carried in the evening the Buttes Chaumont and the heights of Belleville, whence for three days the insurgent batteries had been bombarding Paris. General Vinoy, whose troops held in the morning the Rue and Faubourg Saint Antoine and the Cours de Vincennes, obtained possession of the Cemetery of Père-Lachaise and the Mairie of the 20th

Arrondissement, which were carried by battalions of Fusiliers and sailors.

"Generals Clinchant and Douay guard the line of the St. Martin Canal, and the Boulevards from the Prince Eugène Barracks to the Bastille. What remains of the insurgent forces is surrounded on all sides, and all resistance will have ceased to-day.

"There was a very vigorous cannonade and musketry fire all last night in the direction of Belleville, where there were also numerous conflagrations. The firing still continued this morning."

The insurrection was now completely crushed, and the remaining fighting was but a struggle of despair, struggle still more terrible as the insurgents now fought only for the purpose of fighting.

In the Faubourgs of Belleville the barricades were numberless; they rose in every street, defended by cannon, and from the neighboring houses, which were also fortified. The soldiers were obliged to conquer each of these improvised citadels. Once taken, the houses were searched in every story, the concierges being obliged to mount with the troops, after having given the number and position of the inhabitants. If their statement proved false they were shot forthwith.

Here women approached the troops with smiles on their lips, distributing bread and wine. These, however, were soon discovered to be poisoned, and the soldiers were forbidden to receive anything from the hands of the inhabitants. Cigars dipped in corrosive liquids had been also distributed, and several officers had been shot by women who had approached them under different pretexts.

These acts, which prove the ferocity with which the contest was conducted, together with the recital of the massacre of the hostages, added to the fury of the soldiers, who, in turn, gave no quarter. An insurgent general, dressed in civilian's clothes, was made prisoner and about to be shot, when he offered 1,000 francs to any man who would save him. He was answered by a laugh, and fell dead at the feet of his executioners.

In one of the houses in which a young officer entered to make a perquisition, he was met at the door by a woman, who, throwing herself at his feet, and winding her arms around him, cried, at the same time drawing him within the entrance:

"My son is in the house, but he was forced to fight; do not kill him!"

"Bring him down; we will see," replied the officer.

The woman hastily mounted the stairs, and the young man, making a sign to his men, was about to follow, when he felt a terrible pain, and saw himself surrounded by flames.

While one woman had occupied him in conversation, another, hidden in the alley, had thrown petroleum upon his uniform, and set it on fire. The men threw themselves upon their officer, and tore off his clothes as quickly as possible; but two hours later he succumbed to the horrible burns which he had received.

On Saturday morning (27th), about eight hundred insurgents occupied the Place de la Fête. All the bandits of the Commune, the desperadoes, had come, hunted on every side, to seek here a last refuge, most of them to find death; a certain number had their heads surmounted by the red liberty cap.

In the morning, a young boy who wished to pass, and who was furnished with a safe-conduct perfectly in order, fell into the hands of these madmen, and was with difficulty rescued by their colonel, Du Bisson.

The formidable bombardment directed by Montmartre against Belleville had driven the insurgents almost mad.

In the trouble and confusion caused by the rain of shells and grape-shot, they no longer recognized their chiefs, against whom their rage, powerless to harm their assailants, was now turned. They arrested Du Bisson, whom they accused of having betrayed them; released him, and arrested him again, when he was led away no one knows where. A few moments later their fury, always on the increase, turned upon one of their lieutenants, whom they shot upon the spot as a traitor.

But the hour of punishment for them arrived. The battery of Bellevue had been taken; twenty-three insurgents were shot on the spot; and at six in the evening, while a few sharpshooters called the attention of the Federals towards the Rue de Crimée, the volunteers of Seine-et-Oise and the soldiers of the 64th regiment advanced by the Rue Compans, turning and gaining possession of the barricades. The Federals still wishing to fight, placed themselves with their backs against the houses of the square.

"Fire on the commandant," cried their chief; and the brave officer fell pierced with balls.

"In two ranks," then cried the Federal commandant, losing all self-possession. The unhappy men obeyed, and were decimated by a terrible discharge. The remainder then beat a retreat, setting fire, on the way, to a large building called the "Chateau."

A last and furious engagement continued until Sunday afternoon at three o'clock, in Belleville and in the Rues du Faubourg-du-Temple, De Saint-Maur, D'Oberkampf, Folie-Méricourt, which extend at the foot of this height, formerly solely renowned for its parties of pleasure.

During several hours the battle was horrible, and was conducted in many cases hand to hand. The musketry fire, sword fights, and charges with bayonet were multiplied at all points, with a fury equal on both sides. From the Rue de Charonne to the Faubourg du Temple, and in all the Popincourt quarter, the fight was general, ardent and pitiless. The National Guards were killed behind the barricades, refusing to yield, and the troops remained intrepid and firm under a rain of balls sent from every window.

At Belleville, where the capture of the barricades required the most energetic efforts, and inflicted sensible losses on the regular army, the insurgents held out, as well as in the lower quarters, until all their ammunition was exhausted—until the last fortified work was completely destroyed.

Finally, towards two o'clock, the fire slackened; shots were only to be heard at intervals; the cries ceased at the different points of contest; the battle of seven days, begun on the 21st of May, was approaching its end.

At three o'clock, a body of about four hundred insurgents descended from the heights of Belleville; they came to surrender themselves prisoners.

At their head marched four members of the Commune, preceded by a lieutenant of the staff bearing a red flag. They all carried their guns reversed, in sign of mourning, advancing silently; and, criminal as was this revolt, this sad procession could not be looked upon without emotion.

Arrived at the canal, when about to place themselves in the hands of the troops, they all threw down their arms, and were immediately surrounded and marched away.

A large number of the insurgents had escaped by the side-streets, falling back towards Montreuil and Vincennes, but they were met in their retreat by the Prussian lines, where all passage was refused them. Any refuge was henceforth impossible. On the left bank, the southern forts of Ivry, Bicêtre and Montrouge, which had remained in possession of the Commune until the occupation of Paris, had belonged for two days to the legal Government. The fort of Vincennes, the only point yet untaken, was surrendered on Monday morning, May 29th, at the first demonstration made against it by a brigade of the army of General Vinoy.

The Chief of the Executive Power issued the following circulars, announcing the triumph of the Government:

"May 28th, 1871—2:15 P. M.

"Our troops, charged with the operations on the right bank, were last evening drawn up in a circle round the Buttes Chaumont and the heights of Belleville. During the night they overcame all obstacles. General Ladmirault crossed the valley of La Villette, proceeded beyond the slaughter-houses, and ascended the Buttes Chaumont as well as the Belleville heights.

"The young Davoust, so worthy of the name he bears, carried the barricades, and by daybreak General Ladmirault's corps had reached the summit of the heights. General Douay, starting from the Boulevard Richard-Lenoir, also attacked the insurgents' positions at Belleville. During the same time, General Vinoy's men climbed the ascent of the Cemetery Père-Lachaise, and carried the Mairie of the 20th Arrondissement and the prison of La Roquette. The sailors have everywhere displayed their usual bravery.

"In entering La Roquette, we had the consolation of saving the lives of one hundred and sixty-nine hostages, who were about to be shot. But, alas! the wretches from whom we are obliged to tear Paris in flames and covered with blood, had had time to shoot sixty-four, among whom, we have the grief to announce, were the Archbishop of Paris, the Abbé Duguerry (the best of men), President Bonjean, and a number of other worthy men. After having murdered, during these last days, the generous Chaudey, a heart full of goodness, and a sincere Republican, whom could they spare?

"Now thrown back upon the ramparts, between the French army and the Prussians, who have refused them passage, they will expiate their crimes, and have either to die or surrender.

"The too guilty Delescluze has been picked up dead by the troops of General Clinchant. Millière, not less famous, has been shot for having fired three times from his revolver on the corporal who arrested him. These expiations do not console us for so many misfortunes, above all, for so many crimes; but they should prove to these senseless men that civilization is not provoked and defied in vain, and that justice soon raises its voice.

"The insurrection, compressed into the space of a few hundred yards, is vanquished—definitively vanquished. Peace is about to be restored; but it will not succeed in relieving all honest and patriotic hearts of the profound sorrow with which they are afflicted."

"PARIS, May 29, 1871.

"To-day a brigade of the army of General Vinoy commenced the siege works against the fort of Vincennes. As soon as the insurgents, who still occupied the position, perceived these preparations, they surrendered at discretion. One of the chiefs blew his brains out. Our troops took immediate possession of the fort."

The social war was terminated; the Communal insurrection had at last succumbed, and Paris was delivered.

This immense result was immediately announced to the Parisian population by the following proclamation from Marshal de MacMahon:

"HEADQUARTERS, May 28, 1871.

"INHABITANTS OF PARIS:

"The army of France came to save you.

"Paris is delivered.

"Our soldiers carried, at four o'clock, the last positions occupied by the insurgents.

"To-day the struggle is finished; order, labor, and security will now revive.

"De MacMahon, Duc de Magenta,
"Marshal of France, Commander-in-Chief."

On the same day the Marshal addressed to the troops the following order of the day, thanking them for the efforts which they had made with so much courage during this difficult contest:

"Soldiers and Sailors:—Your courage and devotion have triumphed over all obstacles. After a siege of two months, after a battle of eight days in the streets, Paris is at last delivered. In tearing the city from the hands of the wretches who had projected burning it to ashes, you have preserved it from complete ruin; you have given it back to France.

"Soldiers and Sailors:—The entire country applauds the success of your patriotic efforts; and the National Assembly, by which it is represented, has accorded you the recompense most worthy of you.

"It has been declared by a unanimous vote that the armies of sea and land have merited well of the country."

As early as the 22d of May—in fact, at the news of the entrance of the troops into Paris—the Assembly had unanimously given this noble testimony of gratitude and encouragement to the soldiers. By a just and delicate sentiment, they had associated the Chief of the Executive Power in the thanks which they addressed to the army in the name of France. M. Thiers and the army had equally merited well of the country. Thanks to their patient and resolute zeal, Paris and France were restored to each other; the sovereignty of the nation had overcome the most terrible of revolts; the civilization and national unity of France were saved.

But alas! at the price of what disasters, of what ruins strewn over Paris, were these results obtained! How many unhappy men, misled certainly by the most detestable passions, but still fellow-citizens, were killed or taken prisoners by thousands! how many gallant soldiers fell pierced by fratricidal balls!

As soon as the combat was terminated, energetic measures were taken for restoring order in Paris: arms were everywhere seized, and in each quarter a rigid investigation was made. During several days, each street, guarded at its two extremities by sentinels, was searched from house to house, from story to story, when every suspected individual was immediately arrested, and all stores of dangerous matters instantly seized.

A large number of insurgents were taken prisoners during these domiciliary visits, many of them important personages, while powder, cartridges, petroleum, and guns were seized in quantities. On every point the barricades were overthrown as quickly as possible, and the streets restored to a condition which rendered circulation comparatively easy.

The public mind, filled with joy at its deliverance, was at the same time troubled by the horrors of the last few days, among which stood pre-eminent the frightful massacre of the hostages. On Sunday morning a letter was written by M. Lamazou, Vicar of the Madeleine, describing the events which occurred at La Roquette during the last days of his imprisonment as hostage:

"PARIS, May 28th, 1871.

"We left this morning the prison of La Roquette, ten ecclesiastics, forty *sergents-de-ville*, and eighty-two soldiers, after having escaped death only by a prodigy of audacity and *sang-froid.*

"Prisoner of the Committee of Public Safety at the Conciergerie, Mazas and La Roquette, I will be to-day sparing of details regarding the revolting and monstrous acts of which the last-named prison has been the theatre, and which assure it hereafter a renown amongst the places most sinisterly celebrated. To mention one out of a hundred, a vicar of Notre-Dame-des-Victoires and myself passed a half-an-hour on Thursday, May 25th, preparing ourselves to be shot. It was only a false alarm, and the agents of the Commune charged with these amiable invitations consoled those who were the objects of them, in assuring them that what didn't take place to-day would not fail to arrive on the morrow. For the time they were only charged with bringing one of our neighbors before a kind of court-martial, then sitting in the prison, and which was composed of citizens principally remarkable, some for their stupidity, the others for their ferocity.

"Since the atrocious execution of Monseigneur the Archbishop of Paris, of M. le Curé de la Madeleine, of President Bonjean, of M. Allard, former missionary, and of the Jesuit Fathers Clair and Du Coudray, which took place on Wednesday, May 24th, in a corner of the exterior court of the prison, without motive, without judgment, without verbal process, in presence of a delegate of the Commune, who had no other mandate than a revolver in his hand, and of a crowd of National Guards, who could manifest no sentiments but the most revolting outrages; without any respect for the bodies of these noble victims, who were stripped of their clothes, piled on a common wagon, and thrown into a corner of earth at Charonne, it was evident that the burlesque acts of the Commune were to be succeeded by others both destructive and sanguinary, and that the hostages who had been conducted from Mazas to La Roquette on the morning of the entrance of the Versailles troops into Paris, were destined to undergo the same fate.

"On Friday, May 26th, thirty-eight gendarmes and sixteen priests were conducted to Père-Lachaise, and there shot. On the following day, as the army of Versailles approached the heights of Père-Lachaise—where the infernal battery had been erected which was to reduce to ashes the finest monuments of Paris—an order was given to shoot all the priests, soldiers, and *sergents-de-ville* who still remained in the prison. The members of the Commune who persisted in their horrible designs had installed themselves in the register office of La Roquette. I was able, from my cell, to follow their deliberations, and I affirm that there cannot be a public house of the worst reputation where the behavior would not be more exemplary.

"At half-past three the purveyor of these executions ordered the inhabitants of the second and third stories to descend. One of the keepers of La Roquette, whose name ought to be known to the public, M. Pinet, yielding to a generous inspiration of humanity, opened rapidly the doors of all the cells, declaring that it was frightful to see honest people shot by such ignoble bandits, and that he would sacrifice his life for ours if we would aid in opposing them by an energetic resistance.

"This proposition was received with enthusiasm; each person improvised an arm in iron or in wood, and two solid barricades were established at the entrance of the doors on the third story; an opening was made in the floor to communicate our resolution to the lower story, where the *sergents-de-ville* already meditated the same design. Under the direction of the keeper, Pinet, and of an enterprising Zouave, the eastern pavilion became a veritable fortress.

The Commune, which was to parody and even surpass all that was most odious and grotesque in the revolution of 1793, allowed that ignoble populace, seen in Paris only on sinister days, to enter the court of the prison, in order to regale them with the spectacle of another day of September.

"While the crowd without shouted and menaced, some of the National Guards, charged with shooting us, mounted to the third story, announcing that the prison was to be mined and blown up, or else reduced to ashes by means of their formidable artillery established at Père Lachaise. They then set fire to one of our barricades in order to suffocate us, but this fire was soon extinguished.

"One detail I do not wish to omit. The individual who waved his gun in the most cynical manner was a man condemned to death by the Assize Court of the Seine, and who was prisoner at La Roquette. Many of the same class had the doors of their prisons opened, and left the building, shouting enthusiastically, "*Vive la Commune!*"

"Our energetic resistance caused great astonishment to the members of the Commune, who soon retreated towards Charonne and Belleville. The crowd, impressed by this example, followed the Commune, and we were able to close the doors of the prison. We were half saved, thanks to the disorder which followed; it was then that the populace remaining before La Roquette, passing from words of menace to those of seduction, began to cry "*Vive la Ligne!*" declaring that they simply wished to restore all the prisoners to liberty. Four priests and eighteen soldiers allowed themselves to be deceived by these promises; hardly had they left the prison before they were placed against one of its walls and shot, and the bodies of the four priests served to crown a neighboring barricade.

"During the night a strict watch was established in the two stories; the menacing cries which rose outside frightened no one; at last, on Sunday, the 28th, at dawn of day, the musketry fire of the Versailles troops, to which we listened with an emotion more easily to be understood than described, announced their approach; at a quarter past five the barricade opposite La Roquette was carried by a vigorous attack, and the soldiers of the Infantry of Marine took possession of the prison.

"We were thus unexpectedly restored to life after four days of the most cruel agony which can possibly be imagined.

"Receive, sir, etc.,

"L'Abbé Lamazou,

"Vicar of the Madeleine."

It was indispensable that the disarming of Paris should be effected as rapidly as possible, and for that purpose the Chief of the Executive Power caused the following decree to be published:

"Versailles, May 29, 1871.

"The Chief of the Executive Power of the French Republic,

"Considering that arms distributed throughout Paris in profusion and without control, have fallen into the hands of rioters and malefactors, and that a general disarming can alone guarantee, at this moment, the public security,

"DECREES:

"Art. I. Under the orders of the military authorities, all warlike weapons are to be carried to each Mairie, to be afterwards placed in the arsenals of the State.

"Art. II. The National Guards of Paris and of the Department of the Seine are dissolved. Until the National Assembly shall have decided concerning their re-organization, the citizens who lent their aid to the army for the re-establishment of order, may continue their services under the orders and direction of the military authorities.

"Art. III. The Ministers of War and of the Interior, and the Marshal commanding the Army of Paris, are charged with the execution of the present decree."

The previous evening, the General commanding the Second Corps had caused the following notice to be placarded on the left bank:

"HEADQUARTERS OF THE LUXEMBOURG, May 28, 1871.

"According to the orders of the Marshal, Commander-in-Chief of the Army of Versailles, the disarming of the city of Paris is general, and admits of no exception.

"While the General commanding in chief the Second Corps of the left bank of the Seine causes this measure to be rigorously executed, he wishes, at the same time, publicly to express his satisfaction at the eager and patriotic assistance given to the army by certain members of the National Guard who fought for the cause of order and civilization. These brave companions in arms have given a noble example to their fellow-citizens, and have shown what the Parisian population might have done against a minority of adventurers and anarchists who oppressed it.

"In the name of France, in the name of a menaced society, the General commanding the Second Corps thanks them, and cordially presses their hands.

"E. DE CISSEY,"

"The General Commanding the Second Corps."

The approximative number of arms taken from the insurgents, in virtue of these military orders, is as follows:

285,000 chassepots.

195,000 guns *à tabatière*.

68,000 " *à piston*.

That is, 548,000 guns of different models, with sabre-bayonets, or bayonets with their corresponding shoulder-belt.

56,000 cavalry sabres of all forms and for all ranks.

14,000 carbines, mostly Enfield.

39,000 revolvers.

Finally, 10,000 arms of every kind, such as daggers, stilettoes, sword-canes, etc., giving a total of 667,000 weapons of every kind taken from the hands of the Communists, independently of 1,700 pieces of cannon and mitrailleuses which they had torn away from the State, and of which they had made such terrible use.

As for the *armes de luxe*, such as guns used in the chase, pistols, sabres, etc., whose surrender was exacted in consequence of the exceptional circumstances of the moment, their number was hardly over 15,000, which is easily explained by the departure of the great portion of the richer population at the first evidence of insurrectional tendencies in the city.

In order to assure the prompt and absolute return of order, and to attain the harmony indispensable for the execution of the different public services, Marshal de MacMahon issued on May 30th the following decree:

"AT HEADQUARTERS, May 30th, 1871.

"Until further order, the city of Paris will be divided into four great military commanderies, namely:

"1st. That of the East, comprising the XI, XII, XIX and XX Arrondissements, under the orders of General Vinoy, commanding the Army of Reserve; headquarters at the Convent of Picpus.

"2d. That of the North-West, comprising the VIII, IX, X, XVI, XVII and XVIII Arrondissements, under the orders of General Ladmirault, commanding the First Army Corps; headquarters at the Elysée.

"3d. That of the South, comprising all the left bank, that is, the V, VI, VII, XIII, XIV and XV Arrondissements, under the orders of General de Cissey, commanding the Second Army Corps; headquarters at the Luxembourg.

"4th. That of the Centre, comprising the I, II, III and IV Arrondissements, under the orders of General Douay, commanding the Fourth Army Corps; headquarters Place Vendôme.

"According to Article 7 of the law of 1849, relative to the state of siege, all the powers possessed by the civil authorities for the maintenance of order and the police pass entirely into the hands of the military authorities.

"DE MACMAHON, Duc de Magenta,
"Marshal of France, Commander-in-Chief."

On the same day, May 30th, the commandery of the North-West gave the first sign of life, in repressing energetically attempts on the public security. General Ladmirault caused the following notice to be placed on the walls:

"NOTICE.

"HEADQUARTERS OF THE ELYSEE, May 30th, 1871.

"Isolated shots are now and then fired from houses situated in different quarters on the right bank.

"The General commanding in chief the First Army Corps informs the inhabitants that any house from which a shot is fired will be immediately the object of a military execution.

"The military authority will not flinch from any rigorous measure which will tend to establish security in the streets of the capital, order and peace in the country. It has a right to count on the concurrence of all good citizens."

On the 30th, another law was passed, ordering all cafés, restaurants and wine-shops to be closed at eleven o'clock.

Any proprietor disobeying this order, or any person found in his establishment after that hour, was to be immediately arrested.

At the same time the theatres were obliged to be furnished with a special authorization from the military authorities before continuing their representations, and the same was required from all newspapers—even from those which had already reappeared.

The following notice was later placarded, and was read with general approbation.

"HEADQUARTERS, PARIS, June 2d, 1871.

"Until further order, all commerce in petroleum is formally forbidden.

"Exceptions can only be made for pharmaceutical preparations. In such cases, the request must be addressed to the military authorities, who will grant it only after having received all the necessary guarantees."

Meanwhile, what aspect did Paris present, while the Government and the army took the dispositions necessary to restore its calm, to obtain the pacification of the public mind, and to bring back order and security to its streets?

The central quarters were gradually regaining their customary appearance. The shops were opening, but as yet very slowly. The suffering had been so great during the last two months—the nightmare of the last eight days had been so frightful—that the inhabitants could with difficulty rouse themselves from the succeeding torpor, and return seriously to their work. The barricades were everywhere being destroyed.

Often, at certain points, the passers-by were required to take down a stone—perhaps the very same which they had been forced to raise during the time of the Commune.

From nearly all the houses, although still closed, floated

the tricolored flag. Everywhere the walls bore traces of the recent struggle; bullet-holes, large pieces torn away by the bursting of a shell, or the marks of a conflagration which the Communists had endeavored to ignite in retreating.

The arrests still continued. Numerous denunciations were hourly made against former Communists. These denunciations were mostly made by women—a fact which was also to be remarked under the Commune, in regard to the Versaillese and suspected persons. The streets were, consequently, here and there dotted with detachments of three or four National Guards, who had just captured a Communist, and were leading him away. With regard to incendiaries, no pity was shown. Any individual, man or woman, found carrying a bottle of petroleum, was instantly shot.

The prisoners taken were directed on different points of Paris, such as the theatre of the Châtelet, and from there, if not condemned by the Grand Provost, were conducted to Versailles.

The number of insurgents slain in the contest was incalculable. During the first few days they were buried anywhere and everywhere—on the banks of the Seine, in the public squares, at the foot of the barricades—in order to prevent a too rapid decomposition from their contact with the air.

The aspect of Paris at night during this time was particularly mournful.

Usually, at this season of the year, night seems turned into day; the cafés and restaurants are brilliantly lighted and crowded with loungers; the little chairs and tables in front of these establishments all have their occupants, and threaten shortly, from their increasing number, to drive the crowd of promenaders from the sidewalk into the street. Night is the city's brightest and gayest time; one walks in fairyland, cares fly away, thorns disappear, evil is veiled in this terrestrial paradise.

No wonder the Parisians love their city; no wonder they forget their misfortunes within its walls. What land can boast another like it?

But what a difference immediately succeeding the reign of terror. The houses were all closed; the gas in many quarters unlighted. Here and there on the tables of some of the cafés might be seen the flickering light of a solitary candle. The streets were deserted, and after nine o'clock nothing was heard but the echoing steps of the sentinels who guarded the corners of the streets. Now and then the cry of "*Qui vive! Passez au large!*" interrupted the silence, as at rare intervals a passer-by was seen. No passenger was allowed to walk at night along the pavements; all were obliged to take the middle of the street, lest some evil-intentioned person should throw petroleum upon the houses, and deliver them as prey to the flames. Often the inhabitants, still uneasy, and not sufficiently reassured by the precautions of the municipalities who had caused all the gratings of the cellars to be stopped up, would sit upon their door-steps until an advanced hour of the night.

It was they who, in such cases, ordered passers-by to take the middle of the street, and it was not prudent to disobey their injunction; any one doing so was instantly suspected, and the cries of the inhabitants soon brought the National Guards from the nearest post, who arrested him forthwith.

It was not until Saturday, June 3d, that trains with passengers were allowed to enter Paris, or that the inhabitants were allowed to leave without a *laissez-passer*. Up to that time workmen were actively employed in destroying the barricades and in clearing and cleaning from the streets all traces of the horrible contests of which they had been the scene. When the eager and curious crowd of sight-seers was finally allowed to enter, the disappointment was general. The newspaper accounts had been so horrible, that many expected to see but the blackened ruins of a once beautiful city. The bustle and activity in the streets were surprising to all, few being able to understand that finest trait of the French character, which enables the nation to rise superior to misfortune, and thus the sooner to conquer it.

Ruins, however, there were in quantities; France's finest palaces, the scenes of her oldest associations, had been ruthlessly destroyed, and amidst their charred and blackened masses the fire still smouldered angrily.

Foremost among these stood the Louvre and Tuileries —the former happily but little injured, if we except the destruction of its magnificent library; but the latter almost entirely destroyed.

These two piles of buildings were completed and harmonized under the second Empire. With their inclosures, they occupy an area of sixty acres, and may be said to have formed a single palace of unequaled splendor and magnitude.

The Louvre consists of the old and new Louvre. The old Louvre is nearly square, being 576 feet long by 538 wide, and contains a vast collection of sculpture, paintings, and other works of art. The eastern façade is one of the finest architectural works of any age or country; it is a colonnade of twenty-eight coupled Corinthian columns.

The new Louvre, inaugurated in 1857, consists of two piles of buildings projecting from two galleries, which join the old Louvre to the Tuileries, and forming the eastern boundary of the Place du Carousel. The Louvre was originally a hunting lodge, and was converted into a feudal fortress, about the year 1200, by Philip Augustus. It was enlarged by his successors, more particularly by Henry II and Catherine de Medicis; and here, in 1572, took place the wedding ceremony of Margaret of Valois and the King of Navarre. Charles IX fired upon the Huguenots from one of its windows; and here Henry IV lay in state after his assassination by Ravaillac. Bernini was brought from Italy by Louis XIV in order to complete the palace; but the east front, with its beautiful colonnade, was the work of a Frenchman, Claude Perrault.

The palace remained unfinished down to the time of Napoleon I, who converted the building into a national museum, where he gathered all the art treasures of France together, with the spoils of his numerous campaigns. Many of these stores were carried away by the Allies at the Restoration, but the remainder, with what has since been added, make the collection of the Louvre one of the finest in the world.

Under the late Emperor the whole collection was rearranged, and great additions made. In 1861 the entire collections of the Marquis Campana, of Rome, were purchased for $1,000,000; these form the greater portion of the Musée Napoleon III.

The ground on which the Tuileries stands, or rather stood, was once a tile-yard, and was bought by Francis I to please his mother, Louise de Savoie, who preferred the position to that of the Palais des Tournelles. The new edifice was begun by Catharine de Medicis, with Delorme for her architect.

The Tuileries seldom served as a royal residence until of late years. Neither Catharine de Medicis nor her sons ever lived there; it was occasionally visited by Henry IV, was the scene of several banquets under Louis XIV, inhabited by Louis XV when a minor, and by Louis XVI as prisoner. During the great revolution the sittings of the Assembly, and afterwards of the Convention, were held in the Palace. The First Consul was afterwards installed there, and from his time the Palace has become the home of the monarchs of France.

In the revolution of 1830 the building was sacked and plundered; restored to its former splendor under Louis Philippe, it was again invaded in 1848, and the throne, carried away by the mob, was burned in the Place de la Bastille. A band of ruffians took possession of the royal apartments, where they remained for ten days.

The Tuileries was then used for a hospital, afterwards for an exhibition of pictures, and, in 1851, became the home of Napoleon III.

The flight of the Empress, when the Palace was again invaded by the mob on the 4th of September, 1870, and the concerts given for the benefit of the wounded during the days of the Commune, are the last historical episodes before the final catastrophe.

The centre, north and south wings of the Tuileries were called respectively the Pavilion de l'Horloge, the Pavilion de Flore, and the Pavilion de Marsan. Under the late Empire the building was shown to visitors.

Napoleon III's theatre and chapel were built upon the site of the old Salle des Machines, where Molière's *Psyché* and *Comédie Française* were played, and where Voltaire was publicly crowned. The state staircase led to a fine ball-room, called the *Salle de la Paix*, which opened into the *Salle des Maréchaux*. This room extended the whole depth of the Palace and the height of two floors, and was one of the most gorgeously decorated halls in Paris. The busts of marshals and generals were ranged along the walls, and the ceiling, exquisitely painted, was supported by four caryatides, copied from those by Jean Goujon, in the Louvre. Doors led on the right from *Salle des Maréchaux* to the private apartments of the Emperor and Empress, and on the left through the *Salle du Premier Consul* and the *Salle d'Apollon* to the *Salle du Trône*, where a new throne occupied the place of the one burned by the mob in 1848, and the *Galerie de Diane,* the Imperial dining room.

The Palais Royal, another of the public buildings attacked by the rage of the Commune, faces the Louvre, and is built on the site of Cardinal Richelieu's palace. It was given to the Duke of Orleans by his brother, Louis XIV, and passed from him to the Regent Duke. Here the Regent and his daughter held their orgies, though not in the present edifice. His grandson Egalité rebuilt the Palace after a fire, and erected the ranges of shops to relieve his embarrassments.

The Gardens of the Palais Royal were the favorite resort of Camille Desmoulins, and other mob orators, and in them the tricolored flag was unfurled July 13th, 1789. Here were hatched the plots which ended in the execution of Egalité, when the Palace was sold by lottery. After the Restoration it was bought back, and repaired by the Orleans family, by whom it was inhabited until they removed to the Tuileries in 1830.

Invaded and plundered by the mob in 1848, the building was turned into a barrack, but, during the second Empire, it changed back again to a palace.

Given by the Emperor to his uncle Jerome, it descended to Prince Napoleon, who fitted it up in the most sumptuous style.

Nothing, however, can equal the loss to the city of the Hotel de Ville, which dates in part from 1628. This was a most magnificent structure, containing some of the finest saloons in Paris, and perhaps in the world. The additions made to this building in 1842 cost no less than $3,200,000. The building contained some five hundred statues of French celebrities, from the time of Charlemagne to Louis XIV, and, as a specimen of modern French magnificence, the decorations and furniture of the Hotel de Ville were unrivaled. Here, during the late Empire, the Prefect of the Seine entertained 7,000 guests in the great gallery, ornamented with gilt Corinthian columns, and illuminated by three thousand wax-lights.

The architecture of the building equalled, and, if possible, excelled in worth its interior decorations.

The Hotel de Ville was associated with many of the most famous and infamous scenes of the history of Paris. The first Commune held here its sittings, and here Robespierre was taken prisoner by the soldiers, having sought, with his partisans, a refuge in the building.

From one of the windows Louis Philippe, the "Citizen King," was presented to the people by Lafayette. In 1848 the soldiers were quartered here, and in 1871 the building became the stronghold of the Central Committee, and afterwards of the Commune, who, determined that no other power should possess what they had lost, set fire to the magnificent pile and reduced it to ashes.

The Hotel de Ville was the one, of all the monuments of Paris, which the Commune had the least right and the least pretext to destroy, and it is precisely the Hotel de Ville whose ruin is most complete, most irreparable. Everywhere else, even where the fire has been most violent, something remains which, if required, renders reparation not impossible.

Here, however, the destruction was implacable; it seems as though a breath would overthrow what still remains standing; and yet, while this ruin is the most complete, it is also the most beautiful which has been left by the vandals of 1871.

Recent as the ruins are, they have already the majesty which is ordinarily given by time alone to the cruel work of the hand of man. Here a few hours have produced the slow effect of centuries.

The skeleton of the immense palace alone remains. The walls, which are corroded by the flames, irregularly mutilated, with their windows enlarged and disjoined, their doors resembling breaches, and their summits capriciously cut in points, give them the appearance of the battlements of a dismantled fortress; with the statues of the great Parisians, who were the honor of their native city, tottering on their bases, some still standing erect and proud, others already overthrown and turned towards the Palace, as though to contemplate its ruin, all this forms a spectacle of imposing grandeur which moves, saddens, and at the same time captivates and retains the beholder.

The losses to art in this terrible catastrophe were very great. The Renaissance lost the small central edifice, the two marvelous mantel-pieces at the extremities of the Salle du Trône, one from the chisel of Beard, pupil of Michael Angelo, the other by Th. Bodin, and in the Salle du Zodiaque, the decorative sculptures on wood of Jean Goujon.

The epoch of Louis XIV. lost the statue of the great king by Coysevox, which was a *chef-d'œuvre,* while the present epoch has lost forty-six statues by the ablest sculptors of modern times, which had been placed in niches purposely designed to ornament the principal front of the building. These statues are all either completely destroyed or greatly damaged.

The Hotel de Ville possessed also a fine municipal library, which was situated in the third story of the north-eastern pavilion, and which contained one hundred thousand volumes, principally historical works. Not a book, not a leaf remains.

On the first story, the walls and ceilings were covered by works from the brushes of the greatest painters of modern times, which, like all the marvels of this beautiful building, were entirely destroyed.

A collection of all the sovereigns of Europe who had accepted an invitation to the Hotel de Ville, and who in doing so, always engaged to send their busts in white marble to the Prefect of the Seine, was also lost. Their number was considerable. The busts of Queen Victoria and Prince Albert, of the King and Queen of Portugal, of the King of Belgium, the King of Italy, the Czar of Russia, the King of Prussia, the Sultan of Turkey, etc., etc., all destroyed, mutilated, or lost in this formidable conflagration.

Most terrible of all was the loss of the prisoners who had been left by a refinement of cruelty in the cellars of the Hotel de Ville, and who were buried beneath the flames.

The archives of the State had also been condemned to perish. The Commune did not like history, probably because it foresaw the punishment which would be one day inflicted on its memory by this avenger of outraged right. The archives were therefore to be burned, with the thirty million files of papers which they contained. These documents excited the hatred of one-half the Commune, and the contempt of the remainder. A more particular grievance, however, added to their desire for their destruction.

The honorable director of the archives, M. Maury, one of the most learned men of the present day, under a menace of death several times repeated, had always refused to pull down the tricolor and replace it by the red flag. Such a crime could not be left unpunished. On Monday, May 22d, five men, of disreputable appearance, presented themselves in the cabinet of M. Maury, declaring that they came on the part of the Commune to assume the direction of the archives. The Commune once installed in the place, it may easily be imagined what fate was reserved for the precious collections which it contained.

The order to set the building on fire was sent on Tuesday, and would probably have been executed during the following night, notwithstanding the efforts of the director and of seven or eight devoted attendants whom he had kept with him, when, obeying an idea whose motive is easily imagined, but which had the happiest results, Debock, director of the *Imprimerie Nationale,* and Alavoine, his associate, came to the director and delivered him the following precious document:

"COMMUNE OF PARIS.

"*Ministry of Justice,*
"*National Printing-Office,*
"*Cabinet of the Director.*

"PARIS, May 24, 1871.

"This evening, at six o'clock, an order was given to the Citizens Debock (Louis-Guillaume) and Alavoine (André) to prevent, by every means in their power, any attempt which might be made to burn the National Archives.

"This order was solicited by those citizens.

"DEBOCK,
"Director of the National Printing-Office.
"A. ALAVOINE,
"The Delegate."

"P.S.—It should be remembered that any disobedience to the orders of the Commune, or of the Committee of Public Safety, is instantly followed by capital punishment."

The archives were saved.

We have already mentioned the almost miraculous escape of the Bank of France from the danger which surrounded it, owing to the heroic resistance of a body of National Guards, who remained day and night on watch at their post. The following interesting account was published by the *Gaulois* concerning the proceedings at the Bank during the days of the Commune:

"How many times has this question not been put: 'How was it the insurgents did not pillage the Bank of France?' In fact, that problem is a very interesting one to examine. Those scoundrels were complete masters of Paris; they lived surrounded by an atmosphere of theft. The Bank was almost entirely in their hands; nevertheless it has escaped nearly intact. And yet it contained (official figures) three milliards of securities: one consisting of deposits of private individuals in gold, scrip, and diamonds; a second in precious metals and bank-notes; and the third in paper-money, which required only one other signature to become legal currency. But is a name so difficult to write? Once done, who could have distinguished between the notes thus completed by the Commune and those previously in circulation? No one, certainly.

"M. Rouland was Governor of the Bank when the storm burst. His duty was to save it, but he preferred making his escape. He withdrew, with regrettable precipitation, on the 23d of March—the very day on which Admiral Saisset came to Paris to rally round him the friends of the Government, or the National Guards of order, solidly established at the Saint-Lazare Station and at the Louvre, covering with a vast buckler the Bank and its Governor. Every one knows how the Admiral's attempt failed; the friends of order, losing courage, dispersed, and the Federals had no difficulty in occupying the abandoned positions. Of the administration, only the sub-Governor, the Marquis de Plœuc, remained, who devoted his attention to the difficult task of guarding the three milliards, which represented the savings of France. He found in the persons under him, and in the National Guards of the quarter, the heartiest assistance, and a battalion was constituted to watch over the establishment. It was five hundred strong; but the men had only twenty-five cartridges each, very little for purposes of defence if really attacked, but enough to make a show, and to enable them to reply haughtily, the insurgents being ignorant of their penury of munitions.

"It is generally believed that the cellars of the building can be inundated instantaneously; but that is an error. Immense reserves of sand enclosed in sacks are accumulated below; in case of danger they are piled on the notes and ingots to so great a height that if the whole structure fell in during a conflagration, not a single paper would be burnt. That precaution was taken, and the future awaited.

"One day Citizen Beslay, the oldest member of the Commune, arrived. He seems to have been a good sort of man, somewhat weak in the head, a great talker, easily led by his vanity, and who always spoke of conciliation. He was of the same province as the Marquis, with whom he was previously acquainted. He came to warn the sub-Governor that the Bank was to be pillaged, and expressed his regret. 'But what is to be done?' he said; 'how can you expect starving men to remain tranquil in front of a baker's shop?' The allusion was clear, and the metaphor, of which M. de Plœuc felt the correctness, rendered him very uneasy. He did not, however, let that feeling be suspected, and declared, in a firm tone, that if the Bank was attacked it was ready to defend itself; that it had arms and would know how to use them. Beslay then softened down, and dropped a hint that perhaps an understanding might be come to with the Commune if a delegate were accepted. The Marquis had enough sagacity to fathom his man, and to see at the first glance all the advantage to be drawn from the proposal. 'A delegate!' said he; never! never! I could only accept one man, because I believe him to be honest—because I know his intelligence and integrity—because he will assist me in saving this great establishment, on the fortune of which . . . etc. Is it not true, my friend, that you will lend me a hand for that patriotic duty?' The other, puffed up with vanity and contentment, promised everything asked; in fact, he was cajoled. He made himself, in reality, extremely useful in the incessant struggle sustained daily during two months against all the men in authority, who were constantly quarreling amongst themselves—the Commune, the Central Committee, and the Committee of Public Safety—but who were all agreed on one point—to appropriate the baker's bread. Therefore, a morsel was given them from day to day—the smallest possible. The first was six millions, which had been previously deposited by the city. There were no means of resistance. Afterwards M. Thiers authorized the payment, on account, of such sums as might be necessary to save the situation, and they were disputed inch by inch.

"Ultimately, the men of the Hotel de Ville were overcome by their impatience, and one day Varlin and Jourde, the two delegates to the Finance, presented themselves, wearing their terrible red scarfs, and fully decided to exact everything, and threatening, if they were refused, to get up a riot in the faubourgs. The sub-Governor, who had been informed of their arrival by Beslay, said: 'Do what you like; but understand, the day you lay your hands upon the Bank of France, its notes will not be worth more than the old assignats. All your National Guards have their pockets full of twenty-franc notes, and you will ruin them at one blow; for, the security once destroyed by you, no one will give five sous for the paper.' That argument, so forcibly advanced, seemed to make an impression on the delegates. Every day a new comedy was played. Matters progressed, the Bank sometimes refusing, sometimes giving when the pressure was too great, but never more than small sums. At last the struggle became more continuous and more dangerous. One morning the Vengeurs de la Republique entered and seized the sub-Governor in his bed, demanding the keys. 'I can only give them to Beslay,' he replied. The latter was sent for and arrived. 'My friends . . . . . . my good friends!' And phrases and threats of resignation! and diminution of demands! and finally the free-marksmen withdrew without a sou.

"Another time the young, gay and triumphant Le Mossu presented himself, furnished with a search-warrant signed by the Committee of Public Safety. He obtained nothing; Jourde arrived to his rescue, raved and stormed; arms, he said, were concealed in the Bank; he had been told so; he knew it to be a fact. 'There are none,' replied M. de Plœuc, 'but you may satisfy yourself. Come with me alone, and if you find a single musket besides those belonging to our garrison, I consent to be shot upon the spot. Come!' 'I believe you,' said Jourde, to whom the proposed search did not seem very inviting; 'I believe you,' and, turning to his men, he added: 'Let us go, gentlemen; no weapons are concealed here.' During all this time the Board of Directors, reduced to four members, met every day, but each time in a different place, having been warned by Beslay that they were to be seized as hostages.

"The last three days were the most terrible. The battalion of the 500 had not for a long time left the building to which all the men had been summoned, and where they were lodged with their wives and children. The Bank was surrounded by the insurrection, like an island in the midst of foaming waves. Fire was on every side; great unwillingness was felt in detaching men to combat it, but necessity required that that course should be adopted. The humble employés of the Bank behaved like heroes; some struggling against the conflagration which threatened to annihilate the quarter, while the others remained at their post, awaiting the combat and death.

"What joy when, on Wednesday morning at half-past seven, the first glimpse of the soldiers was seen. The red flag had never sullied the Bank, and haste was made to hoist the tricolor; and to complete the good fortune, M. Rouland returned—behind the soldiers—to resume his post, and deigned to congratulate the various persons on the premises. Marshal de MacMahon gave the National Guards a more flattering recompense, as he permitted them to retain their arms—an honorable exception of which the men were truly worthy."

At the time when Paris was not *Paris* but *Lutèce*—that is to say, little more than a mud-village—the site of the Palace of Justice was occupied by a castle or citadel, which served as a residence for the governor of the province, and sometimes for the Cæsar who reigned over Gaul.

A little later, when the dominion of the Franks had succeeded that of the Cæsars—when their barbarous domination had replaced a learned oppression—the long-haired kings divided their time between the Palais des Thermes, situated on the site of the Hôtel Cluny, and then in open country, and this other Palace which stood within their fortifications, and which a long succession of modifications and changes have made the Palais de Justice of the present time.

The first who established himself perpetually in this Palace was Eudes, Count of Paris, and afterwards King of France. Robert the Pious enlarged and embellished it, and during a long succession of years, each king left there some souvenir of his time. It was Saint Louis, however, who did most for the building. By his orders it was almost entirely reconstructed and the *Sainte-Chapelle* built.

This beautiful building, happily uninjured to-day, is an admirable specimen of the religious architecture of the thirteenth century—a model of grace, elegance, and at the same time of majesty, which nothing since has surpassed, or even equaled, and which will cause the name and genius of its author, Eudes de Montreuil, to live as long as there exist men, lovers of the beautiful and capable of appreciating it.

Saint Louis had also caused an immense saloon to be constructed for the fêtes which he gave sometimes to his great vassals; here also were accomplished all the solemn acts of his reign. This grandiose-type of the civil architecture of the thirteenth century occupied the site of the more modern *Salle des Pas Perdus*, which was unhappily entirely destroyed by the conflagration.

Philippe le Bel, Louis XI, Charles VIII and Louis XII made new additions to the Palace, although it was no longer the exclusive and habitual residence of royalty. The monarchs began to prefer the Louvre or the Hotel Saint-Paul, and Francis I was the last monarch who took up his residence here, which he did, however, only temporarily.

From the time of Saint Louis, the Parliament had divided the Palace with the king, and from Henry II they occupied it alone.

Of the ancient Palace of the middle ages and the Renaissance, nothing now remains but the Sainte-Chapelle. a part of the gallery, the kitchens, the Tour de l'Horloge, and the two neighboring towers.

Forty years ago, works were begun after a new plan which were to end in the definitive completion of the Palace, and to realize the ameliorations which had been contemplated for so long a time. Under the Empire these works were pushed with serious activity, and at the time when the building was burned by the Commune it was about to receive its last embellishments.

The saddest spectacle, perhaps, to be seen in Paris is on the left bank of the Seine; here, from the Rue du Bac to the barracks of the Quai d'Orsay there is a long succession of imposing ruins.

That of the Palace of the Legion of Honor is, perhaps, the most saddening, because this beautiful monument, which recalled to the mind ideas of grandeur and nobility, while it at the same time offered to the eye a picture of exquisite grace, gives rise, by the contrast of the past with the present, to the most lugubrious impressions.

This Palace, a beautiful specimen of the ingenious art of the eighteenth century, was built in 1786 for a rich foreigner, the Prince of Salm-Kirburg. It was inhabited for a time by Madame de Staël, under the Directory. The Grande Chancellerie of the Legion of Honor was established here in 1803.

During the Commune it served for headquarters to the Citizen Eudes, an assassin whom the revolution of the 4th of September had found in prison and set at liberty. Here were brought all the furniture and private effects which were taken from the house of the Marquis de Gallifet. The equipages of the Marquis were also brought here, and, needless to say, everything was pillaged. The silver of the Hotel of the Legion of Honor at St. Denis, which had been brought to the Grande Chancellerie at the commencement of the first siege to save it from the avidity of the Prussians, was also stolen.

The building was set on fire at the four corners after the walls had been smeared with petroleum, notwithstanding the energetic resistance of the concierge, Hamel, who was carried off and thrown into prison. The Archives of the Grande Chancellerie, which stands opposite the Palace in the Rue de Lille, was also set on fire and entirely destroyed, together with the glorious annals it contained.

The Palace of the Quai d'Orsay, which was another victim to the vengeance of the Communists, was commenced under the first Empire and finished under Louis Philippe. It was first destined for the King of Rome, then for the Ministry of Foreign Affairs. Under the Restoration it was intended to be used for the expositions of the different industries; and during the late Empire it lodged the Conseil d'Etat and the Cour des Comptes.

With the exception of the Staircase of Honor, decorated by the remarkable compositions of Theodore Chassériaux, the entire interior of the Cour des Comptes has been burned. The walls, which are thick, still remain standing.

The ravages are most frightful in that portion of the building adjudged to the use of the Conseil d'Etat. Its large saloon, of a rich and imposing decoration, is entirely destroyed, and with it have disappeared the beautiful historical portraits of Sully, Colbert, Vauban, Richelieu, Turgot, Suger, Portalis and Cambacérès. In the Hall of Legislation is to be regretted a beautiful painting by Paul Delaroche, while in another room one of the finest pictures by Eugène Delacroix, representing the Emperor Justinian, became also a prey to the flames.

Nowhere did the Federals show such a ferocity in their rage for destruction. Whole bucketsful of petroleum were drawn from the casks which had been for some time stored in the court, and the walls, staircases and floors were inundated.

After having sheltered for some time the Citizen Peyronton, delegate of the Commune to the Conseil d'Etat, and his secretary Pelletier, the Palace was occupied militarily, at the entrance of the Versailles troops, by the assassins Eudes and Mégy, who had fallen back precipitately with their men from the Palace of the Legion of Honor, and who evacuated this in turn, after having accomplished their odious task.

Unhappily, to the losses of the State were added those of many private individuals, members of the Cour des Comptes and the Conseil d'Etat, who, fearing the pillage of their private houses, had brought here many precious objects and valuable papers, thinking to secure them from all harm.

Not satisfied with the destruction of public edifices, the rage of the Communists expended itself on many private buildings. Every manifestation of riches excited their animosity, and they attempted thoroughly to carry out the programme of the *International* society, recognized as prime mover in this insurrection, which is:

The abolition of all religions.
The abolition of all property.
The abolition of all family.
The abolition of inheritance.
The abolition of nationality.

The Rues de Lille, Du Bac, and Royale are those which suffered perhaps the most from the terrible scourge which afflicted Paris.

Although the Communists had such an objection to capital, they showed that, once in their possession, they could spend it freely. The following is the approximative amount of what their eccentricities have cost the city of Paris:

	fr.
Expenses of the Commune..................	52,000,000
Roads..	2,500,000
Hotel de Ville and Municipalities of Arrondissements...............................	36,000,000
Forward......	90,500,000

Brought forward	90,500,000
Churches	1,000,000
Barracks	1,000,000
Theatres	7,000,000
Reparation of public buildings	1,000,000
Palaces and monuments burned	114,000,000
Reparation of palaces and monuments	1,000,000
War expenses	260,000,000
Houses burned	78,000,000
Houses half burned or damaged	34,000,000
The villages in the environs of Paris	70,000,000
Railroads	10,000,000
Commerce	200,000,000
Total	867,500,000

Among the men who supported the Communal insurrection might be counted a great number of foreigners. Many of these belonged to the International Society, fanatics who had volunteered for the cause of Socialism, numbering perhaps 20,000, and who obeyed implicitly every order of the Society received through the medium of the Central Committee.

The war with Prussia had also drawn towards the unhappy city of Paris a large number of adventurers of every race and climate, who flock always towards any spot where events are thrown out of their ordinary course by some great excitement.

Among the thousands of prisoners who defiled along the boulevards might be seen Russians, Italians, Greeks, Wallachians, Belgians, Dutch, Irish, Spanish, and, above all, Poles.

Among the chiefs, the number of foreigners was also considerable, and seemed gathered from all quarters of the globe. Every nation had one or more representatives, as may be seen by the following list:

Anys-el-Biltar, director of manuscripts at the National Library (Egyptian).

Biondetti, surgeon-in-chief of the 233d battalion (Italian).

Babick, member of the Commune (Pole).

Becka, adjutant of the 207th battalion (Pole).

Cluseret, general, Delegate of War (Frenchman, naturalized an American).

Cernatesco, surgeon-major (Pole).

Crapulinski, colonel of the staff (Pole).

Capellàro, member of Military Bureau (Italian).

Carneiro de Cunha, surgeon-major of the 38th battalion (Portuguese).

Charalambo, surgeon-major of the Federal sharpshooters (Pole).

Dombrowski, general of the forces of the Commune (Pole).

Dombrowski, his brother, colonel of the staff (Pole).

Durnoff, commandant of a legion (Pole).

Echenlaub, colonel of the 88th battalion (German).

Ferrara Gola, director-general of the ambulances (Portuguese).

Frankel, member of the Commune (Prussian).

Giorok, commandant of Fort Issy (Wallachian).

Grejorok, commandant of the artillery at Montmartre (Wallachian).

Kertzfeld, director-in-chief of the ambulances (German).

Iziquerdo, surgeon-major of the 88th battalion (Pole).

Jalowski, surgeon-major of the Republican Zouaves (Pole).

Kobosko, estafelte, placed in the order of the day of the army of the Commune (Pole).

La Cecilia, general (Italian).

Landowski, aide-de-camp of General Dombrowski (Pole).

Mizara, commandant of the 104th battalion (Italian).

Maratuck, aide-major of the 72d battalion (Hungarian).

Moro, commandant of the 22d battalion (Italian.)

Okolowicz and his brothers, general and staff-officers (Poles).

Ostyn, member of the Commune (Belgian).

Olinski, chief of the 17th legion (Pole).

Pisani, aide-de-camp of Flourens (Italian).

Potampenki, aide-de-camp of General Dombrowski (Pole).

Ploubinski, staff-officer (Pole).

Pazdzierswski, commandant of Fort Vanves (Pole).

Piazza, chief of legion, (Italian).

Pugno, musical director at the opera (Italian).

Romanelli, director of war materials (Italian).

Rozyski, surgeon-major of the 144th battalion (Pole).

Rubinowicz, staff-officer (Pole).

Rubinowicz (P.), surgeon-major of the fusiliers of marine (Pole).

Syneck, surgeon-major of 151st battalion (German).

Skalski, surgeon-major of the 240th battalion (Pole).

Soteriade, surgeon-major (Spaniard).

Thaller, sub-governor of Fort Bicêtre (German).

Van Ostal, commandant of the 115th battalion (Dutch).

Vetzel, commandant of the southern forts (German).

Wrobleswski, general, commandant of the army of the south (Pole).

Wilton, surgeon-major of the 72d battalion (American).

Zengerler, surgeon-major of the 74th battalion (German).

CHAPTER XIV.

Projet de loi concerning the hostages—Funeral services of the Archbishop and the other victims, celebrated at Notre-Dame—Immense number of prisoners captured by the Government—Description of the camp at Satory—Audacity of a Communist—Fate of the members of the Commune—Billioray—Gambon—Eudes—Okolowitch—Mathieu—Varlin—Jourde—Johannard—La Cecilia—Treilhard—Paschal Grousset—Régère—Vésinier—Verdure—Courbet—Rossel—Vermorel—Cluseret—Dufil—Langelle—Razoua—Rochefort—His ingratitude to his father—Letter of Henri V.—M. Ducatel made Knight of the Legion of Honor—The American Minister in Paris—His letter concerning the Archbishop—First condemnation of the Councils of War—Conclusion.

ON Friday, June 2d, the Minister of Public Instruction addressed to the Assembly the following words:

"The insurrection of Paris commenced by an assassination, and ended by a massacre.

"Every one here, every one in France, every one in Europe has present in his mind the details of the execution of the hostages.

"Their bodies have been recovered. The funeral obsequies are soon to take place. The Government will have measures to propose which will tend to manifest the public piety in a solemn manner, and attest at the same time the regrets of the country and the indignation which fills all hearts.

"I hope to be able to-morrow to give you an official communication on this subject; but, having received today from the chapter of Notre Dame a deputation which announced the day and hour of the obsequies of the

Archbishop and other hostages, I thought it my duty not to defer the communication.

"The reunion for the ceremony will take place at the Archbishopric on Wednesday morning (June 7th) at a quarter past ten."

The National Assembly then decided that a deputation, chosen from among the members, should attend the funeral. Although the number of persons composing a deputation of this kind is ordinarily twenty-five, the Assembly saw fit, under the present circumstances, to derogate from its custom, and appointed fifty to show this mark of respect to the Archbishop, and other victims assassinated by the Commune.

On the following day M. Jules Simon read the following *projet de loi:*

"At the same time that the insurgents, to increase the ranks of their army, took by force all citizens capable of service, leaving them no alternative but to hide, so incurring the greatest perils, or to march in their ranks under their infamous flag against order, liberty, and their country, they laid their hands, without pretext, without a shadow of judgment, on the most eminent and respectable men, announcing that they would keep them as hostages until the end of the civil war.

"Nearly all the priests of Paris were arrested under these conditions, and, at the head of the priests, their Archbishop.

"Several times, by proclamations, by discourses pronounced in the sittings of the Commune, it was declared that if the insurgents taken with arms in their hands were judged and executed at Versailles, the rebels would execute their reprisals on this flock of innocents, not even following the law of retaliation, which did not suffice them, but in assassinating three victims for every criminal whom the law had condemned.

"We refused to believe in the realization of these savage menaces; but no one would have dared to imagine that, in the last and supreme hour, the hostages would be massacred for no other motives than vengeance, hatred, and love of murder; sentiments worthy of the barbarians who, in retiring before our soldiers, have destroyed so many national riches, who attempted to burn our houses and libraries, to their eternal shame and our eternal grief.

"The bodies of these beloved and deplored victims have been collected with the greatest care.

"Some, still bearing the trace of the inconceivable fury of their butchers, present no longer the human form, and are utterly unrecognizable.

"We are about to place them in the earth amidst universal respect and tears.

"The Assembly decided yesterday by a unanimous vote that it would represent the country at the head of the funeral procession. We ask it to-day to decree that the obsequies be conducted at the expense of the Public Treasure.

"PROJET DE LOI.

"Art. 1. The burial of Monseigneur Darboy, Archbishop of Paris, and of the hostages assassinated with him in Paris, will be made at the expense of the State.

"Art. 2. For this object, an extraordinary credit of 30,000 francs is opened for the Minister of Public Instruction and Worship."

This project was unanimously adopted on the succeeding day by 547 voices, with the addition of the following article:

"A commemorative tablet, erected in the Church of Notre Dame, will bear the names of all the hostages."

During the week preceding the ceremony, every day from ten to four, an immense crowd stood at the gates of the Archbishopric, waiting their turn to see the remains of the Archbishop, who lay embalmed within.

His face was ghastly; his beard and mustache, which had grown in the prison, were on one side discolored with blood. He was laid out in state, and beside him, day and night, nuns and priests were praying.

The body of Monseigneur Surat, placed in the same room, was not uncovered, the face having been too much disfigured to render embalming possible. This was also the case with the Abbé Duguerry, whose corpse was placed in a chapel of the Madeleine, and where, all day long, a respectful and mourning crowd came to take a last farewell of their beloved curate.

On Wednesday, June 7th, the obsequies of the Archbishop, of Monseigneur Surat, Vicar-General, of the Abbé Duguerry, Curé de la Madeleine, of the Abbé Bécourt, Curé de Notre-Dame-de-Bonne-Nouvelle, of the Abbé Sabattier, second vicar of Notre-Dame-de-Lorette, and other hostages, took place at Notre Dame.

The interior of the cathedral church of Paris was entirely hung in black, as was also the front of the church. A shield bearing the arms of the Archbishop, with this device: "*Labore fideque*," was placed above the central door. On each side were shields bearing the fatal dates of the 24th, 25th, 26th, and 27th of May.

In the interior of the church on other shields were engraved the names of the hostages assassinated by the Commune.

Before the choir in the middle of the transept stood the catafalque of the Archbishop; on the right and left were those of Mgr. Surat and Abbé Duguerry; further down were those of Abbé Bécourt and Abbé Sabattier.

The members of the National Assembly, the Ministers,

the Diplomatic Corps, the Magistrates, Marshal de MacMahon Duc de Magenta, Marshal Canrobert, several admirals, a large number of army and navy officers, the Institute and the University, all assisted at this imposing ceremony.

At eleven o'clock the funeral procession, having left the Rue de Grenelle at ten, arrived at Notre-Dame. M. Darboy, brother of the venerable prelate, was chief mourner, and was followed by the secretaries of the archbishops and the hostages who had escaped the massacre ordained by the Commune.

A large and mournful crowd filled the streets as the procession passed. A hearse, drawn by six horses, contained the remains of Mgr. Darboy; another followed, with those of Mgr. Surat.

The procession having reached the Place du Parvis-Notre-Dame, the Canons of the Church of Paris, the Curates of the Diocese of Paris, preceded by the cross of the Chapter, advanced to receive the corpse of the Archbishop. Mgr. Allouvry, former bishop of Pamiers, then celebrated the divine office.

At three o'clock, after the Vespers for the Dead, the body of Monseigneur Darboy was deposited in the vault of the Archbishops of Paris.

The Abbé Duguerry was buried at the Madeleine on the following Friday. His body had been taken to Notre-Dame, owing to a request of the National Assembly, whose members wished to unite in one the funeral honors of all the victims of the horrible massacre committed at La Roquette.

Happily retribution was not long in overtaking the majority of the authors of these terrible crimes. Every day large convoys of prisoners succeeded each other on the route to Versailles, their number finally amounting to over 30,000 men and women; they were first directed to the camp of Satory, remaining there until they had been examined, when they were sent off to other places of confinement, Cherbourg, Brest, etc.

On Sunday, May 28th, a large column of prisoners, numbering 5,000 or 6,000, who had been captured at Belleville, was directed towards the west of Paris. When the head of the column reached the Arc-de-Triomphe, prisoners were still defiling on the Place de la Concorde.

There was every class of insurrectionists in this sad procession. National Guards, men in blouses, women and children, and, above all, a large proportion of deserters, belonging to those regiments which on the 18th of March had rendered the insurrection possible. It was they who, in the last hour, fought with the greatest fury and desperation. They marched sadly along, with their jackets turned inside out, and tied together in couples. All were bareheaded.

The column was guarded by *chasseurs d'Afrique*, who made frequent halts, allowing the prisoners to sit down and rest. At the Porte Dauphine, the procession was met by the Marquis de Gallifet, followed by an aide-de-camp. He passed through the crowd of prisoners, amongst whom were women dressed as men, the *vivandières* of the Commune, and by his orders they were divided into three parties before passing the ramparts.

Eighty prisoners, principally soldiers of every arm, linesmen, artillerymen, and Zouaves, were set apart and afterwards led to the right of the rampart to be shot. Twenty soldiers of the line were invited to return their jackets, and were set at liberty amidst the applause of the crowd, which had gathered while the remainder of the prisoners continued their march to Versailles.

A noted journalist gives an interesting account of a visit made by him to the camp at Satory:

"A prominent feature on the ground is a vast parallelogram, inclosed by a stout wall, where artillery used to be parked and a number of cavalry stables stand. It is here that the Communist prisoners are lodged when they arrive from Paris. When I say lodged, I mean that they are crowded into the stables and grouped in the open, inclosed by ropes and surrounded by sentries. Yesterday was a pouring wet day, as the one before it had been, and the carriage wheels sank deep into the mud and holes of the neglected road. On our right were the tents and huts of a division there encamped. Opposite the entrance to the inclosure guns were drawn up, their muzzles pointed at the prisoners. Around the gateway stood gendarmes and police, and officers in their cloaks, all muddy and unshaven. . . . . The rain and the trampling of thousands of men had converted the whole of the vast square into a quagmire, into which one sank ankle-deep, intersected by ditches over which one had to jump. The various stables being inadequate to accommodate more than a portion of the prisoners, the others were penned like sheep in the corners of the inclosure. There they stood behind a rope, watched by numerous gendarmes-sentries with loaded chassepots, for the most part motionless, many of them probably sick and suffering, some in rags, some barefooted, many with dirty handkerchiefs as sole covering for their heads. As some protection—a very slight one—against the rain that poured steadily down, some had covered their shoulders with wisps of the straw they had slept upon. Most of them looked stolid and sullen. Our gendarme said they were generally very meek and volunteered readily for fatigue duty. If those in the open were exposed to the elements, they at any rate breathed a purer atmosphere than was to be found in the stables. We entered one of these, crowded with men of all ages, some gray-headed, some boys of fourteen. Most of them were standing; but in the background, where the light was dim, many recumbent forms could be distinguished as soon as the eye got accustomed to the gloom.

"The appearance of four strangers, escorted by a gendarme, evidently caused a sensation, and probably awakened hopes and fears. The Communists crowded round us, opening only a narrow avenue for our passage. The atmosphere was unspeakably noisome. It was wonderful to see such a number of ignoble faces, and with such a vile expression, brought together. Among those in the first stable we entered, it was almost in vain to seek a countenance that would not have condemned its owner in the eyes of the most lenient physiognomist. Our guide told us that numbers of them had arrived drunk, half mad, or completely stupefied by the alcohol, with tobacco steeped in it, which had been served out to them by their leaders. It seems incredible that so nauseous a mixture should have found consumers; but there appears to be no doubt that it did, and that it was a stimulus copiously employed.

"An officer of gendarmes entered the stable and stood near us. 'Answer to your names,' he called out in a loud voice; 'it is for your own interest to do so.' And he read the names of four men, drivers of Paris cabs, whom somebody had applied for. Among the crowd of prisoners some innocent persons are inevitably to be found, and when their friends claim them, and give proofs of their respectability, they are frequently released.

"We passed into another stable allotted to insurgents who had been soldiers, and who are therefore looked upon as doubly culpable. All sorts of uniforms were there, dirty and tattered for the most part. There were thirteen artillerymen from one battery. A tall man with a pale face and his head bound up, of smart soldierly figure, and who walked briskly and confidently in spite of suffering and degradation, was pointed out to us. He was an artilleryman of the 20th regiment, which was formed during the Prussian siege, and consisted entirely of Parisians. It had never been a good corps, but always troublesome and insubordinate. The *enfants de Paris,* it is well known in the French army, take long to discipline. On the 18th of March, this regiment was at Vincennes; it seized General Guibour, who commanded there, and threatened to shoot him.

"There was a *pompier,* or fireman, who had received a sabre-cut over the head for insubordination after he had been taken prisoner. The well-known corps of *pompiers* is composed of picked men, generally soldiers who have served in the artillery or engineers, and they receive large pay. This man had commanded an insurgent battery on the heights of Montmartre, which sent petroleum shells into Paris. '*Son affaire est claire,*' said our conductor, thereby meaning that he was certainly to be shot. Indeed, it is surprising he was not killed as soon as taken; but having once been brought to the Satory depôt, he will go through the usual formal examination and trial.

"Of the soldiers who had been captured among the insurgents, many were insolent and defiant. Perhaps, half drunk, they boasted of their deeds, and gasconaded about their past exploits and military qualities. Not a few of these heroes were shot after capture by their exasperated escorts. 'Accidents' happened to them on the way from Paris to Satory. We observed a few of the military prisoners, who, in clean uniforms, and with washed faces, would have passed muster well enough as smart, good-looking soldiers. Also there was a fair sprinkling of young men of gentle aspect, apparently recruits who had been forced to serve by the insurgents. . . . . . . As a general rule, the prisoners at Satory cared not to speak, even when accosted, but turned away or put on a sullen, disheartened smile. The stench and filth in their places of confinement are revolting. The end of one of the large stables through which we passed was made to serve for every purpose. Those who, weary of standing, lay upon the ground, were on damp straw or the bare earth. Horrible faces scowled at us as we passed through the unsavory throng. Probably our gendarme had a revolver under his cloak; but they might have closed in upon our little group, and have strangled or torn us to pieces in an instant had they been so minded. Of course they would have paid dearly for the freak, probably a volley or two would have been sent among them. To prevent outbreaks, and secure many thousand desperate characters, who are neither handcuffed nor under bolts and bars, great precautions and severity are necessary. In the walls of the inclosure holes have been made, through some of which the mouths of cannon grin, charged with grape and canister, while at others sentries are stationed. The night before last a prisoner approached one of these embrasures and persisted in looking through. The sentry warned him to retire, once, twice, and thrice, and then he blew his brains out. The top of his skull, we were told, flew over the wall. The victim had evidently sought his death. All round the inclosure outside there is a double line of sentries, and gendarmes stand thick in front of the stables. The slightest symptom of insubordination suffices to provoke summary punishment, and the only punishment known in such cases is death. The guard consists of gendarmes, police agents, and a battalion detached from the camp outside.

"Before leaving, we visited the women's prison, which is a two-story house in a corner of the enclosure near the entrance gate. There were about two hundred of them, for most part such as are commonly found in the neighborhood of soldiers' barracks, or in the lowest outskirts of Paris, squalid and dangerous localities, of which sketches are to be read in the pages of Suë and other romance writers, whose taste it is to dive into the lowest depths of human depravity and degradation. There were some gray-haired old women, and some rather pretty young ones; but the majority were hard-featured and middle-aged, and of indescribably repulsive aspect. One gaunt Amazon had a sort of uniform coat with a white band and red cross upon the arm, and when she arrived, we were told, she wore epaulets. Madame Millière had been there, who did the honors of the Hotel de Ville, and who came gayly attired; but she had left before our visit. One girl struck me particularly. She did not look above eighteen, but may have been two or three years older. She was slender and well formed, with a profusion of fair hair, terribly dirty and tangled; whereas many of the other women, squalid and dirty as their clothes might be, had evidently taken pains to comb and arrange their hair in the most becoming manner their scanty resources permitted. Her blue eyes were large and shifting, and with the expression of a wild animal, of which she reminded me as she roved restlessly up and down one end of a room, keeping close to the wall, brushing against it as a hyena does against the bars in its monotonous, weary pacing of its narrow prison. From time to time she shot a side-glance at our gendarme, who was giving particulars about the prisoners in a pretty loud voice, and in terms which showed slight consideration for their feelings. They were such glances as might fitly have accompanied a dagger-stab. I know not what there was in the appearance of one of my companions which made some of these unhappy wretches fancy him an official person—a police commissary apparently—but they came up to him and began their tales, all pitched much in the same key. Could they be believed, they were all lambs, innocent and heart-broken; some had the regular whine of the professional mendicant, as they implored '*Mon bon monsieur*' to pity and release them. There were a few very young boys with the women; some rather older ones I saw going about the enclosure with their fathers. It was the boys and women, we were told, who had acted as incendiaries. Many of the latter, however, had fought. In one of the recent convoys of prisoners that passed through Versailles came a female colonel, in a braided uniform, with straps for epaulets on her shoulders, and lace bars upon her wrist, indicating her rank. Another woman was being driven on by a gendarme, who goaded her with the point of his sabre till the blood ran. 'Shame,' cried a spectator, 'to treat a woman so!' 'Woman!' exclaimed the gendarme; 'that woman, as you call her, killed my captain and lieutenant and a sergeant with three shots from her revolver.'"

A most curious scene which also occurred at Satory proves to what an extent many of the Communists carried their audacity.

A quartermaster of artillery presented himself at the camp, and asked from the chief of the guard permission to see his son, who had been arrested by mistake, he said, in one of the *razzias* of Paris. The chief of the guard took off his hat, expressed his regret most humbly that such a mistake should have been made, and ordered the young man to be called.

Suddenly a gendarme on duty in the yard dashed his gun upon the ground, and throwing himself upon the quartermaster, seized him by the throat and endeavored to strangle him, crying, "I recognize you; you are a Communist; you ordered the execution of forty-five gendarmes. I was the only one who succeeded in escaping. At last I've got you, and will kill you."

Seeing this, the chief and several persons intervened, and succeeded in disengaging the grasp of the gendarme.

"What is the matter?" they cried; "explain yourself."

The gendarme then informed them that the pretended quartermaster was no other than a chief of a battalion of the National Guard, and that on Wednesday morning, May 24th, he had ordered the execution of forty-five gendarmes and several other hostages.

"It is false!" replied the individual; "I am a member of the regular army, and as such I assisted at the capture of Montmartre. I a Communist! *Allons donc!*"

"I swear," replied the gendarme, "that you are an insurgent chief. I am *not* mistaken. I saw you under circumstances which I can never forget, and I demand your immediate arrest."

"Very well," said the commander; "the gentleman shall be conducted to the military bureau in the Rue de Satory, and there he can establish his identity."

He was then placed in the hands of four men, escorted by the gendarme.

Arrived in presence of the General, the individual acknowledged that he had, in fact, served under the Commune, and that he had been charged with the execution of a portion of the hostages. "I could have saved myself," he added, "but my paternal sentiments were too strong, and I wished also to deliver my son."

Needless to say that the quartermaster was forthwith transferred to prison.

Besides the chiefs and members of the Commune who perished fighting behind the barricades, or who were shot by the soldiers immediately after arrest, many are now in prison at Versailles; others, however, such as Felix Pyat and General Bergeret, have succeeded so far in eluding the vigilance of the police, and have probably gained the frontier.

The deaths of Dombrowski, Delescluze, Millière, Rigault,

GAMBON
Commune of Paris
1871

etc., as also the arrests of Rochefort, Mourot, and Assi, have already been described.

Billioray was arrested on Saturday evening in the Rue des Canettes, 19, where he was hidden under the name of Benedech. He was immediately conducted before the Grand Provost, where he was made to pass through a summary interrogatory. He denied for a long time being Billioray of the Commune and Committee of Public Safety, and it was only when confronted with a commissary of police, whom he had caused to be arrested and plundered on the 18th of March, that he ended by avowing his identity. One thousand and fifteen francs were found upon his person. He was then conducted to Versailles to await his trial.

Gambon and Lefrançais were shot in the Rue de la Banque. On Sunday morning, while the battle was still going on in Belleville, Gambon, Géresme, the two Ferrés, Lacord, and several other members of the Commune, had withdrawn to the Mairie of the 20th Arrondissement, escorted by a guard of honor, composed of forty National Guards, and of fifteen boys between fourteen and sixteen years of age, almost unable to carry their guns. The insurgents had taken these boys from the foundling hospital in the Rue d'Enfer, and had given them kepis, embroidered with yellow, had placed guns and cartridges in their hands, saying, "Fire upon whomsoever we tell you, and when we tell you." They carried the last red flag which still floated in Paris.

Gambon, whom report had killed on Thursday, was the only one who wore in his button-hole the badge of the Commune. He had even added to the ribbon, fringed with gold, a head of Liberty framed in the Masonic triangle of silver, on the three sides of which were inscribed these words: "*Liberty, Equality, Fraternity,* Commune of Paris."

At eleven o'clock, word was brought them that the last partisans of their horrible cause were vanquished on every side, and that the regular troops were advancing to occupy the Mairie. They had barely time to save themselves, carrying with them their flag. They descended towards the exterior boulevard, which they crossed, stopping only when they reached the Rue Fontaine-au-Roi, at a restaurant, where they ordered a frugal breakfast to be served. The foundlings were placed on guard at the door, while the Guards were sent out as scouts, and a bugle was to give the signal if the enemy approached.

While eating, the members of the Commune deliberated; all were for resistance with the exception of Gambon, who spoke for surrender. At two o'clock they descended into the street. The majority had pronounced for resistance; so the members of the Commune, aided by the foundlings, by a few women, and some Communists of the quarter, began the erection of a barricade.

After a few moments the bugle was sounded. The National Guards were sought for, but they had prudently hidden away. Then Gambon mounted on the barricade.

"I have passed thirty years of my life," said he, "in sacrificing myself for the Republic and Liberty. I have given everything to the people, and to-day the people abandon me. I have made the sacrifice of my life for cowards who flee from danger when it meets them face to face. I swear that, if I escape, I will never again give an instant of my life, or one of my thoughts, to these men. Citizens, the great cause is again lost; the Commune is killed by those who had sworn to make it triumph or to die, and who have not even defended it."

His companions then tore from him his badge as member of the Commune, and threw away his kepi, to prevent his being recognized. The bugle sounded another signal; the red flag was placed on the barricade but half constructed, arms were thrown in confusion on the ground, and all took to flight.

The Commune had disappeared, but Gambon's good resolutions came too late.

Eudes, another member of the Committee of Public Safety, was shot at Vincennes.

Okolowitch, who was wounded at the time of the arrest of Cluseret by the Commune, was placed in an ambulance on the Champs Elysées. He had there a special tent, and a sentinel mounted guard close by. Monday, the 22d, he was suddenly awakened by an officer, who said to him:

"You are my prisoner."

"Ah!" cried he, "the Commune arrests me?"

Soon undeceived, he was transferred a prisoner to Versailles.

But the members of the Commune were not all arrested or executed by regular troops. Many were taken and shot by their own soldiers.

Mathieu, member of the Commune, was one of these. Wednesday morning, the Federals led to the Pont Neuf an individual dressed in civilian's clothes, no other than Mathieu, who had been arrested in the morning, and upon whom had been found a sum amounting to one million five hundred thousand francs.

The insurgents accused him of having received this sum from Versailles for opening one of the gates to the regular troops.

The ex-member of the Commune, notwithstanding his protestations of innocence, was placed with his back against the pedestal of the statue of Henry IV, one of the Federals bound his eyes with a handkerchief, and a few seconds after six shots resounded.

Mathieu fell dead, his head crushed by the balls. His body was then picked up by two or three insurgents, who, after balancing it three or four times over the parapet, flung it into the Seine.

Varlin, Delegate of Finances, accused of having participated in the burning of the Ministry of Finance, was shot at Montmartre, in the Rue des Rosiers, at the same place where the Generals Lecomte and Clement-Thomas were assassinated.

Jourde, the successor of Varlin as Delegate to the Finances, was arrested May 31st on the Quai d'Orsay, by two agents of the police.

The former minister had taken refuge in a house which stood close by the still smoking ruins of the *Caisse des dépôts et consignations.*

When arrested by the two agents of police, who said, "You are the Citizen Jourde?" Jourde replied—"I? never in the world! My name is Roux. I am known in my quarter. Look here! take me to the Marie of the 7th Arrondissement to see the Adjoint M. Hortus; he used to be my schoolmaster, and will recognize me perfectly."

The agents conducted the individual pretending to be Roux to the Mairie in the Rue de Grenelle. They were introduced into the cabinet of M. Hortus, whose honesty and goodness are proverbial.

"Good morning, M. Hortus; do you remember me? I am Roux, your former pupil," said Jourde.

M. Hortus rose abruptly, turned very pale, and, as though making a violent effort, replied:

"You are Jourde, and you were never my scholar."

"You are killing me," said Jourde, in a low tone; "I have my poor mother, my wife. . . . ."

The Adjoint was inflexible; the Delegate to the Finances was imprisoned in the Mairie, and word was sent to Marshal de MacMahon, who caused him to be brought to his headquarters.

When interrogated regarding the resources of the Commune, he said that they consisted on the 18th of March of four millions found in the Treasury.

Two millions taken from the railway companies.

Twenty-four millions obtained from the Bank of France.

And finally, the duties, contributions, and ordinary resources of the city furnished the rest.

As for the expenses, they were obliged to pay daily for the National Guards 350,000 francs, to the great regret of Jourde, who declared that towards the end of the reign of the Commune there were not more than 30,000 men who really performed their service. Beyond this the other expenses amounted to—

609,000 francs during the first week.

700,000 francs for the second week.

This amount continued to augment until it reached the sum of 4,200,000 francs, which constitutes an average expense of 600,000 francs a day.

Jourde denied being a member of the International, and stated that the society had placed very little money in the hands of the Commune, as according to his account the committee in London, which governs the whole institution, had only 30,000 or 40,000 francs at its disposal.

He at the same time denied having received any payment from foreign countries, and added that he could prove from what sources he had drawn the sums which he had expended.

Johannard, member of the Commune, attached as civil delegate to the General La Cecilia, was judged by every one incapable of doing harm. A fine-looking young man, of striking attitudes, and much admired by the fair sex—surnamed in fact the Key-of-Hearts—he was extremely anxious to wear a uniform. He was finally named captain in the 100th battalion, and member of the Commune. Then, as always before, he showed himself to be good-hearted and intemperate. A woman was never refused anything by the civil delegate.

In the last days, however, this citizen, considered so soft and pliable, became truly ferocious.

At the barricade of the Rue du Petit-Carreau, he blew out the brains of a volunteer of the 10th battalion, and ran away after the first shot.

In the Rue des Amandiers, a young girl belonging to the ambulances deplored the fate of the unfortunate victims of the civil war; by order of the delegate she was instantly shot.

At La Roquette he caused eight convalescent soldiers to be shot for refusing to march.

As victory became more and more impossible, he became, under the impression of the fear which maddened him, a very cannibal in delirium. Some time before the end of the struggle, he withdrew as fast as his horse could carry him to the stronghold of Vincennes.

"Kill every one as you fall back," was the order given by this bandit to the "Avengers of the Republic."

At Vincennes, Johannard was not reassured; even in this citadel he dreamed of snares of every kind. By his orders, the chapel was thoroughly searched, and the old fortress explored with minute care, but neither Johannard nor his associates had courage to descend into the vaults below.

At the first cannon-shot, the delegate of the 2d Arrondissement disappeared, and it was only after a long search that he was found behind the arsenal, hidden under a heap of broken gun-carriages.

Two hours later he was shot in one of the ditches which surround the fort.

General La Cecilia, his associate, was for some time reported to have been shot in like manner at Vincennes. This news has, however, since proved false, and was probably circulated, as has happened in many other cases, by his friends, in order to cause the vigilance of the police to slumber.

While colonel of the *francs-tireurs* of the Seine, La Cecilia lived during a month in the Chateau de Banneville, at Banneville-la-Campagne, a small town in the arrondissement of Caen.

Having succeeded in getting out of Paris, it was towards this chateau that La Cecilia directed his flight. He counted on the kindness formerly shown him by Madame de Banneville during the war with Prussia, and believed that she would consent to interest herself in his fate.

He was mistaken, however, in his calculations. Madame de Banneville declared that for the defender of the Commune she had only hatred and contempt, and that if he did not immediately leave of his own free-will, she would have him put out of the house by force or else arrested.

Seeing that all remarks would be superfluous, La Cecilia decided to withdraw. Almost immediately after his departure, and while still overcome by the scene just enacted, Madame de Banneville was informed that the house was surrounded by gendarmes. A brigadier presented himself saying that they had been instructed of the presence in her house of a dangerous man who had arrived that morning at the station of Moult-Argences, and that they had come to arrest him.

The lady then related what had happened.

The gendarmes proceeded, without losing an instant, to search the environs, and the ex-general of the Commune was soon discovered in a small inn of Banneville-la-Campagne, accompanied by his former attendant in the *francs-tireurs*, who, since the war, had taken service at the Chateau de Banneville. He had left the chateau with his former chief. A certain quantity of arms and ammunition was found in the inn, whose proprietor, together with La Cecilia and his attendant, was directed immediately toward Versailles.

La Celicia is of Italian origin, and had received a very good education; his exalted opinions had obliged him to leave Italy, and in 1859 he was professor of mathematics in the University of Ulm. He joined later the corps formed by Garibaldi, since which time he has taken part in every revolutionary plot or intrigue.

Treilhard, Director of Public Assistance, was shot May 26th, at the Place du Panthéon. A search made in his house brought to light a casket in which he had hidden 40,000 francs.

The arrest of some of the Communist chiefs was not effected until after long and patient search.

Paschal Grousset succeeded for many days in remaining in security within the city, while various reports were spread of his capture in Switzerland, his appearance in Belgium, and his arrival in London, all calculated to throw the authorities off the scent, and to enable him finally to effect his escape in safety.

It was not until the 3d of June that he was captured, although, for five or six days, there had been strong suspicions entertained that the ex-Delegate of Foreign Relations was hidden in the Rue Condorcet.

These suspicions were soon changed into certainty. It was said in the neighborhood that he came every morning to breakfast with a Miss Hacard, with whom he had been on intimate terms for many years, and who lives at 39 Rue Condorcet. A commissary of police, accompanied by two agents and a locksmith, presented himself at the entrance to the fourth story of this house.

He had been informed that two women lived there, but that one had just gone out. It was Miss Hacard, who had gone to buy some newspapers.

Having rung at the bell, and receiving no reply, M.

Duret, the commissary, caused the door to be broken open, and perceived a woman, whose back was turned towards him. This woman, possessed of an abundance of black hair, or rather with an enormous *chignon* attached to the summit of her head, was dressed in a black skirt and dressing-jacket.

"You are Paschal Grousset," cried the agent of police, seizing the woman by the arm and forcing her to terms.

Grousset, for it was he, did not attempt either to deny his identity or to make the slightest resistance; he avowed his name, declaring himself a journalist and member of the Commune.

He then asked permission to resume his masculine garments, which was granted, and a search was immediately commenced in the apartment.

Grousset remained perfectly impassible, flattering himself that no one had ever laid hands on his papers, and that it would be the case always; but when the order was given to search the canopy of the bed, he grew pale.

"You've got the hiding-place," he cried.

An enormous quantity of documents was in fact found, the study of which will probably be very interesting for the history of the foreign relations of the Commune.

After a short interrogatory, Grousset was conducted to the Mairie of the 9th Arrondissement. He asked permission to smoke a cigarette—a pleasure of which he had been deprived for ten days during which he had been disguised as a woman.

It was in fact from the 23d of May that all news of him had ceased, and he had probably taken refuge as early as that day with Miss Hacard.

Hardly had Grousset arrived at the Mairie Drouot when he was recognized and immediately saluted with cries of "*A mort, l'assassin! à mort, l'incendiare!* let him go on foot!" etc.

The carriage in which he was placed was escorted by a body of soldiers, but they were insufficient to restrain the fury of the assailants; they pushed through the guard, shaking their fists in his face, and endeavoring to strike him.

Several times M. Duret was obliged to lean out of the window and beg the crowd to respect his prisoner.

"Be patient," he said, "justice shall be done; but my honor as a magistrate is engaged to place Paschal Grousset alive in the hands of the authorities."

He was listened to for a moment with deference, but almost immediately the clamor recommenced with greater violence, and it is probable that justice would have been done on the spot if the procession had not been met by General Pradier, who inquired the cause of the tumult. Informed of the danger incurred by the prisoner, he requisitioned indifferently all the officers and soldiers who passed, and thus formed an escort sufficient to impose its will upon the crowd.

They then proceeded along the boulevards and Rue Royale to the Palais de l'Industrie.

Arrived at the entrance of the Faubourg Saint-Honoré, which was choked by the ruins of the surrounding houses, the fury of the crowd redoubled in violence.

"Look, wretch, at what you have done! Death to the incendiary! Let him be shot on the ruins of the houses he has burned!"

"This crowd is ferocious," said Paschal Grousset.

"One must be philosophical," replied M. Duret. "Fifteen days ago, if I had been seized, I might have been in your place and you in mine, and who knows whether you would have saved me then from the fury of all these people."

The carriage, however, advanced slowly. Grousset remarked that he could not understand how he, a writer and an artist, could be confounded with the iconoclasts of the Louvre and Tuileries.

After a long and often-interrupted march, the procession finally made its entrance into the Palais de l'Industrie, seat of the chief military provostship, whence he was sent the same evening to Versailles.

He was conducted, immediately upon his arrival, to the prison of the Rue Saint-Pierre, and placed in cell No. 8, between Rochefort and his secretary, Mourot.

The ex-Delegate of Foreign Affairs was very depressed in spirits, and seemed convinced that he was to be shot on the spot without any form of trial. When he arrived at the prison and saw the guardians of the peace ranged round his carriage, he said, in a trembling voice:

"Soldiers, don't hurt me!" words which he repeated for the third time since his arrest.

When he saw that the peril was not as imminent as he had feared, he regained a certain assurance, and, in entering his cell, remarked to the guardians who conducted him:

"They did well to come .... Two hours later they would not have found me."

This appearance of tranquillity was not of long duration; invited to take something to eat, he refused, asking only for some tobacco. He then added:

"When shall I be judged? I hope I shall be judged. It is my right; I was not taken prisoner with arms in my hands."

It was then explained to him that he must await the orders of the military authorities, to whom he belonged, for the future. During most of the night Grousset was pacing his narrow cell.

On the morrow he was up at an early hour, having thrown himself, towards morning, dressed, upon the bed, expecting to be interrogated immediately. The day passed, however, without any other formality than a short interrogatory which established his identity.

Régère, a member of the Commune, whose name is well known from the decree of the Commune already mentioned, "The Citizen Raoul Rigault is charged, together with the Citizen Régère, with the execution of the decree of the Commune of Paris relative to the hostages," was also arrested in Paris, but not until nearly the end of the month of June.

For about eight days before his arrest he had been living in the Hotel des Italiens. His arrival at the hotel was preceded by that of two young men, serving doubtless as scouts, who gave out that they were nephews of an old man of sixty, who was about to rejoin them.

The venerable uncle arrived in time, but it was remarked that his hair and beard, cut very short, were of reddish tinge. This, however, was supposed to be the result of vanity on the part of the old man—nothing more. The day after his arrival he caused his whole body to be covered with plasters, and took to his bed, where he remained most obstinately.

M. Régère had inscribed himself in the book of the hotel as M. Teuquien, a singular name, somewhat Chinese, and hardly calculated to divert suspicion; however, he might have remained for a long time undisturbed, had it not been for the intervention of a lady, very nicely dressed, who had undertaken to furnish passports to several persons compromised in the insurrection. She had already procured several papers of this kind at the Prefecture, in virtue of what title it is not yet known, when the snare was discovered.

From that moment the lady was furnished, in the kindest manner, with all the passports which she came to demand, only—two zealous agents of the police were, at the same time, attached to her person.

In this manner Régère was discovered, and his red beard was unable to resist a serious examination. [One of the nephews of Régère was a staff-officer in the Federal Guard, who, as early as the 22d of May, had taken off his uniform in the quarter of the Elysée, and hidden in a cellar, "to await the course of events."]

Vésinier, editor of the *Officiel* of the Commune, and, when he fell from those high functions, of the *Paris Libre,* was arrested at the Hospital of La Pitié. Here he had taken refuge under an assumed name on the 23d of May. He was slightly wounded in the arm, but was never heard to remark at what barricade he had fought.

Citizens Breslier and Greffier, *fils,* both officers in the battalion called the Avengers of Flourens, particularly sought as the instigators of the conflagration of the Palace of Justice, were finally recognized, and arrested before the ruins of the monument they had destroyed.

Citizen Verdure, belonging to the Central Committee of the Confederation of the National Guard, had disappeared immediately after the entrance of the Versailles troops into Paris, and all the searches made for him had proved vain.

Verdure, however, had been arrested. He had been taken on one of the first days of the struggle in a group of National Guards who had voluntarily surrendered. He had assumed a false name, and hoped, thanks to this artifice, to pass unperceived amidst a crowd of others.

Unfortunately he was recognized by one of his companions of insurrection while on his way to the provost-marshal, who, faithful to the principle of fraternity, hastened to denounce him.

Verdure endeavored at first to deny his identity, but having been confronted with several other Communists, and recognized by them, he was finally obliged to drop the mask and appear in his true character.

The painter Courbet, to whom Paris and France are indebted for the destruction of the Column Vendôme, was arrested in the Rue Saint-Gilles, in the house of one of his friends, a piano-manufacturer.

On the same day, Rossel, the ex-Delegate of War, was arrested at No. 54 Boulevard Saint-Germain. He was considered in the house, one of the employés of the Northern Railway, of which he wore the uniform cap. He sought for some time to prove that there was a mistake, but finding all denial useless, he resigned himself, saying, "Don't touch me, I am an officer of the army; I will follow you without resistance."

Vermorel, member of the Commune, was taken wounded to Versailles, where he died from the effects of an operation necessitated by his wound.

J. Miot was shot May 29th, at La Muette.

Of the famous Cluseret nothing positive is known. It is generally believed, however, that he made his escape from Paris disguised as a cabman, and has landed safely in the United States, and that he will probably remain there until Satan "finds some work for idle hands."

Two of the assassins of Generals Lecomte and Clement-Thomas have met the reward their crimes deserved.

One of these, Dufil, arrested May 27th, accused of having commanded the fire on the unhappy Generals, and of having boasted of his crime but a few moments before his arrest, was conducted by a lieutenant and eight soldiers to the Chatelet. On the route he endeavored to escape, but was pursued by the lieutenant, who wounded him in the head by a shot from his revolver, causing him to fall. He then raised himself on his elbows, when four more shots were fired, and he fell to rise no more.

Another of these assassins was Langellé, former sergeant of the line.

He had had some difficulty with the Commune, which caused him to be thrown into prison, and he profited by this circumstance to pass himself as a victim of the men of the 18th of March.

A few days after order was restored, as he was about to return one evening to his home, he perceived two men who seemed to be awaiting his approach.

With the instinct peculiar to people of his kind, he instantly recognized them as agents of the police, to whom, in fact, mission had been given to capture him.

A battalion of the line was camped not far from the spot. Langellé ran to find an officer, and with his order of arrest under the Commune in his hand, endeavored to persuade him that two insurgents were waiting to avenge themselves for his defection by doing him an evil turn.

The officer pretended to be convinced, and a platoon of the line went immediately to arrest the two men; but when Langellé wished to withdraw, he was politely requested to accompany them. They went together to the commissary of police, when the true state of things was discovered.

There are at present imprisoned at Versailles but fourteen members of the Commune. This is all that remain of that odious government which counted no less that one hundred and fifteen persons; one hundred and one have disappeared, and are either killed or have succeeded in making their escape.

Those who remain are: Régère, Ferré, Assi, Rastoul, Courbet, Urbain, Paschal Grousset, Jourde, Trinquet, Arnold, Billioray, Verdure, Ulysse Parent and Descamps.

This last had been also for some time imprisoned under an assumed name; not until six weeks after his capture was the fraud discovered.

Razoua, another member of the Commune, has just been arrested in Geneva; his extradition will probably be demanded by the French Government.

Rochefort is now confined in the prison of the Rue Saint-Pierre awaiting his trial; he occupies one of the cells usually given to persons condemned to death; it is small, narrow, and very obscure, receiving light only from the corridor outside, which is itself only dimly lighted. Since his entrance into prison he has been anxious, preoccupied, and taciturn, showing at times a fear of the fate which awaits him. He was shortly taken quite ill, owing, as he said, to a recent affliction in his family. This bereavement, however, was no other than the death of his father, which occurred on the 12th of April, and whose funeral Rochefort had himself attended. The poor old man died in a state of great misery, almost of starvation, although, as Henri Rochefort himself stated, the publication of the *Mot d'Ordre* brought to his son the sum of $200 daily.

At the time of his death, the Marquis de Rochefort was living almost upon charity, at a house in the Faubourg St. Antoine, which was filled with aged persons who brought here what little furniture they had, and who paid, some $240, others $160, yearly. M. Rochefort was one of these last, but the poor old man's payments were very rare. His furniture consisted of an old bureau and four cane-bottomed chairs, a broken and torn old arm-chair, a small library containing about thirty volumes, and an iron bedstead. This was all pressed into a room about six yards, but it did not even belong to him. He owed it to the charity of persons almost as poor as himself, who had come to the aid of the old man whose children had abandoned him. Two years ago M. Rochefort became possessed of $240 by selling two entrances for life to the theatres Des Variétés and Vaudeville.

At this period, Henri Rochefort, for whom his father had made every sacrifice in order to procure him a good education, was forced by the outcries of the Paris journals, indignant at his unfilial conduct, to remember that he had a father dying of hunger in one of the Faubourgs of Paris. He made him a pension of $20 a month; although the gains of the editor of the *Marseillaise* and *Mot d'Ordre* during the last two years are estimated at $60,000. The old man, however, was so happy at the receipt of this sum that he almost lost his head.

Henri Rochefort never but once entered the sad abode of his father, and that was a few hours before his death, when he came and embraced him. On the morrow he returned with five or six persons, and followed the corpse to the cemetery of Bercy.

Our readers will probably remember the part taken by M. Libbmann under the Commune, and his success in saving from ruin the Chapelle Expiatoire of Louis XVI. Immediately after the entrance of the troops, a subscription was raised to repay M. Libbmann the sums he had expended. The amount raised, however, far exceeded the necessary sum, and the surplus was devoted to charitable purposes. M. Libbmann has lately received the following letter of thanks and congratulation from Henry V, Comte de Chambord:

"CHAMBORD, July 3d, 1871.

"I was much moved, Monsieur, by the feelings which you expressed in your letter, and by the thought, so Christian and so French, which inspired you. I already knew of the admirable zeal and courage which you had displayed in the crisis through which we have just passed. I am happy to be able to express here, myself, all my gratitude to you. Thanks to you, France will not have had the grief of seeing disappear in the revolutionary turmoil the chapel consecrated to the memory of the martyr-king. Saint Louis has, by his intercession, saved the Holy Chapel, which stands alone to-day in the midst of the ruins surrounding it. The prayers of King Louis XVI have obtained the preservation of the expiatory monument in the Rue d'Anjou. You were chosen to be the instrument of this great work. Rejoice at the recompense accorded to your patriotism and your faith. I entirely approve of the destination given to the surplus of the subscriptions which you have received, and I again repeat, Monsieur, the assurance of my sincere gratitude and affection. "HENRI."

For the services rendered by M. Ducatel, by whose means the troops were enabled to hasten their entry into Paris, the Minister of Public Works has recommended that M. Ducatel should be nominated a Knight of the Legion of Honor. This recommendation was followed by a decree of M. Thiers carrying out the proposal.

We cannot close this work without paying a tribute to Mr. Washburne, the American Minister in France, who has remained in Paris during the two terrible sieges which the city has undergone, and who has done so much to render our countrymen proud of their representative. During the days of terror his courage and energy were unequalled, while his efforts for the release of the unhappy hostages were unceasing, and in many cases were crowned with success. Everything in his power was done by him to assuage the sufferings of the Archbishop; and, thanks to his intervention, several Sisters of Charity were released from confinement.

Mr. Washburne's letter, however, explains better than we can do, his visit and his kindness to Monseigneur Darboy, at a time when it was so much needed.

"PARIS, April 23, 1871.

"You are aware that Monseigneur Darboy, the Archbishop of Paris, was seized some time since, by order of the Commune, and thrust into prison, to be held as a hostage. Such treatment of that most devout and excellent man could not but have created a great sensation, particularly in the Catholic world.

"On Thursday night last I received a letter from Monseigneur Chigi, Archbishop of Myre and Nuncio Apostolic of the Saint-Siège, and also a communication from M. Louvrier, *chanoine* of the Diocese of Paris. M. Lagard, the Vicar-General of Paris, and Messrs. Bousset and Allain, *chanoines* and members of the Metropolitan Chapter of the Church of Paris, all making a strong appeal to me, in the name of the right of nations, humanity, and sympathy, to interpose my good offices in behalf of the imprisoned Archbishop. I have thought that I should have been only conforming to what I believed to be the policy of our Government, and carrying out what I conceived to be your wishes under the circumstances, by complying with the request of the gentlemen who have addressed me. I, therefore, early this morning, put myself in communication with General Cluseret, who seems at the present time to be the directing man in affairs here. I told him that I applied to him not in my diplomatic capacity, but simply in the interest of good-feeling and humanity, to see if it were not possible to have the Archbishop relieved from arrest and confinement. He answered that it was not a matter within his jurisdiction, and however much he might like to see the Archbishop released, he thought, in consideration of the state of affairs, it would be impossible. He said that he was not arrested for crime, but simply to be held as a hostage, as many others had been. Under the existing circumstances, he thought it would be useless to take any steps in that direction. I myself thought that the Commune would not dare, in the present excited state of public feeling in Paris, to release the Archbishop. I told General Cluseret, however, that I must see him to ascertain his real situation, the condition of his health, and whether he was in want of anything. He said there would be no objection to that, and he immediately went with me in person to the Prefecture of Police, and upon his application I received from the Prefect a permission to visit the Archbishop freely at any time. In company with my private secretary, Mr. McKean, I then went to the Mazas prison, where I was admitted without difficulty, and being ushered into one of the vacant cells, the Archbishop was very soon brought in. I must say I was deeply touched at the appearance of this venerable man. With his slender person, his form somewhat bent, his long beard—for he has not been shaved apparently since his imprisonment—his face haggard with ill-health, all could not have failed to have moved the most indifferent. I told him that I had taken great pleasure, at the instance of his friends, in intervening on his behalf, and while I could not promise myself the satisfaction of seeing him released, I was very glad to be able to visit him to ascertain his wants, and to assuage the cruel position in which he found himself. He thanked me most heartily and cordially for the disposition I had manifested towards him. I was charmed by his cheerful spirit and his interesting conversation. He seemed to appreciate his critical situation, and to be prepared for the worst. He had no word of bitterness or reproach for his persecutors, but on the other hand remarked that the world jndged them to be worse than they really were. He was patiently waiting the logic of events, and praying that Providence might find a solution to these terrible troubles without the further shedding of human blood. He is confined in a cell about six feet by ten, possibly a little larger, which has the ordinary furniture of the Mazas prison—a wooden chair, a small wooden table, and a prison bed. The cell is lighted by one small window. As a political prisoner, he is permitted to have his food brought to him from outside the prison; and in answer to my suggestion that I should be glad to send him anything he might desire, or furnish him with any money he might want, he said he was not in need at present. I was the first man he had seen from the outside since his imprisonment, and he had not been permitted to see the newspapers, or to have any intelligence of passing events. I shall make application to the Prefect of Police to be allowed to send him newspapers and other reading matter, and shall also avail myself of the permission granted me to visit him, to the end that I may afford him any proper assistance in my power. I cannot conceal from myself, however, the great danger he is in, and I sincerely hope that I may be instrumental in saving him from the fate which seems to threaten.

"I have the honor to be,

"Very respectfully,

"Your obedient servant,

"E. B. WASHBURNE."

The trial of the chiefs of the Commune has been several times postponed; but little doubt can exist of the fate which awaits them, if we may judge by that of a subordinate named Ferdinand Sencier, who has been condemned to death by the First Council of Versailles.

This man was an artilleryman at the Porte Maillot, renowned for his unerring aim, and who boasted that he never aimed a gun at the Versailles troops without killing his man. His behavior at the tribunal was anything but prepossessing; accused of desertion in time of war, of having formed a part of insurrectional bands, of massacre and pillage, he aggravated his situation by fanfaronades which nearly caused his expulsion from court. A still more horrible accusation, however, was brought against him; it was that, while he was firing upon Neuilly in the direction of a house inhabited by his mother, the poor woman was killed by the bursting of a shell. He was condemned to capital punishment.

If the instrument is thus condemned, the leaders will not remain unpunished; and the men who ruled over Paris with a rod of iron, only at the last to deliver up the unhappy city to fire and blood—the men who obliged the poor soldiers, after five months' rude imprisonment in hated Germany, to turn from the firesides waiting to receive them and take up arms against their fellow-countrymen—the men who brought desolation and mourning to so many homes which had been filled with joy at the safe return of their sons and brothers from the Prussian war—these men will surely meet the reward of their crimes, and give to the world a terrible example.

Colonel Rossel, whose career was both brief and sanguinary, Captain of Engineers in the French Army, Colonel under Gambetta, Chief of Staff under Cluseret, Delegate of War, President of the Military Court, and Commander of the Commune Forces, was condemned to military degradation and death by the Versailles Court-Martial, September 7th. The savage and heartless Ferré and would-be Dictator Lullier were sentenced to the same fate.

Trinquet and Urbain were condemned to imprisonment for life. Assi, Grousset, Billioray, Régère, Verdure and Ferrat, to deportation and confinement in a fortress. Jourde and Rastorel to transportation.

Courbet was condemned to six months' imprisonment, Clement to three months; Decamp and Parent were acquitted.

PARIS, Thursday, Sept. 21, 1871.

M. Rochefort's trial has concluded, and he has been sentenced by the Court-Martial to transportation to a penal colony for life.

AMERICAN GUIDE TO EUROPE.

Harper's Hand-Book for Travellers in Europe and the East: being a Guide through Great Britain and Ireland, France, Belgium, Holland, Germany, Italy, Egypt, Syria, Turkey, Greece, Switzerland, Tyrol, Spain, Russia, Denmark, and Sweden. By W. Pembroke Fetridge. With numerous Maps and Plans of Cities. Tenth Year. Large 12mo, Leather, Tucks, $5 00.

This new, revised, and enlarged edition of *Harper's Hand-Book* contains the following Maps and Plans:

Railroad Map of Europe, 25 by 22 inches (in cover-pocket).—London, 35 by 27 inches (in cover-pocket).—Paris, 25 by 35 inches (in cover-pocket).—Atlantic Routes.—Ireland.—Lakes of Killarney.—Dublin.—Belfast.—Great Britain, North.—Edinburgh.—Glasgow.—Environs of London.—Great Britain, South.—The Lake District.—Wales.—Paris.—Versailles.—Marseilles.—Nice.—Metz.—Strasbourg.—Antwerp.—Berlin.—King's Garden, near Potsdam.—Hamburg.—Dresden.—Prague.—Vienna.—Pesth and Ofen.—Trieste.—Venice.—Verona.—Milan.—Bologna.—Turin.—Genoa.—Florence.—Plan of the Uffizi Gallery.—Pisa.—Rome.—Roman Forum.—Ancient Rome.—Palace of the Vatican.—Naples.—Museo Nationale.—Pompeii.—Palermo.—Egypt and Northern Nubia.—Cairo.—Thebes.—Palestine.—Jerusalem.—Church of the Holy Sepulchre.—Turkey in Asia.—Greece and the Ionian Islands.—Switzerland.—Munich.—Augsburg.—Nuremburg.—Carlsruhe.—Frankfort.—Cologne.—St. Petersburg.—Stockholm.—The Alhambra.

It gives the best routes of travel, names the places of interest, tells how much money certain trips cost, and furnishes the traveller with all the necessary advice and full information for a trip to any or all parts of the Old World. We do not see how a person crossing the Atlantic can afford to do without it.—*Home Journal.*

From having travelled somewhat extensively in former years in Europe and the East, I can say with entire truth that you have succeeded in combining more that is instructive and valuable for the traveller than is contained in any one or series of hand-books that I have ever met with.—T. B. Lawrence, *U. S. Consul General, Florence, February* 15, 1866.

Every traveller who carries this guide-book and uses it faithfully will find it not only an invaluable companion on his journey, but a most useful book of reference on his return.—*Congregationalist.*

A volume that should be in every traveller's hands.—*N. Y. Standard.*

To all tourists we recommend this guide-book.—*N. Y. Herald.*

No European hand-book can be found that is equally comprehensive and satisfactory.—*Cincinnati Commercial.*

It is concise, giving all necessary information to the traveller.—*N. Y. World.*

Harper's Hand-Book of Travel, always good, is now excellent.—*Philadelphia Press.*

There is scarcely any information which the tourist may require respecting any part of Europe that will not be supplied by this hand-book.—*Montreal News.*

☞ Harper & Brothers *will send the above work by mail, postage prepaid, to any part of the United States, on receipt of the price.*

LOSSING'S FIELD-BOOK OF THE REVOLUTION. Pictorial Field-Book of the Revolution; or, Illustrations, by Pen and Pencil, of the History, Biography, Scenery, Relics, and Traditions of the War for Independence. By BENSON J. LOSSING. 2 vols., 8vo, Cloth, $14 00; Sheep, $15 00; Half Calf, $18 00; Full Turkey Morocco, $22 00.

LOSSING'S FIELD-BOOK OF THE WAR OF 1812. Pictorial Field-Book of the War of 1812; or, Illustrations, by Pen and Pencil, of the History, Biography, Scenery, Relics, and Traditions of the Last War for American Independence. By BENSON J. LOSSING. With several hundred Engravings on Wood, by Lossing and Barritt, chiefly from Original Sketches by the Author. 1088 pages, 8vo, Cloth, $7 00; Sheep, $8 50; Half Calf, $10 00.

WINCHELL'S SKETCHES OF CREATION. Sketches of Creation: a Popular View of some of the Grand Conclusions of the Sciences in reference to the History of Matter and of Life. Together with a Statement of the Intimations of Science respecting the Primordial Condition and the Ultimate Destiny of the Earth and the Solar System. By ALEXANDER WINCHELL, LL.D., Professor of Geology, Zoology, and Botany in the University of Michigan, and Director of the State Geological Survey. With Illustrations. 12mo, Cloth, $2 00.

WHITE'S MASSACRE OF ST. BARTHOLOMEW. The Massacre of St. Bartholomew: Preceded by a History of the Religious Wars in the Reign of Charles IX. By HENRY WHITE, M.A. With Illustrations. 8vo, Cloth, $1 75.

ALFORD'S GREEK TESTAMENT. The Greek Testament: with a critically-revised Text; a Digest of Various Readings; Marginal References to Verbal and Idiomatic Usage; Prolegomena; and a Critical and Exegetical Commentary. For the Use of Theological Students and Ministers. By HENRY ALFORD, D.D., Dean of Canterbury. Vol. I., containing the Four Gospels. 944 pages, 8vo, Cloth, $6 00; Sheep, $6 50.

ABBOTT'S FREDERICK THE GREAT. The History of Frederick the Second, called Frederick the Great. By JOHN S. C. ABBOTT. Elegantly Illustrated. 8vo, Cloth, $5 00.

ABBOTT'S HISTORY OF THE FRENCH REVOLUTION. The French Revolution of 1789, as viewed in the Light of Republican Institutions. By JOHN S. C. ABBOTT. With 100 Engravings. 8vo, Cloth, $5 00.

ABBOTT'S NAPOLEON BONAPARTE. The History of Napoleon Bonaparte. By JOHN S. C. ABBOTT. With Maps, Woodcuts, and Portraits on Steel. 2 vols., 8vo, Cloth, $10 00.

ABBOTT'S NAPOLEON AT ST. HELENA; or, Interesting Anecdotes and Remarkable Conversations of the Emperor during the Five and a Half Years of his Captivity. Collected from the Memorials of Las Casas, O'Meara, Montholon, Antommarchi, and others. By JOHN S. C. ABBOTT. With Illustrations. 8vo, Cloth, $5 00.

ADDISON'S COMPLETE WORKS. The Works of Joseph Addison, embracing the whole of the "Spectator." Complete in 3 vols., 8vo, Cloth, $6 00.

ALCOCK'S JAPAN. The Capital of the Tycoon: a Narrative of a Three Years' Residence in Japan. By Sir RUTHERFORD ALCOCK, K.C.B., Her Majesty's Envoy Extraordinary and Minister Plenipotentiary in Japan. With Maps and Engravings. 2 vols., 12mo, Cloth, $3 50.

ALISON'S HISTORY OF EUROPE. FIRST SERIES: From the Commencement of the French Revolution, in 1789, to the Restoration of the Bourbons, in 1815. [In addition to the Notes on Chapter LXXVI., which correct the errors of the original work concerning the United States, a copious Analytical Index has been appended to this American edition.] SECOND SERIES: From the Fall of Napoleon, in 1815, to the Accession of Louis Napoleon, in 1852. 8vols., 8vo, Cloth, $16 00.

BALDWIN'S PRE-HISTORIC NATIONS. Pre-Historic Nations; or, Inquiries concerning some of the Great Peoples and Civilizations of Antiquity, and their Probable Relation to a still Older Civilization of the Ethiopians or Cushites of Arabia. By JOHN D. BALDWIN, Member of the American Oriental Society. 12mo, Cloth, $1 75.

BARTH'S NORTH AND CENTRAL AFRICA. Travels and Discoveries in North and Central Africa: being a Journal of an Expedition undertaken under the Auspices of H.B.M.'s Government, in the Years 1849-1855. By HENRY BARTH, Ph.D., D.C.L. Illustrated. 3 vols., 8vo, Cloth, $12 00.

HENRY WARD BEECHER'S SERMONS. Sermons by HENRY WARD BEECHER, Plymouth Church, Brooklyn. Selected from Published and Unpublished Discourses, and Revised by their Author. With Steel Portrait. Complete in Two Vols., 8vo, Cloth, $5 00.

LYMAN BEECHER'S AUTOBIOGRAPHY, &c. Autobiography, Correspondence, &c., of Lyman Beecher, D.D. Edited by his Son, CHARLES BEECHER. With Three Steel Portraits, and Engravings on Wood. In 2 vols., 12mo, Cloth, $5 00.

BELLOWS'S OLD WORLD. The Old World in its New Face: Impressions of Europe in 1867-1868. By HENRY W. BELLOWS. 2 vols., 12mo, Cloth, $3 50.

BOSWELL'S JOHNSON. The Life of Samuel Johnson, LL.D. Including a Journey to the Hebrides. By JAMES BOSWELL, Esq. A New Edition, with numerous Additions and Notes. By JOHN WILSON CROKER, LL.D., F.R.S. Portrait of Boswell. 2 vols., 8vo, Cloth, $4 00.

BRODHEAD'S HISTORY OF NEW YORK. History of the State of New York. By JOHN ROMEYN BRODHEAD. 1609-1691. 2 vols. 8vo, Cloth, $3 00 per vol.

BROUGHAM'S AUTOBIOGRAPHY. Life and Times of HENRY, LORD BROUGHAM. Written by Himself. In Three Volumes. 12mo, Cloth, $2 00 per vol.

BULWER'S PROSE WORKS. Miscellaneous Prose Works of Edward Bulwer, Lord Lytton. 2 vols., 12mo, Cloth, $3 50.

BULWER'S HORACE. The Odes and Epodes of Horace. A Metrical Translation into English. With Introduction and Commentaries. By LORD LYTTON. With Latin Text from the Editions of Orelli, Macleane, and Yonge. 12mo, Cloth, $1 75.

BULWER'S KING ARTHUR. King Arthur. A Poem. By EARL LYTTON. New Edition. 12mo, Cloth, $1 75.

BURNS'S LIFE AND WORKS. The Life and Works of Robert Burns. Edited by ROBERT CHAMBERS. 4 vols., 12mo, Cloth, $6 00.

REINDEER, DOGS, AND SNOW-SHOES. A Journal of Siberian Travel and Explorations made in the Years 1865-'67. By RICHARD J. BUSH, late of the Russo-American Telegraph Expedition. Illustrated. Crown 8vo, Cloth, $3 00.

CARLYLE'S FREDERICK THE GREAT. History of Friedrich II., called Frederick the Great. By THOMAS CARLYLE. Portraits, Maps, Plans, &c. 6 vols., 12mo, Cloth, $12 00.

CARLYLE'S FRENCH REVOLUTION. History of the French Revolution. Newly Revised by the Author, with Index, &c. 2 vols., 12mo, Cloth, $3 50.

CARLYLE'S OLIVER CROMWELL. Letters and Speeches of Oliver Cromwell. With Elucidations and Connecting Narrative. 2 vols., 12mo, Cloth, $3 50.

CHALMERS'S POSTHUMOUS WORKS. The Posthumous Works of Dr. Chalmers. Edited by his Son-in-Law, Rev. WILLIAM HANNA, LL.D. Complete in 9 vols., 12mo, Cloth, $13 50.

COLERIDGE'S COMPLETE WORKS. The Complete Works of Samuel Taylor Coleridge. With an Introductory Essay upon his Philosophical and Theological Opinions. Edited by Professor SHEDD. Complete in Seven Vols. With a fine Portrait. Small 8vo, Cloth, $10 50.

CURTIS'S HISTORY OF THE CONSTITUTION. History of the Origin, Formation, and Adoption of the Constitution of the United States. By GEORGE TICKNOR CURTIS. 2 vols., 8vo, Cloth, $6 00.

DRAPER'S CIVIL WAR. History of the American Civil War. By JOHN W. DRAPER, M.D., LL.D., Professor of Chemistry and Physiology in the University of New York. In Three Vols. 8vo, Cloth, $3 50 per vol.

DRAPER'S INTELLECTUAL DEVELOPMENT OF EUROPE. A History of the Intellectual Development of Europe. By JOHN W. DRAPER, M.D., LL.D., Professor of Chemistry and Physiology in the University of New York. 8vo, Cloth, $5 00.

DRAPER'S AMERICAN CIVIL POLICY. Thoughts on the Future Civil Policy of America. By JOHN W. DRAPER, M.D., LL.D., Professor of Chemistry and Physiology in the University of New York. Crown 8vo, Cloth, $2 50.

DAVIS'S CARTHAGE. Carthage and her Remains: being an Account of the Excavations and Researches on the Site of the Phœnician Metropolis in Africa and other adjacent Places. Conducted under the Auspices of Her Majesty's Government. By Dr. DAVIS, F.R.G.S. Profusely Illustrated with Maps, Woodcuts, Chromo-Lithographs, &c. 8vo, Cloth, $4 00.

DOOLITTLE'S CHINA. Social Life of the Chinese: with some Account of their Religious, Governmental, Educational, and Business Customs and Opinions. With special but not exclusive Reference to Fuhchau. By Rev. JUSTUS DOOLITTLE, Fourteen Years Member of the Fuhchau Mission of the American Board. Illustrated with more than 150 characteristic Engravings on Wood. 2 vols., 12mo, Cloth, $5 00.

DU CHAILLU'S AFRICA. Explorations and Adventures in Equatorial Africa: with Accounts of the Manners and Customs of the People, and of the Chase of the Gorilla, the Crocodile, Leopard, Elephant, Hippopotamus, and other Animals. By PAUL B. DU CHAILLU. Numerous Illustrations. 8vo, Cloth, $5 00.

DU CHAILLU'S ASHANGO LAND. A Journey to Ashango Land, and Further Penetration into Equatorial Africa. By PAUL B. DU CHAILLU. New Edition. Handsomely Illustrated. 8vo, Cloth, $5 00.

EDGEWORTH'S (MISS) NOVELS. With Engravings. 10 vols., 12mo, Cloth, $15 00.

GIBBON'S ROME. History of the Decline and Fall of the Roman Empire. By EDWARD GIBBON. With Notes by Rev. H. H. MILMAN and M. GUIZOT. A new Cheap Edition. To which is added a complete Index of the whole Work, and a Portrait of the Author. 6 vols., 12mo, Cloth, $9 00.

GROTE'S HISTORY OF GREECE. 12 vols., 12mo, Cloth, $18 00.

HALE'S (MRS.) WOMAN'S RECORD. Woman's Record; or, Biographical Sketches of all Distinguished Women, from the Creation to the Present Time. Arranged in Four Eras, with Selections from Female Writers of each Era. By Mrs. SARAH JOSEPHA HALE. Illustrated with more than 200 Portraits. 8vo, Cloth, $5 00.

HALL'S ARCTIC RESEARCHES. Arctic Researches and Life among the Esquimaux: being the Narrative of an Expedition in Search of Sir John Franklin, in the Years 1860, 1861, and 1862. By CHARLES FRANCIS HALL. With Maps and 100 Illustrations. The Illustrations are from Original Drawings by Charles Parsons, Henry L. Stephens, Solomon Eytinge, W. S. L. Jewett, and Granville Perkins, after Sketches by Captain Hall. 8vo, Cloth, $5 00.

HALLAM'S CONSTITUTIONAL HISTORY OF ENGLAND, from the Accession of Henry VII. to the Death of George II. 8vo, Cloth, $2 00.

HALLAM'S LITERATURE. Introduction to the Literature of Europe during the Fifteenth, Sixteenth, and Seventeenth Centuries. By HENRY HALLAM. 2 vols., 8vo, Cloth, $4 00.

HALLAM'S MIDDLE AGES. State of Europe during the Middle Ages. By HENRY HALLAM. 8vo, Cloth, $2 00.

HILDRETH'S HISTORY OF THE UNITED STATES. FIRST SERIES: From the First Settlement of the Country to the Adoption of the Federal Constitution. SECOND SERIES: From the Adoption of the Federal Constitution to the End of the Sixteenth Congress. 6 vols., 8vo, Cloth, $18 00.

HARPER'S NEW CLASSICAL LIBRARY. Literal Translations.

The following Volumes are now ready. Portraits. 12mo, Cloth, $1 50 each.

CÆSAR.—VIRGIL.—SALLUST.—HORACE.—CICERO'S ORATIONS.—CICERO'S OFFICES, &c.—CICERO ON ORATORY AND ORATORS.—TACITUS (2 vols.).—TERENCE.—SOPHOCLES.—JUVENAL.—XENOPHON.—HOMER'S ILIAD.—HOMER'S ODYSSEY.—HERODOTUS.—DEMOSTHENES.—THUCYDIDES.—ÆSCHYLUS.—EURIPIDES (2 vols.).—LIVY (2 vols.).

HUME'S HISTORY OF ENGLAND. History of England, from the Invasion of Julius Cæsar to the Abdication of James II., 1688. By DAVID HUME. A new Edition, with the Author's last Corrections and Improvements. To which is prefixed a short Account of his Life, written by Himself. With a Portrait of the Author. 6 vols., 12mo, Cloth, $9 00.

HELPS'S SPANISH CONQUEST. The Spanish Conquest in America, and its Relation to the History of Slavery and to the Government of Colonies. By ARTHUR HELPS. 4 vols., 12mo, Cloth, $6 00.

JAY'S WORKS. Complete Works of Rev. William Jay: comprising his Sermons, Family Discourses, Morning and Evening Exercises for every Day in the Year, Family Prayers, &c. Author's Enlarged Edition, revised. 3 vols., 8vo, Cloth, $6 00.

JEFFERSON'S DOMESTIC LIFE. The Domestic Life of Thomas Jefferson: compiled from Family Letters and Reminiscences by his Great-Granddaughter, SARAH N. RANDOLPH. With Illustrations. Crown 8vo, Illuminated Cloth, Beveled Edges, $2 50.

JOHNSON'S COMPLETE WORKS. The Works of Samuel Johnson, LL.D. With an Essay on his Life and Genius, by ARTHUR MURPHY, Esq. Portrait of Johnson. 2 vols., 8vo, Cloth, $4 00.

KINGLAKE'S CRIMEAN WAR. The Invasion of the Crimea, and an Account of its Progress down to the Death of Lord Raglan. By ALEXANDER WILLIAM KINGLAKE. With Maps and Plans. Two Vols. ready. 12mo, Cloth, $2 00 per vol.

KINGSLEY'S WEST INDIES. At Last: A Christmas in the West Indies. By CHARLES KINGSLEY. Illustrated. 12mo, Cloth, $1 50.

KRUMMACHER'S DAVID, KING OF ISRAEL. David, the King of Israel: a Portrait drawn from Bible History and the Book of Psalms. By FREDERICK WILLIAM KRUMMACHER, D.D., Author of "Elijah the Tishbite," &c. Translated under the express Sanction of the Author by the Rev. M. G. EASTON, M.A. With a Letter from Dr. Krummacher to his American Readers, and a Portrait. 12mo, Cloth, $1 75.

LAMB'S COMPLETE WORKS. The Works of Charles Lamb. Comprising his Letters, Poems, Essays of Elia, Essays upon Shakspeare, Hogarth, &c., and a Sketch of his Life, with the Final Memorials, by T. NOON TALFOURD. Portrait. 2 vols., 12mo, Cloth, $3 00.

LIVINGSTONE'S SOUTH AFRICA. Missionary Travels and Researches in South Africa; including a Sketch of Sixteen Years' Residence in the Interior of Africa, and a Journey from the Cape of Good Hope to Loando on the West Coast; thence across the Continent, down the River Zambesi, to the Eastern Ocean. By DAVID LIVINGSTONE, LL.D., D.C.L. With Portrait, Maps by Arrowsmith, and numerous Illustrations. 8vo, Cloth, $4 50.

LIVINGSTONE'S ZAMBESI. Narrative of an Expedition to the Zambesi and its Tributaries, and of the Discovery of the Lakes Shirwa and Nyassa. 1858-1864. By DAVID and CHARLES LIVINGSTONE. With Map and Illustrations. 8vo, Cloth, $5 00.

MARCY'S ARMY LIFE ON THE BORDER. Thirty Years of Army Life on the Border. Comprising Descriptions of the Indian Nomads of the Plains; Explorations of New Territory; a Trip across the Rocky Mountains in the Winter; Descriptions of the Habits of Different Animals found in the West, and the Methods of Hunting them; with Incidents in the Life of Different Frontier Men, &c., &c. By Brevet Brigadier-General R. B. MARCY, U.S.A., Author of "The Prairie Traveler." With numerous Illustrations. 8vo, Cloth, Beveled Edges, $3 00.

M'CLINTOCK & STRONG'S CYCLOPÆDIA. Cyclopædia of Biblical, Theological, and Ecclesiastical Literature. Prepared by the Rev. JOHN M'CLINTOCK, D.D., and JAMES STRONG, S.T.D. *3 vols. now ready.* Royal 8vo. Price per vol., Cloth, $5 00; Sheep, $6 00; Half Morocco, $8 00.

MOSHEIM'S ECCLESIASTICAL HISTORY, Ancient and Modern; in which the Rise, Progress, and Variation of Church Power are considered in their Connection with the State of Learning and Philosophy, and the Political History of Europe during that Period. Translated, with Notes, &c., by A. MACLAINE, D.D. A New Edition, continued to 1826, by C. COOTE, LL.D. 2 vols., 8vo, Cloth, $4 00.

MACAULAY'S HISTORY OF ENGLAND. The History of England from the Accession of James II. By THOMAS BABINGTON MACAULAY. With an Original Portrait of the Author. 5 vols., 8vo, Cloth, $10 00; 12mo, Cloth, $7 50.

NEVIUS'S CHINA. China and the Chinese: a General Description of the Country and its Inhabitants; its Civilization and Form of Government; its Religious and Social Institutions; its Intercourse with other Nations; and its Present Condition and Prospects. By the Rev. JOHN L. NEVIUS, Ten Years a Missionary in China. With a Map and Illustrations. 12mo, Cloth, $1 75.

OLIN'S (DR.) LIFE AND LETTERS. 2 vols., 12mo, Cloth, $3 00.

OLIN'S (DR.) TRAVELS. Travels in Egypt, Arabia Petræa, and the Holy Land. Engravings. 2 vols., 8vo, Cloth, $3 00.

OLIN'S (DR.) WORKS. The Works of Stephen Olin, D.D., late President of the Wesleyan University. 2 vols., 12mo, Cloth, $3 00.

OLIPHANT'S CHINA AND JAPAN. Narrative of the Earl of Elgin's Mission to China and Japan, in the Years 1857, '58, '59. By LAURENCE OLIPHANT. Private Secretary to Lord Elgin. Illustrations. 8vo, Cloth, $3 50.

OLIPHANT'S (MRS.) LIFE OF EDWARD IRVING. The Life of Edward Irving, Minister of the National Scotch Church, London. Illustrated by his Journals and Correspondence. By Mrs. OLIPHANT. Portrait. 8vo, Cloth, $3 50.

POETS OF THE NINETEENTH CENTURY. The Poets of the Nineteenth Century. Selected and Edited by the Rev. ROBERT ARIS WILLMOTT. With English and American Additions, arranged by EVERT A. DUYCKINCK, Editor of "Cyclopædia of American Literature." Comprising Selections from the Greatest Authors of the Age. Superbly Illustrated with 132 Engravings from Designs by the most Eminent Artists. In elegant small 4to form, printed on Superfine Tinted Paper, richly bound in extra Cloth, Beveled, Gilt Edges, $6 00; Half Calf, $6 00; Full Turkey Morocco, $10 00.

RAWLINSON'S MANUAL OF ANCIENT HISTORY. A Manual of Ancient History, from the Earliest Times to the Fall of the Western Empire. Comprising the History of Chaldæa, Assyria, Media, Babylonia, Lydia, Phœnicia, Syria, Judæa, Egypt, Carthage, Persia, Greece, Macedonia, Parthia, and Rome. By GEORGE RAWLINSON, M.A., Camden Professor of Ancient History in the University of Oxford. 12mo, Cloth, $2 50.

RECLUS'S THE EARTH. The Earth: a Descriptive History of the Phenomena and Life of the Globe. By Élisée Reclus. Translated by the late B. B. Woodward, and Edited by Henry Woodward. With 234 Maps and Illustrations, and 23 Page Maps printed in Colors. 8vo, Cloth, $5 00.

SMILES'S LIFE OF THE STEPHENSONS. The Life of George Stephenson, and of his Son, Robert Stephenson; comprising, also, a History of the Invention and Introduction of the Railway Locomotive. By Samuel Smiles, Author of "Self-Help," &c. With Steel Portraits and numerous Illustrations. 8vo, Cloth, $3 00.

SMILES'S HISTORY OF THE HUGUENOTS. The Huguenots: their Settlements, Churches, and Industries in England and Ireland. By Samuel Smiles. With an Appendix relating to the Huguenots in America. Crown 8vo, Cloth, $1 75.

SHAKSPEARE. The Dramatic Works of William Shakspeare, with the Corrections and Illustrations of Dr. Johnson, G. Steevens, and others. Revised by Isaac Reed. Engravings. 6 vols., Royal 12mo, Cloth, $9 00.

SPEKE'S AFRICA. Journal of the Discovery of the Source of the Nile. By Captain John Hanning Speke, Captain H. M.'s Indian Army, Fellow and Gold Medalist of the Royal Geographical Society, Hon. Corresponding Member and Gold Medalist of the French Geographical Society, &c. With Maps and Portraits and numerous Illustrations, chiefly from Drawings by Captain Grant. 8vo, Cloth, uniform with Livingstone, Barth, Burton, &c., $4 00.

SPRING'S SERMONS. Pulpit Ministrations; or, Sabbath Readings. A Series of Discourses on Christian Doctrine and Duty. By Rev. Gardiner Spring, D.D., Pastor of the Brick Presbyterian Church in the City of New York. Portrait on Steel. 2 vols., 8vo, Cloth, $6 00.

STRICKLAND'S (Miss) QUEENS OF SCOTLAND. Lives of the Queens of Scotland and English Princesses connected with the Regal Succession of Great Britain. By Agnes Strickland. 8 vols., 12mo, Cloth, $12 00.

THE STUDENT'S SERIES.

- France. Engravings. 12mo, Cloth, $2 00.
- Gibbon. Engravings. 12mo, Cloth, $2 00.
- Greece. Engravings. 12mo, Cloth, $2 00.
- Hume. Engravings. 12mo, Cloth, $2 00.
- Rome. By Liddell. Engravings. 12mo, Cloth, $2 00.
- Old Testament History. Engravings. 12mo, Cloth, $2 00.
- New Testament History. Engravings. 12mo, Cloth, $2 00.
- Strickland's Queens of England. Abridged. Engravings. 12mo, Cloth, $2 00.
- Ancient History of the East. 12mo, Cloth, $2 00.
- Hallam's Middle Ages. 12mo, Cloth, $2 00.
- Lyell's Elements of Geology. 12mo, Cloth, $2 00.

TENNYSON'S COMPLETE POEMS. The Complete Poems of Alfred Tennyson, Poet Laureate. With numerous Illustrations by Eminent Artists, and Three Characteristic Portraits. 8vo, Paper, 75 cents; Cloth, $1 25.

THOMSON'S LAND AND THE BOOK. The Land and the Book; or, Biblical Illustrations drawn from the Manners and Customs, the Scenes and the Scenery of the Holy Land. By W. M. Thomson, D.D., Twenty-five Years a Missionary of the A.B.C.F.M. in Syria and Palestine. With two elaborate Maps of Palestine, an accurate Plan of Jerusalem, and several hundred Engravings, representing the Scenery, Topography, and Productions of the Holy Land, and the Costumes, Manners, and Habits of the People. 2 large 12mo vols., Cloth, $5 00.

TICKNOR'S HISTORY OF SPANISH LITERATURE. With Criticisms on the particular Works, and Biographical Notices of Prominent Writers. 3 vols., 8vo, Cloth, $5 00.

TYERMAN'S WESLEY. The Life and Times of the Rev. John Wesley, M.A., Founder of the Methodists. By the Rev. Luke Tyerman, Author of "The Life of Rev. Samuel Wesley." Portraits. 3 vols., Crown 8vo.

VÁMBÉRY'S CENTRAL ASIA. Travels in Central Asia. Being the Account of a Journey from Teheran across the Turkoman Desert, on the Eastern Shore of the Caspian, to Khiva, Bokhara, and Samarcand, performed in the Year 1863. By ARMINIUS VÁMBÉRY, Member of the Hungarian Academy of Pesth, by whom he was sent on this Scientific Mission. With Map and Woodcuts. 8vo, Cloth, $4 50.

WOOD'S HOMES WITHOUT HANDS. Homes Without Hands: being a Description of the Habitations of Animals, classed according to their Principle of Construction. By J. G. WOOD, M.A., F.L.S. With about 140 Illustrations. 8vo, Cloth, Beveled Edges, $4 50.

WILKINSON'S ANCIENT EGYPTIANS. A Popular Account of their Manners and Customs, condensed from his larger Work, with some New Matter. Illustrated with 500 Woodcuts. 2 vols., 12mo, Cloth, $3 50.

ANTHON'S SMITH'S DICTIONARY OF ANTIQUITIES. A Dictionary of Greek and Roman Antiquities. Edited by WILLIAM SMITH, LL.D., and Illustrated by numerous Engravings on Wood. Third American Edition, carefully Revised, and containing, also, numerous additional Articles relative to the Botany, Mineralogy, and Zoology of the Ancients. By CHARLES ANTHON, LL.D. Royal 8vo, Sheep extra, $6 00.

ANTHON'S CLASSICAL DICTIONARY. Containing an Account of the principal Proper Names mentioned in Ancient Authors, and intended to elucidate all the important Points connected with the Geography, History, Biography, Mythology, and Fine Arts of the Greeks and Romans; together with an Account of the Coins, Weights, and Measures of the Ancients, with Tabular Values of the same. Royal 8vo, Sheep extra, $6 00.

DWIGHT'S (REV. DR.) THEOLOGY. Theology Explained and Defended, in a Series of Sermons. By TIMOTHY DWIGHT, S.T.D., LL.D. With a Memoir and Portrait. 4 vols., 8vo, Cloth, $8 00.

ENGLISHMAN'S GREEK CONCORDANCE. The Englishman's Greek Concordance of the New Testament: being an Attempt at a Verbal Connection between the Greek and the English Texts: including a Concordance to the Proper Names, with Indexes, Greek-English and English-Greek. 8vo, Cloth, $5 00.

FOWLER'S ENGLISH LANGUAGE. The English Language in its Elements and Forms. With a History of its Origin and Development, and a full Grammar. Designed for Use in Colleges and Schools. Revised and Enlarged. By WILLIAM C. FOWLER, LL.D., late Professor in Amherst College. 8vo, Cloth, $2 50.

GIESELER'S ECCLESIASTICAL HISTORY. A Text-Book of Church History. By Dr. JOHN C. L. GIESELER. Translated from the Fourth Revised German Edition by SAMUEL DAVIDSON, LL.D., and Rev. JOHN WINSTANLEY HULL, M.A. A New American Edition, Revised and Edited by Rev. HENRY B. SMITH, D.D., Professor in the Union Theological Seminary, New York. Four Volumes ready. (*Vol. V. in Press.*) 8vo, Cloth, $2 25 per vol.

HALL'S (ROBERT) WORKS. The Complete Works of Robert Hall; with a brief Memoir of his Life by Dr. GREGORY, and Observations on his Character as a Preacher by Rev. JOHN FOSTER. Edited by OLINTHUS GREGORY, LL.D., and Rev. JOSEPH BELCHER. Portrait. 4 vols., 8vo, Cloth, $8 00.

HAMILTON'S (SIR WILLIAM) WORKS. Discussions on Philosophy and Literature, Education and University Reform. Chiefly from the *Edinburgh Review*. Corrected, Vindicated, and Enlarged, in Notes and Appendices. By Sir WILLIAM HAMILTON, Bart. With an Introductory Essay by Rev. ROBERT TURNBULL, D.D. 8vo, Cloth, $3 00.

HUMBOLDT'S COSMOS. Cosmos: a Sketch of a Physical Description of the Universe. By ALEXANDER VON HUMBOLDT. Translated from the German by E. C. OTTÉ. 5 vols., 12mo, Cloth, $6 25.

www.ingramcontent.com/pod-product-compliance
Lightning Source LLC
LaVergne TN
LVHW021233110826
845150LV00002B/323